Slow Waltzing
Back To
Goodhue

POPCORN PRESS' POPULAR HISTORY SERIES OF THE UPPER MISSISSIPPI VALLEY

by Jim Franklin

A multi-volume series telling the story, through historical accounts and photos, of the hearty, courageous people and benchmark events in the Upper Mississippi River Valley.

No. 1___
Pioneering Goodhue County
The villages, burgs, hamlets, whistle-stops, ghost towns, townships and good folks of Goodhue County, Minnesota

Publication 2002

No. 2___
Settling Lake Pepin's Shores
The majestic lake, steamboats, rafting, anchoring towns

Publication 2003

No. 3___
Pike's Peak and the Five Rivers' Valley
The Mississippi, Wisconsin, Kickapoo, Turkey and Yellow Rivers

Publication 2003

No. 4___
Grand Excursion 2004
Paddlewheelers, sidewheelers, captains, pilots, roustabouts, scoundrels again ply the Upper Mississippi River

Publication 2004

Popcorn Press
presents
THE GOODHUE TRILOGY
by Jim Franklin

One boy finds meaning growing up, later moving beyond a tiny, dusty village out on the rolling prairie. His adventures and escapades are those of universal youth. Relive your own in this heartwarming, whimsical trilogy. Come along.

Part I
Last Waltz in Goodhue
Adventures of a Village Boy
Publication 1997

Part II
Slow Waltzing Back to Goodhue
Once Upon a Time in a Village
Publication 2002

Part III
Whistling Down County Road No. 9
Remembering a Village
Publication 2004

SLOW WALTZING BACK TO GOODHUE

Once Upon a Time in a Village

Jim Franklin

POPCORN PRESS

Books of the Upper Midwest

Popcorn Press
McGregor, Iowa

Frontispiece: Jimmy Franklin, circa 1946
Goodhue area drawing, pages 10 & 11, by John Mundt, Esq.

Library of Congress Catalog Card Number: 2002091370

ISBN 0-9634689-5-2

Printed in the United States of America

5 4 3 2 1

Mark Twain epigraph quotation, public domain.
General Editor, Mark Twain Project,
University of California, Berkeley
Hamlin Garland quotation, public domain

Popcorn Press
Main Street
P.O. Box 237
McGregor, Iowa 52157

For the people of Goodhue,
living and dead

And as always,
Anne and Joe

Preface

As with many writers, my first attempts in the eighties were autobiographical, writing about what I knew. I knew the village. Those first pages were a way to reflect upon earlier times in a later life. As the pages multiplied they eventually became *Last Waltz in Goodhue* (1997). I later wrote a sequel but delayed its publication. Meanwhile, my thoughts hadn't left the village as I realized there was more to tell. Those recollections have now become THE GOODHUE TRILOGY with part II, *Slow Waltzing Back To Goodhue* (2002) and part III, *Whistling Down County Rd. No. 9* (2004). The thread is autobiographical. The focus is the village, its people, its values, its idiosyncrasies. Although a tiny village, it has become, for non-native readers, *their* village, a larger, universal village. What occurred in Goodhue is not unique. That's what makes it unique.

Although I have not lived in Goodhue since 1960, I have walked its streets, smelled its aromas, heard its sounds in my dreams. *Slow Waltzing* continues where *Last Waltz* left off, somewhere on a hushed Upper Street. *Whistling* extends that journey.

I entered the village in 1936 and graduated from Goodhue High School in 1954 before attending St. John's University in Collegeville, Minnesota (1954 - 1958). During my college years I would return to Goodhue to spend summers with my mother and to work at Libby's pea viners or Heaney and Gorman or Majerus Appliance, or paint barns and houses in Goodhue and surrounding rural areas.

I was the third child of Thomas B. Franklin of Goodhue Township and Lucille (Haustein) Franklin Ryan of Red Wing. There were five Franklins in our village family besides myself: Father Thomas Bernard (1893-1951), mother Lucille (1900-1970), sister Rose Marie, brother Thomas Edward (1934-1987), and baby brother Daniel (c. 1940 - 1940).

If our paths crossed somewhere around Goodhue, you'll probably recall many of the experiences I have written about. Most are true, and if they aren't, they should have been.

Contents

Human nature cannot be studied in cities except at a disadvantage—a village is the place. There you can know your man inside and out—in a city you but know his crust, and his crust is usually a lie.

—Mark Twain, *Notebook,*
1883

Each season dropped a thickening veil of mist between me and the scenes of my youth, adding a poetic glamour to every rememberable form and fact.

—Hamlin Garland, *A Son of the Middle Border,*
1922

Chapter 1

On the pea viner

Out on a high prairie farm

"Now, LET ME GET THIS STRAIGHT, SON. DID you or did you not touch her breast?"

"I don't actually know, Father, because, well, you see, I'd never touched one before, so how was I to know?"

"I'll ask the questions here, son. You just give me the answers.

1

How on earth am I to give you penance? How am I to know what kind of sin you committed if you don't know whether or not you touched her breast? Now let's go at it again. What were you actually doing when you might have or might not have touched her breast?"

"Gee, Father, I, rather . . . I was . . . you know, trying to get some experience. I hadn't had much, only some holding hands back in grade school, spinning the bottle and hoping for a kiss at my classmates' homes, a little necking later in high school, but that's about all. So I was . . . ,"

"Get on with it, son. There are other Johnnies in line behind you who need to confess their sins."

"It's hard, Father. I had just put my arm around her, trying to get a little closer, when my hand sort of slipped down over her shoulder touching something. It was soft, but it might have just been her blouse. I honestly don't know, Father."

"Well, if you don't know, I don't know, so for this confession we'll just call it a venial sin and for that say three Our Fathers and three Hail Marys and, son . . . get it right next time."

God! It was hard getting it right. I had been trying to get it right for years, confessing my sins to Father Smith at Holy Trinity Parish in the village or at St. Columbkill's out in Belle Creek Township. Now, I was trying to get it right with the Black Robes up at St. John's University located on the edge of Minnesota's tundra. I didn't know if the Black Robes would be more, or less, tolerant than Fr. Smith, but I would find out during the next four years.

I had only been on the remote campus a week since leaving my sequestered burg, entering a new world of endless, serpentine lines of hooded Black Robes—Benedictine Monks—shuffling single file into the monastery, into the church . . . into my life.

Before arriving on campus my spiritual life had included mostly Fr. Smith in his starch-collared, tight-lipped surplice, and an occasional white-faced, black- and white-hooded nun or two processing into Goodhue to teach Catholicism to wayward, un-worthy and uninterested children during the village's blistering summer months. The village was a community of Catholics and those others, non-Catholic folks who out of our hearing range called themselves Protestants: English Lutherans, German Lutherans, Norwegian Lutherans, Swedish Lutherans, English Methodists. The village displayed minimal, outward religious activity during the week, but on Sunday, the "official" religious day, ethnic-religious spirits rose from dormant farmsteads and hushed bleached village houses. Men dressed themselves in singular dark suits and awkward, uneven hand painted ties while women arranged themselves in styleless, drab dresses accompanied by ancient hats and shrouded, black veils. Reluctant children dragged behind wearing their "finest" but most uncomfortable Sunday-only clothes and hellishly tight shoes.

In-town German Lutherans filed to St. Peter's on the edge of town while out-of-towners congregated at St. John's and Grace Lutheran on the eastern prairie. English Lutherans processed to in-town St. Luke's while Methodists trekked to their whitewashed, clapboard church. Norwegian Lutherans traipsed all the way to Norway—Minnesota, that is—for Sunday services while Swedish Lutherans congregated somewhere out on the prairie in a lost Swede town, mostly in the Vasa settlement. In-town Catholics gathered at a former chicken coop rechristened "Holy Trinity," it noticeably lacking a nave and apse, while rural Catholics prayed at St. Columbkill's on the undulating Belle Creek prairie.

In only a few short weeks since Mother and new stepfather Bill Ryan had driven me out crumbling County Rd. No. 9 into a new life at St. John's, I had left the gang at Heaney & Gorman's Market; Erv Richter reclining on Upper Street begging me to play "Melancholy Baby" one last time on my clarinet; left my 1954 graduating classmates to their own futures, and most significantly, left the familiarity and security of the sequestered village. As Mother and Bill drove me around the sprawling Twin Cities, through St. Cloud and deep into the hinterlands to the isolated St. John's enclave, I didn't know if I was ready for college. Now, four weeks after sauntering out of that musty, imprisoning confessional toward St. Benedict's Hall—my new home—I still didn't know. Dennis Heaney said I was. George and Dodie Gorman said I was. Uncle Dave said I was. Frank O'Gorman said I was. Mother was unsure, and . . . well . . . I still had my doubts.

But first things first, I thought, crossing the imposing medieval-styled campus—the notable St. John's twin church towers soaring toward the heavens—to St. Ben's Hall past hundreds of other green, awkward looking freshmen, beanie headed students peering askance at me just as those old-timers had near the Corner Bar several years ago. These new, strange faces from St. Paul, Minneapolis, Avon, Cold Springs, Bemidji and Valley City, Dakota, didn't look as ominous as the village's Corner Bar ruffians, yet they appeared to be sneering at this obvious hick from the sticks. I high tailed it to my dorm room. I had those Hail Marys and Our Fathers to recite.

M y world had changed considerably since last spring's serene high school graduation ceremonies when, later, I joined classmates at post graduation parties before covering a shivering Erv with my graduation robe on Upper Street. Before that night everything had been in its rightful place, had stayed in place. Oh, there was a big bump in the road when Dad died suddenly in '51, but time moves on. He's content out on the prairie in St. Columbkill's Cemetery with other dearly departed: Johanna and Will Heaney, sister Anne Franklin-McWaters, Will McHugh, Tom Heaney, Phil and Sarah Ryan, Lou Schinnert.

Children are adaptable. After Dad died sister Rose returned to nurses' training in Duluth, brother Tom to Heaney & Gorman to butcher squealing hogs and bellowing steers, Mondays, with Dennis Heaney and Bump Schinnert, inturn earning enough to buy a gleaming blue '53 four-door Chevy with which to romance Shirley in Rochester. I struggled through three more years of high school with teachers Ray Batty, Charles Wood, Miss Cree, Supt. Hubert, and Miss North hoping to eventually join my classmates graduation night with a *signed* diploma. I hadn't given much, if any, thought to a post high school future. I was just hoping to graduate.

Four days after that graduation night, I found myself out in Belle Creek at St. Columbkill's forlorn country church standing on the altar in a flowing, white surplice facing a teary eyed, veil-less mother and beaming Belle Creek countryman, Bill Ryan. He was lean and trim from a lifetime of farming, high cheekbones displaying several generations of Irish heritage. This seemed odd, confusing. What on earth was I doing here? I thought. Some unknown priest was administering the oath of marriage in Latin, his basso voice mysterious as if he had just been released from the catacombs. It certainly wasn't Fr. Smith, now reassigned to a dreary, forgotten, endless-horizon parish to scold young altar boys, dress them down as a master sergeant would just as he had done to George O'Reilly, brother Tom and me, even Phil Ryan, haranguing us while chomping on triple decked peanut butter sandwiches and slurping cup after cup of cold coffee.

How did I get here? I pondered while Father Somebody began the nuptial ceremony. *My* father was entombed across the road in the deep bowels of the cemetery, but here I was getting a new father . . . well . . . a stepfather. It didn't make sense; it didn't register. I wasn't sure I wanted a stepfather. Brother Tom was fidgeting down in the first pew. Rose was in Duluth studying how to stick people with a bloody needle. My new step- brothers and sisters—Dick and Tom "Gorm" Ryan, wives Helen "Shorty" and Grace had taken the day off from tilling their Belle Creek fields—beamed in the front pew while I wondered if I could get through this Nuptial Mass, this ordeal without spilling the water or wine, without overdosing on the incense, without making a total fool of myself as I had done on earlier liturgical occasions.

Yet, I was more nervous for Mother, because she always cried at special events. I wasn't at her first wedding with Dad, but here I was at her second, anxious about whether she could get through it without bawling. She had cried when I tooted "Believe Me If All Those Enduring Young Charms," for my first solo clarinet performance accompanied by a hesitant Goodhue High School Band. She had cried and rushed to the toilet ten times during every basketball game I played in the old school gym, thereby missing many of my best shots. She had wrung her hands wondering if I would remember my lines in the senior class play "Tish." She had shaken so much graduation night that she couldn't take my diploma-receiving photo without assistance from Mary Haas. That was my dear mother; sentimental, that's all. Now I stood with hands and arms thrust toward her, supporting a wedding ring balanced precariously on a white, stuffed satin pillow. I looked into her dark eyes to see the petite, young Red Wing woman who herself had had two mothers—a real mother and a substitute mother—now thrusting me into the same familial environment. She was looking at the priest, Bill at Mother as Tom inspected his always shined cordovan wing tips. The witnessing Ryans were watching Bill and Lucille, happy their father had found someone to share his life with after the cancerous death of Mother Julia. It was to be a marriage made in heaven, if not Belle Creek.

It worked. Bill slipped the ring on Mother's finger, kissed her on the cheek—not on the lips in church, for God's sake!—then escorted her through the massive wooden front doors into a bright May day and a new life for the two of them. Mother got through it. I got through it. I wasn't so sure about reticent Tom. We threw yellow shelled corn, pinging Bill's new '54 Plymouth in the process, as the newlyweds sped down the dusty, crushed rock road toward County Rd. No. 9, off to somewhere exotic for a honeymoon, maybe Cannon Falls or Rochester. I didn't know. I stood on the steps of St. Columbkill's wiping the road grit from my eyes, momentarily shaken by the abrupt turn of events. Tom quickly drove off to see his girlfriend in Rochester without speaking a word to his younger brother, while new step- brothers and sisters Ryan shook my hand welcoming me to the family before they trudged back to impatient fields of grain and corn.

I shuffled across the road to the cemetery and Dad's grave, corn stocks rustling beyond the weary fence, the dry stalks rattling like death itself. I recalled three years ago, that cold, rainy, awful day we buried him. This day was a bright spring day in contrast to that freezing, bitter, sleeting day of October 1951. The fresh, earthy country wind billowed my white surplice as I pondered this sudden change in my life. Only a short time ago there had been a family—a father, a mother, a brother, a sister. Suddenly, I found myself alone, everyone gone. What had happened to the *family*, I wondered, peering down at Dad's headstone. How could it all have ended so quickly? I "talked" with Dad for a few minutes before hanging up my surplice in the vestibule and heading back to the village, heading into an unknown and uncertain future.

Before remarrying, Mother had invited me to "summer" with her and Bill in their new Red Wing home, but I chose to remain in the village. Goodhue was my home, not Red Wing. Red Wing had been a place to shop at Woolworth's Dime Store, to visit Haustein relatives, but not a place for a village boy like me. How could I leave the familiar dusty village streets? How could I leave the only hometown I had known for seventeen years? How could I leave Heaney & Gorman and Swenson's Cafe and Jesse's Hardware and Eddie's Drugstore and Uncle Dave and Erv Richter?

Several weeks after Dad died, Mother had asked me to consider moving to Zumbrota for the remainder of high school. "Jimmy, some Zumbrota friends have offered me a job, but it would mean moving to Zumbrota. Do you think you could live there?' she asked, twisting the cotton dish cloth in her nervous hands, her sharp Austrian chin quivering slightly.

"Oh, Mom, I don't want to live in Zumbrota. All my friends are here," I responded abruptly, selfishly.

"But I have a job offer, and we need the money, so . . . ,"

"You can get a job in Goodhue. I bet you could be a waitress at the Hotel Cafe, or maybe Dennis would hire you to cut meat. I like it here," I reiterated while helping her stash the supper dishes in the cupboard. Mother was silent as she finished washing the dishes. I guess my point had gotten across to her, as she never suggested Zumbrota again. We remained in the village so I could graduate with "Sandbox" Bob O'Reilly and Mary Benda and Digger Dave Majerus and Tom Manahan and Dewey Jonas, this on the coat tails of others who had passed through the halls of GHS: the McNamaras, the Gadients, the Gormans, the Diercks, the Bucks, the Shelstads.

Rejecting Mother and Bill's offer, I returned to the village to the house where I had grown up, living in only my bedroom, the remainder of the house already rented to a new couple. Mother, in her ever-caring manner, had arranged a room for the summer.

For the next couple of nights, I pondered all that had happened. The house was no longer a harmonious family home, it now emitting strident, eerie, creaking noises I never knew existed the past fifteen years when I investigated every inch of this old two story, farm-styled house. The folks downstairs were rarely home, so I found myself in a quiet, forlorn, stale wood building that had previously breathed life, that had released the sounds of a family: rippling laughter, sister Rose's piano tinkling; the tangy aromas of Mother's German-based cooking and Dad's occasional haunting cigar; Bridge and 500 parties, three tables bidding, counter bidding, talking, joshing, coffee slurping and beer drinking, Chesterfield cigarettes dangling from tobacco-stained mouths—Tom and Lucille, Bill and Laura Mans, Vern and Mary Haas, Cy and Bessie Benda, Ag and Vince O'Reilly.

I looked through my second story window toward Sandbox Bob's house, ruminating. Where was Bob? We had grown up playing in his sandbox in the back lawn. We had walked to school together that first day in 1941. We had done just about everything together. I peered out the window through the apple tree toward his equally stark, dark house thinking about "calling" him on our Dixie Cup telephones, frayed string remnants still twisting in the night's breeze on the sides of our houses. I gazed down at the lawn, the scene of so many ball games with Jack O'Reilly, Lee Johnson, George O'Reilly, brother Tom, tonight devoid of any boyhood activity, only memories lingering beyond the apple tree. Yet, I felt secure in my room, secure in my village. Everything would be all right. I would enroll at St. John's in the fall to make new friends, new family, I hesitantly told myself.

But this night I needed to stop meditating and jump into bed. Four o'clock would arrive early. Bookie Buchholtz' peas would be running fast. Those fresh, juicy, snapping emerald-green peas out in the east township wouldn't wait at Bookie's pea viner.

"Hey, Jimmy! Get your butt out of bed and hustle down here." Shouting from down on the street startled me out of a deep, but short sleep. It couldn't be four o'clock already, I thought; then, a second, more persistent shout reached my second story bedroom.

"We got peas to box, vines to stack. Hurry up, Jim. Bookie is waiting!" Jack hollered from his car window, simultaneously revving the engine. I rushed to my window, flipped it open, "Be right down, Jack. Give me a couple of minutes," I shouted into the coal black morning before jumping into tattered jeans, buckling Red Wing boots, slipping into a tattered purple and white GHS sweatshirt, flipping on my stained White Sox baseball cap and rushing down the back stairs while trying not to wake my new landlords. Mother had arranged for the downstairs couple to make my lunch, so I halted at the frige, grabbed a brown paper bag and zipped through the door.

"Jim! You're gonna have to get an alarm clock, so you'll be ready when I get here. Your mom's off to Red Wing. You can't depend on her rousting you anymore," Jack lectured, adjusting his proud New York Yankees baseball cap lower on an equally square head and jaw, his short, gnarled fingers gripping the steering wheel as he geared into a wheelie on the dark neighborhood street. Jack and I had spent many an hour, many a day, many a year together. A stout, agile friend, we had suffered catechism as well as other vagaries of the church together for seventeen years.

"I know, but it's just that . . . well, I'm not quite used to living alone yet. I'll get the hang of it," I mumbled, settling into the bumpy seat of his '50 Chevy. "This living on my own will take some getting used to."

"You'll be okay. Besides, we got us a big summer ahead of us out to the viner. I worked there last year, but this is your rookie season, rookie! We do nothin' but pitch and box peas from five o'clock to sometimes midnight! Don't have time for anything else," he said while whipping into a "Ralphie" downtown by Swenson's Cafe. We drove past the dormant, slumbering grain elevator on Lower Street, its tubular, corkscrew elevators appearing like spider legs in the morning gloom.

"I suppose I'll get used to it. Sure need the money for St. John's in the fall. How much do we make, anyway?" I asked as we sped east across Highway 58 toward Bookie's farm.

"Last year we made dollar-five an hour. Think this year'll be 'bout a dollar-fourteen. Don't seem like much, but shoot, all we do is work. Don't have no time to spend it. We can make 'bout $800 to $1,000 for the summer. That ain't too bad a deal, is it?" Jack asked as I adjusted my pant belt and straightened my cap while wondering if I would like pitching peas all day. It was still dark as we headed into a hiding sun. I picked the sleep from my eyes, pulled a banana out of the bag and peeled it while pondering a new summer job. We bounced east on No. 9, Jack's beat-up, rusted Chevy could use some new springs, I thought, the road rutty, dusty, pothole-marked, badly in need of paving.

During recent high school summers I had worked at Heaney & Gorman's Grocery and Meat Market. After Dad died George Gorman offered me a job sweeping floors after school, toting garbage to the incincrator in the alley, and sacking potatoes. That was my biggie—sacking potatoes—dropping 100 pound bags of white or red potatoes onto the floor, then sorting them into five and ten pound paper bags for the sweet ladies of the village. It was a good job, plus I was able to make some decisions on my own, decisions a kid in the eighth grade didn't get to make often, but I could while sacking potatoes—you know, better potatoes for the Catholics, not-so-good potatoes for the non-Catholics who Fr. Smith had lectured us incessantly were going to hell, anyway.

George, Dodie and Dennis kept me working during the ensuing summer months as I slowly expanded my job description. Oh, I still swept floors, toted garbage to the incinerator, and sacked potatoes, but that didn't take all day. I began helping Donnie Luhman restock grocery shelves with Campbell's Soup and Bon Ami cleanser and Wheaties and Kix and Folgers coffee. I helped George trim quarters of beef for hamburger, and gradually began delivering groceries to little gray-haired, shut-in ladies on Saturday afternoons. That was a big deal, driving George's sleek '50 Ford around town hauling wire baskets of groceries to Mary McHugh and Mrs Goodsell and Emma Kindseth and Emily Parker, even to Oscar Decker up beyond St. Peter's Lutheran Church in the hinterland.

After a couple of early high school summers, Dennis Heaney recruited me for the adjoining Locker Plant where my job was to wrap meat in heavy waxed paper after he cut up shoulder roasts and tenderloins and chops and steaks, and . . . well, I could also make decisions at the wrapping table, though not as freely as when sacking potatoes. Township farmers trucked in steers and hogs for butchering in the slaughter house and they surely wanted their own meat placed in their rented lockers. It wasn't a good idea to send Ernest Gorman's steaks to Art Lohman's locker. It wasn't a good idea to send Ralph McNamara's pork chops to Ray Banidt's locker, or Maynard Haas' pork roasts to John Stenlund's locker. No sir. I had to keep on my toes when wrapping and stamping and marking the fresh, raw cuts Dennis threw at me over his ominous band saw, sometimes through it. And I surely didn't want to get a Catholic meat package mixed up with a non-Catholic package. Why, that was sin itself. The two didn't mix anymore than the various religions did in our sequestered burg. Just the thought of a mixup like that would send me into a tizzy, wondering how I would explain it to Fr. Smith during my next confession, even though it might only be a venial sin.

By the time I had thought about those summer and after-school working days at Heaney & Gorman, Jack had turned off No. 9 down an equally crumbling road toward No. 16 and Bookie's farm. Bookie's daughter, Phyllis, a classmate, was a fledging musician like me. The high school gang would occasionally congregate at her farm place where she would plink piano rags. We would sing and josh as high schoolers do, pop popcorn, drink soda and play Monopoly or Charades. This day, as we passed her house, I wondered if I would see Phyllis working at the viner.

"You been awfully quiet the past few miles, Jimmy. Where you been?" Jack asked as he revved the Chevy into a wheelie, throwing up a dust twister while speeding toward the ominous, shadowy viners.

"Oh, I've been thinking about the past summers at Heaney & Gorman. They've got their own children now who need work, so when Dave Hutcheson suggested I work at the viners this summer, George thought it would be a good idea. It would make room at the store for Tom, Charlie and Helen."

"You been working at the grocery a long time, ain't you?"

"You got that right! Began in eighth grade working after school. Dodie said my fifty cents an hour could help out at home, but I spent most of it on malts and burgers at Swenson's. Saved a little bit. Gave some to Mother, but she didn't bug me much," I answered as three enormous dinosaur-sized machines suddenly appeared through the early morning mist.

"Here we are. You ready?" Jack asked, spinning the steering wheel with those gnarled fingers, executing another perfect wheelie into the viner site.

"Guess I'll have to be," I said as he completed his third wheelie of the morning into the rutted, stubbled field, parking about a John Yunger's touchdown run from the looming machines.

We trudged toward the ominous machines set in the middle of Bookie's pea fields, dual-wheeled dump trucks already barking and spewing black exhaust into the heavy, dew-laden morning air. I had visited Dave Hutch last summer at the viners just to see what was happening. I wasn't totally ignorant of the operation. This was the first day of the season's pea run, so there was no gigantic green vine stack rising behind the viners yet, no slurry pea moat releasing that excruciating, pungent odor, no stacked boxes of fresh peas for the Libby Foods plant in Rochester. But I knew it wouldn't be long during the coming, long summer.

I noticed Hutch out behind the expectant viners tinkering with a Ford tractor, while George O'Reilly—one of the first to sign on at the viners—sharpened pitchfork tines. Jack quickly began gathering empty pea boxes as Bookie climbed over the machines like a monkey—a grease gun and huge crescent wrench looped in his overalls—this despite his, according to Bookie, trick knee. ("What tricks can it do, Bookie?" became a well-worn cliché.) Uncle Dave, his long, angular legs dangling through the open door of his pickup, was "supervising" the entire operation from the front seat. Uncle Dave drove out in his bouncy Ford every day to work at the operation, mostly supervising, which meant telling jokes and joshing with us "young whippersnappers" while reminding Bookie where, deep in the viners, he had stashed his blackberry brandy bottle. But I enjoyed having Uncle Dave around since Dad wasn't. Dave and I had painted the bulk oil storage tanks at Lohman's

Standard Oil. Well, he had me swinging from twenty-foot ropes scraping and painting while he supervised from the ground. But it was good work for a kid, good working with Uncle Dave.

"Mornin', Jimmy," Dave hollered from his pickup where he was slurping coffee from a cracked, green Thermos that had probably been on the Franklin farm. "Damn gout's acting up early today in my big toe."

"Morning, Uncle Dave. Well, you got me out here. Got me out of the grocery store, so I guess I'm ready to pitch peas. What's your job?" I chided, giving him a little Irish-tainted feedback.

"Me? I'm a supervisor. My job's to make sure you younguns get these peas pitched. Hell! I've got the most important job . . . keeping you young farts working instead of jackin' off," Dave said as more of the gang—Pat O'Reilly, Dennis Mahoney, George "O" Johnson (an adopted O'Reilly)—bounded into the site, they too rubbing sleep from comatose eyes.

"Shit, Dave. You haven't done a good lick of work in your entire life," George O'Johnson hollered from the pitchfork corral. "I've been working around you for a few years, yet to see you do a decent day's work, you antique fart!" George OJ hollered approaching Dave, slapping him on the back causing coffee to spill on the seat. George OJ, a very handsome, very distant relative from a very distant state, Idaho, spent the last couple of years at GHS, preferring our dusty, lonesome prairie village to the sweeping Idaho mountains. But we accepted him. He soon learned the ways of the village and villagers. Why, in no time at all, he was one of us—for better or worse.

"Watch it, Johnson, or I'll give you the hardest job out here. Me and Bookie and Max will do that, guarantee it," Dave retorted, adjusting his ever-slipping glasses on a particularly long "Franklin" nose, complemented by an equally prolonged face and pointed jaw. Everything was "long" about Uncle Dave unlike my father's shortened physical stature. Dave got the long legs, long arms and long nose off that Goodhue Township farm while Dad got the bulk and reduced height.

"See that stack of pea vines in front of the conveyors, you worthless farts?" Max, the on-site giant Libby's foreman snarled as Bookie clambered high atop a viner machine, vigorously rubbing that trick knee. "They ain't going up the conveyor themselves, now is they? Grab your socks instead of your cocks. Get those hands 'round somethin' bigger than a pencil, a pitchfork fer instance, and start to runnin' peas. We ain't payin' you to fart around all day. Get with it!" Max shouted as Bookie pumped more grease into the noisy, grinding gears of the awakening dinosaurs. The viners were on Bookie's place, but Max drove up from Rochester, daily, to oversee the operation. Bookie had been the foreman the first years, but the Libby bean counters felt one of their own would increase efficiency, the bottom line. Bean counters were just that . . . pea counters. Giant Max—some of the crew called him "Schmelling' behind his back—was a gruff Prussian who shouted orders, his bronchial bull voice resonating off the viners. He wasn't a bean counter himself, but answered to the Rochester bean counters. Oh, we did what he said, when he said it, but we survived in spite of him.

The viners emitted deep, grumbling sounds from within their bowels, sort of like the GHS band's tuba section on a good day. Gears grated and conveyor belts screeched and tarps slapped sounding like Ol' Buck lapping water out behind Ebe's Barber Shop. Bookie—sort of a Napoleon-ish pea viner commander— usually dressed in faded, torn-at-the-knee-faded-blue Oshkosh-Bigosh bib overalls, an extra grease gun slung from his left-side hammer loop (he had the wife sew an extra loop making him look like a Dodge City double gun slinger), commanded his domain with a vengeance. Though portly he possessed a commanding, dominating voice. Through a stubbled beard and lightly graying mustache, he portrayed the countenance of Napoleon, though none of had ever seen a photo of Napoleon around the village.

Someone threw me a pitchfork and suddenly I was pitching stringy, tangled pea vines into the endless conveyor that transported the vines and pods into a large screened rotating drum that gently knocked the peas out of their pods before rolling onto a revolving canvas. Pretty good system, I thought as the summer progressed. The pod-less vines then corkscrewed through the drum onto another conveyor while the free-running green peas rolled down the canvas where Jack busily filled boxes, replaced the filled ones, then stacked the boxed peas. Out on the ass end of the viner, as Bookie was wont to say, Hutch drove a tiny Ford tractor with a tongued fork distributing the spent green vines evenly, building a monument to the pea viners of Goodhue and Belvidere Townships. Throughout the summer Hutch and his Ford would compress the vines into a growing mass, its weight compressing the pungent juices into a circuitous, castle-like moat creating a penetrating odor the likes of which villagers seldom smelled. By the end of that summer of '54, by the time we had finished ninety consecutive sixteen-hour days, by the time we had pitched and boxed and chided each other endlessly, that stack had become a monument to our work. It had risen twenty feet above the rolling prairie, looming above even the viner machines themselves, looming above the workers. That summer and the following three would be good days for my compatriots and me. It wasn't such a bad deal. In fact, it was a heckuva deal.

But those first days took some getting used to. The work didn't become automatic immediately. I spent that first day, the first week on the pitchfork. Everything ached: My hands sprouted blisters, my shoulders and arms cried in agony, my back went into muscle spasms, but I wasn't complaining, just whining a bit to no one in particular. That first day the trucks kept arriving, dumping gigantic stacks of fresh vines in front of the conveyor, two fellows attacking the stack from opposite sides, both pitching tangled vines into the never-ending, never-stopping conveyor. I teamed up with George O'Reilly at the foot of viner No. 2—Mahoney and Johnson working No. 1—George having a year's experience on me, years of experience on everything I did, so it seemed.

"Whaddya think, Jimmy?" George O' hollered from the opposite side of our stack. "Think you're going to like this work, you little fart?" I couldn't see him over the towering stack, but I could hear him. I could always hear him. George and brother Tom had been the best of friends since day one in the village, and George had been sort of sweet on sister Rose, too, Class of '51. We had cut and wrapped meat together at Heaney & Gorman, prayed side-by-side as altar boys for Fr. Smith, later getting our butts chewed out behind the sacristy for picking our nose or letting farts during the consecration, doing something irreverent on the altar. In fact, George probably held Holy Trinity parish's record for the most reprimands from old Master Sergeant Smith. But George had a way about him. He could dish it out as well as take it. He handled Fr. Smith, in his own way.

I couldn't see him but, feeling his presence, answered, "You bet. It'll be fine soon as I get the hang of it. Haven't had a pitchfork in my hands since working Frederick Benitt's farm couple summers ago. I'll be tiptop in a couple of days."

"How you doing living by yourself now, Jimmy? Your mom's gone off to Red Wing, getting married again and all."

"Oh, everything's fine. Got my same bedroom. Folks fix my lunch. Mom pays the rent, so I can save all my viner money for St. John's."

"How the hell'd you ever get into St. John's? You didn't do a lick of studying in high school. I had a hard time getting into Winona State, but at least I studied in high school. You didn't," George scolded as we whittled the stack down to half size.

"I had some help from Principal Charles Wood. He wrote a good letter of recommendation, and Dave Hutch, a sophomore at St. John's, put in a good word for me with their head priest. What the hell, George, I also said a few rosaries. Prayer works. You ought to know that what with all our years serving on the altar," I said as we reached the bottom of the first stack, my arms beginning to stretch, my mind wondering if I could keep this up until eight o'clock.

"You never did *learn* your Latin, you little fart," George nagged, "all you ever did on the altar was *recite* Latin: *Mea culpa, Pox vobiscum*. At least I studied Latin, knew what it meant."

"Don't make no difference whether I understand it or not. God understands it. He's the one who speaks Latin, not me. And Ol' Smithy didn't care whether I understood or not. He and God had that figured out. And the parishioners didn't understand Latin. Why, half of them couldn't read English let alone understand God's native tongue. Parishioners just listened to what Smithy was jawing about during the gospels and homily and put their faith in the Lord. Their faith was why they attended Holy Trinity, not to understand Latin or listen to that horrible pump organist. What was her name, anyway?" I asked, now seeing George directly as we reached bare earth and the finish of load one.

George leaned on his pitchfork and squinted at me in the rising sun, "I don't know, one of the McNamaras or Gadients, maybe an O'Reilly. I never had much of an ear for music like you. You still honking on that clarinet for Erv outside the Corner Bar?"

"Yes sir, still play every day for myself, sometimes for Erv, though I haven't seen much of him since graduation night. Play sometimes for Red Ryan and Oscar Decker and some of the other diggers at the Claypits."

"You going to major in music at college, you little sissy!" George taunted, always chiding me, other guys too, but I learned over the years to stand up to him. He was an outstanding athlete, sort of an early-day Joe Namath—bossy, always coaching other fellows, always telling us what to do. Maybe it was the Irish in him. He had a way of coaching even when just the three of us—George, Tom, Jimmy—played tackle football out on the back lawn.

"Music isn't sissified. Shoot, if I practice enough I could be as good as Benny Goodman," I said as the second load of vines suddenly appeared in front of us, again obliterating George from view.

"Dammit, Jimmy, you aren't even close to playing like Benny Goodman, more like Art Fitch with the Polka Dots, if you ask me." George disappeared from view as the towering second load of vines created an eight-foot barrier between us, but that didn't stop him from jawin'. "You was fair-to-middlin' basketball player in high school, not as good as me, but pretty good. I'm on the team at Winona State, thinking about becoming a high school coach. You should become a coach. Forget that Benny Goodman stuff."

"If you two would knock it off and pitch faster, we'd get more work done," Bookie hollered from atop the viners. "Zip it up for awhile, O'Reilly, and put some muscle into that fork. We ain't payin' you to jaw. Payin' you to work," Bookie hollered as he hopped like a jungle monkey to other machines with his dangling grease guns.

"You got that right, Bookie," Max grunted. "Heave to there boys. Get those peas into the can so I can count them."

"We're working here, boss," George hollered back to Max. "Working faster than laggards Mahoney and Johnson on that other machine."

"My daughter can pitch peas faster that you two townies. I'll bring her up to show you," Max growled as he grabbed two pitchforks, one for each hand.

"Don't think so, Max," George retorted. "These two altar boys'll show up your prissy non-Catholic daughter anytime."

"Watch it you mackerel-snappin', good-for-nothin', shanty Irishman. You keep spoutin' like that an' we'll ship you 'nd your entire Catholic clan, troublemakers all, right back to Ireland," Max snapped, those pitchforks looming closer. Bookie was all ears as he reached deep into the viner mechanism to retrieve his morning "benediction," a smooth move I later learned would become a regular ritual—blackberry brandy in the morning.

Irishman Mahoney chimed in from viner no. 1, "Hey, you giant Prussian. We Irish can kick the living sauerkraut out of you. No trouble at all."

"Take 'er easy, Max," George OJ hollered, pointing his pitchfork directly at Max, "or we'll nail you to the doors just like we did to Martin Luther," he said, guffawing as we attacked the stacks of vines with twenty flashing tines.

"You got that wrong, you wayward Catholic sonofabitches. Martin didn't get nailed . . . he did the nailin.'"

I was taken a-back, guys talking to Max like that, but over the days and weeks I found it to be just good natured chiding. Max, despite his gruff outward appearance, loved it as well as Bookie and everyone else. It made the long hours seem shorter. It developed camaraderie in the crew. We got the peas boxed, sent them to Rochester where pea counters counted them and chefs in tall white hats boiled, canned, packaged and labeled them before shipping to the grocery shelves of the country. We were doing our job out there on Bookie's viners.

By eight o'clock that first day the dump trucks had dropped their last loads; we had finished pitching, boxing and stacking, but then I found we had an additional two hours of cleaning before dragging weary bodies back to the village. We needed to clean everything: the huge drum, canvases, conveyor, viner's internal moving parts, boxes, pitchforks, the ground until all was ready for tomorrow's run. Those fellows at Libby's demanded clean peas. Max and Bookie saw to it that we cleaned thoroughly, but eventually, that too was done.

"That's it, you worthless farts. We're done finished for the day," Max hollered from somewhere deep within the viners. "Go home and get some sleep. And don't fuck the girls or jackoff tonight so's you can work a decent day tomorrow, a hell of a lot better than you did today."

"Come on, Jimmy, let's blow out of here, get a burger at Swenson's," Jack said, impulsively flipping his Yankees cap as we plodded, dog-tired toward his Chevy. I was hungry but preferred going straight to my room, to bed. Yet, Jack insisted on ordering burgers and malts. He spun past the now dozing dinosaurs, throwing stones and dirt onto the tractor and Bookie. He sped down the road past the darkened, silent farmstead before executing another wheelie onto County 16.

"Burger and a malt," Heinie," Jack hollered, plopping on a tall, beer-stained stool, simultaneously sailing his cap onto a tenpenny nail on the wainscoted wall, it hanging like a two-point horseshoe.

"Same for me, Heinie," I said, joining Jack at the forever-lonesome bar. Three regulars—Oscar, Erv, Red—plus a stranger were sipping 3.2 beer from eight-ounce glasses, mesmerized by the blue neon sign behind the bar, the Hamm's Bear circling Mille Lac lake. Two girls, classmates, were sitting in a high-backed booth whispering about Red Wing boys. Four men looking for more excitement than they found at home were dealing a Whist game in an adjacent booth. Otherwise, the humble, unpretentious cafe was subdued, the sizzling of Heinie's grill and the slapping of cards the only audible sounds. The lack of excitement was all right with me, I thought, pulling wayward pea vines from my hair. I was more tired than I had been in a long time; besides, I had only graduated from high school a week ago and wasn't used to hard, physical labor.

"You okay, Jimmy? Gonna make it? Jack asked, tapping his hard knuckles on the bar as Heinie slid two malts down the elbow-worn, smooth bar, both stopping in front of us like a shuffleboard three-score.

"Hell yes. I'll make it, just need a couple of days to get used to it," I answered as George O', Hutch and George OJ joined us at the counter, ordering the same.

"Jimmy, you little fart! You gonna make it, or am I going to have to do all of your work?" George O' said, whopping me on the back while plopping on a stool.

"Yep. Just tired after day one, but I'll outdo you in no time at all," I answered as he shook pea vines and dust from his boots.

"That'll be the day, that'll be the day, you honky-tonk clarinet player. Hurry up, Heinie. Tired here. Worked my butt off at the viners. Hutch and OJ, too. Malts and burgers around."

I scarfed my burger, slurped the malt before trudging home past Joe's Place and the Corner Bar to my bedroom. I plopped into bed and was asleep in a minute, knowing full well that four o'clock would arrive much too quickly.

S o went the Summer of '54—rise at four o'clock, pitch peas until ten or eleven at night, grab a burger and malt at Swenson's, then catch a short four hours of sleep. Yet, it was good the summer happened that way, because I didn't have time to sit in a stark, lifeless room feeling sorry for myself, wondering where the family had gone. The only time I spent in my bedroom was to sleep, because when the peas were running, they ran fast and furious. Ripening peas didn't care about holidays, Saturdays or Sunday Services, regardless of Catholicism, Lutheranism or Methodism. Peas wanted off those vines and out of those pods, hell be damned.

Even though I was only seventeen, working every day, all day, did get tiresome. Max and Bookie only gave us a day off when it rained so much the dump trucks couldn't enter the fields, which rarely happened. During one stretch the guys worked forty-five days straight. Tired! Even Uncle Dave was weary of supervising, looking forward to a day off in the village, getting off his gout-laden big toe to hang around Heaney & Gorman telling far-fetched stories about how hard he was working at the viners.

Occasionally, the pea harvesters and truckers would finish a field by six o'clock. After the crew had scoured the viners, we would finish about eight. Elation! That left enough time to speed to Zumbrota for roller-skating with Zumbrota, Wanamingo, maybe even some Goodhue girls, if they weren't already searching for Red Wing boys. Exuberance of youth—work ten or twelve hours followed by roller-skating, to bed by midnight, then back to the viners by five.

But even on a rainy day off I couldn't sleep long, couldn't stay in my stark bedroom. I would saunter downtown to visit with anyone I could find, folks who weren't so busy they couldn't talk a while, which was just about anyone in the village . . .

Julius Ebe was sitting in his own barber's chair reading the newspaper, his red-and-white rotating barber pole no longer rotating, long ago having given up any attempt of attracting customers. Julius didn't see the sense in fixing it. His customers knew where he was and strangers weren't likely to happen through town seeking a haircut from an old country barber, anyway.

"Morning, Julius. Lookin' pretty darn busy sitting in your own chair," I said, plopping into a lumpy, cracked leather chair that had seen better days. Julius set the *St. Paul Pioneer Press* on his lap and squinted at me over his bifocals while brushing back thinning, wispy hair, his own sparse coiffure not a decent advertisement for a barber.

"Good morning, Jimmy. How's things out at the viner?" he asked after being interrupted from his reading.

"Oh, good. Raining today, so we have the day off. I'm glad, though. Been working lots of days straight."

"Hell, Jimmy, you young fellows can handle that. You'd only get into trouble if you didn't work. What are you going to do with all your moola?" Julius asked, slowly rising from the barber chair to, once again, comb his thinning hair in a stained, cracked mirror that passed for a barber's mirror.

"Enrolling at St. John's this fall. Dave Hutcheson said it was a good college, Catholic too. Think I'll like it."

"Why don't you stay closer to home, enroll at Winona State; that way you would be closer to your mother."

"Oh, Mother remarried a few weeks ago. She's got a new husband, Bill Ryan, so she doesn't need me. She'll be all right living with Bill in Red Wing. I like Goodhue better," I said, jumping out of the chair as Burt Austad entered for either conversation or a haircut, both inexpensive in the village.

"Morning, Burt," I said, hitching up my pants and heading for the door. "How's the Goodhue County Artificial Breeders getting along?"

"Morning, Jimmy. We're just shootin 'em up right and left, front and back, if you catch my drift. Where you going? You don't have to leave just 'cause I came in," he said, tossing his Dekalb seed cap to the now vacant chair.

"Day off. Got to make my rounds, see what's been happening," I said, reaching the torn screen door.

"Well, don't go away mad then," Burt guffawed. "Just go away!"

"See you, Burt. So long, Julius," I said, stepping into the pouring rain and running toward Marshall-Wells Hardware to see what was happening. I ducked under the canopy to shake off rainwater. Three rusted pickups were parked at the curb. I supposed their owners were busy in the hardware store, so I stood out of the rain for a moment looking up and down this two block, barren prairie town I called home. I recalled sitting in Julius' barber chair that fateful day of October 1951, getting a fresh crewcut when Julius and I happened to look out his window, across the street, to see Ole Haga loading Dad and his casket into the hearse for a ride to our house and a wake. It had caught me by surprise, caught Julius by surprise. He stopped cutting, laid both hands on my shoulders and didn't say anything for a minute or two. I felt the warmth of his hands on my shoulders, knew that he cared. That was four years ago, I recalled, looking now at the listing pickups. I dashed next door to visit with Sidney Berg in his tiny shoe shop. "Hey, Sidney! How goes it this morning?"

"Hallo to the morning, Chimmy. Not so bad to see yoos today, but how's come yoos not to be workin'?" Sid asked as he glanced up from his workbench while resoling a pair of worn boots.

"Wet. Cutters and truckers can't get into the fields, so we have the day off," I answered, slipping around the corner of his bench, banging my hip on an iron shoe anvil. "What are you doing there, Sid? Looks like those old boots should be thrown away instead of resoled. Whose are they, anyway?"

"To Cy Benda dey belong. Cy don't like to throw tings away, den. 'Sides, I can fix dem up real good, juss like dey yuss to be. Be like new ven I finish with dem."

"I know that Sidney. You've got good hands. You've kept my four bucklers in good repair through grade school and high school. I'll have to bring these boots in one of these days. Working at the viners is darn hard on them," I said as I looked over the boots and shoes lining his rack.

"Juss keep polishing dem, Chimmy. Dat's good to keep da water off dem. Den dry dem tonight, too. They last yoos long time dat a way, den."

"What do you have for juice-pissed boots, Sidney?"

"Juss piss? Don't understand dat 'juss piss'?"

"When Hutch stacks the vines at Bookie's, pea juice runs into the moat. Stinks worse than a Lutheran's fart!"

"Yoos shouldn't say such tings, Chimmy. Dat's sort of sacri . . . sack . . . well . . . tiss not nice."

"Just joshing, Sid. You aren't Lutheran are you?"

"No, Chimmy. Methodist, but closer to Lutherans dan you Catlics."

"Probably right. Don't know much about Methodists, other than they don't confess to a priest and they don't think much of Mary, our Blessed Virgin. Lutherans don't either, but Catholics do. Confession is hard, Sid. You ever been to confession?" I said, circling the counter and picking up discarded sole leather.

"No sirees, but I talk to da Lord 'bout my misgivings. I confess directly to Him, feeling mighty sorry for some of da tings

I tink about and not so good at doin'," Sid answered while rising to buff Cy's boots on a machine looking something like a John Yungers' contraption. He got more black polish on his already black-stained hands and apron.

"But how do you know if He's listening, if he forgives you? When I confessed to Fr. Smith, I sure knew because Ol' Smitty answered me with a vengeance-full penance, sometimes little, sometimes big. Ol' Smitty sure used to let me and everyone else at Holy Trinity know, too, 'specially when he'd gotten his dander and booming voice up," I said, admiring the buff Sidney was placing on Cy's boots.

"I read da Bible ever day, juss the gospels, sometimes da ancients, too, but I's trouble with dat fella Leviticus and hiss laws. Da Bible says if yoos are sorry for da sins, den da Lord will hear yoos and forgive yoos some. Dat's what John Wesley's Methodists say," Sidney said while tying Cy's laces together, tagging the boots and placing them 'juss' so on the overflowing rack. He then sat in a wooden chair and pulled out a long Camel cigarette from his stained cobbler's-vest pocket.

"Sounds like a heckuva deal to me, Sid. Makes confessing pretty easy, I'd say. It was hard confessing to Fr. Smith behind that black screen. Sometimes he would get real surly when I told him *tings*, got loud, wheezed behind that curtain. He zapped me pretty good with penance . . . why, one time he sentenced me to say the entire Sorrowful Mysteries, a full rosary, Sid. Took me a week to finish."

Sidney—medium build with a slight paunch escaping over an always polished, wide leather belt, round Winston Churchill-ish happy face, full head of silver hair except for receding temples—leaned back in his wooden craw-legged, swivel chair, puffed long and deep on a Camel cigarette, then let the smoke swirl in rings ever so slowly toward the corrugated tin ceiling. I looked around his ten-by-ten cobbler's shop, the same one I had been visiting since those days in first grade back in 1941. I would sneak out of the house to meander downtown, finding grownups to talk with. Even then I liked chatting with old-timers. Sidney would welcome me into his shop, give me penny candy, then let me handle his shoes. I would pick up boots, inspect them, set them back, wrong, of course. I would pick up discarded leather from the floor. I would run my hands over the curved-needle stitcher, hand-cranked cutter and presser, and his heavy duty sewing machine. I would stick my hands in jars and pails, smell tangy, raw-cut leather, and coal black boot polish, Sid all the while, ever-patient with a little, inquisitive boy.

Sid hadn't had any children of his own, so he enjoyed having me around. I was his boy, vicariously. "Yoos going off to college den in da fall, Chimmy, I hear'd. We miss yoos in da village," he said, drawing one last deep breath from his Camel, coughing deeply before snuffing it out in an already filled ash tray.

"Dat's . . . I mean . . . *That's* right, Sidney. I'm entering St. John's up at St. Cloud. Good Catholic college, so they let me in. Mom's going to drive me up the last week of August, but till then I'll be working at Bookie's viners earning tuition and board money," I said now inspecting a shiny pair of penny loafers.

"Dat's good, Chimmy. Juss glad to see yoos going off to da college, den, though we'll miss yoos. Make sure yoos come back to visit to me ven yoos come home to vacation."

"Sure will, Sidney. Always like visiting with you. Say 'halloo' to the wife, Eyece Berg, for me. I'll be around all summer at the viners. See ya," I said, bounding through the squeaking door into the still pouring rain.

Shooting the breeze with Sidney and Julius about Dad's wake four years ago had gotten me into some sad thinking as I left Sid's shop, something I didn't want to do. Julius said it was good I was working long days. Sid said so, too. They were right about that. I hadn't expected to be on my own at seventeen, only a few days out of high school. I had entered grade school much too early, as Mother had pushed me out the door to first grade when only a toddling five. I had expected the family unit to continue longer, but here I was, on a pouring, dreary, gray day, shuffling along Upper Street, on my own. Dad was out in St. Columbkill's country cemetery; Mother was remarried and planting gladiolus in Red Wing; Rose was sticking needles into cadavers up in Duluth; Tom was learning how to aim and fire an M-1 rifle for the U.S. Army at

Ft. Leonard Wood. It didn't make sense, I thought, suddenly ducking into Mans & Benda Shell Station out of the pinging, grateful summer rain.

"Hey, Jimmy, how you doin'?" Cy Benda asked as I shed rain from my cap and coat like a drowned Black Labrador.

"Wet, Cy, doggone wet today. Can't work at the viners 'cause the trucks can't get into the fields. Okay, though, needed a day off," I said, shaking rain from my cap. "What are you up to today?" Cy was co-owner of Mans & Benda Shell Station with Bill, but he also operated an electrical service out of the gas station. He didn't just pump gas all day long. Bill did most of that, and Vern Haas did the mechanical work on cars and trucks in a double-bay station. Cy had a small shop in the rear of the garage. He was fastening metal electric boxes and conduit when I shuffled in.

"I'm getting conduit, wire and boxes ready for a job out in Vasa. Fella is putting on an addition to his house. You ever been out to Vasa, Jimmy?" Cy asked, continuing to cut conduit with an obviously dull hacksaw before leading wire through the tubes and tying them into four-outlet boxes.

"Guess I drove through a couple of times with Dad when hauling milk to the Welch Creamery. It's out by Welch, isn't it?" I asked, inspecting outlets from Cy's tidy work bench.

"Sure, it's down near Welch, but not that far. Just a little burg set in a valley around that big Swedish Lutheran Church. Fact is, the house I'm working on is just down the hill from the church, across the road from the Vasa General Store. I'm driving out in about a half hour, Jimmy. Want to ride along, maybe help?" Cy asked as he finished wiring two heavy-duty boxes. "You don't have work today anyway, can't pitch peas, and . . . you're on your own now, aren't you? Living up to the house? It's good Lucille married again. Tough after Tom died. He was a good friend. Why, Bessie and me and Bill and Laura played lots of Five Hundred and Bridge with your folks. Good people, Jimmy, but you'll be okay, then. Glad to see you're staying in the village for the summer. How about riding to Vasa with me now? Here, grab this conduit and wire, throw it in the back of the truck and we'll head out to Vasa; maybe even have a little lunch later."

"Whatever."

Actually, I was glad Cy suggested riding to Vasa, because I was getting blue on a gray day. This was my first day off from the viners, so it was also the first day I had a chance to ponder how things had changed. Oh, not in the village; they never changed. Rather, in my life. I was trying real hard not to feel sorry for myself. Cy's offer saved me from thinking.

Cy squeezed his six-foot-one frame and lanky legs into the pickup, legs not as long as Uncle Dave's, but long by village standards, nevertheless. He wore his usual baseball cap, Cleveland Indians I think, to cover a slightly balding head, but he was well enough coiffured around the ears and back, sort of a village male trademark. Cy's pickup had custom metal storage boxes along the sides where he hauled assorted electrical paraphernalia. Bert Majerus, across the street at Majerus Gas & Appliance, had a service truck also, but he filled his with overflowing plumbing paraphernalia. Cy drove a faded, yellow Ford, Bert a rusted, black Chevy, but I recognized the two trucks anytime I saw them out in the townships. Cy loved a clean truck; Bert didn't care as long as it ran at least on six of the eight cylinders. Cy changed oil regularly, filled the tires with air, kept it clean, neat and tidy. Bert couldn't have been more different. He was lucky to have gas in the tank, even though he distributed propane gas in the county. He seldom changed oil and probably hadn't inspected his tires in years, other than if he had a flat or a blowout. Bert and Cy were complete opposites when it came to trucks.

The windshield wipers were working overtime, splashing, tapping incessantly as Cy peered through the windshield in Evergreen Cemetery heading west toward Vasa Township on County Rd. No. 9. We passed neat farmsteads devoid of activity in the fields today. I was silent. This day off was turning out to be hard, yet I was glad to be riding with Cy. We bounded toward Vasa for several miles before he spoke . . . "Bill and me got into the gas station business in 1940. Thought it would be a good business, because Goodhue didn't have much for a service station then. We brought Luverne Haas on to do the mechanical work, because I'm not much with motors, but always liked working with electricity.

It works out pretty good then, operating both the station and the electrical businesses out of the same building. You like to tinker with electricity, don't you, Jimmy?" Cy asked, leaning forward in his seat, peering through the wipers, having difficulty seeing and avoiding the frequent potholes.

"A couple of years ago, you gave me some discarded conduit, Cy. Remember when I built a lighted lamppost out front of our house? I didn't know what I was doing, but that didn't stop me and you helped me. I set the lamppost near the front sidewalk, dug a trench along the walkway to the house, buried the conduit, then wired it to our fuse box in the basement. Mother thought I was crazy; Tom thought I was crazy, but after a couple of shocks at the fuse box, I got it wired. It worked for a week until the moisture shorted it out. Clara Hennings thought it had something to do with that newfangled television folks were starting to get. Yup, I always liked tinkering with electricity and switches and radios and microphones," I said as we passed the turnoff to St. Columbkill's country church and cemetery.

"I remember that. Your mother chided me for giving you the wire and conduit, for encouraging you. Thought you'd kill yourself, but Lucille always did worry about you, you being the youngest and all."

"I know, Cy, but she didn't have to worry so much. What trouble could I get into in the village? I spent a lot of time playing with your daughter, Mary. We were good kids, didn't get into any serious trouble, even though Fr. Smith thought we did."

The rain was letting up as we came over a small rise on No. 9 before turning off to No. 7 toward Uncle Vic O'Neill's place in Belle Creek Township. We passed Vic and Cis' ancient eighty-acre plot they called a farm, then wound through the increasing hills to Vasa, the Swedish Lutheran outpost of Goodhue County, maybe even Minnesota. Sidney Berg might have been from Vasa, but I was unsure of that. Eddie Fischer at the Drugstore was a Featherstonian, I remembered. Heinie Swenson was Swedish, and B. C. Majerus hailed from the Bellechester area while George Lucman at the Corner Bar had shown up in town one day from outside the county. Even though I wasn't a kid anymore, I hadn't given much thought to where folks originated from. They just were. I knew most Catholics in Belle Creek Township had Ireland roots—the McNamaras, Gadients. O'Reillys, O'Connors, O'Rourkes, O'Neills—because that was my heritage. And in high school I was minimally aware some friends and classmates were Norwegian, Swedish, German—the Johnsons, Carlsons, Ericksons, Fredericksons, Knutsons, Buchholtz', Diercks, even a smattering of Bellechester Luxembourgers. Now that I was bound for college I would probably run into even more ethnic guys, maybe even some African-Americans or Orientals from the Twin Cities, unknown groups around the village.

"Did Sidney grow up in Vasa?" I asked as Cy pulled to a stop across from the Vasa General Store.

"Don't know, Jimmy. Might have, but I'm not sure," he said, jumping from the pickup, grabbing a heavy, leather tool bag and shuffling toward the house. "Come on, grab that conduit and switch boxes from the back. You got to pay for your ride now."

I jumped into the back to gather several ten-foot lengths of conduit and a box of electric boxes before following Cy to the house with the new addition going up on the south side. I guessed it was to be a family room or additional bedroom. For the next couple of hours, Cy bent conduit into right angles with a long-handled, curved wrench, slipped 12-gauge wire through it and twisted the conduit onto metal outlet boxes. He had me screwing the outlets into boxes then wiring them. I liked the work, felt good getting something done on a rainy day. It felt good being with Cy, a pleasant, gentle man I had known all my life, even though it had only been seventeen years.

Cy and Bessie had been good friends with Dad and Mom. Cy and Dad even fished together down at Collischan's Landing where the Cannon River meets the Mississippi River. Mary Benda and I were both born in '36, so we spent twelve years together in the same boring classrooms, graduated together a few weeks back at the high school. Now that I didn't have a father anymore, but a new, untested stepfather, I figured Cy could step in as a step-stepfather.

"You hungry, Jimmy?" Cy asked as I struggled with stiff, unyielding 12-gauge wire, inserting an outlet into a box.

"I could eat," I said, while cutting my finger with a sharp-ended wire.

"Bessie always makes a big lunch. I've enough to share. Let's take a break to eat sandwiches," Cy said, leaning the curved conduit wrench on his tool box.

I hadn't eaten breakfast, hadn't taken my lunch from the frige back at the house. Suddenly, I *was* hungry. Bessie's bologna sandwiches and Jonathan apple tasted mighty good. We sat on plank benches in the new, uncompleted addition chomping on white bread sandwiches. Cy drank coffee, but I declined his offer. I wasn't much for coffee yet, water did just fine. "I'm glad you're going to St. John's in the fall, Jim. It'll be good for you. I don't know what Mary is going to do. She's awful sweet on a guy in Bellechester. Wants to get married, but I wish she'd wait a while. You sweet on anyone?"

"Naw, haven't had time. I suppose there'll be lots of girls at St. John's, although they don't allow girls at the actual college. But St. Benedict's girls college is just down the road, Dave Hutch said. I'll probably get around to it," I answered, finishing the first half of my sandwich.

Cy bit into his apple and offered some advice. "Take your time. You've time. Marriage is fine, but it lasts a long, long time."

We returned to work throughout the afternoon as the rain continued falling on Vasa. I was learning about 10- and 12- and 14-gauge wires, conduit, breakers, fuses, outlets, circuits, shorts, black on black, white on white, 110–220 volts and amps, and I even began thinking I might not need college. I started thinking that maybe I should stay in the village, become Cy's journeyman, learn a good trade. The village had stood me in good stead so far. Why couldn't it for the future? I asked Cy about it. "Hey, Cy, maybe I shouldn't go to St. John's. Maybe I should stay in the village, work with you. I kind of like this electric stuff," I said, finishing an outlet.

"Jimmy, I sure could use your help, but you need to enroll at St. John's. Your Dad would want you to. Your mother wants you to. You head off to college, then come back and work with me during the summers. I could use you. You come back next summer. I'll have a job waiting for you."

"I don't know if I can make it in college, Cy. I didn't study much in high school. Spent more time playing basketball and baseball, tooting my clarinet. I'm nervous about it. Maybe I should become an electrician like you," I answered while rummaging through the box for more outlets.

"I didn't get a chance to go to college, barely finished high school. Your dad only went to eighth grade out in the township, 'cause he had to help out on the farm like most boys. He'd want you to continue your education. You really should, and because your dad isn't here to tell you, I'm telling you! You're going to St. John's, you hear me, young man!" Cy shouted as he set his prolonged, angular face directly in front of mine.

"Yes, sir, Cy. Yes, sir."

By the time we finished the job, had approached Evergreen Cemetery on the village's west side, the rain had ceased, clearing skies indicating I would be back pitching at the viners tomorrow. Cy dropped me off downtown, thanked me for helping him before driving home to Bessie and his family. I waved good-bye before shuffling into Swenson's for a hot beef sandwich with gravy and maybe applesauce. I was hungry and felt better having spent the afternoon with Cy. Maybe I'd still become an electrician, anyway.

Despite untold seventeen- to nineteen-hour days at the viner, the summer moved rapidly, much more so than I had anticipated. Pitching peas had been about the best work I could have had. It kept me from meditating about things I didn't want to think about. Oh, I still experienced trepidation about impending college classes, and I still had mixed feelings about possibly staying in the village to work with Cy or George or Dennis. After all, this burg on the rolling Minnesota prairie was the only home I had known. I had traveled little, maybe to Red Wing, periodically to Rochester, seldom to the Twin Cities. My horizons had been limited, mostly confined to Goodhue County. We worked so much I seldom saw Mother; besides, she and Bill began traveling to California, North Dakota and other exotic places.

As I had mentioned to Cy, Mother worried about me as a boy.

What trouble could I possibly get into in Goodhue? She didn't worry about Rose. Once Rose had driven past the slumbering Goodhue Elevator, had headed out of town to nurses' training in the frozen Duluth tundra, she never returned to live in the village. Elated to leave, she soon kicked the dust and grime from her saddle shoes. Oh, she liked the burg well enough, enjoyed her classmates, but she said she had other horizons to reach. Brother Tom didn't return for a long time, because he was learning how to shoot that M-1 rife when Col Leavenworth or Generals Pershing or Eisenhower sent him to Germany to mop up after Hitler and Stalin. Tom was two years away from the village, from the country, before I saw him again.

Many school gang members hung around that summer, sort of a transitional period before entering real life. Sandbox Bob O' was preparing to enter St. Thomas up in St. Paul. Nights when the peas weren't running, I would get back to the old neighborhood about eight. Bob and I would sit on his front porch recalling the past twelve years, since that day we had walked to first grade . . .

"So, how come you're going to St. Thomas and not St. John's, then?" I asked Bob as he lounged in a rusty metal lawn chair.

"I want to be in the big city, Jim. St. John's is too isolated."

"You always did love big cities. Shoot, even back when we were toddlers playing in your sandbox you built the biggest houses, drove the biggest cars, lived on Sunset Boulevard out in Hollywood. Where'd you get those ideas, anyway, being just a country bumpkin like all of us?"

"I always dreamed of it. I would really prefer attending college in Southern California, but can't afford it. I think I'll like St. Paul. It'll beat the Dickens out of Goodhue," Bob said while sipping on a glass of lemonade. "Want some lemonade, Jim? It's sweet and cool. Mom made it."

"Sure, don't mind if I do," I answered, looking past Bob to my house, bedroom dark, no one there to welcome me home. What had been the center of my life only stood there now, darkened, a simple two story, blanched clapboard building that used to be a home. "You always did like California, I can say that. You and your movie stars. Don't you like Goodhue? You anxious to leave?"

"I'm ready to leave. We have our friends and classmates, but they'll be moving on, too: Larry O'Reilly and Mary Benda and Bettie Lunde and Rita Ryan and Beverly Moran and Joanne Mans and Lyle Puppe—we've had loads of fun, but I'm looking forward to St. Thomas, seeing real movies in St. Paul, maybe attending plays on Hennepin Avenue. Aren't you anxious to leave?" Bob asked as his mother brought me a tall glass of lemonade.

Bob's question startled me. I wasn't prepared for it. I pondered for several moments, just listening to the crickets and katydids, even the bronchial croak of a lonesome bullfrog back in the marshy ditch, loud sounds in a quiet village. "Thanks, Gladys, much appreciated. I guess I'm anxious, Bob, but have mixed feelings. I like our burg, even thinking of staying to work at Heaney & Gorman or maybe with Cy Benda. I'm a little mixed up at this point. Geez! It's hard, you know, leaving for college, meeting everybody new. Almost as hard as confessing to Fr. Smith. But Larry said he was planning on entering St. John's, too, and Dave Hutch will be a sophomore. I'll probably go, only a few weeks left at the viners to decide."

Bob didn't speak for a while. He lounged in his lilting chair in always neat trousers—no jeans for Bob—in deference to my scruffy pants. Even when casual, just hanging around the neighborhood, Bob dressed well, was well groomed, his clothes clean, pressed, crewcut flat across the top, a collared shirt, neat, just so. We were both about five-foot-nine then, and maybe all of 135 pounds, though I was to grow a couple of inches after high school, Mother having shipped me off to first grade a year too early just to get me out of the house.

I had talked myself out. We sat on his porch in our old neighborhood gazing at the forlorn street, the childhood street and neighborhood we thought held all our dreams, a single 100-watt streetlight bulb swaying in the midwestern summer's breeze. At seventeen we were too young to be nostalgic, but Bob was thinking about the same things I was. We had been next-door neighbors the past fifteen years; had hiked to school together with respective Gene Autry metal lunch boxes and Crayolas; had played endless days and nights in Bob's sandbox; had shared the tree house behind my house, remnants still dangling ten feet up; had built model airplanes, meeting that fateful day on the Holy Trinity lawn for a showdown; had quadrupled-dated for high school proms, taffeta, Old Spice and dime store perfume overflowing the Buick and high school gymnasium; had sat, ramrod straight, in catechism classes Friday afternoons while Fr. Smith ranted and raved about self-abuse and temptation and impurity and picking our fingers and noses during mass, on and on about the sanctity of the *Baltimore Catechism*. There wasn't much Bob and I hadn't experienced together other than participating in sports. Bob showed no interest in basketball and baseball; rather, he was a scholar, much more so than me. I worried about that . . . I broke the silence of the evening.

"You were a good student in high school, Bob, but I didn't study very hard; you finished second or third and I finished twentieth out of twenty-one. Only Digger Dave was behind me. I'm worried about making it at St. John's."

"You'll be all right, Jim. I know you didn't address study much, but you'll improve once you're up there. You'll have to or you'll soon be filling cars at Mans & Benda's or butchering at Heaney & Gorman. St. John's and St. Thomas are excellent schools with exemplary academic reputations. I'll need to study diligently, even though I applied myself more in high school," Bob said, placing his lemonade glass on the porch railing, then getting up to stretch.

"You can pray for me, Bob. You know, a few Hail Marys, a Glory Be. I'll need them."

"You're the altar boy. You know more about theology and liturgy, holy water and blessed wine, Latin and the stations of the cross, even Holy Thursday than I do. I never became as entranced with being an acolyte as you. You'll do fine at St. John's with that background. We can compare notes when returning for vacations, maybe have some parties with our classmates."

Bob suddenly changed the subject from our futures to the present, an issue I had been trying to avoid all summer. "How are you faring living alone, Jim? Is it difficult?"

"Guess I'm doing okay. Busy at the viners, so don't have time to think about family that's gone. Oh, I get lonesome, 'specially at night; feels odd being in my room with the rest of the family gone. Guess I'll make it, though."

"Odd for me, also," Bob said, glancing toward my deserted house, no longer a home. "Rose and I did a lot together; I liked your mom and dad. Peculiar not to have them next door anymore."

"Yup, but I better not start talking about that; better go to bed, Bob. Four o'clock arrives awfully early. See you later."

"Good night, Jim."

I sauntered thirty feet to the house, jumped the stairs to the bedroom, then looked out the window to see Bob still sitting on his front porch. I was glad to have him as a friend, glad to still have him in the neighborhood, his family, too. I slipped into bed thinking about our years together, good years. I said prayers that we'd have many more as I fell asleep . . . in the old neighborhood.

I never did buy that alarm clock. Every morning Jack had to holler up to my window, waking me as well as the neighbors, "Dammit, Franklin! Why don't you buy an alarm clock at Jesse's Hardware, so I don't have to wake everyone ever-day," he hollered, exasperated, fishtailing down the street.

"Never get around to it, Jack, We're always working."

"Shit! We only got a couple weeks left. Guess there isn't much sense in buyin' one now," he said, spinning around the corner by Swenson's slumbering cafe. "You going to St. John's?"

"Guess so, but I'm still unsure. Sort of want to stay in town, maybe a year or so," I said, digging the sleep out of my eyes as we crossed Highway 58 for the eightieth time that summer heading to Bookie's voracious dinosaurs.

"Shit, Jimmy. Go to college. I'll be entering my second year at Mankato State. You got to do it. You can't stay here all your life. Your family's gone, anyway," Jack said, gunning the Chevy through the loose gravel on No. 9.

"Guess you're right. I've got to make up my mind in a few days. Got about $800 saved from our viner work. Another couple hundred and I could make it through the first year. I'll decide in a few days, that's for sure."

I slumped into Jack's depressed seat as he barreled down the road toward Bookie's. He loved driving his Chevy, even liked driving his dad's trucks when Bill would permit it, that is. I didn't have a car yet, so Jack had driven me throughout the summer. We had been bouncing down this road for ten weeks, rising at four, arriving at the viners by four-forty-five, tolerating Bookie's bullshit, Max's Germanic haranguing, Dave's outrageous stories, George O's tall tales and chiding, yet it had been an enjoyable and profitable summer. We liked working outside, even if it rained, drizzling for countless days. Hutch's stack had grown wider and taller until it reached twelve feet. The moat smelled more acidic as the weeks passed, so much so that we could even smell it well before arriving at Bookie's place.

The following Wednesday, as the cutters and truckers finished early, a couple of truckers brought a case of beer to the viners. Max let us sit on the truck to drink it, although I didn't like beer then. I would take a first cold swallow then set it aside. The other guys loved it, but it would take a year or two of intensive training at St. John's before I liked it. I had to drink enough that day so O'Reilly and the other fellows wouldn't raze me . . .

"You been getting any lately, Jimmy?" a grizzled, bear-sized trucker asked, his heavy boots swinging from the rear of the truck.

"Getting what. Sleep?" I asked.

"No, you little shit. Pussy. You been getting any pussy, snatch lately?" he said, laughing, guffawing as he looked at the other guys sitting in the bed of the truck.

"Ya, sure, all the time. I been getting some," I retorted, slapping my knee and laughing right along with him and the other guys, friends looking suspect at me.

"Shit! You don't even know what I'm talking about, do you, you prepubescent fart."

"How about you, Jack? You been getting any?" Grizzly Bear asked as he popped the cap off another Grain Belt.

"Fuckin' A," Jack shot back immediately, his hardened fingers tapping his ripped knee. "Hell, I've got those Mankato State girls just standin' in line. They can't wait for me to get back in a couple of weeks."

"You're full of shit, O'Reilly. Bet you can't even get your cock up for those prissy white college girls. Now me? I get pussy all the time, anytime and anywheres I want. All I need to do is strut into a bar in Zumbrota or Oak Center, down in Hay Creek, and the women fall all over me, just beg me to fuck 'em," Bear boasted, drawing high and long on his Grain Belt.

"You're nothing but bullshit," OJ retorted. "When Max hollers 'Grab you socks and not your cocks,' you can't even find your cock," he snarled, reaching for a second Grain Belt.

I guess the guys were compelled to boast, although I wasn't much interested in it. I liked girls, that's for sure, but I wasn't into pussy yet, just a little necking and feeling around interested me, but well . . . confession was hard and Father Smith's replacement confessor was hard of hearing, hearing aid and all. He blurted "Eh? say that again, young man," behind the ominous black curtain. I spoke softly, not wanting everyone at Holy Trinity to know what I had been doing. I figured I'd wait until I got up to St. John's to experiment more, well beyond the prying ears of the parish. That way, when I went to confession, everyone in town wouldn't know what I had been up to. There would be time enough for more experimentation at college.

Lower, softer rays of summer began creeping over the viners, the sun taking longer to peak over the surrounding, depleted and desecrated pea fields as our summer came to a close. Jack, Hutch and George O' began talking about returning to college, OJ of one more year at GHS. The more I heard, the more I reassured myself that I should go too, that I would be lonesome in the village without them. I wouldn't be returning to GHS; everything would soon be changing. By the time Bookie had said, "Tomorrow's the last day, you lazy sonofabitches," I had reaffirmed my intention to enroll at St. John's. What the hell, I thought, I could always come back and work for Cy.

The next day, Friday, we did, indeed, finish. The trucks stopped dumping by noon giving us the remainder of the day to complete a final cleaning, tear down the equipment, store it in

Bookie's barn, and pack the viners in mothballs for the harsh winter. I'd probably be back, as well as the rest of the guys, next summer.

Mother had left a message indicating she and Bill would be out early Sunday morning—after mass, of course—to drive me north to St. John's. I guess she didn't know I had been deliberating about not going. It was good I hadn't concerned her. She would have been disconcerted thinking I might hang around her and Bill in Red Wing. But she needn't have worried. They had a new life now, as Bill had retired from his Belle Creek farm. They could travel to see family, friends and the country. I wasn't about to get in their way.

Saturday morning, Jack and I drove, for the last time, to Bookie's farm for our final paycheck. He and Max were sitting in rusted green metal lawn chairs under an ancient split oak tree sipping black coffee spiced with, presumably, whiskey or black-berry brandy as Jack wheeled into the yard. "You little fart, O'Reilly. Everyday you roar out here kickin' up a dust storm with that beat up Chevy. When you gonna learn to drive right like?" Bookie shouted as we jumped from the car to join him and Max under the spreading tree.

"Hell, Bookie! You ought to spray some of that pea juice shit on your road. It'd stink but keep the dust down. Or you could pour some of your sweet brandy on the drive—that'd do it," Jack snapped while plopping his five-foot-eight frame on a dilapidated wooden bench.

Max piped in, "Me and Bookie like our 'coffee' straight and laced. They's only one place my whiskey goes, and that's down my throat, into my gut," he snarled. "I may piss it on the road later, after it's been filtered, but not before," Max snapped while drawing another swig.

"What're you farts up to? Think you got dough comin' for the lousy workers you been this summer?" Bookie asked.

"You betcha, we got money coming, Book," Jack retorted, "and you could give us some of yours, too. Jim and I worked real hard, didn't we, Jimmy?" he said, smiling to me and poking me in the ribs with his elbow.

"What'd you think, Franklin? Think you're worth this last pay check? Let me see now, $125 dollars. What you gonna do with all that money?"

"Heading to college, Bookie. Mom's coming out in the morning to take me to St. John's. This last pay check will just about get me through my first year," I said while sitting on a listing metal chair next to Bookie.

"You young farts ain't smart enough to learn pea vinin' much less learnin' anythin' at college, but guess it'd be good for you's to get out of the village. Me? Hell, I'm just a farmer, pea 'nd hog farmer. You guys ain't half bad workers, though. Just all bad," Bookie laughed while pulling our checks from a stained vest pocket, Max fumbling with his bean counter notebook.

"Don't go spending it on girls, getting into their pants, buyin' perfume for 'em, things like that," Max admonished as he jotted receipt of our checks in his stained book.

"You got that right, Max. Use it for college . . . and boys . . . come back next year. I kind o' liked having you around," Bookie said, rising to slap the dust off our backs.

"So long, Bookie . . . Max. We'll be back next summer." Jack tugged his Yankee cap lower, peered over the steering wheel and roared out of the driveway causing five dogs to bark and chase their tails, chickens to scatter out of the hay loft, itinerant rabbits and squirrels to seek shelter under the corn crib. He spun three wheelies on the gravel road creating a maelstrom of dust as Bookie and Max covered their eyes and gave us the finger. Yes, we surely would be back.

Instead of driving straight back to the village, Jack wheeled into a Ralphie and headed toward Bellechester, just to kill time. We had money in our pockets; maybe we would spend a few bucks, although that was hard to do in Bellechester, the burg a ghost town other than Cooney's Bar. But we thought we might see classmates Dennis Mahoney or Hal Pepper or Tom Manahan or one of the innumerable Majeruses or Poncelets on the single downtown street. But all we found was more dust, abandoned 1946 Plymouths and dried dog turds on the broken sidewalks. Bellechester never had gotten around to paving its streets like Goodhue. We bounded past the Creamery, hung a Ralphie, executed a wheelie in the middle of the deserted street before driving to the rocky baseball diamond where Jack and I had played many a game against the infamous Bellechester nine, left-wing-liberal-right-handed-hitting priest and all.

"Hell, there's nothing happening here," Jack said, revving his engine, spinning onto the diamond's sandy infield.

"You can say that again. Let's head back to town. I got to deposit my check in the bank 'cause mom's driving me to St. John's in the morning," I said, adjusting my pea-stained baseball cap at the attitude Tom Manahan used when pitching on this old diamond.

"Guess you're right, Jimmy. Me too. I have to head to Mankato Monday morning for fall registration," he said, spinning out of the diamond. Jack loved driving his Chevy; loved driving fast. He dodged a hundred potholes on No. 9 as we sped back toward the village where he dropped me in front of the bank, "See ya, Jim. We had a good summer. Drop me a line at Mankato. See you at Christmas vacation," and he was off in a cloud of dust up the street, fishtailing past the antiquated Goodhue Hotel.

After depositing $125.39 and verifying my savings balance: $982.36, I found I had earned and saved enough to pay for one college year. Tuition and board would be $450 each semester, but I would need to earn money for textbooks plus spending money. Maybe I could get a job toting holy water for the Benedictine Black Robes, or sweeping out the sacristy, or cleaning their liturgical-year vestments, or dispensing pinion-scented incense at mass. I sure had had enough incense training at Holy Trinity. Years of "incensing" and reciting Latin and lugging heavy gospels from one side of the altar to the other—never did understand why the pope sanctioned that—should stand me in good stead with my soon-to-be Benedictine Brothers.

Sauntering out of the bank onto Upper Street, one-year balance in my hand, I suddenly felt at a loss, not knowing whether to walk right or left, either direction quickly taking me to the outskirts. Too soon, summer was over, my reason for being in Goodhue was over. Tomorrow I would leave, enter a new life, meet new people. I wasn't sure I wanted to. I tucked my hands into deep, tattered pockets, then sauntered toward the Creamery where I recalled having helped Dad with his milk hauling some years back. Well, I didn't actually help him; it was more a matter of riding with him while he picked up milk in 80-pound cans from area farmers, hauled them to the Creamery, then unloaded them onto a rolling, steel conveyor. He would rise early, finish by noon on a good day, well into the afternoon on a hard winter day. He would spend the remainder of the day trucking for township farmers—grain to the Goodhue Elevator, cattle to South St. Paul. They were good times for me, riding in Dad's red International tuck, just a boy with his dad.

I strolled past the creamery toward the Cooperative Elevator before stopping in to visit with Burnette at Buck's Garage. I liked joshing with him; besides, he hung calendars of big-titted, naked women on his walls in the days when auto parts stores promoted spark plugs and piston rings with "girlie" calendars. I liked looking at them, although Burnette always chided me, "Hey, Jimmy, you comin' to look at my big-titted girls?" he said, sticking his head out from under a hood while working on a beat-up Ford. "Oh, no, Burnette, just walking by; stopped in to say 'hello,' " I said, approaching the Ford. "What are you doing there? So, whose old wreck is this, anyway?"

"Belongs to Les Bandit. I'll get 'er working fine, only missing on cylinder no. 2," he said, wiping his greasy hands on an equally greasy rag. Burnette was the quintessential village mechanic— rags hanging from all pockets, fingers black as a dirty oil pan, steel-toed boots scuffed from sliding under worn-out pickups. "Why ain't you working, nice day like this and all?"

"Finished at the viners yesterday, Burnette. All done at Bookie's for the summer. Going up to St. John's tomorrow to become a freshman. Kind of nervous about that," I said while picking up a greasy crescent wrench, inspecting it.

Burnette stuck his head back underneath the faded, dented hood, tattered pants and ass thrusting above the front bumper before answering. "You'll do hunky-dory, Jimmy. Your dad'd be proud of you, I know that. Hell! He brought his International in all the time for working on, peaceable man. Liked you kids. Too bad he's gone, but you'll be okay. You do that, then come back to make us proud of you. Hear me now?"

"See ya, Burnette. I'll come back and tell you about college," I shouted, continuing my departing end-of-summer sojourn around the village.

I sauntered past the Corner Grocery, and Swenson's Cafe barren of customers this afternoon, toward Lodermeier's Implement Shop. Shuffling past Taylor's Eat Shop, I noticed Florence sitting in the window seat. I backtracked. "Afternoon, Florence. How you doing?" I said, removing my cap and joining her on the ancient settee. Florence, a diminutive, silver-haired lady with hair done up in a bun and hair net and looking much like the little lady in Grant Wood's *American Gothic* painting, had been operating an eating and boarding establishment for all the years I could remember. Even now she served family-styled meals to regulars hunched over a long, antique oak table. Oh, she didn't offer rooms for rent anymore, hadn't since her dad, Tom Taylor, operated the White House, a boarding house next to Heaney's Meat Market on the side street. But she still served regular meals to Eddie Fischer, Erv Richter, other bachelors, periodically Red Ryan, lonely single men in a town of married folks. I had even eaten a few meals there myself during the past summer, rainy days when the peas weren't running.

"Why aren't you working on such a nice day, Jimmy?" she asked, setting down her *Better Homes and Gardens* magazine.

"Done, Florence. Finished yesterday. Got my last paycheck this morning. Just killing time till Mom drives me to college in the morning," I said, picking up a *Saturday Evening Post* and leafing through it.

"Would you care for lemonade? I've made a fresh batch."

"Sure would, ma'am. That'd be just fine."

"How are you getting along living alone?" she asked while stepping lightly to the rear kitchen to fetch lemonade. I followed her past the oak table and kitchen cupboard.

"Not half bad. Been busy this summer at the viners, so haven't had much time to think. I'm going to college, so everything will be different anyway." Florence poured me a cold glass of sweet lemonade and one for herself as we sat in the kitchen near an antique wood- and coal-burning stove where she toiled over beef roasts, pork roasts, pork chops, ham steaks, gravy, mashed potatoes, whole kernel corn and steamed green peas.

"I'm happy you've decided to enter college, Jim. We'll miss you around the village, and I'll especially miss your meat deliveries from Heaney's, but it's good you're going on to improve yourself. Lord knows you need it!" she chided, an unusual aside on her part. She busied herself straightening cast-iron pots and pans, out of habit, as she talked with me. Florence couldn't have weighed but ninety-five pounds, I thought as she set her kitchen in order, wearing an ever-present apron that kept foods from splattering on her flowered print dresses. But she was efficient, could serve a table of famished threshers if called upon. And she was a staple at Holy Trinity suppers, no lady more efficient at cooking or table serving than Florence. "Will you be back next summer?"

"Oh, sure. Probably work at the viners again for Bookie. I can make enough for an entire school year."

"Jimmy, maybe next summer you might chose to eat your meals here at my place. The men are older than you, but you're a good talker. You would get along fine. Think about it. You could rent a room in the village, then eat at my place. I would even give you a special price," Florence said, placing a warm, motherly hand on my shoulder.

"That's a good idea, Florence. Maybe I will, maybe I will," I said, reaching the bottom of my lemonade glass. "Need to be going now; more folks to see before tomorrow. I'll stay in touch. Thanks for the lemonade . . . and Florence . . . say a couple of Hail Marys for me. I'll need 'em," I said, bounding through the squeaky screen door onto the stark prairie street.

I shuffled around the corner past Lodermeier's Farm Implement shop and Heaney & Gorman—I'd return tonight, Saturday nights always busy at the store—to Upper Street to chat with Bert and Addie at Majerus Gas & Appliance. As I entered, the diminutive, amiable Addie was writing statements at her tidy desk while Bert rummaged through cluttered plumbing shelves searching for an adapter. Bert's stocky, disarrayed stature appeared to blend right in with his surroundings. "What the hell you doing here?" Bert asked, looking up, exasperated, unable to find the right fixture.

"Hi, Bert. Hi, Addie. Just walkin' an' talkin.' Finished at the viners yesterday. Off to college tomorrow. Just loafing this afternoon," I said, pulling up a stool at the high, cluttered counter. I liked visiting their hardware and plumbing store, something I had been doing for most of my years. Bert had hundreds of items hidden in dark, spider-webbed corners, stashed under overflowing wooden boxes, scattered on dusty shelves, stacked on the impassable stairwell. Shoot! He didn't know half of what he had. But between Bert's and Jesse's stores I had been able to find the items I needed to build my tree house, peach box racer, crystal radio antenna, lighted front lawn lamppost, model railroad layout. They even had assorted parts for my hand-me-down bicycle. If I couldn't find the screw or bolt or wrench or wire at Bert's, I could find it at Jesse's.

"Addie! Where is that goddamn three-quarter inch right-angled pipe?" Bert hollered, head deep in a dungeon corner. B. C.'s eyesight wasn't the best in the village, but it was better than his patience. When he couldn't locate something immediately, his eyesight and temperament both diminished accordingly. He wasn't helping himself this day by not wearing his heavy rimmed, black glasses, which he usually couldn't find anyway. Addie smiled at me, raised her eyebrows as she rose from her claw-footed swivel chair and snaked through the clutter toward Bert. "Why, Bert, it's right here in front of your nose," she said, handing him the pipe.

"I'll be goddamn. It wasn't there a minute ago. Shit!" Bert said, stumbling over boxes before joining me at the counter. "Goddamned pipes ain't never where I want 'em when I want 'em. Doin' a job up to the school. LeRoy Schinnert needs it for the main floor toilets. Want to ride up with me, Jimmy?" B. C. said, grabbing his overloaded, rusted tool box.

"Whatever. Haven't been in the school since graduation night. I got time to kill." I followed B. C. through the back door to his truck parked in the alley, stepping over pipes and fittings and wrenches and gas cylinders. Cy's truck was neat and tidy, everything in its place. Bert's was just the opposite. I could hardly sit, what with pipes and copper tubing and galvanized joints, pipe wrenches and sewer rope lurking in every imaginable place, even lining the dashboard.

"Just shove that damnable stuff aside, Jimmy, and hop in. Goddamn stuff never stays where I put it," Bert snarled as I finally found enough room to sit, the truck listing considerably toward the right front as we bounded out of the pockmarked alley. B. C. didn't concern himself with his junky truck as we listed and lurched slowly up to the school. "Cy keeps a pretty neat truck, Bert. I rode to Vasa with him yesterday. You could take a few lessons from him," I chided reaching the school.

"Hell! Cy's an electrician, but I'm the best damn plumber you ever seen. Don't have time to keep the truck clean and prissy-like. Long as she fires up, long as she runs, I'm happy as a fly on a turd," Bert snorted as we jolted to a stop in front of the school, the plumbing tools in the back catapulting toward the front, denting the already dented cab. "Here, make yourself handy and carry these damn fittings," he shouted while rummaging through the cluttered truck bed. I grabbed a handful, then followed him down the hall past vinegar-lipped Superintendent Hubert's office to the main floor toilets. B. C. toiled on his back under the sink and said 'goddamn' and 'fuck' ten times while I handed him pipes and wrenches like a surgeon's assistant until he finished. "There. That ought to keep those little shits happy shittin'," he said, tossing his pipe wrenches into the box.

The empty school halls seemed odd as we walked from the school. I had been used to shouting, classmates joshing, endlessly. It was eerie, this late summer afternoon, walking empty, silent halls I had tread since that first day in grade school—hallowed halls I would no longer walk. It didn't make sense.

Later that evening—after a short nap up in my grim room—I moseyed downtown to see what was happening. During the forties and fifties Saturday nights were the village's most exciting, although "exciting" may be an exaggeration. The Civic Club sponsored free outdoor movies on Lower Street, the film projected onto a temporary, billowing screen tacked to the street side of the Chicago Great Western Railroad Station. Farm families bounded into town to stock up on groceries for the coming week and to release their imprisoned children on unsuspecting villagers. Eddie filled prescriptions, carefully wrapping and tying each in tight brown paper, while men picked up ten-threaded bolts and a roll of baling wire at Bert's or Jesse's or Gerken's. Moms bought spools of white and black thread, plus assorted dry goods from Diercks' store, while dads sipped a couple of Grain Belts at Art's Bar or George's Corner Bar.

During my last high school years—trimming and wrapping beef roasts at Heaney & Gorman—I had sensed this weekly routine changing, classmates' families occasionally driving all of fifteen miles to Red Wing, maybe to Zumbrota or Cannon Falls instead of the five or eight into Goodhue. Yet, Belvidere, Goodhue, Belle Creek Township farmers mostly shopped in the village, Saturday nights, arriving in *Grapes of Wrath* pickups and bland, four-door Bel Air Chevys, because this night was more than a shopping night; the night was for talking with other folks, farmers, townsfolk they hadn't seen for a week or two.

"Evening, Emma," I said, greeting Mrs Kindseth on Upper Street, the evening growing dimmer, only a reddish band of diminishing sunlight peaking over the water tower.

"Why, hello, Jimmy. How are you this fine evening?"

"Just fine, Emma, just fine. Going to college in the morning," I said, tipping my pea-stained baseball cap to her.

"Good luck, but you make sure you come back, you hear now?"

"Sure will, Emma, sure will." As she entered Eddie's Drugstore, I passed Bert and Addie's again, Shug Ryan inside buying plumbing supplies for his Belle Creek farm.

"Evening, Emily," I said to Mrs O. T. Parker in front of the bank.

"A very good evening to you, Jimmy," Emily answered, adjusting her always present black hair net. "How has your summer been, may I ask?"

"Just finished working at the pea viners. Mom's driving me up to college tomorrow, but I'll be back for vacations and holidays," I said, tipping my cap again.

"You make sure you do. Don't forget us. Come back, Jimmy," she said, moving on with one last tug on her hair net and corset.

"Good-night, Emily. Nice seeing you again," I said, passing Art's Bar, the boisterous clamor of the inside crowd as well as beer and whiskey aromas spilling onto the street through the open screen door. At seventeen I was still too young to frequent Art's, but Dad had taken me in for a soda when he was still around. But I knew Art's was one of the popular "watering holes" in town, a meeting place to loosen up after a hard week of milking and plowing and harrowing and calving out on the farm; a place to talk about pork bellies and fattening calves and threshing barley, wheat and oats, the price of milk per hundred. Several years later I would frequent Art's myself, after the good brothers of St. John's had introduced me to Benedictine Brothers Brandy, that is. This night, though, I continued sauntering toward Heaney & Gorman. I knew the "old philosophers" would be there. I needed to pick up additional wisdom before leaving town.

"Hi, George, Dennis, Dodie, Lefty, Dave, Frank. How's everybody this evening?" I said, joining the group sitting around the potbellied stove at the rear of the store. This was *the* meeting place, the site to solve the town's, the county's, the state's, the world's problems. Dennis had rescued the Black Oak stove from the earlier, fire-ravaged Heaney's Market after the devastating fire in the forties, the tall, black, iron stove about the only thing he did recover, other than several smoked hams. The old stove attracted the ecclesiastic "old philosophers," especially during Minnesota's long, bitter and brutal winters. Chairs of every size and style encircled the stove: cane-backs, rocking, stuffed, hard-ass chairs. I had grown up around this stove, had gained whatever wisdom of the outside world I had acquired, to date.

Uncle Dave, his long legs propped on a peach crate to relieve the pressure on his big toe, was holding court when I shuffled in . . . "Hi, Jimmy. You pick up your 'bacon' from Bookie yet?" he asked, momentarily interrupting his long-winded tale about supervising at the viners.

"Yes, sir, Dave. Jack and I picked up our checks this morning. Already in the bank for college," I answered, pulling up a chair in the familiar circle.

"So, you're going off and leaving the village soon?" Lefty O'Reilly asked, he a regular at the Saturday night klatch when not selling postage stamps or sorting mail at the village's tiny post office.

"That's right, Lefty. Tomorrow, after mass, Mom's driving me up to Collegeville. Don't know what to think about it yet. Sure'll be different from high school," I answered, removing my baseball cap and setting it on a vacant peach box. The store was busy with folks buying a week's worth of groceries. They didn't waste money or time driving to town during the week for only one or two items, and in 1954 the village was still light years away from convenience stores. Farm folks regularly filled two overflowing shopping carts with groceries and retrieved meat from Dennis' deep-freeze lockers, thereby stocking up until next Saturday night's visit.

"Brother Larry has decided to enroll at St. John's, too. You fellows will see much of each other, I suppose," Lefty said, peering over the *Minneapolis Tribune* through heavy glasses that enhanced his less than twenty-twenty vision. He loved his daily newspaper, reading it at the store on coffee breaks, which he didn't drink, preferring frequent sodas and thick chocolate malts instead, subsequently adding to his portly stature.

"Guess so. Should be good having Larry there."

Ancient Frank O'Gorman was the senior member of the group, an octogenarian who mostly smoked cigars and listened to the conversations like a circuit judge, inserting succinct observations at the appropriate time. Uncle Dave, Lefty, Dodie, and Dennis would join the confab when not waiting on customers, but George could remain in the conversation from the nearby meat counter.

"Hello, Marg. What would you like this evening?" George asked Margaret Ryan at the meat display, Marg dressed for "Sunday Mass" although she was only shopping for Saturday groceries.

"I'll take a beef shoulder roast, lean; three pounds of your fresh hamburger meat, and ample pork chops for Sunday dinner," Marg said as George began filling her order at the butcher's block. Marg saw me sitting with the gang around the stove.

"Hello, Jimmy. Will you be serving mass in the morning?" she asked, her oldest son, Phil, having been the stalwart altar boy of Holy Trinity, serving more masses, pouring more wine, dispensing more incense, deterring more Lutherans, reciting more *Mea culpas* and *Pox vobiscums* than any other fellow in town. Marg knew the routine well. She would probably receive a higher place in heaven just for having given birth to Phil. Townsfolk thought Phil would become a priest, but he only captain'd a U.S. Navy aircraft carrier.

"Maybe, Marg, but the new priest has his own hand-picked altar boys now. I'm sort of a sub acolyte after all these years. Didn't serve as long as Phil, a long time, though. Should buy me several good years of penance, a shorter Purgatory at least," I said, leaving the men and joining Marg at the meat counter.

"Heavens, Jimmy, you're a good boy. The Lord will permit you to bypass Purgatory and enter directly into heaven," she said as George wrapped her order before placing it on the counter.

"Hope so, Marg, hope so, but Fr. Smith wouldn't have agreed with you."

"You shush! Fr. Smith has been reassigned to a different parish in the dioceses. Our new priest isn't as hard on Hell and Damnation and Lutherans as he was. You have a good time and study hard. My son, Jimmy, is in his third year at St. Thomas, and Bob is enrolling there, also. You boys make us proud, and remember to come home. I will see you at mass. Good-bye, then," Marg said, heading for the busy checkout counter, a couple of heavily-loaded carts in front of her. I returned to the stove where the conversation was now centered on Hubert Humphrey.

George loved politics. He was active in the Goodhue County Democratic Party, had met Humphrey several times, even in the village, in fact. The loquacious Hubert had been the commence-ment speaker for the Class of '53, and the Gormans invited me to a private dinner with Humphrey before his commencement ad-dress. "Humphrey and the DFL'rs have done more for the farmer than any other senator we've ever had in Minnesota," George said, wiping his hands on a white apron.

"You can say that again," Lefty replied, shifty his fleshy weight in an uncomfortable, narrow Windsor chair, Uncle Dave already having plopped down into Lefty's favorite wider chair. Lefty was a voracious reader of the *Minneapolis Tribune* and *St. Paul Pioneer Press,* even occasionally the village's weekly *Goodhue County Tribune*. He was well read, astute, perceptive and a liberal Democrat: "Damn Republicans in this state would like to run the farmer into the ground," he responded, brushing back a few hairs on his increasingly balding head. Well, I liked politics, but wasn't as well read and informed as Lefty or George and Dennis; besides, this night I needed to see my high school gang at the free movies before the evening escaped. "Got to go, fellows, see what's happening on Lower Street," I announced, rising to retrieve my cap.

"Good luck at St. John's, Jim. Study hard and make us proud of you. Come back," Dodie hollered from the busy checkout register.

"Study harder than you did in high school," Dennis shouted from the Locker's cutting room. "Don't come back a failure, flunking out or anything like that," he said, slapping me on the back with a red-meat hand.

"I'll study hard. Thanks for everything, everybody. I'm not going that far. See you, then," I said, suddenly rushing for the front door, a surging emotion overwhelming me from somewhere deep inside. I hadn't expected that. I reached the front sidewalk—heavy midwestern humidity striking me in the face—to take a long, deep

breath. I hadn't anticipated this feeling, wasn't prepared for it. I felt
dizzy crossing the street toward Lodermeier's Garage. "Don't
flunk out!" he had said. Can I really get through this? I thought,
reaching the railroad station.

The white movie screen was billowing in the summer's hot
evening breeze, cars backed into the curb facing the Great Western
Station as a flickering, barely visible Gene Autry jerked across the
screen, his voice barely audible above buzzing flies, darting
mosquitoes and braying cattle just beyond the city limits. Classmates and friends sat on car hoods and fenders, on chairs placed in
the rear of manure-smelling pickups, on the crumbling curb. They
stood by Jesse's store and Joyce's popcorn wagon as folks honked
when guys in white hats killed guys in black hats. Autry finally
rode off into the sunset, somewhere toward Hay Creek, I guess,
before I joined Mary B, Janice C, Bettie L, Bob O' for burgers and
malts at Swenson's. Sitting together in a well-worn booth, we
realized we would soon be heading in different directions: Mary
getting married to that Bellechester guy Cy told me about, Bettie
getting married to a Hay Creek dude, Janice zipping to Rochester
at the Mayo Clinic, Bob entering St. Thomas, me, St. John's. These
five "kids," "The Five," had begun school together, the only
village children making up the Class of '54. Now we were about
to walk in five different directions. Would we meet like this again?
Would we see each other in the coming months, years?

We chomped on Heinie's greasy burgers and drank thick
chocolate malts from frosty, well-used metal containers while
reminiscing about high school—Miss Cree, Miss North, Supt.
Hubert, classmates—until we found ourselves out on the sidewalk
hugging, waving "good-bye." Bob and I shuffled up to our neighborhood where we stood under the swaying streetlight for an hour
talking about the past years, just as we had done for many a night.
Finally it was time to go in . . .

"See you at mass, Jimmy."

"Okay, Bob. I'll be there," I said, traipsing toward my lonely
bedroom. I looked through the window to see Bob in his bedroom,
now melancholy about the coming change in my life, our lives. I
looked down on the shadow-covered lawn, moonlight softly

illuminating remnants of the old tree house . . . thinking . . . pondering the years I'd spent here, hoping the next years would be as good.

Chapter 2

Monk'y business

On tour at St. John's U

B Y THE END OF MY FIRST MONTH ON CAMPUS, I had found Catholicism running deeper, more fervent than even at Holy Trinity and St. Columbkill's, something I hadn't thought possible. Arriving that first apprehensive day, I had known only that St. John's was a Catholic college "up north." Now,

I knew it to be a full monastery where hunchbacked, balding, black-hooded monks prayed endlessly in row upon row of prison-like cells entombed in diverting cloistered walls and angular quadrangles reminiscent of a mediaeval fortress. A shrouded prep school hunkered beyond the towering pines, a sepulcher where tow-headed, pimple-faced high school boys were doing what I should have done in high school—studying English and Literature and Math and History—preparing for their future entrance into St. John's. A hushed seminary embraced the oval shores of Lake Sagatagan—Phil Ryan might have enrolled, but escaped to Annapolis' Naval Academy instead—a mausoleum-styled building where untested, virgin seminarians sought the Lord through dedication to the priesthood, studying theology, classic liturgy and the Bible twenty-four hours a day, never thinking about girls and kissing and touching breasts. A working farm with Vic O'Neill-era antiquated McCormick-Deering Farmal tractors, horse-drawn scythes, rolling fields, gabled barns, hogs and cattle helped monks fulfill the Rule of St. Benedict, "Idle hands make . . . ," A brick-lined bakery where half asleep monks baked the famous deep-grained St. John's holy-rye bread as we slept, scintillating yeast aroma floating over campus like the world-wide St. John's liturgy, kept monk hands busy and holy. Finally, the campus embraced Brother Leo, a shuffling monk-about-campus who had flunked out of seminary years ago, but who still dedicated his life to the Lord. Brother Leo was one of us, traipsing endlessly throughout campus, eyes downcast, incessantly repeating a spiritual mantra, a constant heavenly aura on his hollow, angelic face. He liked being around college students, even though he wasn't one himself.

My lack of academic dedication and efficient study habits at GHS soon took its toll. After a battery of entrance exams that first week, I found myself in English 101, "Bonehead" to those passing out of it; "Bonehead" Math 101; History of the Western World; Introduction to Political Science—an elective that sounded interesting, plus I thought George and Dennis would appreciate me taking the class, as it might help me in subsequent conversations around the potbellied stove; Music Appreciation, Napoleon-built Fr. Dominic professing the intricacies of Bach and Beethoven, harmony and polyphony (and I thought I knew a little about music!); Survey of World Religions (I was soon to learn there was more than Catholicism, more than Christianity flourishing beyond the limited village boundary); and as an elective I joined concert and marching bands, wanting to keep my clarinet skills in shape while still harboring thoughts of becoming another Benny Goodman, in spite of what George O'Reilly thought.

"Now class, punctuation is one of the hallmarks of good writing. Without the proper use of commas, periods, semicolons, dashes, colons, et cetera, the meaning of words is flawed," Fr. Cuthbert—bald, bespectacled, boring—intoned like Fr. Smith on a good day. He sat at his desk in front of the tiny, cloistered classroom spewing the virtues of punctuation that first week in "Bonehead" English. My entrance exams indicated I needed to be there, but I didn't want to be any more than I had wanted to be in Miss Cree's GHS English Class, that entire class a farce and not a Shakespearean farce, either—Belle Creek and Bellechester classmates more interested in pulling pranks than learning what Miss Cree was attempting to teach them. As Fr. Cuthbert intoned the differences between commas and periods, I gazed out the window, down into the monastery quadrangle, an inner sanctum where Black Robes shuffled like lethargic penguins in peaceful repose. I began daydreaming about the day in Miss Cree's class when Tom Manahan threw Virginia George's grammar book out the window, an act causing Miss Cree to break down and cry right in front of those "sensitive" bullies. This act suddenly ended her recitation with a definite period rather than a comma. That was for sure.

"Mr Franklin. Would you be so kind as to offer us an example of the different usage between the comma and the period?" Fr. Cuthbert suddenly asked, bringing me back reality.

"Well, sure, Father. You see, a comma is used when you don't want to stop, and a period is used when you want to stop. Simple as that," I said, wondering why I had been singled out.

"Partially true, Mr Franklin, but an inadequate explanation, nonetheless. A comma is much like taking a breath when speaking, to let the listener know the words are connected in meaning, a pause being needed to indicate variances in phrases. A period indicates the end of a complete, declarative sentence," Fr. "Baldy" said without raising his eyes from the grammar book.

"Right, Father. I've got it. And *that's* a period."

"I'll then expect improvement in your next written assignment," Baldy said as he tinkled a small hand bell indicating the end of class, students quickly filing into the long, cimmerian quadrangle hallway. As I gathered my textbook I suddenly wished I had studied more, paid more attention in Miss Cree's class. Wherever she was today, she would certainly be happy to hear that.

I struggled throughout that first semester with Bonehead English, Bonehead Math, History of the Western World, Political Science, trying to develop study habits I hadn't acquired in high school. In fact, I didn't even *want* to study that first semester, but it was forced upon all students. Nightly, we were expected to sit at our dorm desks from seven to half past nine, radios and phonographs off, not socializing. Fr. Henry shuffled slowly up and down the hallway reading his Breviary, watching that we were doing just that. After forced study period we had only a half-hour to socialize, because Henry later became an electrician like Cy Benda. He pulled the main circuit at ten o'clock throwing the entire floor into perpetual monastic darkness. That meant "retire," rise early and fresh for daily mass. The regimented routine was difficult, but absolutely what I needed. I had yet to find the joy of studying, of learning, but there wasn't another option. Fr. Henry, the abbot, the pope, the ghost of Fr. Smith were watching over me.

Days turned into weeks, weeks into months. I wasn't setting any academic records, but not flunking out either, holding true to Dennis Heaney's admonition. I certainly couldn't return to the village, facing him after having failed.

But St. John's became more than a place of higher learning. I found a family of fellow students, found a camaraderie I hadn't anticipated. What with the events of the past summer and the break up of my personal family, the new college family was unexpected and encouraging. I tooted clarinet daily on the marching field; then when northern Minnesota's winds blew snow over the cathedral's twin towers, we began rehearsing concert overtures, tone poems and four-movement symphonies unheard of in the village. My new band colleagues got me to thinking about music as a possible career. I certainly wasn't going anywhere in Political Science, despite having had dinner with Hubert Humphrey's liberal DFL'rs, George Gorman and the Goodhue County Democrats.

By Thanksgiving I had been away from the village for ten weeks, longer than ever before. After taking pre-Thanksgiving midterm exams in bonehead classes; after gathering my overused, overdue, well-stained shorts, shirts and socks for Mother's caring hands and trusty Maytag; after biding my new-found friends a temporary farewell, I joined scores of Johnnies out on the pine-shrouded highway, thumbs out, hitchhiking home for the holiday. By eight o'clock that evening I had returned to the village, and although unknown then, it was something I would continue doing for the remainder of my life.

I had been fortunate to hitch a ride down to the Twin Cites, another with a medical salesman south through Cannon Falls and Hader. He dropped me off at the intersection of Highways 52 and 58 in Zumbrota where I stood, cold and shivering in the late November air near the Wagon Wheel. The Wheel had been the first drive-in eatery I had ever been to, the first place I had ever eaten in a car instead of at Mother's table, the first drive-in I had ever taken a date to—a Zumbrota girl, later necking with french fried onion breath. Tonight, I glanced toward the Wagon, high school kids ordering fried onion rings, burgers, malts, rough necking in the back seat on a chilly night. Huh! I was way beyond that high school behavior. I was now a college boy coming home to a tumultuous welcome.

Milo Swenke, recognizing me standing at the intersection with my thumb out, screeched to a halt, hollered back, "Jump in, Jimmy. I'm heading to Goodhue. What you doin' out here without a car?" he asked, tugging on his ever-present white buttermaker's cap, shifting the two-seater Plymouth into the first of three, whining, straight stick gears.

"Been up to college, Milo. Coming home for Thanksgiving vacation. Four whole days off from classes and away from the

Black Robes. Feels great. I've missed it," I said, settling into the front seat as Milo pulled through downtown Zumbrota past the Armory where the GHS Wildcats had won many a basketball game, particularly that great team of '44 with southpaw Lefty O'Reilly and the towering Phil Ryan and shifty Eugene Haas and smooth Burton Eppen and rugged Dick Eyestone and reserve forward Elroy Schulz and backup guard Toby Buck and International Harvestor dealer-coach Karl Tomfohr.

"You a college boy now, huh? Gonna be one of them smart-ass'd, highfalutin' college kids, Jimmy? Don't you go and do that 'round here, you hear? Remember where you came from, your humble roots," Milo lectured, shifting into a recalcitrant third gear as we pulled past the Goodhue County Fairground up a long grade out of the Zumbro valley.

"Oh no, Milo. I wouldn't do that. Fact is, I've been humbled since entering college. They're showing me everything I didn't learn in high school. I'm in several 'bonehead' classes while classmates from Minneapolis and St. Paul are in regular or advanced classes. I've considerable catching up to do," I shared with Milo, now pushing the Plymouth up to forty-five through the rolling, golden hills of Zumbrota Township. I looked out the window as we passed White Willow, or at least where the ghost town had been, seemingly seeing these bountiful fields for the first time. I felt very good coming home, back to the county, back to the village. It suddenly occurred to me that it had been good to leave, to gain a different perspective, even with my initial trepidation last summer. Bypassing the Bellechester turnoff, I had become aware that my new colleagues didn't share all the beliefs my relatives and friends held. Incredibly, a few Johnnies actually questioned some of my statements about Catholicism, political parties, ethnic perspectives, family values, sex, love, Hubert Humphrey and FDR. Although they were "good" Catholic boys, they weren't all as die-hard about Roman theology as me, as I had been trained and indoctrinated during those long, tiring Friday afternoon catechism classes and summer, nun-laced tolerances. Yet, college was, in only ten weeks, turning out to be a valuable experience, one of gaining a differing perspective about, well . . . just about everything. As Milo exited Highway 58 into the village at Art Luethe's Home Oil, I saw the village for the first time . . . new again.

"Okay, Jim. Where you wanna be dropped? Don't have a home in the village anymores, do you?" he asked as we dodged potholes on Lower Street near the forlorn depot, the ghost of agent A. B. Overby hunched over his telegraph haunting the village.

"Mom's living in Red Wing, married for the second time to Bill Ryan, but I've kept a room at our old house up past Holy Trinity. Just drop me off at Swenson's Cafe. And, Milo, I appreciate the ride . . . thanks," I said, jumping to the street as Milo slowly pulled away from the decaying curb.

The sun had set beyond water tank hill—Cranson Heights to pretentious folks—but there was still enough red in the western sky to cast a warm glow over the village. I stood on the corner for a few minutes, the village hushed, deserted. I had mixed emotions—on the one hand, happy to be home, on the other, momentarily at a loss, separated from my new "family," pondering my old.

"Hello, Heinie."

"Hi, Jimmy. Welcome home. What'll it be, then?" Heinie asked as I shuffled through the door, Swenson's Cafe devoid of life other than Heinie. For the first time it occurred to me that the light-haired, stocky Heinie was always at the cafe. I had been frequenting this long, narrow, comfy cafe since grade school. During all those years Heinie and his building had been connected as one. But now, looking at the cafe anew, I realized he was always here when I was.

"Do you ever go home, Heinie? Ever take a day off?" I asked, pulling up a stool near the rear kitchen.

"No, just like the working," the somewhat reticent Heinie answered. "What'll it be then, Jimmy?" he repeated, obviously eager to begin my order rather than having a new college kid ask him about his personal life.

"One of your juicy ham sandwiches, Heinie, some french fries and a Coke."

"You betcha," he said, limping to the grill area on a chronic arthritic hip. I grabbed a *Pioneer Press* and aimlessly leafed through it, soon putting it down. The only customer, I viewed the cafe differently—the bar longer, the booths older, the stool covers more tattered, the decor nonexistent, the ambiance more stark. Since August I had been attending class, studying in the dorm, spending some off campus Friday evenings in St. Cloud, the "big city" with soda fountains and department stores and bookstores and big hotels and restaurants instead of just cafes. Yet, when back at Swenson's, I was home. It didn't make any difference that I now viewed it differently. This night, I was simply aware, that's all.

I ate my sandwich in silence—only the scraping of Heinie's spatula on the grill breaking the prairie stillness—and read the *Press*. Heinie was a pleasant proprietor, but not much of talker for being a Swede, for living in the village where talking was next to godliness. Glancing down the deserted, endless bar, I pondered this holiday return, the cafe, the village strangely calm this eve of Thanksgiving. Guess my friends hadn't returned yet. Guess my momentous homecoming was a bust. Guess folks were starving themselves tonight for tomorrow's feast, I thought. I would also because Mother and Bill were picking me up in the morning for Thanksgiving dinner at the Ryan's Belle Creek farm.

"Thanks, Heinie. Probably see you in next few days," I shouted toward the grill while heading for the door.

"So long, Jimmy. Nice to see you home," he answered, simultaneously swooping up my dirty plate before trudging to the sink.

Out on the barren street the redness in the western sky had turned to rust, then reddish-brown, then black, heavy darkness now enveloping the village casting shadows around the cafe. I figured I would have run into Jack or Bob or Larry, one of the O'Reillys, but apparently they hadn't returned yet. But that was all right. I would simply enjoy the evening by myself. I began walking past Husbyn's Hatchery and Huebner's Blacksmith Shop to Upper Street. A few dogs barked from back lawns and alleys, staking out their territory, but I knew most of them. They soon became as silent as the village. Ol' Buck behind Ebe's Barber Shop was too lazy to bark.

I reached John Berlinski's Corner Bar, still too young, too disinterested in beer or spirits to enter. I could see through the window, though, that the usual gang was inside drinking Grain Belt, Seagram's Seven and whiskey sours. I detected a stale, musty, ingrained beer odor seeping under the threshold onto the sidewalk. Patrons were animated, talking, enjoying the companionship of others while avoiding the companionship of others at home—a nagging wife, a nagging husband, demanding children—this friendly bar seemingly a better, temporary substitute. As I matriculated through the next four years of college, I too would learn how to socialize with college brethren and the good Benedictine Brothers, summers with old and new friends in the village. I had gradually learned to enjoy a couple of beers and the light-headed socializing with friends, good hearted companionshipping in an innocent era before drugs of later decades. But not tonight, I thought, passing Berlinski's toward the old neighborhood.

Sauntering past Holy Trinity, I saw my old house up the street, my room, my neighborhood illuminated by the dim streetlight, all seeming smaller, more confined than what I had remembered. Oh, everything was still there, but what had once seemed to extend forever now appeared confined—Sandbox Bob's house, smaller; Murphy Buck's home, closer; the Gorman's house, closer; the Haga's house, almost on top of ours; Henning's home, tight; Regina and Heinie's home, diminished. And a quietness I had become accustomed to, tonight seemed tomb-like. My entire, expansive childhood neighborhood now appeared contained within a small memory, only a breath of earlier days.

Bob's house was dark. I stood under the swaying streetlight seeing new what I had seen a thousand times, this night offering new sight-lines, new perspectives. Odd. Had the neighborhood changed so much in ten weeks? Had I changed in such a short time? I couldn't get a handle on it as I plodded up the back stairs to my cold, bleak room, it too appearing smaller than when I had left it.

Bill Ryan knocked on the front door. My downstairs landlord banged on the ceiling with a broomstick indicating Bill and Mother were here. I skipped down the stairs and out the back door to meet them. Mother had a difficult time returning to this house, this place she and her family had called home for fifteen or so years, but to me, a lifetime. In the front downstairs bedroom, her bedroom, we had waked Dad with a proper in-house Irish wake, this less than four years ago. Her memories remained intense—Dad's fatal heart attack, his wake, his funeral service and burial—and although Bill had entered her life a couple of years later, she didn't erase those memories, only pushed them deeper into her heart, covering them with newer experiences. Bill had helped her immensely, yet when she visited me she still couldn't enter the house.

"Good morning, Jim," Mother said, momentarily removing her fifties-era glasses as I jumped into the back seat of Bill's blue Ford sedan.

"Hi, Mother. Whew! It's cold this morning," I said as the heat of Bill's car soon warmed me.

"Are you ready for a tasty Thanksgiving dinner at the farm?" Bill asked, his chiseled Irish face appearing as if it could use a feast, but his body tight, taut as we passed Hagas, Hennings and Swensons, up water tank hill skirting Evergreen Cemetery—the Protestant cemetery—out County Rd. No. 9 toward Bill's farm in Belle Creek Township.

"Sure am, Bill, and thanks for picking me up. St. John's food is pretty good, but nothing like a dinner on your farm."

"It's good to see you, Jim. Are you doing all right up at St. John's?" Mother asked as we rolled out No. 9.

"Oh, sure, Mom, no sweat. Classes are going great, and I've made many new friends. I get along with the priests and monks, too. It's great."

"How are those priests and monks, Jim?" Bill asked as we neared the turnoff to St. Columbkill's country church. "They any harder on you than Fr. Smith?" he asked, pushing up his ever-slipping glasses.

"That's hard to do, Bill. Fr. Smith was a hard one; you and everyone else in Belle Creek knew that, but he was the only priest we had. We didn't have other choices, but at St. John's there are so many priests and monks and abbots and acolytes and sub acolytes and brothers that a guy gets a different theological opinion once in a while. Students don't actually talk with monks, mostly just see them processing to and from church in endless lines to attend lauds and matins and vespers and compline, hoping to save their souls. But most of my professors are priests and they're all different, some personable, some irascible like Fr. Smith. My Music Appreciation professor, Fr. Dominic, is cantankerous, maybe because he's short and stocky with a barrel chest and stumpy legs—Little Napoleon. When he raises his black hood he's a spittin' image of Napoleon."

"Well, Jim, you ought to get along just fine with those priests and monks. Shoot! You spent lots of years on the altar with Fr. Smith serving mass, carrying wine and water, moving the gospel book about the altar, and I remember watching you during those long Holy Week services at St. Columbkill's carrying jugs of holy water. Yes sir, you ought to fit in real well with the monks," Bill said as we turned off No. 9 onto No. 7 toward the Ryan farm deep in the heart of Irish Catholicism.

"Think so, Bill. College is interesting and different from high school, that's for sure. I just hope I can hang in there with my classes. They're difficult," I said as we pulled through the increasingly hilly terrain, nearing the actual babbling creek of Belle Creek.

"What are you going to major in, Jim?" Mother asked as we passed Aunt Cis O'Neill's place. "You sure liked your clarinet and listening to the radio, late nights when you were supposed to be sleeping."

"Oh, I don't know yet, Mom. Haven't decided. I'm taking mostly required courses, Political Science as an elective, but I don't think government is my niche. I'm playing clarinet in band, still like music a lot, but it's too soon to tell. Hope I'll know by the end of the year."

"Well, I'm very proud of you, Jim. You just study harder than you did in high school. I'll say a novena for you, and Bill will pray for you, won't you, Bill? And your dearly departed dad will pray for you, too. I've been saying novenas for you, did you know that? I'm sure you'll do just fine," Mother said, maybe wiping a tear from her dark eyes as we turned off No. 7 toward Bill's farm.

Mother loved novenas, said them for everything and everyone. They were her staple of religious security. She had learned them from the nuns of St. Joseph's School in Red Wing. She had said a novena for me when I traipsed off to first grade with Bob. She had said a novena that I would be worthy of my First Communion, another novena when Bishop Byrne confirmed us at Holy Trinity, another when I entered high school, a novena on my first date, partial novenas before each basketball game—not enough time for a full novena—and I'm sure she was continuing them, incessantly, for my success at St. John's. But I appreciated them, nevertheless. I needed all the prayers she could offer-up over the next four years.

Bill bounced into the farm yard, the 320-acre Belle Creek spread he had nurtured and tilled and toiled for many years before wife Julia died, before he retired, married Mother and moved to Red Wing. Second son Dick farmed it now, son Tom having tired of plowing and harrowing and threshing and milking, preferring instead a Budweiser beer distributorship in Red Wing. Son John "Billy" had escaped Belle Creek, Goodhue County and Minnesota entirely, journeying all the way to California before even looking back, seeking a more lively life than what Belle Creek offered, which other than St. Columbkill Masses, funerals, weddings and church suppers or periodically hanging out at the Belle Creek General Store down on No. 8, wasn't much.

"Hello, everyone," Bill announced as we stepped into the bursting kitchen, folks talking, joshing, laughing . . .

"Hi, Dad. Hi, Lucy. Hi, Jimmy! Come on in; take your coats off. Happy Thanksgiving!" Shorty shouted as we squeezed into the tiny kitchen already overflowing with pumpkin pies, mashed potatoes, red cranberry relish, the delectable aroma of a cooking turkey filtering through the house.

"How's the college kid?" Dick asked as he carried my coat to the bedroom.

"Oh, just fine, Dick, just fine."

"You getting along all right with those monks up there?"

"Yes, sir, I am. But I see mostly priests in my classes and at mass, although I've learned that a priest and a monk are sort of synonymous. Some monks are only monks, some are priests, some are brothers. Yet some priests are only priests, not monks, while other priests are both priests and monks. Brothers are only brothers, although they could be a priest, if they chose," I said as we joined the others back in the kitchen.

"That's more than I need to know about monks, Jim. You don't need to run that by me again. We've a new priest now, just a priest as far as I know. Want a beer? Hell! Gorm and Dad and me are having one. Here's a Budweiser," Dick said before letting me answer.

"You fellows get out of the kitchen now. Retire to the living room, so we ladies can get this dinner cooking," Shorty announced, scooting us from her cozy, warm kitchen. Mother, Shorty, Grace and other Belle Creek ladies I didn't know were fixing the dinner. They didn't want men-help. Dick would milk his Holsteins later, but his or my help wasn't expected, or tolerated, in the kitchen.

As we men settled into the living room to sip on Gorm's Budweiser, Gorm asked of Dick, "How's the year been, Dick?"

"Been a good year. Wheat and oats did well this year, corn was good, too. Milk 'bout average, could be a better, but all 'n' all, can't complain. A guy could do a lot worse," Dick said. He and brother Gorm had grown up on this rolling, high prairie Belle Creek farm. Gorm had remained on the place for a while after high school, helping dad, but then moved to Red Wing, married Gracie, leaving the homeplace to Dick and Short. Three hundred twenty acres wasn't large enough anyway to support two families, although Dick and Short proceeded to sire numerous children themselves, putting additional strain on the farm.

But this Belle Creek land was rich, deep soil for growing crops, good land for raising children of which there were hundreds in this predominantly Catholic township. In every direction from the Ryan farm, other Irish tilled the land and sired families of ten, eleven, twelve children, thereby creating a built-in work force while keeping Fr. Smith and the pope content. In the twenties, thirties, forties, even the fifties yet, practicing birth control was unheard of out here, unspoken, unsanctioned. Only free-thinking, left-winged radical Catholics, of which there were few, if any, ever considered it. Once those good ol' Irish boys got their machinery started, there was no stopping them. In fact, most didn't know how to turn off the damn thing. Oh, they had read something about the Rhythm Method in the *Catholic Digest*, but it was easier to just do it whenever they had the urge rather than fuss with counting days. North, south, east, west of St. Columbkill's, huge families of Ryans, O'Connors, O'Reillys, O'Neills, MacNamaras, O'Rourkes, Gadients brought both good crops and good children to the surface of this high, rolling prairie.

My own paternal heritage emanated from this township . . . well, almost. Grandparents David and Catherine Franklin's farm was only a few miles east of the Ryan place, directly on the Goodhue Township side of the dividing road between Goodhue and Belle Creek Townships. David sired seven children before he died in 1926, before his Franklin children filtered into the surrounding farmsteads. But Catherine—stubborn, determined—remained on the homeplace for another ten years awaiting my arrival, then farmed with son Patrick an additional ten before giving up a hardscrabble life and moving to Red Wing. I chased chickens, gathered eggs, romped in the hay mow and stepped in cow turds on the Franklin homeplace. Although a town boy, I had deep, rural Belle Creek roots.

As Dick and Gorm talked incessantly about corn, beans, grain prices and milking, I faded from their agrarian conversation and began thinking about the ethnic-religious diversity surrounding the village. My class in World Religions was opening up new thoughts about religious preference. Oh, we were receiving a good dose of Catholicism, just what one would expect at a Catholic college, yet if it were to be an objective college course, it would need to consider other faiths. We were currently surveying Christianity with its many diversions from Roman Catholicism, something Fr. Smith and the summer nuns had never spoken of, other than adversely of that Martin L. fellow, this in the same vein as when speaking of fallen angel Lucifer. In grade and high school "we Catholics" had talked disparagingly—in private—of non-Catholics, because we had been taught their fate . . . er, faith. How could Catholics be the chosen ones and non-Catholics, too? It had to be one or the other, black or white. If Catholics needed to confess their sins directly to Fr. Smith—disobeying our parents, avoiding evening prayers, fibbing, out-and-out lying, stealing, *enjoying* impure thoughts or *committing* impure acts, for God's sake!—then that was the *only* way to forgiveness. We might need to stop off at Purgatory before reaching God's heaven. If that's what we believed, then how could Lutherans confess sins *without* Fr. Smith? Well, it was obvious . . . they couldn't; consequently, they trudged around the village carrying a heavy load of sin, doomed to hell. Logical back then? Yes. Logical now? No.

I was learning there was more to *being* a Christian than *not* being one, a concept that had been heretical at Holy Trinity. Being non-Christian was as unheard of as, oh, let's say, Italian or French or Arabic or African-American or Oriental . . . something other than of non lily-white European ancestry. Through lectures, readings, squinting at immeasurable small print footnotes, late-night conversations with dormies, religious preferences began opening up to me. Not that I was about to do something as drastic as become a Methodist or Lutheran or a Jew. But just maybe, it was time I looked at "those people" objectively rather than casting them automatically into the nether world . . . hell. After all, I still wanted to enjoy my non-Catholic friends outside the protective, novena-laced boundaries of Belle Creek Township.

Hans Mattson's immigrant Swedish Lutherans had settled in Vasa, Belle Creek's northern neighbor. They were as ensconced in the Cannon River valley as Irish Catholics in Belle Creek. Norwegians elected to settle farther west in Wanamingo, Kenyon and Holden Townships to build shrines of Lutheranism to ex-Augustinian priest Martin Luther. Germans, mostly Lutheran with a smattering of Catholics, settled in eastern Goodhue Township, some north in Hay Creek and Featherstone while a smattering trekked into Bellechester and Belvidere to erect ominous, dark, fortress-styled churches in the middle of corn and pea fields. Non-Christian sects never entered the county. If there were *any* in Minnesota at that time, they settled in the Twin Cities where folks tolerated ethnic and religious diversity more than rural Goodhue County.

I was learning that Hans Mattson had brought his Swedish Clan, including Reverend Norielius' Lutheranism, to the rolling hills of Vasa. I was learning that the Rev. Bernt Muus had chosen Wanamingo and Kenyon in western Goodhue County to install his stronghold of pietistic Norwegian Lutheranism while simultaneously fighting within his Lutheran brotherhood against the Reverend Vilhelm Loren at Decorah, Iowa. I was learning that Methodists had spread themselves into multiple townships, finding continuity of faith in their faith rather than demography. Judaism, Hinduism, Buddhism, Taoism, Islam had never attacked Goodhue County, having eons earlier fought their battles on the steppes of Asia and Europe. They weren't about to invade the Christian superiority of Goodhue County.

> *Bless us o Lord for these thy gifts,*
> *Which we are about to receive from thy bounty,*
> *Through Christ our Lord . . . Amen*

"Happy Thanksgiving, everyone," Shorty said as we plopped at her dining table extended by several feet of table leaves. Helen's nickname "Shorty" was a local idiosyncrasy of calling folks by an obvious characteristic rather than by their given name. Helen was physically diminutive, but her nature was towering, particularly in *her* house. We passed, forever, the mashed potatoes, gravy, chunky red cranberry relish, yellow whole kernel corn, emerald-green sweet peas, and finally, a heaping platter of golden-brown, aromatic turkey. The womenfolk served the always rambunctious children in the kitchen while twelve adults gorged on a scrumptious feast in the dining room, similar scenes occurring at neighboring farms: the Charlie O'Neills, the Vic and Cis O'Neills, the Philip Ryans, the Clem Ryans, the MacNamaras and their band; the O'Connors, the Gadients, the O'Gormans.

Mother and Bill sat at the ends of the table, seats of honor this day, having been married six months. They were noticeably happy, beaming with their extended, hybrid family, and although not a Ryan by birth, I was rapidly becoming one by association. We gorged on the feast, talked endlessly about farming and the church

... why, one might have even considered the talk dangerously close to gossip, as almost every farm place and person had been mentioned before the feast ended: Francis McNamara had bought a new fire-engine-red International tractor; Clem Ryan had put up a new corn bin; Phillip Ryan had his best corn crop in years; Cis and Vic O'Neill's family had been devastated by polio, three children having contacted the dreaded disease, everyone praying for them; David Gadient had a fire in his hay barn; and Fr. Smith was long gone, but not forgotten.

Approaching gluttony—a sin for the next confession—we all suddenly stopped, relaxed and leaned back in our chairs. Shorty brought coffee and pumpkin pie to the table. I believe we did reach gluttony. Afterward, the men retired to the overstuffed chairs and davenport in the living room, the women remaining in the kitchen to clean up and get ready for another feast later in the afternoon. One meal certainly wasn't enough on a farmstead. It required two meals for a decent Thanksgiving feast. After all, daily farm work required considerable food consumption to maintain a strong health and a strong will. Farm life, and anyone associated with it, was based on eating three full meals plus morning and afternoon lunches, because the work was physically difficult whether it be spring plowing through heavy wet fields, cultivating long rows of corn and beans during humidity-laden, oppressive Julys, or a week of threshing wheat and oats. Food in the belly was as much of a staple as harvesting.

Drowsiness set in after the midday feast causing heads to dip and dart like Dick's incessantly pumping, creaking windmill out in the yard. Some enjoyed short, refreshing naps before playing Euchre and enjoying the camaraderie of family and friends. Gorm even retrieved more Budweisers during the afternoon as the ladies finally escaped the kitchen, joining us in the "best room."

"Ever milked a cow, Jim?" Dick asked, changing into his milking overalls in the basement.

"Oh, one time, hand milking over at O'Neills a few years ago, but I wasn't good at it."

"Come on, then. We'll teach you how to milk. Here, throw on these overalls 'cause the shit will be flying in the milking parlor," Dick said, snapping on three-buckle boots. Tom "Gorm" and Bill were also dressing for the late afternoon milking. I hadn't planned on this, but on the Ryan farm, with the Ryan men, I wasn't given a choice. I soon sported a pair of huge bib overalls, enormous oversized three-buckle boots, a DeKalb seed cap, and was stomping toward the dairy barn with three real milkers and a green horn bringing up the rear.

Dick was milking forty head of Holsteins, I overheard reaching the milking parlor on the barn's ground level. Dick, Gorm and Bill, three Ryan clan look-a-likes, attacked the work immediately as I picked my nose and pondered this sudden change. But Dick soon made it known I wasn't to be an observer. I was out here to work, to earn my keep, to earn the meal I had eaten, plus investing in the next meal.

"Here, Jim, grab these stainless steel milkers and carry them down to Dad at the far end," Dick hollered as Gorm herded willing, agreeable Holsteins into the milking parlor from the yard. They were braying and mooing as low and untuneful as the Holy Trinity congregation when singing a "good" hymn. The udder-laden cows sloshed through clean gutters into prison-like stanchions, each apparently having his or her private stanchion. What were these cows? Dick slapped them on the ass. Bill used his lean, strong heft to shove them right and left as Gorm shouted, slapped and herded the beasts from the muddy yard. The sons were spittin' images of their father in looks and action.

"Shit!" I hollered trying to reach Bill while bouncing off Holsteins like a steel ball in Bartlett's pinball machine. Twice the stainless steel milkers fell from my grip to the floor. Twice, swishing tails sloshed me in the face until I finally reached Bill. Gorm latched the double door, all forty head now locked into place, milking tits at the ready.

"Here, give me that, Jim, and get me the rubber connectors." I rushed through the alley—yawning Holstein asses snarling, tails swishing—to gather rubber tubes that connected to the stainless steel milkers that connected to the . . . Dick handed me a handful of rubber tubing, then I rushed to Bill. Gorm and Dick were cleaning more tits that I had ever seen—even in Eddie's Drugstore magazines—with a wet cloth before placing rubber-necked suction devices on each tit. They hooked the ominous cups to stainless steel milkers, inturn connected to more tubes on a portable suction-motor contraption. The milking had begun. I was bewildered, although I didn't have time to ponder as Bill or Dick or Gorm kept firing orders at me . . .

"Get this,
Bring me that,
Kick that sonofabitch,
Move 'er over,
Here, Jim, carry this full one to the vat,
Bring me another milker, Jim,
Hurry up, this isn't college,
You got to work to earn your keep,
Another full one, Jim, dump here in the vat."

The Ryans kept me busy. After the men filled each milker, I lugged it to the huge vat in the milk house to dump it. They were heavy sonofabitches, I found. I dumped, rinsed, then rushed back to one of the determined Ryans. This was pure "gold" they were harvesting from each Holstein, pure white gold that brought regular money to the farm, not like seasonal corn, not like seasonal grains. Milk was a staple, a year-round income just like the chickens Dick and Short still raised. Shorty liked gathering eggs, raising fryers, but Dick had tired of it, preferring his milking cows, a few fatted hogs and summer harvesting in the sprawling fields on the edge of the Belle Creek. But Shorty was persistent about her layers and fryers. She hatched a new brood every spring, kept her hen house as clean as her living room, gathered eggs daily for baking and breakfast, then sold the remainder to Lensch & Rusch in the village. And she hid the egg money in a Red Wing Pottery jar in the kitchen, not to be touched by Dick or the children. Dick didn't think it brought in enough money, what for all the work, but he was a considerate husband, knowing Shorty enjoyed the work, enjoyed getting out of the house, doing something other than changing diapers and raising children.

Since the first Ryan trekked into this township from Ireland in the 1840s, a milking cow, and a laying hen had been life itself. It had taken their ancestors several seasons to get what would be called a farm up and going. It took time and sweat and heartache to break the virgin sod, to build the first soddies and stone-based homes, stone barns, stables and root cellars before erecting improved log cabins. It took persistence to plant vegetables, potatoes, turnips and rutabagas before winter winds screamed in from the west. It took persistence to breed cattle when water and shelter were sparse. The milking cow each farmer had brought into the township represented life. The few chickens they had been able to bring provided sustenance. Milk was a life source, pure gold then, white gold now. Cows had been almost kinfolk, often sharing the same quarters with the family, house and stable one, each species living off the other—the cow offering milk and heat to a family who inturn offered caring, food and shelter. Chickens provided eggs for baking and frying when there were enough. Yes, cows and chickens had been part of the Ryan ancestry. Shorty wasn't about to let go of that, even one hundred years later.

The Ryan men worked together like well-oiled farm machinery, efficient, talking little, working fast from cow to cow, up and down the milking parlor now filled with cow shit, of which I was having difficulty avoiding and smelling. My nostrils weren't accustomed to the caustic, defecating, fecal odor, but I couldn't escape or complain. These cows were certainly domesticated, but they weren't house- or even barn-broken. They shit when and where they chose—out in the yard, in the milking parlor. It was supposed to land in the gutter, but these Holsteins weren't good at aiming. "Don't worry about getting cow shit on you, Jimmy," Dick hollered as he acquired milking paraphernalia, "goes with the territory. You'll get used to it." Then from somewhere deep within the black-and-white herd he commanded, "Bring me a milker!"

Get used to it? What did he have in mind? I wasn't going to be a farmer. I was a college man studying to be . . . well . . . something I'd figure out later. Milking Holsteins was *not* in my plans. I hadn't enrolled in the U's Ag School, no sir. I was attending a Catholic, liberal arts college studying to be . . . something.

"Hurry up, Jim. Got to move faster," Dick hollered, setting a full container in the alley.

"Comin', moving fast here, boss," I hollered, rushing down the alley with an empty milker, fatally slipping on the slimy surface, sliding into a shit-filled gutter to lie there gazing up at an angry Holstein ass ready to open wide. I crawled and slithered to the safety of the center aisle luckily escaping a rush of shit pouring into the gutter. The Ryans-three looked up, bemused, then returned to milking without saying a word. Guess they had seen it all before. Bill and Gorm helped me by emptying some milkers, but Dick had me going; besides, he was the boss, his parlor, his herd, his "white gold." After a couple of hours, cow shit covered me from head to toe and I reeked like the village's sewage plant. I glanced at Dick, Gorm and Bill, but they weren't dirty. I wondered about that. What was I doing wrong? Must be some trick to this milking business, I pondered, as Dick passed the last full milker to me.

"There, that'll hold these sonofabitches for another day," Dick shouted as the men began releasing the Holsteins from their stanchions, slapping them on ample asses, herding them out the doors into the yard, milking done for another day. "Grab that shovel, Jim, and start shoveling this shit from the gutters," Dick hollered as Bill grabbed a shovel and started working the far gutter. Shit! Shit to shovel? Oh well. I grabbed a shovel and began pushing Holstein shit toward the already muddy yard, and let me tell you, there was plenty to shovel. My nostrils weren't any better after a couple of hours of acclimation, but as Dick said, 'It goes with the territory.' Shoving, hefting and slipping, I finally cleaned my gutter about an hour after Bill had finished his, but then, he was experienced and I was only a town fellow with semi-rural roots.

Dad had grown up on the Franklin farm down the road a piece, but I didn't get to work there, he having left the farm for W.W.I in France and Germany long before I entered the county in '36. But he had driven our village family out to the homeplace to visit Grandmother Catherine during my toddler years, those years for romping in the chicken coop, climbing the hay mow and windmill, jumping on tractors and binders and wooden-wheeled wagons. They were *not* working years. Uncle Jim farmed somewhere around Belle Creek, raising many crops and kids; Uncle Pat raised crops, no kids, with Catherine on the homeplace. Uncle Dave quickly tired of farming, preferring the urban setting of the village. Aunt Cecelia married "Goddamn cows, sonofabitching tractor" Vic O'Neill from down the road, moved to an eighty-acre parcel across the field from Bill "W. C." Ryan and proceeded to raise ten red-headed, freckle-faced Irish kids, dragging them by their ears to Sunday Mass and holy days of obligation while tending her chickens, just like Short. With all that farming background in my heritage. I was sort of "farm." Mother's Red Wing kin weren't farmers. It balanced out.

Finally, we finished scooping the gutters, rubbing down the stanchions, gathering rubber hoses, washing milkers, and most importantly, safely securing the "white gold" in the stainless steel vat in the cool milk house. It was ready for pickup from the Creamery. Bill had followed this routine for thirty or more years; Gorm had helped for twenty; Dick was continuing the tradition, milking forty head every day of the year, without fail. Milking cows tied you down, that was for sure, but it was a trade off. It put money in the bank. These were cash cows.

"Well, Jim," Dick said as we trudged back to the house, snow falling in the bleak November sky, "you didn't do half bad, just all bad." He slapped me on the back, grabbed my arm, just as Dad used to do. "Actually, you're a pretty good worker for a town fella. I'd keep you on. You can come back and work for me during summer vacations. Do you good, getting shit on your shoes, driving tractor in the fields. How about it?" he asked as us four "Ryans" walked to the basement to clean up before dinner.

"I'll think about it, Dick, but I like the pea viner work, and I've promised Bookie I'd return next summer. I'll come out and work for you though if it doesn't work out with Bookie," I said as we milkers began cleaning up, showering in the basement, getting spruced up for the womenfolk and a second Thanksgiving feast. I had earned my keep.

I woke Friday morning wondering where I was, for a moment, confused. Where was Bernie Franta, my gangly six-foot-six roommate? Where was Fr. Henry? Where were all the fellows on third floor St. Ben's Hall? It took a moment to realize I was back home in my sparse room rather than at St. John's.

I had taken most personal items to college, so my village bedroom consisted of only a bed, an antique dresser (not antique, old!), a hard-ass'd chair, and my duffel bag dumped in the corner. The room was cold. I stayed under the covers pondering my day. This room had always been cold, never receiving any heat even when the family lived here. In the forties we had only a Jungers oil-burning Heatrola in the living room, a wood-burning stove in the kitchen. Mother kept the door to the upstairs bedrooms closed during the day, but honored Rose, Tom and me with an open door and a little rising heat an hour before we trudged to the arctic bedrooms. We would bound into bed, hardly touching the freezing floor, jump under ten blankets and quilts, then reverse the process in the morning. Three flannel-bedecked kids scurried down to the Heatrola, fighting for a spot near it, subsequently burning our butts on the hot surface.

This day, from deep under my quilts, I looked onto the street toward Heaneys, wondering what I would do today, the sky gray, sleet tapping my window like a Civil War rudimental drummer. Mom and Bill had retreated to Red Wing last night. I was free to make my rounds in the village. Mother seemed happy being married again. I was happy for her. I liked Bill, too, a good man turning out to be an okay stepfather, something I had never considered. And Dick and Gorm were treating me like a real brother. That was good, too, as brother Tom was still shooting his M-1 rifle somewhere in Germany picking off the ghosts of Hitler and Stalin. Rose was still practicing her Florence Nightingale routine sticking cadavers with long, menacing needles. Could've been worse.

Without a car, I sauntered downtown, but I had been doing that since learning to walk. This day wouldn't be any different;

besides, the village was so small that by the time I reached Third
Avenue I was on the edge of town. We were so tiny that the
"Welcome to Goodhue," and "Thanks for Coming," signs were
nailed to opposite sides of the same, listing post. We were so small
that the police car and fire truck couldn't run at the same time,
because the village could only afford one battery. Well . . . I could
go on about being small . . . but it felt good shuffling down the
sidewalk even though sleeting. I pulled my jacket tighter approaching Holy Trinity.

Although chilled, I paused. Holy Trinity caught my attention
this gray day. I had been attending mass, stations of the cross,
catechism, confession here forever. It was an unadorned fifty-by-
thirty-foot former chicken coop converted into a church after the
chickens stopped laying. Holy Trinity, a tiny, white-washed,
humble building village Catholics naively assumed the Lord
would actually visit. Holy Trinity, a leaning building with a
catawampus cross and expansive lawn where children played
Captain May I? and the site of that eventful, competitive model
airplane flight between Bob and I, the still-towering pine tree
almost sealing my fate.

St. John's looming cathedral had pews by the hundreds,
towering gothic stained-glass windows, an arched ceiling with
flying buttresses soaring to the heavens, a real pipe organ with
thirty-two-foot bass pipes that, when unleashed, drove the devil
out of our souls as well as any threatening Protestants. The
cathedral also had sequestered, monastic pews *behind* the altar.
The only thing behind Holy Trinity's altar had been the portly Fr.
Smith himself, plus just enough room for two skinny altar boys.
The cathedral displayed divine statues and medieval mosaics and
housed that pipe organ played by a real organist who knew how to
put the pedal-to-the-metal on a post-mass Bach fugue causing
those pipes to rumble and roar and beckon God and his angels onto
the roof of the cathedral. Heavenly!

I pulled my jacket closer, impulsively diverting my downtown sojourn to shuffle up the broken steps and undulating
sidewalk into a frigid Holy Trinity. I felt as if I were entering a
confessional with a heavy load instead of a church. Holy Trinity

appeared extremely small as I passed the minuscule foot-pump organ. I genuflected then knelt in the stark, bleak church saying a few Hail Marys and Our Fathers before rising to meander, it being too cold to kneel and pray, yet realizing the Lord was probably looking down on me saying, "If it's heat you want, Jim, I can arrange that!" I glanced at the bland stations of the cross renderings on the bland walls, the humble, insecure communion rail where Bishop Byrne had brought the Holy Ghost to insecure parish children at Confirmation. I noticed the side altar confessional where I had released my sins of impure thoughts behind a thin confessional veil, mumbled words filtering out to the parishioners like incense, so that they all knew what I had been doing, snarls and smirks on dubious faces as I returned to my pew. The tiny, unadorned altar—where I had sweated bloody penance, in advance, fearing Smitty would belittle me after mass for some irreverent mistake—startled me today in its simplicity. I walked back to the leaky, wheezing pump organ where an inept housewife organist pumped out depressing hymns during Lent services when I had wanted to get off my knees and go home. Everything was here, as it had been forever, my childhood religious relics and education, that education now being continued with the black robed Benedictines in a real church.

Although startled by the unmistakable bleakness of the interior, it had meant much to me through childhood. I had known nothing else, had never entered a Lutheran Church—out of fear of eternal damnation—had never set foot in Goodhue Methodist, had never been in a synagogue. I had had no comparisons. This tiny, holy chicken shack is all I had known before St. John's. And all I had learned about The Church, the pope, God and salvation had come from here and sister parish St. Columbkill's out on the prairie, Fr. Smith having served both parishes to earn extra moonlighting money.

I sat on the high organ bench pumping the resistant foot pedals, picking out a few monophonic, monastic tunes I had recently learned in piano class, although I was inept at the keyboard. The clarinet was still my only instrument . . .

Holy God, we praise thy name,
Lord of all, we bow before thee!
All on earth thy scepter claim,
All in heav'n above adore thee . . .

That hymn had always received more parishioner accolades than any other. Parishioners loved it, singing it for years, uninterested in learning anything new the organist occasionally attempted to teach before mass.

Infinite the vast domain,
Ever lasting is thy reign,
Infinite the vast domain,
Ever lasting is thy name.

I picked out a few bars, then just sat in the chilled church gazing at the altar, ruminating about my years here. Catholicism had stood me in good stead. The people of this parish had stood me in good stead, had put me on the "right" path to life and salvation. I appreciated that now that I was on my own. Mother couldn't do much more for me. Dad had done all he could, now praying for me from the cemetery. It was up to me from here on in. St. John's was taking over where Holy Trinity and St. Columbkill's had left off. That wasn't so bad; could've been worse, I thought, executing the sign of the cross before continuing downtown through sleet turning to snow.

I passed the ominous two story parish house—never used as a parish house—diverted through the alley behind the Corner Bar, Majerus Gas & Appliance, Art's Bar, the bank, then crossed the street to the Goodhue Hotel Cafe (Elsie's Cafe during the forties, Carole's Coffee Shop early fifties, Mrs Chuck Bremer's Cafe later fifties). I guess Mrs Bremer was still the proprietor, but to me it was just the Hotel Cafe. Although Swenson's was the regular teen hangout, occasionally Joe's Cafe, and Bartlett's Bowling Alley, I would periodically visit the Hotel Cafe for a change of pace. Today, my stomach growled for breakfast.

"Morning, Mrs Bremer. Think I'll have breakfast," I announced, sitting at the low-stool counter, the nondescript cafe devoid of other customers.

"Good morning, Jimmy. When did you get home?" she asked, adjusting her hair net and placing a menu on the counter. "What'll you have to drink?"

"Glass of milk, and some of your famous french toast with sausage. Even though I stuffed myself yesterday, I'm pretty hungry this morning," I said, placing the tattered and stained menu back in the wire holder.

"Coming right up. Here's your milk. How are you getting along living by yourself and up to college?" she asked while tossing two thick slices of battered bread onto the steaming grill.

"Just fine, Mrs Bremer, just fine. I like college a lot, although it's pretty hard. I've lots of new friends. It's not so bad, then."

She set Log Cabin maple syrup in front of me, then scooped stray bread crumbs into her apron from a previous customer, plus a dime someone had apparently thought fulfilled the tip requirement. "You be back next summer at the viners?"

"I think so. It was good work and I liked working with Bookie, Uncle Dave and the gang. Dick Ryan's offered me a job on his farm next summer, so that's an option, too. I just hope I don't flunk out of St. John's before that. Didn't study much in high school, so I have a lot of catching up to do," I answered, reaching for the *Pioneer Press*. Mable Diercks and Edna Allers walked in and sat at a table in the corner while I was reading the headlines.

"Hello, Jimmy. Home for Thanksgiving?" the lanky Mable asked from her red-and-white, linoleum-topped table.

"Morning, Mable, Edna. Yes, had dinner at the Ryans yesterday. Have a couple more days before returning Sunday. Did you ladies have a nice Thanksgiving?" I asked as Mrs Bremer placed a heaping order of french toast on the counter.

"Oh, now did we ever," a beaming Edna exclaimed. "Family came and we ate and ate. Mable and I are so full yet we're only having coffee this morning," she said as Mrs Bremer carried the pot and two white, heavy mugs to their table. "Enjoy your breakfast."

I ate my breakfast pondering this old hotel forever ensconced on the corner. To my friends it had always been simply "The Hotel." But it had had many names throughout the years, having been built about the same time Mother was born in 1900. Mr Buchholtz built the hotel in 1901. Various owners subsequently named it the Howard House, the City Hotel, the Pomeroy House, the Thompson House, Walker's Commercial Hotel and the Merchant's Hotel. Other than the school building, it was the village's largest brick building, its front facade adorned with three, arched entries leading into a cigar-stained parlor where Pat Rowles had held court for years while reclining in heavy, leather chairs. A mottled oak front desk greeted itinerant rail travelers traveling to or from the village depot, sojourners who booked rooms on the second floor. The north side contained apartments and the near-bank corner housed Dr. Halvorson's office, later occupied by Dr. DeGeest who gave hard-ass'd physical exams to unruly GHS so-called wanna-be athletes.

Many a boyhood afternoon had been spent in the parlor gazing through smoke-stained windows toward Tomfohr's International Harvestor Shop, Sjoblom's Photo Studio, Heaney & Gorman, and Uncle Dave's Dray Barn. I listened to Pat Rowles, Tommy O'Rourke and itinerant travelers, old-timers talking of earlier, younger days, something I was sure I would never do or be—that is, get as old as Pat or Tommy. Pat ruminated about farming in Belle Creek while Tommy recalled his ancestors immigrating to the township from County Limerick or O'Doon or Cork in the Old Sod. He spoke of farming and racing horses and playing baseball down in the wooded hollows along the Belle Creek. As the old-timers recalled youthful days, they puffed long and deeply on huge, dark cigars, cigars as deep as their memories, as they spun smoke rings toward the already stained tin ceiling. But they were good afternoons for a boy. A kid can learn a lot listening to old-timers. It wasn't so bad, then.

I finished breakfast and tipped my hat to Mable and Edna before sauntering into the lobby where the ghosts and yesteryear smoke aroma of Pat Rowles and Pete Nibbe and Tommy O'Rourke were still embedded in the woodwork and thick leather chairs.

On Saturday night the ol' high school gang congregated at the Skyline Ballroom, dancing to Whoopee John Wilfart "Only on Decca Records," as we nauseatingly said every time his name came up. We had danced our way through high school, mostly at the Skyline, sometimes at Oak Center, never too tired to dance the Lindy-Hop (Charles "Lindy" Lindbergh had been a Minnesota boy), the waltz, the jitterbug, the fox trot, the polka, the schottische, the mazurka. Every style was fair game as long as we were on the big dance floor swinging a partner. We even danced after Friday night basketball games in the village, heading out to the Skyline for several hours of high stepping, regardless of a win or loss.

Whoopee John's Orchestra was well known in the area; in fact, he brought his orchestra down from St. Paul where he had held court for years at the Prom Ballroom, broadcasting Saturday nights over clear channel 50,000 watt WCCO. After his contract expired at the Prom, Skyline management arranged for him to appear Saturday nights, live, but without a broadcast. Whoopee had a good orchestra, good musicians who could play both old time and swing. He still traveled with the band in those years, sitting out front squeezing his diminutive old-world concertina, nodding his head to-and-fro to the old-time tunes, his drummer son running the band. They played half old time, half modern with fox trots and swing that I liked best.

"Come on, Janice, let's do the Lindy," and out on the floor we'd hop and swing, darting, jiving to Whoopee's band. Janice was cute, a good dancer, a good friend, though I wasn't sweet on her in high school. She was one of The Five. Mary could do a spirited Lindy, too. I liked dancing with her, Bettie too, just about everybody was a good dancer.

"How's college, Jimmy?" Janice asked as we swung in and out of couples on the floor.

"Good. Like it a lot. I just hope I can make it without flunking out. You were our valedictorian, weren't you? I remember you reciting the alphabet graduation night before the class joined in on the stage. You could recite that the day we started first grade. You should be the one going to college instead of me," I said as we swung from corner to corner, Whoopee working through Benny Goodman's "Let's Dance" arrangement.

"I thought about it, maybe in a year or two, but right now, I'm enjoyed living and working in Rochester. But you hang in there, Jim. You'll make it," she said as the tune ended, the floor clearing to the booths skirting the huge ballroom floor.

"Thanks for the dance, Janice, see you later," I said, walking up and down along the booths, folks catching their breaths after the vigorous dance, some sipping cokes, others Squirts, others reaching underneath the table, retrieving a brown bag to make whiskey sours. Everybody was there . . .

"Hey, Jack,"

"Hi, Dallas,"

"What's happening, Dale?"

"Roger, how the hell are you?"

"Hoffer!"

"Hey, Hutch. How's it going?"

"Doris, great to see you," I said to Doris Bremer, my sort-of-sometimes high school sweetheart. I squeezed in beside her in a booth overflowing with other high schoolers joshing and talking, sipping cokes through long, ruby lipstick-smeared bent straws.

"Nice to see you, Jim. How's college?" she asked, displaying that celebrated, enticing smile she had become famous for, her blond locks framing a pretty oval face. She wore a pleated long skirt, sandal shoes, and pink, open-collar blouse.

"Fine, Doris, just fine. I like it, just hope I can hang in there. It's a lot more difficult than high school," I said, somewhat stunned at running into her, something I hadn't anticipated. Suddenly, those old high school feelings came rushing back. Oh, I hadn't been much of a lover in high school. If the truth be told, I hadn't been a lover at all, hadn't really known what to do with girls. Oh, I knew *what* to do, I just didn't do it, being shy and all that. I dated periodically, liked Doris a lot, but . . . well . . . it hadn't gone much beyond that. Some of the other guys, older guys more worldly and more experienced than me—Carl "Cueball" Holtz, Neil Bremer,

Dallas Diercks, Hutch—knew how to get the girls, but I mostly watched and tried to pick up a few tricks and tips from them.

"You a senior now, Doris?"

"No, only a junior, Jim, Class of '56. You should remember that. It hasn't been that long since you graduated," she said, her full, red lips delicately drawing that coke up a straw.

"Guess not. Just seems like I've been gone a long time already. You . . . ah . . . you . . . well, I mean, dating anyone?" I muttered, dormant high school shyness suddenly emerging like that freshman-year day I attempted to ask her to the prom in front of the water fountain but couldn't do it.

"No one in particular. You found a girl at St. John's?" she asked, drawing me into her again with those bright eyes.

"Well, I've been mostly studying, you know, but I've dated a Benny from Avon a couple of times."

"Benny? What is a Benny?"

"Oh, a Benny is a St. Benedict's student from the girls college three miles down the road from St. John's. We don't allow girls at the college, so they started their own a couple miles away."

"That sounds sexist, Jim. You wouldn't be sexist now would you?" Doris asked, her famous smile and slightly seductive grin spreading across her face.

"Well, no, Doris, I mean, its just that St. John's was founded by monks not nuns who can't be priests but monks if they choose can be priests but of course they don't have to so anyway monks started the college for just men but then . . . ,"

"I get the picture, Jim. That's about all I need to know about monks, me being non-Catholic, as you so often reminded me."

"I did? I said that when we dated? Can't believe it. Wouldn't now," I mumbled as Whoopee broke into a slow ballad. "Want to dance, just for old time's sake?"

"Sure."

We began swaying to "Memories of You," and I was soon back at the 1952 high school prom, Doris in my arms, wondering what to do next, but enjoying her close proximity, nonetheless. I hadn't expected this, hadn't anticipated running into her at the Skyline. It brought back feelings I hadn't exercised much lately.

You see, I had met all these new fellows and it had become mostly a guy thing at St. John's but . . . well . . . Doris, her soft, creamy skin, her midwestern-straw-haired-farm-girl-luscious countenance smelled good and felt good and danced good, and "Memories" was over much too soon.

"Thanks, for the dance, Jimmy, see you later," and she was skipping toward the booth, joining classmates, leaving me standing in the middle of the floor grasping for her lingering scent, the sweet scent of high school, the scent of a could-have-been continuing romance.

Before I had forgotten Doris, the floor suddenly exploded with dancers doing the Bunny Hop—a stupid dance with everyone forming a serpentine line, then jumping around the floor like hormone-induced rabbits. Absurd, but fun. We snaked around the huge ballroom floor, stomping, sweating, hanging on to a waist in front, someone behind holding yours. Hop . . . hop . . . hop . . . it was over. Whoopee wheezed and coughed and counted-off an old-time set of mazurkas, waltzes and polkas, the old-world folk style he popularized around New Ulm before infiltrating the rest of Minnesota. Real folk dancers of every size and shape emerged to stomp and two-step to the vigorous old-world beat. I three-timed two waltzes and one schottische before finishing the evening doing a four-in-the-box fox trot and a final slow dance to Glenn Miller's "Moonlight Serenade," a strange but cute Red Wing girl in my arms. She squeezed in real tight making me wonder if she was confession-close, me smelling sweetness in her long auburn hair, sparkles blinking in her green eyes. Her name was Sharon "something" and she said I was cute and I said she was cute and I said I'd call and she said she'd be waiting and I kissed her on the cheek and she murmured "mmmmm" and I walked her to her car and said I'd see her at Christmas vacation and she said she'd be waiting and I said "bye" and she said "bye" and I went back to the village and she went back to Red Wing and I thought about her later in my room and Sharon dreamed of me that night and I said my prayers.

"**N**ow, let me get this straight, son. When you danced with her, what exactly was it you felt?" "Gee, Father, I was just dancing, you know, close and she was pressing into me because we were dancing real slow, and I felt . . . well . . . ,"

"Get on with it, young man. Other Johnnies are waiting behind you carrying loads of heavy sin," Father Black Robe intoned from inside the catacombed, curtained confessional deep in the cathedral. I had returned to St. John's after Thanksgiving vacation unsure of my spiritual status because of dancing with Sharon at the Skyline. I sort of wanted to clarify it, so had headed directly to the confessional.

"Well, she pressed in and I pressed back, and we danced slowly in the middle of the floor, and . . . ,"

"What were your hands doing, son?"

"I was holding her regular-like, slow dancing."

"Above her waist?"

"Yes, Father."

"I don't think you sinned, son. But you're moving into a new area where you'll have to be especially careful with your hands and your mind. The Lord wants you to be attracted to women, but you have to exercise patience, fortitude and willpower concerning sexual encounters. Willpower, you hear me, son, willpower?"

"Yes, Father."

"You don't need a penance today, but say a decade of the rosary for the future, just in case. Go in peace, and may the Lord be with you."

That felt better, I thought, returning to the dormitory. This "girl thing" was becoming increasingly confessing . . . I mean confusing. We're supposed to be attracted to them, pursue them, but not do anything with them once we catch them. How do you figure that? Oh, well, I'm taking Marriage and the Family with Father Coleman, the Benedictine "marriage" guru, second semester. Maybe he will shed more light on this growing predicament.

I felt good returning to campus, just as returning to the village.

Delighted to see my classmates, happy to return to class, motivated to study more intently—to see if I could "make it" as villagers had perpetually admonished me during vacation—I vigorously attacked my scholarly endeavors. In Bonehead English I continued searching for the right places to insert commas, periods and colons while improving my spelling. I struggled with Bonehead Math, receiving tutorial help from dormies by flashlight after lights were out. I became increasingly bored in Political Science class, it becoming obvious I wasn't about to be a lawyer like the village's Frank O'Gorman, or a judge like Richard Heaney, or a delegate to the Goodhue County Democrats like George Gorman. I saw no future in government work. And I dedicated myself to reading the World History textbook, though, during exams, I couldn't remember what I had read. Those improved study techniques I sought were slow in arriving. I enjoyed Worlds of Religion, although becoming more confused with so many of them. I had no idea there was such a world multitude. I had naively thought there was only Catholicism, Christianity. Now, I was learning about Judaism, Hinduism, Buddhism, Taoism, Islam plus several unpronounceables. I certainly had substantial sorting to do, but then I had four years—Johnnies required to take twelve to eighteen credit hours of religion and ethics courses. When I graduated, if I graduated, I would certainly have this religious-spirituality thing figured out.

"Hurry up, Jim. Practice in five minutes on the field," Chuck said, rushing from the rehearsal room with his clipboard, megaphone and whistle. I put my bonehead textbooks down, grabbed my clarinet and followed him to the marching field sequestered in a natural pocket embraced by towering, eternal pines emitting a fragrant aroma light-years ahead of cheap auto fragrance cards. The marching band had one more half-time show before we could remain inside to play sit-down music instead of marching and tooting in the frozen northern Minnesota tundra. But I was enjoying band and fellow musicians. For two hours we rehearsed stick figures and letters on the field, show arrangements and the Johnnie "Fight Song."

"That's it for today, band. Rehearsal tomorrow, same time," director Robert O'Brien hollered through a megaphone from atop a high podium. Half past five brought November darkness to the college-monastic community and the dinner hour in the quadrangle cafeteria. The band would be back tomorrow rehearsing for Saturday afternoon's final home game versus Hamline, one of the many non-Catholic team's invading the staunch Catholic stronghold of north-central Minnesota. We had already beaten Concordia, Augsburg, Gustavus Adolphus, St. Thomas, having lost only to Moorhead State. Coach Gagliardi had been coaching for two years by the time I stumbled onto campus, leaving my inept football skills back on the deserted GHS field. That first high school team of '48 had inspired me, but my skills faltered. Gagliardi was to devote fifty years to this field—hollering, prodding and cussing his Johnnies to nationally-successful seasons.

The student body processed to the cafeteria, hungry young men emerging from sequestered dorm rooms, confessionals, chapels, labs, library, to take seats at preassigned tables before being served family style. The scene was similar to eating at Florence Taylor's Eat Shop in the village. Everyone was reverent during the general blessing, increasingly irreverent when reaching "Amen," eight hundred Johnnies digging into an evening dinner with their best boarding-house reach. This was a set routine like many campus events: we processed in together, out together, later enjoying a few, relaxed minutes before required study hours and ten o'clock lights out. Regimented? Of course. Could the Black Robes get by with that in the new millennium? Of course not. Was it good for me? Absolutely. Had I enrolled at Winona State with George O', Mankato State with Jack O' or at the University of Minnesota, I would have failed. I would have flunked out after the first semester due to a lack of prior academic motivation and efficient study habits. I would have wasted time in the sprawling student union drinking cokes, playing pool, just as I had at Al Shelstad's Cafe. I was a mere seventeen, but certainly had made a good decision when choosing St. John's. Once those Black Robes had me in their heavenly grasp, they weren't about to let go. They attacked my inadequacies like rampaging Middle Age Crusaders.

"Franklin! You going to the dance tonight after the game?" my towering roommate Bernie asked as I dressed in my marching band uniform for the game.

"Hadn't thought about it, Bernie. I suppose I could, but who would we dance with?" I said, slipping into my cardinal-and-blue band jacket and pants.

"The Bennies are coming over in a bus, chaperoned, unfortunately, but they'll stay till about half-past eleven. A Johnnie jazz band is playing. I'm going hoping to find some real action. Come along after the game," Bernie said, thrusting his lanky legs over the end of the top bunk. I had acquired Big Bernie alphabetically. I hadn't made a choice for a roommate before arriving, so the head academic priest simply assigned us. *F*ranklin and *F*ranta became roommates. Big Bernie, 6-6, 250 pounds, towered over me, but was a gregarious fellow hailing from Olivia, Minnesota. If anyone had worse study habits than me, it was Bernie. He detested studying; don't know why he even enrolled. He mostly joshed and talked and played pranks during study hours. His claim to fame was an ability to fart at will. That's correct. Bernie could, and would fart anytime he chose to, or someone asked, which initially, was often. That in itself wasn't significant, but the blue farts were. I couldn't believe it the first time he demonstrated it, which was about five minutes after we had settled in that first day.

"Watch this," he said, retrieving a long wooden farmer match from his front pocket, lighting it on a pant leg like a township farmer, lifting his six-foot right leg into the air, angling his ass toward me and shooting out a long, blue flame, bluer than B. C. Majerus' best propane . . . Big Bernie's blue fart. "Ain't that a hoot?" he asked, lighting another match for a second attempt to prove he really could fart, at will. Big Bernie never failed. He could fire ten blue-fart flames in a row until his audience tired of the gaseous trick. That was Bernie's claim to fame, but it didn't earn him any points with Fr. Henry or the other monks. Bernie spent the first semester firing blue farts, then retreated to Olivia to screw his girlfriends—more about that later—never gracing St. John's campus again. I moved down the alphabetical list to the *Gs*, acquiring a new second semester roommate.

Gagliardi's Johnnies massacred Hamline 47–3; the marching band performed admirably, but when long, encroaching shadows began creeping over the pine forest late in the fourth quarter, we became chilled to the bone. We were ready to leave. The band marched a column-of-fours back across the now leaf-less campus in front of admiring parents, Brother Leo, and indifferent students. We disbanded, then rushed to the cafeteria for a special roast dinner with the always-present rye Johnnie Bread.

My table mates were also freshmen: Dick, Chuck, Bill, John and Bernie. Dick, wearing his ever-present sheep-lined sleeveless vest, hailed from someplace up in the far tundra, International Falls, I recall; Chuck, his basso Cossack voice catching our attention when he addressed the table regardless of his message, hailed from Eau Claire, WI; Bill, his ever-present smoking pipe tucked neatly into a vest pocket, journeyed to these monastic grounds from Valley City, North or South Dakota; John, his ever-present plastic slide rule stuck in a rear pocket, from Forest Lake near the Twin Cities; Bernie, long, tall, impatient, from Olivia. I was the only Goodhue student at the table, which, with the fellows, was just fine.

"How big is Goodhue, anyway?" John asked, passing a huge bowl of dusky Johnnie Bread to me.

"Goodhue is so small that . . . ,"

"How small is it?" John asked, picking up my lead-in.

"Goodhue is so small that when we call a wrong number we end up talking for fifteen minutes anyway," I said, passing the overflowing bread bowl to Chuck. "Goodhue is so small that we don't roll up our streets; we shovel them."

"Shoot! Forest Lake is small compared to the Twin Cities, but a lot bigger than Goodhue, that's for sure," John said, reaching for the meat plate.

"Eau Claire is about 30,000 and we think that's small over in Wisconsin," Chuck offered, his roaring basso voice resonating beyond our table, causing all to give him more attention than he probably deserved. He retrieved a chunk of roast.

Bill, anxious to finish eating so he could light up out in the quadrangle, offered his community's statistics, "Valley City has a population of circa 15,000, three Catholic churches, one public high school and one Catholic high school."

"How about Olivia, Bernie? Olivia have a Catholic high school?" John asked, as we finally began eating instead of passing.

"Shit no!" Bernie exclaimed. "We didn't have none in town, even if we did, don't know if I would have attended," he exclaimed, fiddling with the matches in his front pocket.

"Why's that, Bernie?" Chuck asked. "You're at a Catholic college now."

"Fuckin' 'A', but it wasn't my idea. Dad's dumb idea I come here, 'cause he's paying the moola. But I don't know if I'll hang with it. Hey! You guys ever seen my trick?" Bernie said, suddenly changing the subject, his fork hand moving toward his pocket.

"Uh . . . not now Bernie . . . later," I said as Bernie suddenly looked downcast.

"Let's go to the dance tonight," Bill suggested. "Guess they're bringing a bus of Bennies over. That ought to be good. What do you think, Jim?" he asked, now attacking heavenly chocolate cake.

"You bet. I'll come. I like dancing and could stand to meet an appropriate girl. Sounds like fun."

"An *appropriate* girl, Jim? What the hell is an *appropriate* girl." Bill asked, looking dumbfounded, chocolate crumbs falling from his open mouth.

"An appropriate girl is cute, intelligent, has a nice figure, likes to neck a little, but one who has studied her catechism and knows when it's appropriate to go no further, an intelligent *Catholic* girl," I said, beginning my cake.

"Where did you learn that bullshit, Franklin?" Bernie snarled, his huge, lanky frame rising above us even while sitting. "Girls are for making out with, for kissing and feeling up and screwing. 'Girls' ain't got nothing to do with being 'appropriate,'" he barked over the din of the cafeteria, suddenly looking as if I said I had killed the abbot.

"I don't know, Bernie. Sounds kind of harsh to me," John said, joining the suddenly enticing conversation. "I've been going steady for three years in high school, and I don't agree with you about that. My girl's sweet and we neck and, like Jim said, she's kind of appropriate," John offered as he cut a second piece of cake, the plate rapidly diminishing.

"Bullshit!" Bernie retorted, now almost standing over the table. "I've been screwing girls since I was a freshmen in high school and they like it," he bellowed, the head priest table suddenly looking our way.

"What about confession then, Bernie?" Chuck asked, his Shakespearean voice causing all to again give him undivided attention. "Making love outside of marriage is a sin, mortal sin I think," he continued.

"Bullshit on that too, Bernie hollered, louder now so that other tables suddenly looked toward ours. "I don't kowtow to all that servile venial and mortal sin shit. That's too priestly, too monk'y business for me. I just do what I want, what my pecker tells me to do," Bernie exclaimed, finishing his cake, chocolate frosting stuck in his gaping teeth.

"Maybe that's why your dad wants you at St. John's, Bernie, to gain a different, more spiritual perspective, perhaps," John offered.

"It ain't gonna work then. I don't like studyin'. Don't like college, but I do like girls, and I aim to find me lots of *inappropriate* girls. Take that, Franklin and the rest of you lily-white Benedictines," Bernie said as we all rose at the clanging of the bell for the departing blessing before traipsing into the darkened, cold night across an inky campus. We would all meet later at the dance, dancing with "appropriate" girls.

A quartet played soft harmonies in the corner of the dimmed, antique gymnasium as Chuck and I entered. Few students had arrived. A punch table surfaced under the far basket. We sauntered over. The Bennies hadn't arrived yet, and I wasn't about to dance with Chuck, although Goodhue girls always danced together, no one then thinking anything about it. Chuck, long of neck and nose, was a table mate and band mate, but he had passed out of bonehead classes having dedicated himself more at Regis High School than I had at GHS. We sat in wooden folding chairs sipping punch and listening to the quartet. Their polish surprised me, playing jazz ballads and some of the new bop music the village hadn't detected. Oh, Whoopee John was pretty good, but he played mostly standard, stock arrangements, plus that old-time music I was growing increasingly disenchanted with. This quartet played a Charlie Parker or Dizzy Gillespie bop tune as three couples began slow dancing. Some Johnnies were day students—living off campus—and they apparently had brought their day girls with them. Long-legged Chuck traipsed off to talk to a theatre major as I began listening more intently to the music. I particularly enjoyed the tenor sax player massaging lyrical melodies, this with a big, full sound, light years beyond Noisy Rusch's tenor sax in the GHS band. GHS hadn't had a jazz or dance band, so I had played only Bb clarinet in Concert Band, but I was beginning to like that tenor sax sound. Four girls appeared in the front door, obviously Bennies, as there weren't any other females within miles of here. My focus quickly changed from the tenor sax to the Bennies.

Although a college fellow now, I was still wrestling with that old high school shyness, so I didn't jump up immediately to dance. But Johnnies and Bennies soon began mingling, drinking punch, chatting, dancing. About the third tune, I joined in, dancing with a curly-haired, gangly, bespectacled Benny from Cold Spring—her hand equally cold—a burg just over the back forty famous for its Cold Spring Brew.

"Hi, I'm Jim from Goodhue."

"Hello, I'm Geraldine from Cold Spring."

We danced fairly well to a fox trot, although she tended to miss the strong beats, followed by a slow waltz where she persisted in four-to-the-bar instead of three-to-the-bar. We chatted for a while before I determined she was very, maybe *too* appropriate, so I moved on, mingling, dancing next with Charlotte, a long-haired, tall brunette from Avon who liked to lead better than follow. We struggled through a fox trot before quickly separating, both seeking more interesting and adept partners. Soon the petite Becky was in and out of my arms jitterbugging to "Woodchopper's Ball."

"You're a fine dancer, Jim. Where did you learn?" she asked, effortlessly following my every step.

"Skyline Ballroom," I said, dipping and darting to Herman's blues.

"Where is that?" she asked as we jived in synchronized rhythm around the floor.

"Down in Goodhue, well, actually Red Wing. Goodhue is too small to support a dance hall. We're so small that . . . ," I discontinued, spinning Becky around my back, she catching my every move even when I couldn't see her.

"I've heard of Red Wing, but never Goodhue. I'm from Mitchell, South Dakota. Have you ever heard of the Corn Palace?" she asked, darting under my arms, smiling, sort of like Doris.

"Sorry, I haven't, but I'll bet it's nice," I answered, as I dipped her to the floor to end "Woodchopper's Ball."

"Thanks for the dance," Becky said, "ask me again," and she was off joining other Bennies at a table. Maybe I will.

"Hey, Franklin! You found your appropriate girl yet?" Bernie said, slapping me on the back, suddenly appearing out of nowhere.

"Hi, Bernie. How are you doing with the ladies?"

"Found me a luscious, hot blond. Danced three times with her. Big tits, push right into me. Look here how my chest is caved in! Day student from St. Cloud. Might get some action tonight," Bernie said, rushing off to the punch table, a flask embedded in his rear pocket. "Don't wait up for me."

"You'll get in tr . . . ," I began hollering after him before realizing it was futile. I danced and mingled and drank punch for a couple of hours until the quartet struck up "Moonlight in Vermont," the tenor saxophonist massaging the melody with his lush sound. Too soon, the last dance of the night arrived. I searched for Becky, located her at a far table, then escorted her onto the darkened floor, she easily slipping into my arms for the slow ballad . . .

Pennies in a stream,
Falling leaves, a sycamore,
Moonlight in Vermont.

Warbling of a meadowlark,
You and I and,
Moonlight in Vermont

This is good, I thought, dancing closely, swaying slowly in the dim gym, "Moonlight in Vermont" shedding star-struck moonlight over the floor. Becky felt soft, danced well, smelled enticing. She was several inches shorter than me, so her shining brown hair often brushed my chin as I showed her a couple of additional "Skyline" steps. I glanced around the floor to notice some Johnnies dropping their right hand dangerously low below their partner's waist. What is this, I wondered; that's not something we did at GHS or at the Skyline. Becky placed her head on my shoulder, snuggling closer as that tenor milked the harmony of "Moonlight." "I'm glad you came over tonight, Becky, and that I met you," I whispered in her dainty ear. "Think I might call you at St. Ben's?" I asked while executing a *pas des deux* or some step I made up trying to impress her.

"I would like that," she said, placing her head back on my shoulder.

Other guys were slipping hands lower and lower as the song approached its end. I figured I would try it, so I slowly dropped my right hand lower until I felt her waist ending and something else beginning. Becky reached behind her back, grabbed my hand, raised it to its rightful place between her shoulder blades. "That's not appropriate, Jim."

Christmas vacation rapidly approached as snow drifts reached first floor windowsills of St. Ben's Hall, encasing the isolated campus like a monastic Burgundian village. The encompassing pine forest bent, groaned under the snow's pressing weight; Lakes Sagatagan and Watab froze to a foot depth. Life beyond the campus enclave appeared to have halted, yet inside, the compound resembled a mole's tunneled environment, expanding, alive with the rhythm of a college, young men in search of their future. The study, class, dining, confession routine was broken only by Saturday night pickup basketball games in the armory-gym where former high school stars displayed their limited gifts. Many of us had tried out for the real St. John's team, but soon found our exemplary high school talents were subpar for the college game. I gave the tryouts my best shot, demonstrated my best soft, long-arching jump shot that had been so effective against Mazeppa, Wanamingo and Zumbrota, plus several right- and even left-handed drives to the basket. Lastly, I fired a couple of jumping hook shots before running sprints from basket to basket. Alas! It wasn't to be. I was relegated to Saturday night pickup games with other "stars." A couple of years later, though, Tom O'Reilly made the *real* Johnnie team; thereby, holding up GHS's prestige. Tom and I had played guards together back at GHS in the early fifties, not really the menace of the Wasioja Conference then, but effective, nonetheless. We had made our mothers proud. In two years Tom had become big and burly, a tough Catholic Irishman to enhance the Johnnie team.

I began calling on Becky at St. Ben's, Saturday or Sunday afternoons in the "Benny" Reception Hall, huge, ominous, dusky-framed pictures of Sister Scholastica—St. Benedict's plain sister—haunting our every attempted romantic move. We would stroll campus gingerly holding hands, sneaking through the nun's ancient cemetery for a few undetected kisses and embraces behind the tombstones of the grateful dead. Evenings, when dances were held on either campus, we would swing and jive joyfully to the Lindy-Hop, jitterbug, then dance ever so closely on slow, dreamy ballads while dark-hooded Benedictine eyes scanned the dance floor for any inappropriate activity. Parents had entrusted their daughters to the good nuns for safe keeping, sanctity and finishing. The nuns weren't about to let them down. I still hadn't worked out the ramifications of courting, yet wasn't giving up. I liked being with Becky, being near her, smelling her scintillating aroma, touching her in all the "appropriate" places, necking within the limits of Church Law, but as she had indicated that first night we danced, there would be a limit to our exploration. She was an "appropriate girl." Mother would have loved her.

Bernie's exemplary farting skills were the talk of third floor

St. Benedict's Hall, its diverting rooms reminiscent of solitary confinement. Others attempted the feat, but could never succeed other than producing a measly bluish pop. Bernie remained the king of blue farting. In fact, we began calling him "Blue Flame."

I persisted in my bonehead classes, Political Science, and struggled through Music Appreciation, an oxymoron if ever there was one. Fr. 'Napoleon' Dominic exercised absolutely nothing to help us "appreciate" music. One hundred students sat or slept in a darkened auditorium as Little Napoleon played dusty, cracked records of Bach and Brahms, Handel and Mozart, most of us knowing nothing about those ancient composers. Why, they could have been Matthew, Mark, Luke and John for all I knew. If the truth be known, I didn't know the apostles well either, our village Catholic education being interpreted for us by Fr. Smith rather than being encouraged to read the Bible. Contrary to my Lutheran friends, Bible reading was considered dangerous lest we realize the wrong conclusions about salvation, sin, marriage, and why The Church killed all those folks during the rampaging Crusades and Inquisition.

Anyway, we were supposed to "appreciate" the music masters. Goodhue, after all, hadn't been the music cultural center of Minnesota in the forties and fifties. The only radio station on our frequency was KDHL and it played only old-time music: Whoopee John, The Kufus Brothers, the Six Fat Dutchmen. Oh, WCCO came in good for Minneapolis Laker games when George Mikan was shooting fifteen-foot hook shots, Cedric Adams narrating the 10 o'clock news, and Ma Perkins noon show, but it didn't play classical or jazz music. And the only phonograph I had access to was Mary Ann McHugh's forty-five record player. She played it for me often, but only pop rock of the day—Perry Como, Andrew Sisters, Frank Sinatra, Mario Lanza—no Mozart, Beethoven or jazz. Bob or Lee or Larry or Janice or Mary or Dallas didn't own recordings. Consequently, my only cultured-music exposure was what Charles Wood confronted us with in chorus and band; considerable, yet left wanting for "Napoleon's" Music Appreciation class.

For our semester exam Napoleon dropped the needle at

random, expecting us to identify the composer and composition by that snippet of music. Then he asked us to define "polyphony," "homophony" and "counterpoint." Give us a break! we intoned like Inquisition friars. He subsequently flunked eighty percent of the class; of course, I wasn't in that other twenty percent. We appealed to a higher court in the academic dean, the abbot, even Brother Leo, the case subsequently overturned after the dean consulted the Vatican, but I still received only a "C." Despite Fr. Dominic's atrocious teaching talents, Mozart, Beethoven and the difficult, inaccessible Bach gradually drew me to their entrancing compositions. I was moving towards the music world by the time I returned to the village for Christmas vacation.

" **J**im, have you ever seen a *Playboy* magazine?" Sharon asked, her bare, creamy, slim legs stretching out on the lush carpet as we lounged on her Red Wing living room floor during Christmas vacation.

"Well, my buddies had some I would peek at once in a while, but I don't know much about them," I said, startled by her brazen inquiry.

"You're just chiding me. You know what a *Playboy* magazine is. Here, I've brought some to look at," she said, tossing several garish-colored, glossy *Playboys* in front of us as she brought those creamy legs in closer. This was startling. She was threatening to actually look at them . . . with me? I had never done something so bold. Sure, our grade school gang had looked at a few nude "girlie" magazines back in my tree house, and I'd sneak as many glances as possible at the stack behind Eddie Fischer's Drugstore counter, Eddie suspect of my activities but not talking. I had always returned them quickly when Emma Kindseth or Emily Parker or Agnes O'Reilly or Mother, for God's sake! would unsuspectingly enter the store. Looking at girlie magazines certainly wasn't something I shared with other folks. Now, here I was, lounging next to Sharon who actually suggested we look together.

She started at the beginning, leafing slowly through the ads and *Letters to Playboy*, and endless, wordy stories. Little or no titillation yet, until she reached the middle section where the nude ladies were. She flipped a page, very slowly it seemed, that page momentarily suspended in the air as my breath stuttered. Suddenly, facing us was a well-endowed woman lounging under a Christmas tree, Santa's cap flowing over her shiny hair, elongated, pointed tits almost falling off the page. I was sort of embarrassed, knowing Sharon was watching me out of the corner of her soft, green eyes.

"What do you think, Jim? Do you like that?" she asked, her voice as soft and creamy as a Swenson's milkshake, a twinkle in her eye.

"Well, yes, it isn't so bad, could be worse," I said as she flipped more pages of the same Santa woman lounging on puffy holiday chairs, crimson-satin beds, even outside in a sleigh, bare ass naked, and in the winter! I hadn't seen Sharon naked, didn't know how endowed she was. Was she suggesting something here? Was she leading up to something after eating hot-buttered popcorn? I began fidgeting as she tossed that issue aside, grabbing another. Where was this evening leading, her parents gone, us alone in the house looking at *Playboys*. As she fetched the second magazine, I did scoot closer to her feeling the warmth of her soft hips as we lounged on the shag carpet floor. The second issue was a little easier as I began enjoying both the photos and Sharon's proximity.

"Do you ever buy *Playboys*, Jim?" she asked, a slight, seductive grin spreading across her delicate, creamy face.

"Naw. Eddie doesn't stock 'em in Goodhue, and of course, there's no place to buy them up at St. John's. Hard to find," I said, snuggling up closer and nipping her on the ear. She felt good, yielding, and was . . . at least up until tonight . . . an "appropriate" girl. She kissed me back. We forgot the magazines for a while, tussling on the floor like late-aged, hormone-induced teenagers. We were getting in some heavy petting when she suddenly jumped to her feet . . .

"Think I'll make the popcorn now. Come on; you can help," she said, sprinting toward the kitchen. I composed myself, slowed my breathing, tucked in my shirt, straightened my hair and entered the kitchen, real cool-like, "Joe College."

"I hadn't expected to look at *Playboys* tonight, Sharon. Kind of interesting, aren't they?" I said, retrieving the bowls and sodas.

"A friend gave them to me today. I just thought you'd like to see them, you being shy and *real* Catholic," she said as the kernels began snapping, popping, getting about as hot as I was.

"Shy? Why do you say that?"

"You just are, but that's good, Jim. I don't like fellows who come on real strong and want to feel me up on the first date, want to take my pants off."

"Uh, well, gee, I'm not really interested that," I said, thinking 'What on earth am I saying? That's not what I meant to say.' I meant to say . . . 'Well, sure I want to but it needs to be appropriate and I wouldn't want to take advantage of you and I'd be a gentleman of course unless you felt that I shouldn't and if then you maybe thought it would be all right.' Shoot! I was confused. This sex stuff was awfully hard to figure out.

We returned to the living room, chomped on hot-buttered popcorn, listened to Ted Heath and Stan Kenton records while practicing petting before I headed back to the village, the piquant Sharon putting a stop to any further action. "That's enough for tonight," she whispered. "I thought I'd just open your eyes a little, Jim," she said, kissing me at the door. "Sweet dreams."

Now what did she mean by that?

F rosty, fluffy snow encased the isolated campus from Christmas until May. It had become obvious why the Benedictines settled in north-central Minnesota. The dense pine forests and frequent heavy snows acted as further deterrents to encroaching Minnesota Lutheranism; that's why. This enclave became the fortress of Roman Catholicism north of the Twin Cities, non-Catholic sects unable or unwilling to attack this theological fortress. The site had the additional benefit of protecting Johnnies from the vagaries of the world, women included, according to the Benedictines. But we were wily—Inquisitions or Crusades or Theoretical-Theological Vatican encyclicals not deterring determined fellows from *seeking* those vagaries of sin. Although a five-foot barbed wired fence separated St. John's from St. Ben's, there were numerous holes in it.

I hadn't flunked out after the first semester, many thanks to Dennis Heaney's prodding. Second semester I gained two new roommates, Eau Claire Chuck and Valley City North or South Dakota Bill, as Big Bernie was true to his word—with prodding from the academic dean—"Blue Flame" not returning to campus. Instead, he spread his blue flames to other parts of Minnesota. The Concert Band rehearsed inside, thankfully, toured northern Minnesota's remote parishes as had the original Benedictine missionaries in the mid nineteenth century. By the end of May, I was preparing to return to the village and Bookie's pea viner for the summer.

"Will you be back next year, Jim?" Chuck asked, stuffing shirts and trousers into an already bulging Samsonite suitcase.

"Planning on it if I earn enough money on the viner this summer. You?" I said, collecting my drawers from my drawers.

"Same . . . if I make enough money."

"How about you, South Dakota?" I asked Bill as he finished packing, finally wrapping a cord around an overflowing suitcase.

"North Dakota, Jim! Valley City is in North Dakota! Same as you fellows. Need money. Hope to see you back here come fall."

"Well, that's it then, guys," I said as we headed down the ancient St. Benedict's stairwell. We'll all be back in the fall. Have a good summer," I bid, striding across campus to begin hitchhiking home. I was momentarily saddened leaving Chuck, Bill and my new-found friends, but I perked up thinking of a summer with Sharon.

Chapter 3

Hostile attack

Josephine "Dodie" Gorman, Florence Taylor
Heaney's Market, Lower Street, c. 1942

"CAN'T COMPLAIN 'BOUT SEEIN' YOU BACK,
Franklin. You too, 'Reilly, but hope you whippersnappers pitch harder this summer than last. Fellas
don't look any smarter for havin' been to college, 'course you don't
need smarts to work my viners, just hard workin'," Bookie snarled

as we met him by the viners, giant Max casting his long, hulking shadow from the pitchfork corral.

"Hi Bookie," Jack hollered, his Chevy sliding to a halt inches short of Max.

"Hey, Bookie!" I hollered, bounding from the car, extending a soft and wimpy academic hand. "Jack and me are ready for another season. Hope you can keep those peas running fast, so we don't have to wait for trucks like we did last summer. Uncle Dave back supervising?"

"You got that right. Ol' Dave'll be bouncing in any minute in that worthless pickup of his. Can't get along without Dave," Bookie said, shuffling like a wayward penguin toward the slumbering viner machinery, Jurassic-era behemoths waiting to be awakened from eons-old sleep. He began his routine by checking all moving parts—double grease gun artillery holstered at his sides—lubricating lazy gears, slapping sullen tarps as Jack, George O', OJ plus new faces quickly fell into our routine of preparing the viners for the day, the season, as if we had never been away.

I felt happy returning to Bookie's verdant pea fields, to the village, to my high school chums, having escaped hooded, prying Benedictine eyes and academic demands of the past nine months. I would enjoy the next three months among the waving fields of Goodhue Township, never thinking about commas or periods or semicolons or conjunctive verbs or complimentary adjectives; never considering obtuse triangles or algebraic formulas; never pondering esoteric essays and lectures on Buddhism, Hinduism, Taoism, gods and idols beyond me; never analyzing the theological counterpoint of the reformed Martin Luther, whatever that was. But as I reached for a long-handled pitchfork, I realized I would never stop encountering non-Catholics. Protestants were all around me: in the village, the county, the state's dominant faith. After studying World Religions, I had become aware there were many more of them in Minnesota than Catholics. My priest professor had reluctantly intoned, ". . . almost two out of three." Truly a Revelation. Yet, that was all right. Protestants had been friends throughout high school. They would continue to be so, even if we didn't theologically agree.

As I inspected the sharpened pitchfork tines, I anticipated renewing my relationship, whatever it was, with Sharon. I had made progress overcoming feminine shyness, having dated the seemly Becky at college, but I was hoping for more *extended* experience with the brassy Sharon this summer. She was more worldly than Becky—less hooded, less nun-influenced, less saturated. Shuffling toward the conveyors, I thought I might have a breakthrough this summer. Maybe I would make progress along the way, going at least part way along the way. I'd call Sharon first thing.

The crew stacked empty pea boxes, sharpened pitchforks, cleaned and adjusted tarps, placed huge screen drums into the viners for the next two hours. Hutch changed spark plugs on the Ford tractor, getting it tuned for his vine stack that would soon loom over Bookie's domain. Most of the crew of '54 had returned in '55, they too having struggled through academic years: Jack O' at Mankato State; George O' at Winona State; Hutch at St. John's, George OJ at GHS, plus new faces I didn't know this first day, but would when the fields had been raped of peas.

By noon the viners were ready—conveyors and tarps running smoothly, boxes stacked awaiting fresh, juicy peas. We were ready for the first truck load of long, stringy, emerald-green vines encasing eager pregnant pods anxious to give birth to rich-ever-loving-'eat-your-peas, children' green peas.

"Jim, you little fart. Did you learn anything at St. John's this year?" George asked as we adjusted the canvas tarp on viner 1.

"Pretty good year, George. Hard but I liked it. Hope to make enough this summer to return in the fall. You were right about me not studying enough in high school, but I'm learning."

George pulled the tarp taut. "See, Franklin. I told you so. You should have studied more in high school instead of spending all your time at Swenson's and Shelstad's. But maybe you'll make it, after all."

"Think so, George. I didn't want to study when I arrived but, well, those priests saw to it that I did. Don't think I'd have made it if I had gone to Winona State like you."

"You can say that again. No priests at Winona. You either do it yourself or you're out. I got one more year. Graduate next year, then I'll begin teaching and coaching," George said as we snuggled the tarp into place before adjusting ten-foot screens in the rotating drum. Jack O' walked up as we were adjusting. "Hi fellas. Getting anything done? Hell, I've got viner No. 2 ready to go, all by myself."

"Shit, Jack. You can't even jackoff by yourself," OJ yelled from viner No. 3, a new addition to the site. The '54 season had been so profitable for Libbys they had Bookie add another viner in '55, three dinosaur-sized leviathans now looming over the fields. More area farmers had seen the financial advantages of growing sweet peas, so Libby's contracted additional acres for the season. It would surely keep us busy.

As the first trucks hadn't arrived, Bookie, Max, Uncle Dave and the crew ate lunch on the still green grass near the viners. I had fixed a peanut butter sandwich, an apple and carton of milk for lunch. We sat on haunches and feasted before beginning the grueling summer. We were as fresh as the impending peas, not yet tired of the ensuing forty or fifty or eighty days of pea pitching. The Goodhue fellas sat together, and the new Zumbrota guys sat together, not yet knowing us, our ways or even what to think of us. Shoot! I was an old fart now, an experienced viner, plus I had one year of college under my belt. That was no small deal in these parts.

"You young farts learn the ropes in school last year?" Uncle Dave asked, slurping cold coffee and chomping on an Oscar Mayer bologna sandwich while squatting on his long haunches like an Asian peasant.

"Hell, Dave, we already know everything," OJ exclaimed. "We keep the girls happy, that's for sure."

"Shit, OJ! You can't even make our village girls happy."

"Hell, Dave, I taught the Goodhue gals everything they know. Why, if it hadn't been for my Idaho ways, they'd just be tiresome farm girls."

"You're as full of shit as last year, OJ," Max exclaimed, joining us in the lunch circle. "Figured maybe 'nother year of schoolin' would learn you up some but I see it ain't. Anyways, can't complain 'bout seein' you back for 'nother summer. This place wouldn't be the same without your sawed-off top," Max said, plopping onto the ground.

"You too, Max. Hell! We're all gonna have a great summer, aren't we, Jack?"

"You bet! Glad to be back in the village for a while. College is all right, but summers are better. I got two more years before finishing, but hell, Max, we're making more money this summer, aren't we?" Jack said, finishing his ham and cheese white Wonder-bread sandwich from Joe's Place.

Max pulled out a new spiral notebook from his bib overalls, "You guys ain't worth any more money, but that's right. This summer you worthless farts'll make $1.21 an hour, and 'nother ten cents for overtime, which we'll have a load of."

When I heard that I became very excited. Dollar twenty-one a day, plus overtime, plus as much as we would work would surely give me enough to return to St. John's for a second year. Yes sir, Tennessee Ernie Ford, it was going to be a great pea pickin' summer. Three dump trucks rolled into the yard diminishing my sudden glee.

"Grab your socks, not your cocks," Max growled. "We got us peas to vine."

That first day of '55 soon turned into days, then weeks as the crew pitched and boxed tons of peas. Hutch stacked vines out behind the incessantly hungry, groaning viners, his stack, once again, rising like phoenix through the blistering weeks, an over-whelming, nauseating acidic pea juice moat again flowing like the River Styx generating a tart odor that saturated the township, the viners, our very souls.

My rooming situation changed that summer. The couple in the "Franklin" house kicked me out, not wanting a kid around anymore. Oh, it wasn't that they didn't like me, or that I had been troublesome; they just wanted the entire house to themselves. They had been kind and compassionate to me last summer, being alone without a mother, but it was time to move on, time for them to enjoy the house without a Franklin haunting it. That was okay with me. I simply moved next door to rent a room from Ole and Agnes Haga. Their children were long gone from the house and village. Ole and Agnes were aging; moreover, I had mowed Ole's lawn for years and had always respected the undertaker of Goodhue. I had known the Hagas since a tike. It would work our just fine.

Stepfather Bill Ryan decided it was time I had my own car rather than hitching back and forth to St. John's. With Bill and Mother living in Red Wing, me in the village, it would offer more flexibility. After week one at the viners, Bill and Mother arrived in the village with a 1950 two-door Ford, the most beautiful car I had ever seen, because it was mine. Bill removed his glasses and tossed me the keys. I started her up, blessed myself driving past Holy Trinity, past the Corner Bar, past Art's Bar, the bank, to the school and back to Hagas where Bill and Mother were anxiously waiting. "Wow, Bill! Thanks a lot. I sure hadn't expected a car this summer," I said as Mother began wiping tears from her eyes. She always cried at moments like this, but they were tears of joy for her youngest.

"By golly, Jim. You didn't flunk out of St. John's, so Lucy and I thought you should have a car for the summer and to return to St. John's," Bill said, placing a firm arm around Mother's shoulder.

"Lucy? Did you call her Lucy?" I asked, suddenly distracted from my beautiful car. That was 'Mother' he was talking about. I had never heard anyone call her "Lucy."

"Sure, Jim. 'Lucille' was just too long and formal. We Ryans call her 'Lucy' now; hope you don't mind."

"No, that's fine, but . . . well . . . L . . . Luc . . . thanks for the car, Mom," I said, hugging her, something I seldom did, had *never* seen Dad do, something I had never seen Mother's Haustein kinfolk do. But that hug suddenly emerged from nowhere. Mother cried again.

I had never even considered buying a car until finishing college. It wasn't in the works, what with trying to earn money for tuition, room and board. But now Bill had come through, surprising me. I would be ever-grateful to him and his Belle Creek clan. I shook Bill's hand, hugged Mother a second time, jumped into my Ford and took it out for a longer drive, waving to Bill and Mother in the rear view mirror. My very own car. I couldn't believe I was driving *my* car, a gray, two-door, stick shift, sleek, postwar 1950

Ford. Why, it was almost as fine as George Gorman's '49 four-door Ford, the one I had driven delivering groceries to shut-ins about the village.

I shifted ever so slowly, not wanting to grind the gears, not wanting to do anything wrong. Oh, I knew how to drive, had been since eighth grade when Dad would let me drive his '47 Dodge home from the school house, this after considerable nagging on my part. Besides, number one cop Hank Befort didn't mind. He didn't pull me over for driving without a license long before schools offered drivers education. All village children did it. Driving with dad in the forties *was* drivers education.

We had finished early at the viners, a rarity, so I had a couple of hours sunlight remaining for a drive. I drove past Streater's sprawling lumber yard, past the stilted, rusting Standard Oil tanks, slowly down Lower Street then to Upper Street waving to the few folks I saw, they doing double-takes at Jimmy Franklin driving his own car. But I didn't stop, didn't ask anyone to ride with me. I wanted this car all for myself this first day. I drove past the high school, the football and baseball fields, left field, in fact, where Elroy Schulz had smacked so many long, screaming balls. I drove out the dirt cutoff road past centerfield toward Elmer Bremer's on No. 6, then turned left to hook up with County Road No. 9. I wasn't driving anyplace in particular, only following my whim and the roads I had traveled for eighteen years.

I turned right onto No. 9 heading toward Belle Creek Township past Sigvard Stenlund's and Mary Moran's farmsteads as slowly as Uncle Dave drove Sunday afternoons when shooting those little critters after which the University of Minnesota Gophers had been named. This was a great car, I thought, driving into the fading sun past Tom O'Reilly's farm, the V-8 engine smooth, humming, a rich, resonant tone emerging from beneath the hood. I listened to its sonorous hum, felt the dash, tuned the radio, caressed the "lush" upholstered seats all the while a broad smile spreading across my face. I couldn't believe I was driving my own car. Wow! Bill Ryan was turning out to be a good stepfather. I would have to make sure I did something nice for him. With this car I would now be able to drive to the viners, taking Jack instead of vice versa. Nights, when finished early, I would be able to drive the guys to Zumbrota for roller skating. And, it suddenly dawned on me, I would be able to see Sharon in Red Wing, by myself, in my own car instead of depending on Jack or double-, triple-dating with Hutch or Dallas. I had thought a lot about Sharon and me looking at those *Playboys* together. I was darn interested in pursuing that. I hoped that by the end of the summer I would have found out what she had meant by, "Sweet dreams, Jim."

Oh, the moon shines tonight on pretty Red Wing.

And after finishing a summer of pea picking, I would drive my Ford back to St. John's, not hitchhiking this time, instead, taking Johnnies for a spin into St. Cloud or over to St. Ben's to visit Becky if she was still interested in me. Oh! What I would do with my Ford!

I soon found myself parked at St. Columbkill's rural church out on the prairie, admiring my car, thanking the Lord for my good luck and his intervention. The sun had disappeared over Phil Ryan's neighboring cupola as I shuffled into the cemetery. I hadn't planned on driving out here, but well, I might as well tell Dad about my new car, I thought. He had so patiently taught me how to drive back in forty-eight or forty-nine. I shuffled to his grave—third row right—recalling the cold, bitter, painful day we buried him. His headstone stone: Thomas Bernard Franklin, c. 1894–1951, the "c." meaning circa, "about," because Dad had been unsure of what year he had been born down the road a couple of miles from where he now eternally rested. Record keeping hadn't been good then. Most church records had been lost.

I said a few Hail Marys, Our Fathers, threw in a Glory Be, then just "talked" with him for a while as the high prairie breeze caressed the adjacent fields and trees. I told him about Bill Ryan, Dad's own young-adult pal, having bought a car for me. Hoped he wouldn't mind Bill doing that. I told him I liked it and that it would help me make money for college. I told him Mother was doing fine, having married again, and that Bill was taking good care of her. I hoped he didn't mind. I told him I was working hard like he had taught me, that his brother, Uncle Dave, was being good to me, and that Bill Mans and Cy Benda and Francis Majerus and Casey Ryan and Arts Haas and Fred Luhman and Clarence Lunde and John Angus and Ray Bandit and Art Lohman and Cy Buck and Dennis Heaney and Les Bandit and Fred Rusch and Hank Befort and Luverne Haas and Reinhold Schulz and Francis Moran and Jim Ryan and all the other volunteer firemen still talked about him and missed him. I thought Dad would like hearing that. I said that I hoped he was doing fine and that if he was in Purgatory that it wasn't too bad and that he'd be getting out soon. I said I was praying for him and his release from Purgatory. If he were already in heaven, he should just pass my prayers on to another needy soul of the parish, if there were any. I made the sign of the cross over his grave, said "Amen," then shuffled back to my car, the one I just knew Dad would have loved.

I left Dad in peace to drive past Vic O'Neills, Charlie O'Neills, Dick Ryans, Phil Ryans, Clem Ryans, plus a few of the Irish "O's" before heading back to the village. Reaching Evergreen Cemetery near water tank hill, I pondered this new development. A car was going to change many things. I would share the driving with Jack for the remainder of the summer, see Sharon when I could, and well . . . having a stepfather wasn't so bad, after all. A guy could do a lot worse.

"Whaddya think, Jack?"

"Other than being a Ford, she don't look half bad."

Jack loved his soup'd-up Chevy, but now I was able to share the driving, thereby saving him gas money. But I wasn't the type of driver he was. I drove slow, nice and easy like an old lady, Jack said. If the truth be told, my driving drove him crazy—no speeding, no two-wheeled corners, no wheelies. He said I drove like Jesse Campbell. He said I was becoming an old man before my time.

Once the peas began running there was no stopping them. Soon, we were into our fourth week, Hutch's vine stack now two feet high by one hundred long, fifty wide. It and the stench it created reached into the eastern sky. On early-finishing or rainy days, I would hang around the village chatting with folks I hadn't seen since traipsing off to college. I had been away when the firemen dedicated the new fire hall with a polka dance last December. Today, I stopped by to check it out. Francis Moran was inside tinkering with a valve on the fire truck. He was assistant fire chief, Bud Allers chief, but Bud was off framing a new house.

"Hi, Francis. Got a new fire hall I see," I said, barging through the high double door.

Francis continued fiddling with a water valve on the fire engine before speaking. The affable, mild-mannered Francis finally looked up, "Hi, Jimmy. Good to see you home from college. Beverly will be glad to see you, too."

"Sorry I missed the dance last December. Kind of cold to have a dance in here wasn't it?" I said, inspecting the truck with Francis, but not knowing what he was inspecting.

"Weather was bad, but we had a nice gathering, real fun time with Art Fitch's Polka Dots playing for our dance."

"Well, I know the Polka Dots and their old-time music. I'm buying an alto sax this summer so I can audition for the college's jazz band next fall. I prefer modern, swing music to old time, but the Polka Dots are okay, for what they do."

"Don't go and get high and mighty on us now, Jimmy, just 'cause you're off to college. We like old-time music, swing too, but you just remember your roots. Don't go a-changing," Francis admonished, wiping his greasy hands on an equally greasy rag.

"You bet. I hear you, but I might start my own jazz band someday. I'd play mostly swing and jazz standards. Guess I could throw in a polka or schottische if the folks wanted it," I said, retreating a bit from my harsh polka comment as Francis began showing me the new fire hall.

"We got a two-staller here, Jim, big enough for two pump trucks and tank equipment. Sure is an improvement over our old station down the street. Too bad your dad isn't here to enjoy it."

"You got that right. I talked with him the other day, and . . . ," Francis suddenly stopped twisting a wrench on a water valve, dumbfounded by my statement. "You what? Talked with him?"

"Well, I was out to the cemetery 'talking' to him, actually just telling him about my car."

"I see. Well, as long as you're talking to him, tell him about our new fire hall."

"See you later, Francis. Nice fire hall," I said, heading to my car.

"So long, Jim. Thanks for stopping. Stop up to the house to see Bev."

I drove around the deserted block to visit with Sidney Berg, but when I stomped into his tiny clapboard shop, a strange, gaunt and sorrowful face greeted me from behind Sid's leather-strewn counter instead of Sidney's round, happy face. It wasn't Sid. "Hi, I was looking for Sid," I said to a lean man looking like the Wizard of Oz scarecrow working on *Sid's* boots.

"Hello, I'm Ed Hanson. I bought Sid out a couple of months ago. Sidney retired," he said, rising from his three-legged stool to extend long, bony fingers toward me in greeting. I was startled, confused. Sid had always been here, since 1941 when I first began visiting his cozy shop. How could a strange man be working on Sid's shoes? How could a newcomer take his place?

"I'm Jim Franklin. Wanted to talk with Sidney. We were friends, and well . . . ,"

"Sidney said you'd probably stop in this summer. Said he had adopted you, him not having children of his own and all. Here, he left a letter for you, said I should give it to you." Ed handed me the black-polish-stained letter as I sat on a hard-ass'd wooden chair in the corner. Written on the outside of the envelope was simply: "Chimmy." I read the stained letter . . .

Juss thought to right you cuss I jusst sold her the shop out to Mr Ed. Juss got tired of makin the souls fer so years to be many. Juss moved to old folks home to Feathrston and yuss would be liked to havin you commin' visit to me den. Yoos vass a good boy fer all dees yers. Juss hop yoo vass doing fined. Coment in den to see me.

You pal, Sidney.

Ed glanced at me from his cutting table as I folded the letter, carefully placing it in a pocket. Sidney's absence was making me glum. This was a change I hadn't anticipated. I knew *my* life was changing, but I hadn't thought others' were also. Sid had retired from re-treading shoes and was now living at the Old Folks Home. Certainly, I would visit him now that I had a car. I looked at Ed who was looking at me. "I know you liked Sidney a lot, and I'm not Sidney, but I'd sure appreciate it if you would stop in occasionally to talk with me," Ed said, his lanky, hinged legs cracking as he shuffled from behind the counter. "Don't know many folks in town yet."

"Well, Ed, I can do that. It's just that, well . . . Sidney . . . shoot! Things are changing in the village. What the heck is going to happen next? I leave for college, come home and things are different. I don't know if I like that. I'd like the village to stay the same," I said, getting up and trudging toward the catawampus door.

"Can't do that, Jim. Things will change, need to change. Folks get older, retire, die, move off to Cannon Falls or Red Wing, the Old Folks Home like Sidney. I only know what Sid told me about you and your changes—new stepfather, new college, living by yourself summers in the village. You're changing; we're all changing," Ed said, placing a bony, but caring hand on my shoulder. "You come by and chat with me like you did with Sid. I think we can be friends."

I wasn't sure I wanted change in the village. A village is a village. It doesn't change. That's what a village is—sameness. That's why folks live in them, so they can talk with everyone and about them. Shoot! Ole Haga told me last week he had sold out to a Mr Lura back in January, Ole no longer able to stuff the unbending corpses into caskets by himself, no longer able to lower folks on their last journey by himself. That undertaking had taken its toll on Ole. He told me he had grown weary, didn't want to put anybody down anymore. He recalled how hard it had been to put Dad down back in '51. But I didn't understand. Once an undertaker, always an undertaker. Once a cobbler, always a cobbler. Shoot! I was just beginning to be something, didn't know what yet, and these folks were ending being something. What on earth would be the next change?

I dashed for my car through a light rain, perplexed about this sudden change. I sat in the car facing Sid's, I mean Ed's Cobbler Shop for several minutes pondering this unanticipated change. Sidney retired? Ole retired? Numerous changes had occurred the past year, but I hadn't sensed *other* people changing. This was home, unchanging home, always-the-same home. This was the place I would return to in years to come, regardless of what career I chose, regardless of where I settled. This was roots, heritage, stability. Oh, the Lodermeier brothers had stormed into town on their orange Allis Chalmers tractors some years back—like the Jesse James Gang riding into Northfield. That was a big change, a big adjustment for the townsfolk, but the village finally accepted them. Arlene closed her Apparel Shop back in high school, but it didn't affect me personally, not buying women's apparel anyway. We had several doctors hang out shingles over the years, yet we only kept one. Frank O' Gorman retired from lawyering above the Marshall-Wells Hardware, the village never replacing him, but not needing a lawyer, anyway. Folks just worked things out between themselves without litigation. Marshall-Wells became Gerken Brothers Hardware, only a name change, the store staying in town. That didn't disturb the village. Naurice Husbyn had recently sold his Produce Company to Harold Lensch and Lyle "Noisy" Rusch, but that hadn't been a drastic change. Naurice stayed in town to open a new chick-hatching business while Harold and Lyle can-dled eggs in the old shop. Art Lohman had moved his Standard Oil Station across the street. I could still talk with Art and Vince O'Reilly at the tiny gas station. That move hadn't affected me. But Sid's retirement was affecting me as I drove through the drizzle to Lower Street. This change seemed bigger than others. But then, maybe I was the one changing. Maybe my year away had opened my eyes to people beyond the village. I was beginning to look at religious faiths differently, but not yet deterring to Lutheranism; I was looking at ethnic groups differently, but not yet ready to cast off my Irish-German-Austrian roots. I was aware of changing horizons. It was becoming apparent that "change" was a constant.

I was changing but I didn't want the village changing. I had a predicament.

Wednesday, end of the viner workday as Jack and I trudged to my car, Doug, Libby's pear-shaped field supervisor, lumbered toward us carrying his 280 pounds like heavyweight boxer Max Schmelling. As I fired up the Ford he hollered, his voice hard as leather, "Jim, can I talk with you a moment?"

"Sure, Doug, what can I do for you?" I said, shutting her down.

"Wonder if you'd like a different job with Libby's. I've had a fellow resign. You'd do field work with peas and corn. Florence at the Eat Shop suggested I speak with you," he said, leaning on my new car, his heft tilting it toward the viners. "Job is driving throughout Goodhue, Dodge and Olmsted Counties checking pea and cornfields for lice. We spray with airplanes if we find the lice excessive, sometimes even use tractor-sized tricycle sprayers. Good work, pays more. I think you'd like it. Florence said you might. She kind of likes you. She a relative?" Doug asked, finally removing his massive body from my fender, the Ford settling back to level.

"No, sir, just an admirable lady who takes care of me when my mom isn't around, which she is . . . isn't much. How much does the job pay . . . sounds interesting?" I said, as Jack grew impatient with our conversation.

"Dollar thirty-two, plus twelve cents overtime. If you're interested, think about it for a couple of days. I'll come back Friday or Saturday to get your decision. So long, Jim . . . Jack," Doug said, finally releasing my car from bondage and trudging off to find someone to smack.

"Let's get to town, Jim. I'm damnable hungry," Jack snarled, pulling his pea cap lower onto his head and slumping into my soft, cushioned seat, "You can think about the job while driving. Spin these damn wheels. Let's see you do a wheelie out of the lot for once."

A change in my job? Another change? Geez! I like working

with the guys at the viner, but maybe I would still see them, still with Libby's and all, I thought, crossing Highway 58 heading toward Swenson's. "You gonna take that job?" Jack asked as we plopped onto high stools near Heinie's greasy grill.

"Don't know. Too soon to tell, though I could use the extra money."

"Hell, take 'er, Jim. I got my own car. We'll see each other during the summer. It won't be that big a change," he said as we ordered burgers and malts from the reticent Heinie.

"Lots of changes coming fast, Jack. Don't know if I like them all. Town's changing. Job's changing. I'd like things to stay the same."

"Can't do it, Jimmy. Thing's always changin'. I know that, me too, at home, at college."

"You too, Jack? Things changing for you? I assumed . . . ,"

"'Course they are. We're growing up, buddy. Aren't the same kids we were in grade school and high school, at catechism, Sunday Mass, the proms. We're changing, that's for damnable sure."

"Shoot, Jack! I didn't realize you were aware of all that," I said, tossing the hamburger-stained menu back on the bar.

"That's 'cause I'm a year older than you. Smarter too. You'll change."

"Hi, Florence. My ear's ringing. You been talking about me?"

"Afternoon, Jimmy. Are your ears ringing? When did you return from college?" Florence asked, setting her *Better Homes and Gardens* magazine on the forever-long oak eating table, forks, knives and spoons exactly so, all ready for boarders.

"Oh, shoot! I've been back a month now, but working the viners all day, every day. I haven't been able to visit you. In fact, that's why I'm here. Doug said you thought I might be interested in a better paying job with Libbys."

"That's correct. Doug eats here whenever he's in town. The other day he was saying that he needed a replacement man. I thought of you immediately, you being such a good boy," she said, absent-mindedly pressing her apron with dainty hands as we sat on her window settee.

"Well, thanks for the compliment, but I'm not sure some other folks would agree with you. For sure, not Fr. Smith."

"The Reverend Father has left Holy Trinity and town. You just forget about him, Jimmy. He was simply an eccentric priest; that's all, but still a priest. Don't you forget that!" she said, reprimanding me slightly.

"Florence? Martin Luther had been an ordained priest, too. They called him Fr. Luther, if you can imagine that, and look what happened to him."

Florence wasn't interested in discussing Martin Luther. She changed the subject, "How are you getting along with the St. John's monks?"

"Real fine. I don't actually see monks much. They mostly pray all day in the monastery's inner sanctum reciting matins and lauds and vespers. My professors are mostly priests with some monks or brothers but brothers aren't priests necessarily because they're not ordained you see but monks could be priests if they chose to go to seminary school and . . . ,"

"Okay, okay. I understand, Jim. I don't need to know that much about priests and monks. I'm just hoping to get to heaven. I was only being polite asking you," Florence said, smiling and sipping tea.

"I like college a lot, although it's difficult. I've had to buckle down studying, but I'm getting there. I hope my second year will be easier," I said, reaching for the *St. Paul Pioneer Press* to check out the headlines.

"Care for lemonade or tea, Jimmy? I've some fresh-made with Heaney's best lemons."

"Sure would. Love your lemonade, Florence." She ambled to the rear kitchen while straightening her hair net as I gawked around her "Eating Place," what locals called it. The place was a throwback to earlier days in the village, not unlike boarding houses throughout the county. When Red Wing businessmen, latter-day railroad barons such as T. B. Sheldon decided to lay tracks from Red Wing through Goodhue Township, they subsequently erected a station just beyond Florence's forthcoming front door. The railroads undulating tracks ran through Hay Creek and Claybank to Goodhue Station—as the site was first called—then onto Zumbrota, Mantorville, Rochester before disappearing into Iowa. Before that first locomotive chugged onto the high prairie in 1889, adulterating the pristine air with coal black smoke, adulterating the fields of grass with shrill, piercing whistles, this dry, lonesome prairie site hadn't been much to talk about or see. Oh, there were a few homesteaders—John Mann, Frank Jergen, John Kelley, George Wilkinson, Jonathan Finney, Patrick Malloy, David Franklin—scratching out a hardscrabble living in Goodhue, Belvidere and Belle Creek Townships. But even before the Duluth, Red Wing & Southern chugged through here, Peter Easterly had tried to get a hotel going over east in Goodhue Centre, but his efforts were as heartless as other attempts in White Willow, Claybank, Ryan, Hader, Forest Mills, Belvidere Mills. When that first locomotive hissed to a stop, a boom town exploded. Well, not actually exploding, but the site did acquire thirty or forty settlers. Theo Sheldon erected a granary-elevator and station-depot near the tracks. Soon, farmers arrived with overflowing grain wagons. Goodhue Station needed a place to room and board them for a night or two before they attempted the long ride back to the hollows of Hay Creek and Belle Creek. And rail passengers needed a nightly respite when they de-trained. Lower Street soon sprouted Anderson's Hotel, Ahern's Hotel, the White House—Florence's father Tom Taylor's eating-boarding place—plus several saloons, although, as far as records indicate, the whistle-stop never became a Barbary Coast as in San Francisco.

Florence wasn't around those first days, but she appeared later serving her famous home-cooked meals to tall, stringy, gaunt *Grapes of Wrath*-type fellas who didn't have a real home, a real wife, a real cook. Yet, even in 1955, Florence still served meals to village bachelors and itinerant travelers like Doug, though no longer seating railroad passengers, the railroad having pulled up tracks and giving the village back to the prairie.

"Here's your lemonade, Jim. Doug was saying that he needed a new man to check his fields for lice," Florence said, rejoining me on the settee while straightening her apron, just so. "What do you think? You'd have more freedom, set your own hours, even have a car for work. You could eat breakfast and supper here. I would even offer you a special deal, you being such a good boy and all?"

"I appreciate you thinking about me, Florence. I just might do it. It'd give me more money for tuition, and I could eat at least supper with you. Doesn't sound like such a bad deal. Think I'll do it. Talk with you later, Florence, and . . . say a couple Hail Marys for me. I need 'em," I said, reaching the street where I stood for a few moments thinking about the job offer, thinking about Florence's concern for me. That was good, she being sort of a replacement *Goodhue* mother. But I was increasingly concerned about how long she could hold out at her Eat Shop. She only served five regular customers now: frail "Step-'n'-a-half" Eddie, tippler Erv, imbiber Red, plus periodic diners like Doug during summer months. Her business fell off drastically during the bitter, endless, agonizing winter. Lodermeier's Implement, next door, was crowding her, huge New Idea farm machinery with menacing wires and wheels, gnawing teeth and slapping belts encroaching her space; tractors with monster rubber wheels and thousand-horse engines looming next to her Eat Shop waiting to charge in and devour Florence's place like Patton's tanks at the Battle of the Bulge. And Florence wasn't a spring chicken anymore, either. I didn't know how old she was—always looked the same—but while I was experiencing change, she must be also, I was beginning to realize. Yet, the Lodermeiers were good fellows: Les, Eddie, Norb and Jerry tolerated my inane questions about machinery and pistons and transmissions when they first arrived from somewhere over in Wisconsin. After supper during the forties they had let me fetch baseballs out at the old diamond, even let me spit in their cracked, dry baseball gloves, massaging them to a softness like the gloves of Warren Spahn or Eddie Matthews or Mickey Mantle. Yes sir, the Lodermeier boys were all right. They would probably own the village one day, I thought, take over much of Lower Street, Florence's place, maybe even the railroad station, only after Florence had retired, that is.

"Here's what I want you to do, Jim?" Doug said as we tramped through a dew-laden pea field in Olmsted County, fresh pods crunching under his massive weight. "These damnable little green lice like to forage on the leaves, but they aren't a problem if they're not excessive. When they are they can destroy the plant, subsequently the peas. We determine spraying needs by randomly counting lice when walking the fields as we're doing today. Take a few leaves in your hand, count the lice on it, and when their numbers approach fifteen to twenty per leaf, call in the sprayers. Same thing for sweet corn, but corn can handle more lice per leaf, about eighteen to twenty-two, it being sturdier. Here's a plat map of all my pea and cornfields in the three-county area. You've got a company car now. We'll set up an air strip in the area, move it when we need to. I contracted an open cockpit biplane outfit from Iowa to spray when we call them. You'll be working with the airplane crew most often. Questions?" Doug asked as we stomped to the end of the field, he running interference for me like the Gopher's Leo Nomelini. Even though I hadn't started yet, just walking through the rolling fields felt good, the earth soft, the air as fresh as the ripening peas. Only the hushed, soothing sound of tumbling, maturing pregnant peas muffled the fields. The new job excited me.

"Sounds good, Doug. Think I'll like it. I'll work hard to do a good job for you and the peas," I said, reaching the barbed fence line.

"Oh, I know you will. Bookie said you were a good worker, and Florence said you were, too." He laid a hefty arm on my shoulder driving me into the soft earth, "We'll get along just fine. Head out tomorrow. So long."

That was it. I was still working for Libbys, but no longer pitching and boxing at Bookie's viner. Tomorrow I would begin driving Goodhue, Olmsted, Dodge Counties searching for lice. Doesn't sound exciting, but folks don't want lice in their pea and sweet corn cans. It was a pretty big deal for me. And it got me into the countryside, too, not just pitching peas all day, listening to

Max's haranguing. Yes, sir, Uncle Dave, I was moving up in the world, even if I didn't know what I was going to do up there. Jack was right. Things were a-changing.

"Hi, Cy. How's things going?"

"Jimmy! What the hell you doing here? Aren't you working the viners this summer?" he asked, his ever-present smile greeting me as he slowly raised his head above the workbench.

"Got promoted, Cy. Counting lice now. Still with Libbys, but not at the viners," I said, inspecting a three-toggle switch on his workbench at Mans & Benda.

"Doesn't sound like a promotion to me . . . counting lice? How do you do that? You got lice now, Jimmy?"

"Uh no, Cy, just on pea leaves and corn stalks. I drive around the county checking for lice infestations, those little bastards! If I find too many per leaf, I call in the lice bomber squadron to spray the little shits."

"Sounds good enough to me. Making more money too, I suppose?" he asked, finally surfacing from his dungeon, wire, conduit, electric outlet boxes hanging from him like the straw man in the *Wizard of Oz.*

"About ten cents an hour more, a bit more for overtime. Every bit helps. How's the electrical business?"

"Business is good. Fact is, I could've used your help this summer, but then Bookie needed you, too. More folks building homes. I'm still working alone, but sons Jim and Joe are growing up. They can start helping," Cy said, dumping an arm load of tubing onto his clean bench. "Did you have a good year at St. John's?"

"Good year, Cy. Learned a lot, mostly what I didn't know. Tussled with Fr. Baldy in Bonehead English about periods and commas. Shoot! We never use them in the village, but I'm making progress. Bill Ryan bought me a car last week to return to St. John's this fall. I told Dad about it the other day. He thought it was a nice car," I said, collecting fallen tubing for Cy.

"You talked with Tom? I think you're pulling my leg, Jim. He's been dead four or five years now."

"I know, but I still go out to the cemetery to talk with him. I figured he'd like to know about my car. I told him you and the other firemen still missed him and talked about him. He thought that was nice."

"You've got an imagination, Jim. Don't ever lose it. Got to go to Bellechester now, though. Wiring a new addition near St. Mary's church. Come back," Cy said, grabbing his toolbox, swinging ten pieces of ten-foot conduit into his long arms as those lanky legs propelled him like a stilt-man toward his pickup.

"Hey, Bill, how's things?"

"Good, Jimmy. How you doing?" Bill Mans said, his elongated face always amiable even when not smiling, a rarity for Bill. Why aren't you working the viners on a nice day like this?" he asked, adjusting a carburetor in bay number one.

"Got promoted to counting lice. Too windy today to spray them, so I got me some time off," I answered, peering under the hood with Bill. "What's wrong with her?"

"Floods all the time. Jim Ryan's car. Just needs some fine tuning. She'll be fine when I finish with her." His gnarly fingers fumbled with the small adjustment screws, "What's this about counting lice? Why would you want to do such a dumb thing?" Bill asked, adjusting the in- or out-flow with a long-handled screw driver.

"If too many lice get on pea and corn leaves, I call in the lice bomber squadron. Those little bastards will devour the entire leaf, corn stalks too. Need to count them, then spray. Good job, but too windy today."

"Jimmy! What the hell you doing? Why ain't you workin' the viners?" Luverne hollered from somewhere under a reluctant pickup in bay number two, his voice surprisingly similar to that rusted muffler.

"Hi, Vern. Too windy to spray. Got a little free time," I said, leaving Bill with his carburetor and moseying toward Vern's pickup, still not seeing him.

"Goddamn tailpipe don't want to come off. Sprayin'? What's

that got to do with pickin' peas? Shit! I'll blast this sonofabitchin' tailpipe with dynamite if she don't come soon," he shouted, only his craggy, steel-toed boots showing from under the pickup.

I kneeled on the greasy floor to make eye contact with Vern sprawled on his back on a steel-wheeled dolly, struggling with a rusted tailpipe. Vern had been mechanic number one for many years at Mans & Benda, keeping village cars and pickups in "fuckin' A-1 shape," as Luverne was fond of bragging. He often coerced vehicles back to working order in spite of themselves. Oh, Bill did good work on carburetors and admirably on grease jobs, but he let Luverne do the *real* mechanical work.

Vern finally freed the recalcitrant pipe, "What the fuck is this about spraying?"

"Got promoted, Vern. I'm counting lice now. I call the lice squadron when I find too many. Windy today, though, so got some free time."

Vern huffed and puffed until the bay walls bowed, finally releasing the rusted tailpipe and muffler. "That goddamned sono-fabitchin' pipe has met its match," he shouted, rolling from under the pickup. "Ain't met a muffler yet I can't tame." He stood up covered with rust, grease, pipe remnants dangling from greasy boots to greasy cap. "Good to see you, Jimmy, you little bastard. Have a good year at college?" he asked, dragging the muffler and pipe to the ten-gallon barrel in the alley.

"You bet. I'm straightening out those monks just like I did with Fr. Smith."

"You got that wrong, you little fart. Smitty did the straighten-ing on all us, but he's gone now. We got ourselves a reasonable priest now. Don't holler and berate us all the time 'bout incidental sinnin.' We're on cloud nine at Holy Trinity." Vern grabbed a stepladder to retrieve a new tail pipe and muffler. "What you gonna be when you get done at college?" he asked from the rafters while searching for the correct sized muffler. Vern was a brawny, amicable, matter-of-fact guy, a village original, a man I had chatted with throughout high school, he offering a ready ear to my troubles whether they be with my Ford, my girlfriends or college.

"Don't know yet, Vern. Tried Political Science, but that's not for me. Studied the world's religion, but I'm not going to be a priest, though it would make Mother happy. And I'm sure not going to become an English teacher. I've found that out. I still like my music, though, so I joined band. I'm thinking about becoming a music major. Buying an alto sax in a few weeks to learn jazz. Maybe music major, Vern," I said, steadying the swaying ladder as he rummaged for a tail pipe.

"Here, catch this goddamn box before I drop it," he said, descending the ladder. He quickly scooted back under the pickup. "Hand me that wrench; make yourself useful instead of picking your ass," he hollered while sliding farther under the transmission or differential, whatever. "Slide that pipe to me, Jimmy. I'm gonna teach this goddamn pickup a lesson or two. Ain't no rusted pipe gonna get the best of me."

I handed wrenches and cutters and wire straps and the new muffler to him, held the end of the tailpipe as he wrenched the other to the manifold or block or whatever mufflers are connected to, listened to him holler and swear while nudging the pipe and muffler until finally finishing. "There that'll hold the sonofabitch for another year. Goddamn knuckles are cut and bruised. Hell of a job, Jimmy. You're pretty good on that clarinet. Just don't become a mechanic like me. Make something of yourself, hear me?"

"I hear you, Vern. Thanks for the advice."

"Hell! I got lots of free advice . . . any time, Jimmy, any time."

Leaving Vern, Bill and Cy to their work, I noticed a strong westerly breeze still blowing from beyond water tank hill at about 25–30 miles an hour, much too high for spraying. Once the winds rose above 15 miles an hour we had to shut down the lice bombing squadron, otherwise winds would carry that spray to Wisconsin. The guys were pitching out at Bookie's, so a lazy afternoon in the village was a pretty good deal.

Bert Majerus bounced by the station, his pickup still listing toward the right front. Guess Bert hasn't had time to get that spring fixed, I thought, the pickup bed overflowing with sewer pipe, propane tanks, copper tubing, pipe compound and pipe wrenches of every size. Bert waved as he passed Heaney's on his way to some job or other. But he would soon be back to get something he had forgotten for the job. Always did.

I decided to put some miles on the Ford. I shifted, excruciatingly slow, Jack would have said, driving as unhurried as Art Haas Sunday afternoons until I passed Home Oil on the highway. I turned toward Red Wing on a breezy but pleasant day—sun shining, temperature reasonable. I flipped on the radio and tuned in WCCO where disk jockeys broadcast big band music for a change instead of pork bellie futures and June wheat, feeder pigs and choice steer markets. I liked big band music—my parent's music, my music. A clarinetist, maybe Benny Goodman or Artie Shaw, was swinging through a tune backed by rich, mellow saxes, biting trumpets and a driving jazz rhythm. Sister Rose was helping me buy an alto sax in a couple of weeks. I was eager to get it, because I needed to learn sax quickly to get into St. John's big band in the fall. I didn't think learning sax would be too difficult, though. If Noisy Rusch could learn it, I could learn it. I already played clarinet, a kissing cousin to the sax, so how hard could it be, anyway? Noisy just made it seem difficult, but that's because he chose to. He honked and barked and groaned in high school band, because he liked loud, raucous, "noisy" sounds. He was simply transferring his normal, reedy voice to the sax. Janie Yungers played tenor, too, softer, more mellow, but drowned out by Noisy. Jimmy Ryan played tenor for several years, hitting some high notes as well as low before traipsing off to St. Thomas where he never touched his sax again. I had been happy with my clarinet, but now that I was in college I wanted to expand my talents. Saxophones played mostly melody and harmony in jazz bands, clarinets used intermittently.

I drove forty-five mph through northern Goodhue Township passing farmers inspecting their neighbor's fields, and past the Claypits to Hay Creek. I began seriously considering music as a major, the fall term only two months away. Nothing else was looming on my horizon. Oh, I had always enjoyed electricity, switches and wiring. Clara Hennings knew that when I erected that lamplighters light post in front of the Franklin house; Cy Benda knew it because I often bugged him for discarded wire and switches. If St. John's hadn't accepted me I might have worked for Cy or entered Dunwoody Institute in Minneapolis to learn electronics. But St. John's short-circuited that idea when they, surprisingly, accepted me. It was a liberal, liberal arts college with little or no engineering curriculum.

As a tike I had listened to late-night radio broadcasts on clear, cold nights, clear channel 50,000 watts broadcast all the way to the village—crackling signals from Del Rio, Texas, Earl Hines from Chicago's Sherman House, black swing bands from Kansas City, rarely New York City. I loved big band music. Oh, I could play clarinet well enough for my proud relatives, village folks and outlying township folks, but I didn't know if I were good enough to be a professional musician. I might have practiced more in high school. But I was still young, had time to practice in college, to learn jazz, learn to improvise. Shoot! Benny Goodman rose from the Chicago slums to become a star. Goodhue was many things, but a slum it wasn't. If Benny could do it, maybe I could, I speculated, descending the long, winding grade into Hay Creek past rock-faced bluffs.

Artie Shaw's "Begin the Beguine" was playing through my radio as I pulled into the Hay Creek store lot. I sat in the car listening intently as Artie played the melody and arpeggiated phrases before the sax section took over. What a great sound, better than Whoopee John, for sure. I would like to be a band leader, I thought, bigger even than Whoopee, bigger than the Kufus Brothers, bigger than the Polka Dots, bigger than Jules Herman. I didn't know if I could become as big as Artie or Benny or Harry James, but I could at least put together a good territorial band playing Minnesota, Wisconsin, the Dakotas, Iowa. Mother liked my clarinet playing, although she never said so directly. Dad liked it, but then he went and died before I had learned more than three songs. Rose and I attempted piano-clarinet duets for the Goodhue County Artificial Breeder's Association Annual Banquet in the Goodhue Township Hall, and the Farmer's Union Spring Banquet in Bellechester where I murdered the "Clarinet Polka," *accompliced* by Rose. Brother Tom displayed indifference to my playing, as with

most of my other activities, me being the younger, tag-along
brother. Actually, he was more disparaging than indifferent. But
Tom didn't understand music, playing only bass drum mostly on
the weak instead of strong beats for Charles Wood's GHS band of
the fifties. But Erv Richter liked my playing, especially "Melancholy Baby," and Red Ryan said he liked it, although he never
stayed around long, usually meandering to the nearest bar on
Upper Street.

But most importantly, I pondered, while enjoying the warm
afternoon down in Hay Creek, I like it. Music makes me feel good.
I like the soft, mellow tone of my clarinet, the thick, earthy sound
of the saxophones. Think I'll give music a try this fall. What the
hell! Lawrence Welk made it big in these parts squeezing a silly
accordion playing saccharine polkas, and he wasn't even from the
county; rather, someplace up in the Dakotas, of all places. Vic and
Cis and most of Belle Creek still listened to Welk every Saturday
night on television. They might as well be listening to "Jimmy
Franklin and his Village Stompers."

Later that evening—after devouring Florence's huge, juicy pork
chops, applesauce, mashed potatoes with gravy, boiled peas and
canned fruit cocktail with reticent Eddie and other men—I walked
to Upper Street as dusk intruded upon the village. I sat on the curb
across from the Marshall-Wells Hardware, now Gerken's Hardware, but always the Dreamland Ballroom to me. The village
surely needed a hardware store, but I began daydreaming about it
being a ballroom again, its mirrored globe revolving over the
dance floor casting glittering light beams across dipping dancers.
Dancing had been a way of life for village revelers during the
twenties and thirties. Mom and Dad liked to dance, as did their
friends. The Dreamland had been a popular hall, though not the
only one, as many burgs had dance halls, even if only a barn dance.
Dreamland had turned off the globe before I was old enough to
enjoy dancing, but it could reopen, I speculated, sitting in front of
Eddie's Drugstore. I wondered where Erv Richter was tonight. I
hadn't seen him around this summer; in fact, I hadn't seen him

since graduation night an entire year ago. Was he at the Old Folks Home with Sid? I would like to play for Erv again. I would like to bring the Jim Franklin Village Stompers to reopen Dreamland. Even if Erv didn't want to dance, he could sit where I am tonight, sip his favorite spirits and enjoy my music. I would play special requests for Erv, for Red, for everybody. I would make folks proud of their Dreamland.

"What are you doing, Jimmy? Lonesome tonight?" Emma Kindseth, her village *de rigueur* permanent just right, said shuffling past.

"Gee! That would be a good song title—'Are You Lonesome Tonight?' Hi, Emma. No ma'am, just dreaming about Dreamland," I said, head on chin, feet in the gutter. "Wouldn't it be great if it was the Dreamland again instead of Marshall-Wells?"

"I would love that, Jimmy. Heavens! We used to do the Charleston, the Shimmy, the Cakewalk, even the Lindy-Hop at the Dreamland. I surely miss it, but you were too young to dance there, I believe," Emma said, standing, not taking a seat on the curb.

"That's true, Emma, but I'm thinking about putting a dance band, a jazz band together in college. I would like to return to the village someday, open the Dreamland again, play with my band, even bring other bands in. It'd be good for the village, good for me," I said, rising to be polite as Mother had admonished me so many times.

"Lordy! You sure are dreaming big about the Dreamland. Folks have changed considerably, though, Jimmy. Some even have television sets now, watch Milton Berle and Jack Benny. They have better cars to drive farther away for entertainment in Red Wing, Cannon Falls, even Rochester, don'tcha know. I don't know if you could make it profitable again," Emma said, straightening her hair net, although no one else was on the street to see a slight disarray.

"I don't know either, but wouldn't you and Mable Diercks and Evelyn Ebe and Emily Parker still like to dance a slow waltz, if you had dance partners, that is?"

"We're all getting older and stiffer with arthritis and rheumatism, you know, and the men folk, those who still have them, don't move so well anymore, kind of all worn out. But we would certainly listen to you and . . . what did you say the name of your band is?"

"I don't have a band yet, but I could call it the Village Stompers, you know . . . dancing, stomping?"

"Whatever you want, Jimmy. You just keep dreaming about bringing your band to the village. I'll get the girls and we'll come down to the Dreamland to try slow waltzing with you. You just keep coming back, Jimmy, just keep dreaming of your Dreamland."

Friday morning the school flag dangled limp on its contorted pole, a sure sign the Libby Air Force would fly today. I fired up my company car—undertaker blue four-door Plymouth—and slowly bounced out of town toward Zumbrota, the village dormant at five o'clock. Fred was probably already greasing and lubricating his yellow open-cockpit biplane. Doug had secured a picked-clean field between Zumbrota and Pine Island as a landing strip. From that field I would drive to outlying fields checking lice, then drive back to inform Fred where we would be spraying. I bounced into the field to see Fred hand-rotating the propeller, checking its lubrication and balance.

"Morning, Fred. How's your air force this morning?" I asked, joining him at the biplane cocked like a teeter-totter in the dew-laden field.

"Morning to you, Jim. Got a full day's flying for me today?" he inquired while greasing the prop and rotary motor.

"Sure thing, Fred. Wind's down, sun's coming up. I'll keep you guys busy all day, that's for sure. You'll earn your money flying with that thing you call an airplane."

"Watch it, Jim. This is my baby. Why, with this baby I can do just about anything in the air. Two wings give me considerable lift. I can drop down quickly beyond telephones lines and get up just as quickly. You ought to know that by now, after having worked with me a couple of weeks," Fred said, finishing greasing this side, moving to the other side. I ducked under the prop to follow him.

"Oh, I know, Fred, just giving you Iowans a hard time. You're in Gopher land now, you know, not Buckeye land."

"Hawkeye, Jim. Iowa is Hawkeye land. Buckeyes are Ohio."

"Whatever. You have this heap ready when the sun's up?"

"Yup. You just get your little ass back here soon and show me where to begin spraying."

"Check that, Red Baron. I'll reconnoiter in half 'n hour," I said, jumping back into the Plymouth, heading out to check my fields for lice. Actually, Fred didn't look anything like the legendary Red Baron. Fred was a tall, lanky redhead who walked with a slight limp, maybe from a hard landing. I never asked him. He sported a red beard, wore a close-fitting leather pilot's cap with ear laps, a cap somewhat like the village boys wore in sub-zero winters, a little like GHS' first football team helmets of 1947.

I drove a few miles from the air strip, checked several pea fields, marked them, then drove back to Fred. "All set, Captain, just follow me." And follow me he did. It was an odd experience being followed by an airplane, but that's how we operated that summer. I would speed down the county road as Fred took off in his yellow W.W.I vintage biplane. With considerable wing lift from double-stacked wings, a light fabric-covered fuselage, he could throttle that plane down to about seventy-five miles an hour. Like many barnstorming pilots, he was a daredevil who liked having fun in the free air. For Fred, that was his end-of-day treat.

Sometimes he would fly off my right fender, other times off my left about one hundred feet above the fields. Sometimes I would even see him in my rear view mirror, landing wheels almost touching the road. That would get me putting the pedal-to-the-metal, asking everything out of the listless Plymouth. On corners Fred would scoop up above me and do a cloverleaf flip into a right angle. Yes sir, Fred loved flying that contraption.

I slid to a dusty stop at my first field, jumped out with two red semaphore flags and ran to the left edge of the field as Fred swept to the far end. I readied my flags as he looped, getting ready for his first pass. He could see the fence line, so I measured off fifty feet where I then stood waving my flags like a sailor waving off an incoming, errant dive bomber. I marked the outside boundary of his first pass. That was our procedure. When spraying cornfields, I counted off twenty rows. By the time I had begun waving my flags, Fred would be nosing into the field, DDT or some killer spray spewing from beneath his bottom wing, the snarling biplane swooping directly toward me. On a level field I would see him continuously, but on a rolling field he would occasionally disappear from view only to suddenly reappear one hundred yards in front of me, wheels brushing the corn stalks. Reaching me at the end of the field, he would gun the motor, pull up into a severe climb as I ran to the next marking point. He would execute a flip above me, then bear down for the return run, zooming directly overhead, sometimes spraying me as well as the lice. Five, ten, fifteen passes and he had completed a field, as today. I semaphored my best Don Center Boy Scout Morse Code to Fred, indicating I was moving out to the next field while Fred dipped his wings in affirmation.

I slipped the Plymouth into gear, spun out faster than was my nature, and sped down the country road a mile to the next field, Fred right on my tail. Whenever he was low on gas or out of killer spray, he would buzz back to the air strip, fill up with the help of sidekick Sam, then return as I marked the next field. This day the wind remained calm all day, a good day for bombing those little green bastards from our peas and corn. By six o'clock we had sprayed ten fields for the Libby folks, a good day for Fred, a good day for me. When Fred had a good day he made considerable money, making him powerfully happy. When I signaled him that we had finished, he revved the biplane into a straight vertical climb several hundred feet above me. At the top he flopped the plane, twisted, sagged, dropped out of control into a somersault. Stunned, I wondered if he could pull out of it, but I should have known better. This was Fred the stunt pilot and sometime lice bomber. He picked up downward speed, heading directly toward me, coming so close I could see his menacing Nazi grin, eyes shrouded behind dark, red goggles, scarf flying over the fuselage. I ran for the Plymouth, seeking safety, just like those blots of England during Hitler's bombing raids over London. One hundred feet above me, he pulled back on the stick, zooming over me, pea vines suddenly fluttering from his open cockpit. Bombed!

"Hi, Archie. Why are you wearing that W.W.II helmet and olive-drab fatigues?" I asked Archie Bjorngaard who was marching into Campbell's Hardware after Fred flew back to Iowa for a few days.

"We're holding a Civil Defense Committee meeting tonight, so I'm wearing it for that," Archie said, shuffling into Jesse's for bolts or paint or lubricating oil.

"Civil Defense Committee? What do you defend?" I asked, curious about this, unknown to me, village organization.

"You know Norb Matthees? He's Minnesota Area Five Coordinator of CD. A group of local citizens formed a committee to study how best to handle disasters such as tornadoes and fires and hostile attacks," Archie said, he one of the few Norwegian Bjorngaards to settle in this part of Goodhue County rather than out west in Wanamingo or Holden Townships. But that, in itself, wasn't the most surprising thing. Archie, Norwegian and all, was no longer a Lutheran.

"The volunteer firemen take care of fires," I said, perplexed, "and I don't recall a tornado ever touching down around here. Just what type of hostile attacks are you preparing for?" I asked, my curiosity increasing.

"Well, Jimmy, you never know, you just never know. We've got to be prepared, though, so that's why we meet, maybe have a couple Grain Belts when we've finished," Archie said, attacking Jesse's tattered screen door, tugging on his web belt, anxious to escape my verbal barrage.

"How do you prepare for a hostile attack, were the village ever to have one, that is?"

"We plan and organize procedures such as storing potable water and canned foods enough for an extended siege of the community. We prepare first aid packages for wounds or worse. We store batteries for lights in case of an attack when the power is knocked out. We repair generators to replace downed electric power. We even collect books so folks would have something to occupy their time in the air raid shelters," Archie said, eager to get away from my incessant questions and tend to his immediate business.

"We have air raid shelters in the village, Archie?"

"Not under ground yet, but we're temporarily using the school basement. We're working on that. The Holm boys, Willard, Walter and Wilfred, said they'd volunteer their big cats to dig shelters, but we don't have the finances yet to construct concrete bunkers. That's gonna take some time yet," Archie answered, now halfway through Jesse's door.

"Just once more question, Archie, then I'll retreat."

"Shoot, Jimmy."

"Would non-Catholics, for instance Lutherans or Methodists or Congregationalists or Presbyterians, be considered hostile enemies in your Civil Defense Standard Operating Manual?"

"Oh, Jimmy, you're too much. Got to go now. See you," Archie said, finally escaping my rat-a-tat barrage, the CD logo reflecting from the back of his helmet.

Hostile attack? In the village? I pondered, continuing my sojourn past Streater's Lumber Yard. Why, the only attack I had known around here came from mosquitoes and sometimes Lutherans, less frequently from the Methodists. But we hadn't called out the militia for either the mosquitoes or Protestants. We hadn't donned helmets or stored water or Libby's peas or first aid kits. Nor had we built bomb shelters, although some townsfolk suggested it for especially horrendous mosquitoes attacks. The village's differing theologies and dogmas hadn't come to religious bunkers. We stopped at a few heated arguments, rarely that, in fact; most folks simply went their own way, said their private prayers in insulated, hushed clapboard churches dotting the village and surrounding townships. The faithful seldom talked about religion on the street. Oh, everyone talked *about* other faiths, when those folks weren't around, but it hadn't come to hostile attacks in line-to-line, battalion-to-battalion, army-to-army combat, for God's sake, anybody's God, for God's sake!

I had finished spraying cornfields with Fred earlier this tranquil day; the gang was still pitching peas, so I was on my own. The village was so quiet you could barely hear songbirds warbling, butterflies flapping iridescent wings, Ol' Buck's rhythmic panting. Archie had escaped. I had a copy of John Hersey's *Hiroshima* from St. John's, but hadn't found the time to read it. Tonight might be a good night. I ambled back to my room at Ole's place up in the old neighborhood.

Now, *Hiroshima* definitely had been a hostile attack. I had vaguely recalled the August 1945 day when they dropped the atom bomb from the Enola Gay B-29 bomber, but that had happened a long way from the village. It had been difficult for an eight-year-old to comprehend the bomb, even though Mother tried to explain it to me. But even then the village hadn't called out a Civil Defense team, although I heard later that some folks did march to water tank hill to search the western sky out beyond Finney's Woods for Japanese parachute bombs. But the only things they ever detected were used rubbers blowing in from Lover's Lane in Finney's. Fifty pages into *Hiroshima*, I dozed off. Soon, the book fell open on my chest, eyes closed, dreaming . . .

> "General Beauregard! We have got us a problem on the right flank at Devil's Den. The Lutherans are moving up fast, threatening to break through. What are your actions and orders, sir?"
>
> "I'm not a general, you imbecile. I'm a colonel and the name is Bjorngaard, not Beauregard . . . private! You got that? Bjorngaard! . . . Lutherans on the right flank, you say? Maneuver Squad A, that's as in Acolyte, private, down there fast. Get them into position to defend against a thrust into the Devil's Den defensive lines."
>
> "But, sir. I say . . . S I R! You are Lutheran, are you not? You must be, sir, with a name like Beauregard!"
>
> "I'm not telling you again, private. The name is Bjorngaard! I was formerly a Lutheran, but now an agnostic. Get a move on to Devil's Den, private," Archie commanded while straightening his uncertain helmet.
>
> "Did you say 'atheist,' sir?"

"'Agnostic!' you imbecile, not 'atheist.' I know
there is a god. I just don't know who he is yet. But I'm
in command here to defend the village against attack,
Lutherans or Methodists or Presbyterians be damned.
Get a move on, private, before I burn you at the stake."

"Yes, sir," the private said dodging and darting
toward the high school from downtown, the Lutheran's
penetrating lines located just beyond St. Peter's Lutheran on the edge of town. By the time he maneuvered
Acolyte Squad into place around the high school, he
saw a three-man enemy point patrol moving toward
him humming "A Mighty Fortress Is Our God," the
battle hymn of the Reformation. "Take cover behind
that rusted Chevy," he shouted to the measly Civil
Defense squad. "Don't let those Lutherans advance
one step closer."

"Colonel Blomquist! A Methodist contingent is
making a thrust, from their church into the middle of
our lines, trying to beak through our position."

"Damnation! Those Wesley Methodists always
did try to break away, just couldn't stay with the fold,
even when Luther broke away at Wittenberg. We got to
stop 'em. Can't let Methodists break through our Catholic Civil Defense (CCD) lines. Move B Squad, that's
for Beatitudes, corporal, to the alley behind the Corner
Bar. Cut 'em off," Bjorngaard shouted, talking rapidly,
slurping cold coffee and wondering where in hell his
reserves were. "Where are the Knights of Columbus
when you need 'em?" he shouted. "And where is my
Calvary?" His forces were low, Lutherans on the right
flank, Methodists penetrating the center. I suppose
those damn Presbyterians will show up next, he thought,
pacing the street in front of headquarters —Art's Bar.

"Captain Bjornssen! We just got a report that
Presbyterians and a smattering of Wisconsin Synod
Lutherans are moving in from east of the village,
reconnoitering at the grain elevator. You got any more

squads to plug that hole? We're under attack here, Bjornssen. You think maybe I should sneak through the lines to Holy Trinity to requisition some holy water? Think that'd do any good?"

Archie tugged at his baggy fatigues, snapped the web belt tighter, straightened his canteen and bellowed in a voice sounding like a 105 howitzer: "I'm a colonel, you idiot, not a captain, and the name's Bjorngaard, not Bjornssen. Get it right . . . sergeant! . . . And to answer your idiotic question . . . Hell no! You Catholics believe in the power of holy water, but I don't and I'm in command here. Hell! Lutherans don't even recognize five of the seven sacraments you mackerel snappers do. Lutherans recognize only Baptism and the Eucharist. But, I guess if you Lion-Hearted Crusaders would feel better gettin' drenched with holy water, you might sneak through the lines to get a gallon or so. On second thought, why don't you just do that then skirt the lines throwing some on the boys. But don't let them leave their positions. Maybe it'll stave off these non-Catholic penetrations."

The situation had completely caught Bjorngaard by surprise. He was normally a patient, predictable man who had just been working his regular job in the village, plus planning the Civil Defense Committee's actions against improbable hostile attack. Len Lodermeier and Norb Matthees were cohorts, but Archie never, even on a bad day, thought they would actually be called to action. The menacing tornadoes hadn't materialized; the Japanese, Koreans or Russians hadn't bombed the village. He and the defenders had grown complacent.

But then the St. Paul bishop had nailed that papal encyclical to Holy Trinity's doors last week. The pope exclaimed, under the protection of papal infallibility, that Catholicism was the only true faith, all others false. The encyclical went on for a thousand words saying only Catholics would find true, eternal salvation, would find peace and everlasting happiness in heaven. He didn't actually say Lutherans and Methodists and Presbyterians and Congregationalists and Southern Baptists were going to hell—everyone agreed non-Christians were—but he certainly implied it. And the Protestants were no dummies. They could read between the lines and they were damn mad. They weren't going to take that encyclical nailing sitting down. They were going to stuff it up the pope's nose, and they were starting the papal war right here in the village, soon to spread throughout the county, massacring Catholics with Luther's Bible translation till every known Catholic ran for his crucifix, holy water and rosary. This war would make the 1800's Sioux Indian War over in Mankato and New Ulm seem like a mere scuffle.

Bjorngaard was in a difficult position, but a command position, nevertheless. When Len Lodermeier had promoted Archie to Chief Observer of the CD's, Archie never figured he would be in a position of defending Catholics, even though he had taken the theological middle ground as an agnostic believing that . . . "Disputes and dissension are deeds of the flesh," Gal 5:20, Archie recalled from his early Luther League days.

And he now pondered Proverbs 17:14, "Stop the quarrel before it breaks out." But a commander has to command. He wasn't about to let any faith be run over. He didn't make policy, just carried it out.

From beyond the perimeter, he heard muted Aggressor conversations . . .

"Are the cities open or fortified? Numbers 13:19."

"Sir, 'The cities are fortified and very large.' Numbers 13:28."

"Well, sergeant, 'If a city will not make peace, besiege it.' Deuteronomy 20:12."

As Archie pondered an impending attack, a verbal, phrasal barrage began, aimed at the surrounded Catholics on Upper Street just to soften them up a bit . . .

"For in it (the gospel of Jesus) the righteousness of God is revealed through faith, for faith. He who through faith is righteous shall live. Romans 1:17."

Catholic Defenders scurried to placement positions as the attack continued . . .

"For by grace you have been saved through faith. This is not your own doing, but the gift of God, not because of works, lest anyone should boast. Ephe 2:8."

Protestants fired more phrasal darts from their strong positions . . .

"Down with priestly penance!"

"Burn indulgences!"

"Remember the injustice of the Crusades!"

"Inquisitions are a red mark on your Roman souls!"

From their creamery position came, "Attack the Philistines! Samuel 23:2."

They took umbrage, firing "Blessed Virgin Mary!" "celibacy!" "five too many sacraments!" and "let priests marry!"

"You will be besieged, Deuteronomy 28:52," sliced through the blistering afternoon air from just beyond the perimeter. Lutherans on the right flank were haranguing and harassing these Backward Christian Soldiers, themselves returning epithets . . .

"Pray the rosary!"

"Observe Lenten fasting!"

"Revere the relics!"

But the Lutherans weren't to be deterred by these barbs, returning fire . . .

"Wittenberg forever!"

"Down with indulgences!"

"Make love, not war!" from a born again beatnik hippie.

Archie rushed to the barricade to see Lutherans preparing their heavy artillery: a five-pound Martin Luther Gutenberg Bible translation, plus a mortar loaded with Luther's "Book of Concord," both to be launched over the barricade.

The Methodists were vexed with all encyclicals, and the pope's supposed infallibility. They shouted from the middle, "Be methodical in your fasting and prayers!" longer barrages slicing through the smothering humidity, landing ever closer to Bjorngaard's headquarters. He could hear them shouting on the fringes of his defensive deployment, ears blistering.

"There is no peace for the wicked, Isaiah 48:22," reached Archie's ears as he momentarily sipped on a 3.2 Grain Belt at headquarters, Art's Bar, while reviewing his battle plan. An off-tune rendition of "A Mighty Fortress Is Our God," penetrated his ears, the marching song of the Lutherans that even he had sung before his change of faith. And although he agreed with some of the barrages himself, it was his command responsibility to defend, to uphold the charter of the CD Committee: Defend the village against any outlandish act or sect or sex.

"They seek peace but there will be none, Ezekial 7:25," bounced off the Goodhue State Bank as its clock struck three o'clock.

The Presbyterians pressed into the village's center from the grain elevator, they themselves not having a church in the village, but supporting the Protestant attack, nonetheless. They began firing insult after insult, holding New Testament Bibles high above their heads, reciting anti-Catholic passages . . .

"Guilty enough for the hell of fire, Matthew 5:22," sliced through the boys on the front line.

"How will you escape being sentenced to hell? Matthew 23:33," slithered through the brown afternoon dust.

C Squad, the Crusaders defending against these accusations, was pinned down, stinging assaults attacking their ears, their beliefs their dogmas . . .

"God forgives sins, not priests!"

C Squad began retreating toward Swenson's Cafe chanting Deus vult! *(God wishes it!), unable to ward off the stinging barbs. Soon, their vacated left defensive line had collapsed past Swenson's to the Hatchery, the tightening circle flaming just like Joan at the stake. As they retreated they shouted over their shoulders, "The shield of faith can extinguish flaming darts, Ephesians 6:16."*

Through his cloudy field glasses, Bjorngaard caught his troops retreating. He lifted his considerable mass from the bar stool, shouting . . . "Get back to your lines, you mealy mouthed mackerel snappers. Defend your faith! Don't shrink in the line of fire. 'Sticks and stones may . . .'" He rushed to the penetrated line, kicked wimpy, even a couple of fallen-away Catholic privates in the ass as they reluctantly returned to face the advancing Presbyterians.

Finally, one Crusader found the faith, born again faith, a renewed belief. "You Evangelical deserters!" he shouted, standing at his unprotected position in front of Joe's Place. "Get back in the fold where you belong. We know what's good for you. We know where your salvation lies. Come back to the church, the one and only true church!"

But his missile was quickly answered, "You will be defeated before your enemies, Leviticus 26:17."

He stood straight up on the front line like Pope Urban leading the eleventh century First Crusade. Presbyterians began retreating, taking cover behind the corn silos.

The defense line held; Bjorngaard was relieved to have defended this thrust, but Protestants were still probing long into the evening, all over town. The

Catholics were surrounded. It wasn't all quiet on this western front. The Lutherans would always press faith over works, never give up, he knew. The Methodists would always press the methodical observance of fasting and prayer, never give up, he understood. The Presbyterians would continually press governance by elders, never give up, he pondered. And he knew his exhausted Catholic defenders would fight for the right and only way to salvation. Bjorngaard had helped them temporally beat back a hostile attack this day, but there would be others. It would never end.

Five o'clock. I realized, picking the sleep from my eyes, that I had dozed off reading *Hiroshima*, something about a hostile attack. Thank God, I reflected, slipping on my boots, we'll never have a hostile attack in the village.

The lice-killing summer was keeping me busy. I rarely worked Goodhue County, so I saw little of the viner crew. But they undoubtedly were getting along fine without me. I flagged pea and corn fields for "Red Baron" Fred, enjoying the summer with his barnstorming flight crew. Late summer, after Fred had barn-stormed back to the Hawkeye State, Doug assigned me to a high-wheeled tricycle machine to spray those little green bastards from the ground rather than the air. I liked the diversion, in a sense, returning to my father's agrarian heritage out in section eighteen. I even drove a corn picker during late August, aiming a two-row International Harvester through the crackling, golden cornfields trying to maintain the middle of the row despite being bombarded by hordes of Dakota grasshoppers attacking me like locust plagues of earlier days. Why, I could hardly breathe for sucking in grasshoppers.

But I was making money off those little green sonofabitches. I had bought an alto sax and had begun learning how to play the confounded thing. Ole's daughter had played piano in the forties, so he and Agnes were used to music in the house, although, I'm not

sure they appreciated my first attempts on the alto sax anymore that
Charles Wood had with my first clarinet attempts. Sax fingerings
were easier than clarinet, but developing a descent tone became an
effort. My first tones sounded more like Bill Henning's vibrato-
less lawnmower than an alto sax. I was a long way from being a
Paul Desmond, but I tried to emulate his light arid tone. I was
learning alto to become a Desmond, a Woody Herman—Benny
didn't play alto—and I wanted to play more progressive music
than Wayne King with his sweet, syrupy vibrato. I knew little then
about Bud Shank's alto on the West Coast. Noisy Rusch played
hard-ass'd tenor like Coleman Hawkins and the Texas tenors,
while Janie Yungers had played smooth tenor more like Stan Getz
and Lester Young. Richard Reese had developed a singing alto sax
tone during my high school years. Ben Gorman had played alto sax
years ago at the Dreamland, but he was long gone. The Frank
O'Gormans and Frieda Vieths and Ole Haga had played various
contorted saxophones in the thirties, but I was on my own learning
fingerings and tone production and reeds and technique and scales
and arpeggios, practicing nights up in the old neighborhood. Yet,
I made progress. With summer speeding toward fall, I had to be
ready for an audition into St. John's jazz band. I had to get into the
Moonmisters.

Friday afternoon, thirteen minutes past two, second week of
August, summer of 1955, Fred and I finished spraying near
Oronoco. He was eager to fly back to Iowa to grab his big titted-
girlfriend, as he so often bragged, tits so big he'd gladly die and go
to hell just for the joy of holding them. They were so round and
pearly-shaped he'd lose it, he said, taunting me daily about Blaze's
huge rose-colored, pointed tits. I had wet dreams about Blaze, her
tits haunting me nights back in the village. Fred asked me if my
girlfriend's tits were as nice and big. I said, "Hell yes! They're
mighty fine. Big as Blaze's." What the blaze am I saying, I thought.
I had only felt them, never seen them in daylight, but I was hoping.

Fred's taunting made me eager to visit Sharon, an infrequent
summer's occurrence, yet she had definitely been . . . *always on my
mind.* I had been speculating, while driving county roads, whether
when naked she looked anything like *Playboy* women. We had

only been together a couple of times during the summer, sipping root beers at the A & W Drive-in downtown Red Wing. We had sauntered hand-in-hand along the levee at dusk watching tow boats navigate the narrow channel, tossing bread crumbs to darting, dipping ducks, necking along the levee, but little else. I hadn't made the progress on diminishing my shyness I had hoped for. I called her from an Oronoco Texaco station.

"Hi, Sharon, Jim here. We wound up early this afternoon. Thought I'd clean up and drive to Red Wing to see you. You free tonight?" I asked, that old trepidation quickly attacking my stomach. What if she said, "I'm busy." What if she said, "Get lost, you jerk!" What if she said, "I've got a different boyfriend now, somebody who can see me once in a while." What if she just said, "I don't like you anymore." Those half- or three-quarter seconds before she answered seemed like an eternity.

"Hi, Jimmy. Good to hear your voice. Sure, I would love to see you. Haven't been around much with all your work," she said, that creamy, milkshake voice speeding over the wires all the way to Oronoco. I was relieved again. She hadn't turned me down. She hadn't told me to get lost. She hadn't called me a jerk. Jesus, Mary and Joseph, my prayers have been answered.

"Great! I'll head up to Goodhue, clean up, then buzz into Red Wing. Should be at your place, oh, 'bout quarter past five," I said, searching for more change in my tattered pockets, the three-minute lady bugging me for more coins.

"Marvelous! See you then. Bye-bye, honey," she whimpered as the three-minute lady intoned, "Please deposit an additional twenty-five cents," but I was already jumping into my blue Plymouth, pedal-to-the-metal, zipping to the village and feeling on top of the world. "Honey?"

I bounded into the village past the Elevator's Butler grain storage bins, waved to Ray Banidt leaning on the corner of Burnette's Garage, dodged potholes near the Corner Grocery, hit spring-bottom at Lensch & Rusch, waved to Jules Lohman near the post office and raced to my second-floor room up at Ole's.

"You're done early today," Ole said from his living room stuffed chair as I darted past him, taking the stairs in pairs.

"Finished early today, Ole," I hollered from the top of the stairs. "Heading to Red Wing to see my girlfriend. I haven't seen her much this summer, and in about three weeks, I return to St. John's," I shouted as I slid out of my boots and jeans. Ole was reading the *Daily Republican Eagle,* having a difficult time filling his days since he had retired. He spent much of his day cleaning and polishing his always-new Chevrolet. And he was meticulous about his lawn. He still had a woodworking shop out back in his barn-garage that helped occupy some time, but he was verging on boredom. I would have to sit and chat with him soon, but . . . well, Sharon was waiting and I was getting curiouser and curiouser.

"Hi, Sharon. Wow! Do you smell good!" I exclaimed, meeting her at the front door and throwing both eager arms around her slim waist. Her delicate, lilac-scented aroma quickly enveloped me. After manhandling stringy pea vines, getting leaf cuts from rough-edged corn stalks, being attacked by voracious grasshoppers, Sharon's countenance overwhelmed me. I wasn't prepared for her warm, inviting embrace, her pliant, welcoming body, her honeyed aroma, her enticing femininity. We held that pose forever, kissing, embracing in the doorway.

"Marvelous!" she said, taking my hand and drawing me into the house.

"You can say that again," I mumbled.

"That was marvelous, fabulous," she said softly a second time.

"Let's head down to the A & W for burgers and root beers," I said, reeling from this huge dose of femininity, "then we can walk along the levee. I like looking at the river. We can drive to Colvill Park to throw bread to the ducks and geese, maybe drive up to Memorial Park later to look over Red Wing at night. What do you think?" I asked, coming in closer for another hug.

"Marvelous! Let me fetch a sweater; might need it tonight," she whispered, breaking my hug, skipping upstairs to retrieve a cardigan.

We hopped into the Ford, ambled down College Avenue to the

A & W. Zumbrota's Wagon Wheel and Red Wing's A & W were two of Goodhue County's first drive-in eateries. We pulled into one of three lines in the small lot as a saddle-shoed car-hop quickly arrived, taking our order of burgers, fries and root beers in tall, frosty mugs. Sharon slipped over closer after we had ordered.

"I've missed you, Jim. I know you've been working long hours, but I've been lonely," she said, kissing me on the cheek, her short, sassy haircut brushing my stalk-roughened face. I liked hearing that. I nuzzled her on the ear, again being swept away by her yielding presence.

"Me too, Sharon, but those darn lice have been heavy this summer, keeping me hopping like a grasshopper all hours of the day. And I need the money for St. John's, and . . . ,"

"You needn't apologize. I understand. I was only saying I wish we might have seen more of each other. I'm not complaining. I'm returning to college in a few weeks. This summer's going so fast. Iowa City is a long way from St. John's, but maybe we can see each other at Thanksgiving and Christmas again." Most of the other heaps and jalopies in the lot also contained twosomes, some foursomes. We inched closer as those at the front of our line finished eating until we were third in the middle line. The car-hop sidled to my car, hung the tray on the driver's side as I paid her $3.50. We slurped root beer, chomped burgers and fries getting mustard and catsup on our faces while sneaking in periodic mustard-laced kisses. I dialed the radio, but could only pull in old-time polkas from Faribault. I quickly turned it off.

"What are you going to major in this fall?" she asked, leaning back in the seat, her green eyes sparkling like Betty Grable's.

"Been thinking about music. Guess I'll try it when I register. Don't see anything else I'm interested in right now. I've bought an alto sax and have been practicing to get into the Moonmisters this fall. I'll be in Concert Band again, plus Marching Band. If music doesn't work out, I can always try something else," I said, devouring my burger. "How about you down at Iowa?"

"Journalism, I believe, but I'm uncertain, like you. I took mostly requireds last year, but I'm searching," she said as we finished our burgers and fries, then drove toward the levee where towboats were pushing long, heavy-laden grain barges through the narrows. We parked near the railroad depot, then sauntered through the park holding hands, watching tows churn upriver, their rippling wake washing against the shore. We watched pleasure boaters bobbing in the tow's wake, watched cars passing over the high bridge to Wisconsin. I had been coming to Red Wing all my life, mostly visiting Mother's Haustein kinfolk, but this was different. Mother now resided with Bill on the outskirts in Burnside, but I was more interested in Sharon than visiting relatives. Things were a-changing. We shuffled along the levee holding hands and other parts, squeezing periodically like two kids in love. Maybe we were. I didn't know what love was, what it all entailed. I guess I had never been in love, infatuated, you betcha, but honest to goodness love?

"Have you ever been in love?" I blurted as we reached the towering flour elevators near the high bridge, surprising myself as soon as I said it.

"I don't know, Jim. I dated through high school, and I've dated at Iowa, but I'm not sure what love is," she said, her green eyes sparkling like diamonds in the twilight. "How about you?"

"I don't know, either. I was sweet on classmates in grade school. And I liked one girl a lot in high school, but I didn't date much. I've been dating at college, but that's mostly it. What do you think love is?" I asked as we sat on the levee, legs dangling over the rippling river, watching fishermen trolling for walleyes, leisure boaters lounging on lazy pontoon boats.

"I guess love entails being physically attracted to each other, as I certainly am to you. It's being on the same wave length, intellectually, finding each other fascinating, interesting, enjoying music, walking like we do, and someone fun to be with. But it's more than that. It has to be. It's getting to know someone so deeply that you would do anything, give anything for them. Of course, love is sex also. That's certainly part of it, but not all of it," she said, dangling her delicate ankles and bare feet over the levee, swinging them easily, sensuously in the encroaching darkness. "Now, your turn."

"Boy, I don't know Sharon. It's hard to put into words. Maybe

I shouldn't even try. Maybe a guy doesn't know what love is until he's in it. Maybe you have to be there to know it, but you can't know it if you aren't or have never been there. Does that make sense? It's sort of like monks and priests up at St. John's. They can be a priest and a monk and they can be a monk without being a priest and . . . ,"

"Okay, I get it , Jim. I've heard that lingo before. I'm more interested in love than monks and priests. Let's go up to Memorial Park to neck."

"Doesn't sound half bad," I answered as we ran back across the park through scattered, crackling autumn leaves, pigeons fluttering out of our hasty way.

Memorial Park, on a river bluff four hundred feet above Red Wing, had been a popular lovers' lane site throughout high school, a place to escape prying parental eyes, a place to walk along the high bluff precipices while gazing down on the city, a place to be with someone special while exploring the sand caves, exploring the meaning of love. I tried the radio again, this time pulling in music from Minneapolis. Frank Sinatra was singing with the Nelson Riddle Orchestra . . .

> *When somebody loves you,*
> *It's no good unless she loves you,*
> *All the way . . .*

All the way? I thought, as we snuggled in the front seat gazing down on the twinkling lights, lights making Red Wing appear more exciting that it actually was. High school bullies had often boasted and taunted us younger fellows about . . . going all the way: "Hey, Jimmy! You ever gone all the way?" Burt or Hal or Dale would ask, taunting me in the locker room after football practice.

"Hell yes," I would answer, playing along with their taunts. Of course, I had meant 'going all the way to the Twin Cities or Rochester,' but I didn't let them know that.

"Shit, you little squirt. You ain't even gone half way!" they would shout and laugh and snap their towels on white, tender asses while parading around the locker room like stallions on the prowl.

They would preen like male peacocks, grunt like bulls out on the farm, showing off, taunting younger guys like Jack and Fred and Tom and me.

Happy to be near you,
When you need someone to cheer you,
All the way . . .

Sharon and I listened to Sinatra, snuggling even closer, if that were possible. The music floated through the Ford, Sharon in my clutch, arms and hands roaming, exploring hidden treasures, searching semi-familiar territory. We tussled, groped and kissed in a Swiss manner, moving ever closer to a French manner, soon finding ourselves prone on the seat breathing heavily, exploring, connecting, finding love . . .

"Is this what love is, Sharon?"

"Shut up, you jerk! This isn't the time for analyzing," she admonished, pulling me forcibly to her, planting her lips heavily on mine. I caught her drift, immediately resolving to keep my trap shut when so engaged. Some things just can't be analyzed, I realized. Some things just can't be explained. I would save the analyzing and verbalizing for fall classes. Sinatra's lyrics were taunting me, nevertheless.

Taller than the tallest tree is,
That's how it's got to feel,
Deeper than the deepest sea is,
That's how deep it goes,
If it's real.

It seemed as if Frank was in the car, singing directly into our ears . . .

All the way,

The high school bullies were taunting me. "You ever gone all the way, Jimmy?" I heard them say . . .

All the way,

This loving thing had been a long journey from those first games of Spin the Bottle in grade school . . .

All the way,

And high school necking at Finney's Woods . . .

All the way,

And college explorations . . .

All the way,

Until this night . . .

Stop, Frank! Stop taunting me, I thought, but then realized it was Sharon speaking.

"Stop, Jim! Not all the way, tonight."

Chapter 4

Catching Johnnie wry

GHS first football team, 1947

T HE SUMMER OF '55 HAD BEEN EXTRAORDINARY after spending an academic year away, something I didn't think I would ever do. I had enjoyed spraying those pestilent green lice, seeing the viner gang early nights to roller skate, loving Sharon a little bit at a time, yet I happily anticipated my return to campus. I would certainly increase my sophomore-year efforts and next and next to graduate in the spring of 1958; thereby, able to return to the village with my head held high.

A couple of weeks into the summer my grades had finally arrived from Red Wing by Pony Express—first making watering stops in Hay Creek and Claybank—postmaster Otto Drenckhahn retrieving the ominous envelope from his "Special Delivery" cardboard box. It was addressed to "James L. Franklin, Goodhue, Minnesota," no further address necessary, the town being so small that . . . well, you know how small we were. I began ripping open the yellow Western Union-styled envelope while sauntering past Eddie's Drugstore, Eddie at the counter wrapping his ever-present packages in heavy, brown, secretive paper. My hands shook, my mind raced as to what I would do if the Black Robes had thrown me out with the used holy water. I slumped on the stoop in front of Majerus Gas & Appliance to read my grades, face suddenly flushed, hands trembling. I needed to take a piss when Bert appeared at the door.

"You all right, Jimmy. Hands shaking pretty fast there?"

"I don't know, Bert. Just got my grades from last semester. They may not want me back," I said, looking up at a kind and accepting face.

"Hell, they'll want you, Jimmy. Here, let me see those damn grades. If they kick you out, you can always work for me," he snarled, ripping the grade sheet from the envelope, squinting at it in the clouded sun. What did it say? I wondered. Why isn't Bert speaking?

"Hell, Jim! You ain't no Einstein, but you needn't worry. You don't have to be a plumber with me, after all."

They weren't great grades, sort of what I had expected, had not wanted, what I had deserved. Yet, I hadn't flunked out, either. The Black Robes said I could return for another year. I jumped with joy from Bert's stoop, skipped across the street through Mans & Benda's gas pumps, past Lodermeier's tractors and combines toward Taylor's Eat Shop. I could face Dennis, the gang at Heaney & Gorman, and Florence, after all. I hadn't let them down. I hadn't let myself down. Oh, it had been a great summer in the village.

E arly September was a glorious season in north-central
Minnesota, the encircling pine forest ever-green, maples
and hard oaks decorating the campus, turning golden
yellows, deep rusts, ochre. This second fall certainly was different
from last year when I first arrived on campus, the sun then hiding
behind the monastery for weeks on end. I had been filled with
trepidation simply leaving the village and coming to the campus,
but that ensuing incessant gray, monastic weather dampened my
spirits some. The clouds finally lifted, though, along with my
spirits, both vaulting me into a successful first year on this lovely
campus.

Before Sandbox Bob jogged my head about going to college,
I hadn't even considered entering college or picking a major, much
less selecting a campus for its scenic beauty. I guess it was
serendipity that I had chosen one where some evergreens stood as
tall as the church towers, where hooded monks melded into the
woods when walking in the surrounding forest, where Lakes
Sagatagan and Watab protected the enclave like Middle Age
moats, where the brick-faced quadrangle merged into the setting
like a Frank Lloyd Wright prairie home. The sequestered, bucolic
setting enhanced both our academic and spiritual lives.

Even the harsh winters seemed more palatable, they too
enhancing our academic pursuits. Below zero temperatures aren't
conducive to frolicking through the woods, aren't supportive of
many outside activities. Fifteen foot snows and bitter cold temperatures were an incentive to academic excellence. What else was
there to do? I wondered, years later, whether the founding monks
had thought all of that through when selecting this site in the mid
nineteenth century. Maybe they did, but maybe they just got lucky.

Chuck G. and I strolled the long, crooked monastic road on
lazy Saturday and Sunday afternoons, roommates now after having lost Bill to a North or South Dakota roommate more of his
liking. We had moved across campus into newer, less monkish
dorm digs in St. Mary's Hall, having escaped antique ivy-laden St.
Ben's Hall, abandoning it to greener-than-Libby-pea-faced fresh-

men plebes. Yuk! What a difference a year makes. Our second fall was devoid of that first-year trepidation when everything and everyone was new, scary. Although we had three more years of academic struggling, graduation didn't seem as remote, more plausible, if you will. (I was learning college words now such as "plausible.") I had settled into a new life away from the village, away from my remaining family, away from those I had grown up with. But there would be many summer returns. I wasn't done with the village yet, not by a long shot.

I had followed my summer inclinations, returning to the medieval-styled campus to register as a music major. Oh, I hadn't received the acclaim, excitement and encouragement from Fr. James, Music Dept. Head, I had anticipated. When I announced at registration that I intended to become a music major, I had expected shouts of joy, the organ blasting a Bach chorale, the heaven's opening, but he only said, "Okay, try it. If you don't like it, you can always change," and signed my registration form. "Next!" That was it. He didn't clap and shout, whistle and stomp his feet as the folks had at the Goodhue County Artificial Breeder's Association Annual Banquet in the Goodhue Township Hall, even though I had massacred the "Clarinet Polka." But those folks loved any type of polka. They were forgiving. Fr. James wasn't ecstatic like the Belle Creek gang had been when I played "Believe Me With all Those Endearing Young Charms" in sixth grade, me standing in front of the band coughing, choking and farting while the band attempted to accompany my irregular rhythms. James hadn't shouted my accolades to the heavens just because I said I intended on becoming a music major. I had anticipated being accepted into the music fold like the Prodigal Son. It didn't happen. Just, "Okay." Yet, I was in, now studying music as a career, on my way to becoming another Benny Goodman, Artie Shaw or Johnny Hodges.

I played clarinet in the Marching Band, struggled as a high first tenor in Men's Chorus and successfully auditioned for the Moonmisters, a forties-styled big band, this after having practiced alto sax long into the evening in the old neighborhood. I was ecstatic about the Moonmisters, but those music courses turned out to be more difficult than I had anticipated. Music wasn't to be the breeze I had thought just because I liked it, but that's where my heart was. I would stick with it. Things would be fine, what with memories of Marldine Richter and Charles Wood and Ben Gorman paving my musical paths in the village, plus the prodding of Dennis, Uncle Dave, George and Dodie and the rest of the potbellied stove folks. And Mother's incessant novenas certainly helped, too.

St. Mary's Hall, second floor, became my new dorm with forty or fifty other Johnnies, the Blessed Virgin's statue looming larger than life in the entry way. Additional sophomores hung from the third floor rafters, seniors and juniors gaining digs on first floor. Although a four-year liberal arts college, "college" life was more like a prep school with daily life revolving around fellow comrades, priests, monks, professors, abbots, deans, and Brother Leo who incessantly shuffled across campus in his own heavenly world. The head priests relaxed the Benedictine Rule for sophomores, junior and seniors, but according to us upperclassmen, The Rule still needed reformation, similar to the Church's sixteenth century Council of Trent Counter-Reformation. We could now study to one o'clock or more, the power no longer failing at ten o'clock, thereby casting us into forever darkness like heathen Lutherans. However, we still needed to sign in and sign out when leaving campus, this for some unknown biblical reason. We sort of followed The Rule.

I had returned to campus in my gray, monastic Ford, though officially prohibited from parking it on campus, cars being neither encouraged nor permitted according to Benedictine Rule No. 5: Though Shalt Not Have Graven Images (or vehicles), In Thy Midst. But as with all rules, religious or secular, there were exceptions; besides, Matthew, Mark, Luke, John, or Fr. Coleman never mentioned cars. Some Johnnies considered Rule No. 5 only Church Rule rather than a theological rule; therefore, subject to interpretation, a concept never permitted to village Catholic parishioners, for God's sake!

Theological interpretation had been out of the question with Fr. Smith and his boss, the archbishop of St. Paul. Children of the faith were to recite the answers from the *Baltimore Catechism,* by rote, perfect, no interpretation or divergence allowed . . .

"Robert Roger O'Reilly! Who made you?" Fr. Smitty barked during a high school Friday afternoon catechism session in the cold, hard pews of Holy Trinity.

"The *Lord* created me," Bob recited, standing tall and ramrod straight in the pew like a seasoned Pfc, his collared shirt impeccably pressed, his trousers hemmed and starched, the veritable image of a fine and holy Catholic boy.

"That's incorrect, Mr O'Reilly. The correct response is, '*God* made me,'" Smitty said, shaking his long, articulated finger at Bob like a Master Sergeant. "And he didn't *create* you; he *made* you."

"However, Father. Aren't the 'Lord' and 'God' one and the same?" Bob had the courage to ask. I was dumbfounded. No one had ever said something like that to Fr. Smith, but Bob wasn't anybody's fool. He thought for himself. He was smart as a tack, as folks liked to say. I had seen Fr. Smith turn red when he berated me for reciting *Dona nobis pacem* (Give us peace) instead of *Pox vobiscum* (Peace be with you), but nothing compared to what I saw that day. Red streaks erupted in his bulging size 19 neck, spreading to his triple chin, to his jumbo cheeks, bloated eyes, whiskey-splashed ears. Redness rose faster than the Goodhue State Bank's thermometer on a blistering July day. And even though Smitty was already a large man, it seemed as if he were expanding like a helium-filled balloon, ready to rise above Bob and the forlorn church. I glanced at Bob, but he was calm. Bob was nobody's fool, whether in his sandbox, in Miss Cree's English class, or in Smitty's catechism class.

Fr. Smith couldn't speak after Bob's irreverent response, one of the few times I had ever seen Smitty speechless. He was choking, unable to catch his breath. I was getting sacred scared, not knowing what to do, feeling an altar boy responsibility to improve his condition, as when pouring a tad more wine from the cruets when he nodded during mass. Did he need water? Maybe holy water would help. I started to leave the pew, tripping over Bob, heading toward the sacristy to get a jug of holy water when Smith suddenly regained his composure, barking at me.

"Sit down you impertinent child. Where do you think you're going?" he questioned while wiping a heavy brow with a huge white handkerchief.

"I was getting you some holy water, Father. You looked . . . well, like you needed water," I said, tripping over Bob back into the pew.

"I don't need holy water, you imbecile! What were you going to do, anoint me like Jesus?"

"I thought maybe you'd like a drink, Father," I said, slinking into the pew after his harsh admonition.

"We don't *drink* holy water, child. We bless ourselves with it. We sprinkle it on our brows. We sprinkle it in our homes. We cross ourselves with it upon entering God's House. We throw it on farmsteads and cows and chickens to bless and ward off Protestant attacks. Holy Water isn't for drinking, you little . . . now sit down and say a penance.

"And as for you, you impertinent Doubting Thomas," he snarled at Bob, slowly rising like a gargantuan, helium-filled Buddha, inching ever closer toward my buddy, "I'll have a few words for you during your next confession. You haven't heard the last of this—questioning the *Baltimore Catechism!* questioning me! It's not your lot to question, to interpret. It's your lot to have the faith, to believe, no questioning allowed. No thinking allowed. Now, depart from my presence, you heathens. Class is over for today," he announced, suddenly waddling into the sacristy.

We didn't doubt his tart words. We genuflected, half heartedly before rushing out of Holy Trinity into the fresh, secular air. "Wow, Bob! You were something in there. Where did you get the nerve to say something like that?" I asked, patting Bob on the shoulder.

"I am correct, am I not?" he said as the class gathered around him on the front stoop adoring him like Saint Columbkill, all gazing in wonderment at his hallowed countenance, his starched collared shirt now reflecting his face. Bob would unquestionably become a legend in the parish from this day forward for his courageous stance. He hadn't advocated reform like Martin Luther, but he would become theologically significant in the parish, if not the dioceses. Saint Bob spoke: "I've been reading and contemplating the Bible evenings in my room. The Bible is beyond us mere mortals, beyond Catholicism, beyond Protestantism, beyond non-Christian beliefs. I have been pondering, musing about differing theological perspectives," he said, gazing beyond the catawampus cross, his adoring apostles gathered at his feet, bowing, waving grimy handkerchiefs to cool him. In a brief moment, in pew number one, Sandbox Bob had become more than just Sandbox Bob. He looked heavenly, a halo appearing to appear over his head, but it had only been the sun breaking through the mist over water tank hill. Yet Mary and Magdalene, Matthew, Mark, Luke, John, St. Jimmy and the rest of Bob's apostles had seen a vision. Saint Bob. From that day forward, from the monumental day he questioned Fr. Smith, he would forever be adorned in our eyes.

Dogmatic interpretation of the Holy Bible had been historically disallowed, because the first Catholics were illiterate, some remaining even so today in the parish, if the truth be told. Second-, third-, tenth-century peasants couldn't read the Holy Bible or anything else; they couldn't read the parchments monks toiled over in dim candlelight deep inside endless, dark dungeons and lion-filled catacombs. Peasants couldn't read that there were actually ten commandants instead of the nine they mistakenly believed, those nine chiseled in crumbling stone. Only near-sighted monks could read and write, thereby interpreting the Church's readings for the illiterate faithful. No thinking allowed. Just do as we say, the Holy Fathers preached throughout the centuries. Listen to The Rule, Saint Benedict said. Well, that worked for many centuries, but gradually, peasants began escaping the bounds of their immediate church, sort of like escaping Goodhue and driving to Zumbrota, Pine island or Frontenac for a differing point of view, a differing perspective. Yes, peasants began seeking more than simple peasantry. They wanted to read the best sellers, even though the best seller was only the Bible. They faithfully followed onward, as Christian soldiers, the Crusaders of the eleventh and twelfth centuries, and as their horizons expanded they got learnin', began to read simple words like "straw," and "ox" and sentences like, "In the beginning . . . ," They wrote their names and children's names and God's name, acts causing increasing consternation to priests and monks and popes who had never before been questioned by the faithful. Protestants, yes. Catholics, no.

Concerning my Ford on campus, I followed Saint Bob's lead and interpreted: "Thou Shalt Not Have brazen images (or vehicles)," to mean, "not on campus." I parked it at a Texaco Station in St. Cloud, hitchhiked in to use it for special Benny dates or Moonmister dance jobs, later reparking it before hitchhiking back to campus. It wasn't especially effective, but useful, nonetheless. And after two weeks of readjusting to academic life at the beginning of year two, we were ready get the Ford and escape the bounds of monasticism.

"Jim, how about going to town tomorrow night, pick up your car and find us some girls?" the bespectacled Chuck suggested, setting down his Music Theory text on his desk and wiping tired, strained eyes. Long-stringed Chuck had also become a music major, so we were in this music thing together. Music Theory I was proving to be difficult—writing scales, intervals, chords, phrases, cadences, harmonic part writing, and practicing melodic dictation. To date, I had only played the clarinet plus my new alto saxophone, knowing nothing about writing scales and chords. Fr. James had started fast that first class period, letting us know there was more to music than playing clarinet or singing basso profundo or loving Woody Herman, Duke Ellington, Stan Kenton, or even the Polka Dots. Academic music wasn't to be a lark.

"Sounds good to me, Chuck. I could use a break from this theory. What say we do mass in the morning, then hitchhike to St. Cloud, find us some girls at the Nurses' School or St. Cloud State, maybe even catch a dance later at the Bloody Bucket?"

"Superb! Let's ask Bill and John to join us. They could use a break, too," Chuck answered, resetting his spectacles on that long nose while returning to writing major and minor scales in quarter notes in all keys on yellow music manuscript paper.

"You got these scales figured out, Chuck? I never wrote a

scale in my life before Music Theory I," I said, sharpening my No. 2 yellow Ticonderoga pencil while attacking the music manuscript paper.

"Mostly, but I'm having trouble with harmonic minors."

"Shoot! The only miners I know were the claypitters in the village, although we didn't call them miners. Claypits were located near both Bellechester and Goodhue, potters clay having been discovered near Bellechester in the twenties, later outside Goodhue by John Paul. They shaped it into that famous Red Wing Pottery and less famous Red Wing Sewer Pipe. Those Clay Pit miners were 'diggers' to us, but these harmonic minors are proving mighty troublesome. Shoot, Chuck! I've had enough of these scales for tonight. Let's knock off and get a malt," I said, flipping my pencil to the desk.

"That was quite a lecture about minors, Jim. You're getting into this college thing. That was really more information than I needed about the Claypits," he chided as we headed for the malt shop.

Although a Friday night and only a quarter past nine, we had more freedom now with Fr. Casper "prefecting" on second floor Mary's, the good father not treading the hallways demanding required study as Fr. Henry had done last year. Oh, we didn't have the run of the house yet. Mary's wasn't a frat house by any means. Girls were hardly allowed on campus, much less in the dorms. Heaven forbid, in our rooms! Mary's was far from an animal house, regardless of Brother Leo's Holsteins braying out back in his still-operating barn. Sophomores were still bound by Benedictine Rules—though not fully monastic—expected to study, to be silent during study hours, to behave like the good Christian boys we were.

"Hey, John. Want to hike to St. Cloud in the morning, get my car, catch a couple of beers, a few girls, before heading to the Bloody Bucket for dancing?" I asked, hollering into John's room, his head drooping over a foot-long engineering slide rule, studying a major far removed from harmonic scales.

"Sounds good, Jim. You going, Chuck?" John asked, setting his fiery plastic slide rule on his desk."

"Absolutely. These first two weeks have been difficult. Need a break; see you in the morning," Chuck said as we hit the stairwell heading for the basement to a food bar passing for a cafe, a hole-in-the-wall a long way from Swenson's Cafe. Although an engineering major, John had played french horn in the Forest Lake High School Band and was also in his second year. Music for John was an avocation. For Chuck and me, it was business. Harmonic, melodic business.

Bill asked John about his summer, "You have a good time in the cities, John?" the Ford hugging the road because of extra weight.

"You betcha! Worked the trucks with Dad hauling freight to the Twin Cities, managing the terminal down by the Mississippi, plus seeing lots of my girl. Great summer, but I'm happy to be back," John said as we reached St. Cloud's Main Street, bumping past the Germain Hotel, four tow-headed Johnnies having been given a dispensation for an afternoon of carousing. "How about you, Bill? What did you do up in boring South Dakota?" John chided.

"North Dakota! John. None of you guys ever get it right. Valley City is in North Dakota," he said, retrieving his pipe and filling it with loose tobacco, some of it falling to my seat.

"Doesn't make any difference to us, Bill. North, South, West, the Dakotas are all the same. Boring!" John retorted.

"Watch it you liberal-loving, Humphrey-McCarthy Minnesotan. At least we have some identity in the Dakotas. What do you have in the Twin Cities? Siamese cities at that," Bill snarled, the two fellows bantering about incidental states, both Upper Midwest, after all. It wasn't as if they were fighting the South again, or the Lutherans.

"Chuck! What did you do in Eau Claire the past three months?"

"Worked the paper mills at Chippewa Falls. Made good paper and good money, but like you guys, I'm pleased to be back. Paper Mill work is hard, wet and long. I sure don't want to do that for the rest of my life, but it's good money. Bought myself another year of college," he said as we crossed the Mississippi River to the east side of town, not going anywhere in particular, just enjoying the afternoon in a secular world.

"How about you, Jim?" John asked. "You do anything but screw around all summer in your dumpy little village? How the hell did you make enough money to buy this car?" he asked, slapping me on the back, a small puff of dirt escaping from the upholstery.

"Stepfather bought it for me. Thought I should have it to get back and forth from SJU, because I live by myself in the village. She's sharp, isn't she?" I asked as the three fellows were suddenly distracted by three fair girls promenading past on the sidewalk.

"It'll do for a college car," John smirked, now peering intently at the obviously young high school girls.

"Hey, John. Those girls are much too young for you. You're a college dude now. Get your eyes off teenagers," I said, circling Cathedral High School.

"You work the viners again, Jim?" Bill asked, he too craning his neck to get a last look at the shapely girls, an unfamiliar sight on campus.

"Began the summer working the viners, but got promoted to killing lice," I answered, unable to watch the road *and* the girls.

"Killing lice? What the hell does that mean?" he said, his pipe now fully stocked, the sweet aroma enveloping the Ford.

"Pea lice. Had to kill the little sonofabitches regularly."

"You got lice in your pee, Jim? How do you kill those little bastards . . . with a hammer? That must hurt like hell," Bill said, laughing, howling at his own witticisms as he blew a long, lingering smoke stream out the window.

"No! *P-e-a* lice, Bill. Pea lice, corn lice too."

"You got lice on your corns, too, Jim?" Bill asked, again slapping the back of my seat bringing more dust to the surface.

"Oh, shit, Bill. You know what I mean. Pea and corn lice for Libby's. Got promoted to count 'em, spray 'em and kill the little bastards with an airplane."

"Took a big airplane to kill little peas?" Bill asked, slapping the seat a third time, dust rising throughout the Ford.

"Do you guys think we could have a more intelligent conversation?" I asked while making a u-turn and heading back up Main Street.

"Well," Chuck said, "we could talk about religious philosophy."

"Naw."

"We could talk about Medieval logic."

"Naw."

"We could talk about English Lit."

"Naw."

"Or, we could talk about women."

"Right!"

"How'd you guys make out this summer?" John offered as we passed Sam's Pizza, the first pizza joint I'd ever been in.

"Good. Got my high school sweetheart back in Eau Claire. Been going steady for three, four years," Chuck said, his prominent Adam's apple bobbing up and down.

"How about you Bill? You got anything up there in South Dakota worth screwing, other than Buffalo?" John asked, forever chiding Bill about the vast, desolate plains.

"North Dakota! John, and the Buffalo've been gone for a hundred years. Pretty calm for me this summer, though, mostly working and reading philosophy. No dating."

"That must be boring, Bill. A boring life in boring state."

"Jimmy! You get any action this summer other than killing lice?" John asked, sticking his head into the front seat as we headed toward Waite Park on the outskirts of St. Cloud.

"Sharon and I spent a few nights together looking at *Playboy* magazines. That was interesting," I said while bouncing across the rough railroad tracks.

"*Playboys*? Together? Didn't know you were a Casanova?"

"Who? Caruso?"

"Casanova, the world-renowned lover, not opera singer," John said, suddenly attacking, adulterating my erudition (another new college word).

"Hell, John, I'm not a Caruso or Casanova, but I hope to be a Benny Goodman or Johnny Hodges someday if I keep practicing.

You guys are far ahead of me in the sex department, but I'll catch up. Sharon was just feeling me out a little about sex, that's all."

"Did you say 'feeling you out'? Did she go that far?" Bill asked, slapping the seat for the fourth time. I wish he'd stop that, I thought.

"Not literally 'feeling' Bill, figuratively, you know. That was just a figure of speech," I said, dragging Main Street.

"You hear that fellows? Jimmy who was in Bonehead English last year is now speaking figuratively. Hell! He didn't even know the definition a year ago. Now listen to him expound."

"How about stopping for a beer at the Modern Bar?" I asked, changing the subject quickly. I liked *doing* sex better than *talking* sex.

"Park this heap, Jim. Let's lift a few beers to a new year."

None of the four were college-level beer drinkers yet, but we still had three years to improve upon those skills. We enjoyed each other's camaraderie while sipping Hamm's beer, on tap, for a couple of hours while continuing our bantering. Later in the afternoon we picked up burgers and malts, dragged Main again, then drove to the edge of town and the Bloody Bucket hoping to find non-celibate female action. The Bucket was a college hangout where hope-to-be nurses, hope-to-be staters, hope-to-be Benny graduates, and hope-to-be Johnnie graduates gathered to hope-to-be connected with the opposite sex, all escaping cell-like dorm rooms, being released from the constraints of academia. In our cases, monasticism, too.

We ordered more Hamm's, chatted with girls from various campuses, danced to Frank Sinatra, Perry Como and Count Basie juke box recordings. John made several of his best moves on a Benny; Bill moved in on a cute nurse I'd my eye on; Chuck mostly drank Pepsi and dreamed about his high school sweetheart back in Oh-so-Claire, Wisconsin while I displayed a couple of my best Skyline Ballroom moves to a St. Cloud Stater. Alas, none of us were as suave, as Casanovian or Carusonian as we thought; consequently, by the end of the night we were sitting, unconnected, in a forlorn booth near the jukebox. Yet, for a few hours we had been liberated. John said, reaching our celibate campus, that it would have been difficult getting eight guys and gals into the Ford anyway with frilly, sexy flowing dresses, sweet smelling perfumes filling the air instead of Bill's stale pipe smoke, lithe thighs, full, pointed breasts, soft shoulders and firm, shapely derrieres.

Music began dominating my life, what with playing clarinet in Marching and Concert Bands, alto saxophone in the Moonmisters, singing a high, ball-straining first tenor in Men's Chorus, even learning enough string bass to join the fledgling, monk-dominated string orchestra. We filled days attending classes, late afternoon band or orchestra rehearsals, the chorus rehearsing monophonic Gregorian Chant after vespers and dinner leaving only later evening hours for study. Yet, I reserved enough time to show off my best GHS basketball moves during pickup games in the old gym, those moves not good enough to make the St. John's official team, but good enough against North Dakota wanna-be's. Weeks quickly turned into months, months into semesters, semesters into years. After what seemed a lifetime in grade and high school, college was passing much too rapidly.

St. John's had become a special place for me. I had made my share of dumb decisions back in the village—pouring salt into Heinie's pepper shakers, spilling holy water as an acolyte, picking my nose or butt during the senior class play, acting up in Miss Cree's English Class, or attempting to get a "feel" with a Zumbrota date before having laid the proper foreground groundwork. But one decision I was proud of was choosing St. John's. It offered me a quality education and a much needed, extended family for my youthful, splintered life. The sequestered campus, the "family" dorm life, the regimentation of the monks, priests and abbot created a closeness, a bonding, a camaraderie that was to last a lifetime. The Benedictine Rule had been stringent, but it bonded us together for four years, and long after.

A couple of years before I arrived, Coach John Gagliardi had charged onto campus to lead the football team. He had quickly become a snarly, eccentric character, not yet the legend he was to become during a fifty-year coaching tenure under the twin towers.

But even in 1955 he dispensed pungent, choice, non-biblical words to listless right guards, lumbering left tackles, sluggish defensive ends and laggard single wing backs, dispensing a vocabulary unfamiliar to the priests. Gagliardi hollered and shouted and, God forbid! even swore at his troops, demanding much from them, getting more from them than what they had in them. Black Robes would divert from parading to vespers in the basilica, to Gagliardi's on-field entertainment. Our marching band caught some of the action also, practicing nearby.

Gagliardi's strength was his ability to take regular guys who thought they wanted to be priests or monks, philosophers or English Lit majors and turn them into football players. He didn't have athletically-gifted football stars, but he had a way of getting the most out of seminarians and monk'ys and, well, guys like me but not me. He encouraged them to sing, "Fight you Johnnies, fight you Johnnies, stand and fight for ol' St. John's," and to work together as a team, a family.

After marching band practice one late fall afternoon—the weakening sun gradually disappearing over the twin-towered basilica, monks processing to vespers or compline or lauds or matins, I never could remember—I watched the team practice. As they tackled and ran, threw pigskins and ran plays in the enclosed, natural-bowl pine stadium, I recalled the first football team at GHS, when I was in grade school . . .

GHS had fielded a couple of early sports teams. They began playing basketball in second story, closet-sized courts in the village during the 1929–30 school year, Coach Will Pickavance prodding Dennis Heaney, Charles Gorman, Frederic Johnson, Milton Harth and Bob Haas to great efforts. By 1935 more fellows had become interested in originator Naismith's new basket game. The cagers now included Burt Holmes, Orv Barry, LeRoy Diercks, Gerald Heaney, John Gentzkow, Marv Bolland, LeVerne Diercks, John Eyestone, Herman Finstuen, Jack Mickley, Bob Johnson, all prodded on by Coach Roscoe Perrine.

Boys played baseball, too, on cow-pasture fields passing for baseball diamonds, the season only six weeks due to heavy Minnesota snows refusing to melt the encrusted infield before spring school dismissal. During the thirties and most of the forties, GHS had had only two sporting teams: Boys' basketball and boys' baseball, girls being relegated to cheering on the boys, sexist discrimination for sure, but alas, villagers knowing no better. But the fellows were happy for the girls' adoration when scoring a basket, and the girls were happy, I guess, cheering on their boyfriend stars. A home run, a few baskets were worth consider- able necking later in the back seat of a Chevy out at Finney's Woods. It could've been worse.

About 1946 the superintendent, school board and townsfolk began saying the school should field a football team to compete with Wanamingo and Dodge Center and Zumbrota and Pine Island and West Concord. Our boys were mostly strong, hefty farm fellows, they said. Our boys were tough and strong as a bull, they said. Some even said bull-headed. Certainly, we should field a football team to compete with neighboring towns, they said. Let's do it, they said. They did, they said.

During the postwar summer of 1947, the school purchased used and tattered football equipment from Lake Wilson, a western Minnesota burg that had decided to give up what Goodhue was just beginning. Lake Wilson hadn't enough boys to field a team, so they sold greasy, tattered leather helmets and shoulder pads to GHS to equip Hilbert Reese, Harold Ramboldt, Marlin Benrud, Joe Burkhard, John Yungers, Duane Hinsch, Harlin Reese, Arnie Jonas, Richard Cook, Junior Lunde, Sigvard Stenlund, Harold Lensch, Butch Jonas, Terry Shelstad, Chuck Johnson, Harold Harvey, Jimmy Ryan, George O'Reilly, Bob Jonas and Jimmy Lohman. To those boys, though, that used equipment was as good as new. They would wear it proudly to honor the first GHS football team. The only problem was, Coach didn't know anything about football. He had only been a teacher, knew how to keep score, but that was all. GHS's first team didn't know how to play the game, either. Few had seen the Minnesota Gophers play up at the U. None had television sets in '47, so they knew little of the game other than they should run from one goal post to the other end without stepping in a cow turd while carrying the pigskin rather than a Holstein skin into the end zone.

But Coach was determined to get the program going. The high school guys had been banging girls long enough, Coach said. It was time they banged football teams, he said. With the help of village men they carved out a field running from the baseball left field to centerfield, extending twenty yards into an adjacent cornfield. The school board, with the assistance of townsfolk, marked the field, procuring lime from Streater's Lumber Yard at $1.95 per bushel. Fred Rusch tacked up two sorely looking two-by-four goal posts, and GHS had a field, if not a team. The men tried to square up the field with a role of baling twine and a carpenter's square, but it ended up one hundred yards on one sideline, ninety-nine on the other, the field askew, but they left it that way. It became an unknown advantage for the Goodhue team, the field being a yard short in the northeast corner. Speedy John Yungers was to often take advantage of that short yard.

Though a pigskin novice, Coach took his coaching seriously, reading what books he could find on Red Grange and the Four Horsemen, studying U of M Gopher play books, even scouting Pine Island and Zumbrota Friday nights. His Goodhue boys were big and rugged, he knew that, plus John Yungers and Joe Burkhard were speedy; Hilbert Reese had an arm good enough to be quarterback, and Hilbert was smart for a farm boy, Coach knew that. Hilbert could remember the plays.

Three weeks before school began that fall of 1947, twenty-one boys signed up for the team. They began practicing down past the stand of elms to become football players, although only half that number showed up for practice, the remainder on their farms stacking and threshing wheat. Coach had a hard time fielding that first team, but things improved when classes began and the wheat and oats were in the granary. Those farm boys, in particular, took to football. Hell! They'd been tackling hogs and pigs and chickens and calves all their life, Coach said. Tackling a runner wasn't all that much different, Coach grunted and shouted those first weeks. Just slam them, grab a leg or two, throw the sonofabitch to the ground, then stand above him sneering and making grunting sounds like a bull, the boys said. That's all they needed to do. Just transfer their agrarian skills to the football field. Well, the boys got the gist of tackling and blocking easily enough, but running plays and scoring proved to be more difficult, because that took fineness, a quality most lacked. Many were raucous and ready boys, fellows who could screw a cow or heifer in the back forty without finesse. Finesse was totally lacking in their life. They were born to tackle.

Clean, lean Hilbert worked on developing his quarterback skills; "Hollywood" Yungers and polished Joe Burkhard practiced evasive running, while beefy, burly Duane Hinsch became a bull of a bull at fullback. They were ready for their first game against Dodge Center.

The townsfolk had been anticipating this first game for months, years, in fact. Bernie Bierman's U of M Golden Gophers had brought fame and recognition to the ten-thousand-lakes state; it was time some of that ran off on "The Boys of '47."

Even though village stores seldom boomed any afternoon, several proprietors locked their doors for the one o'clock game. Most just walked out, though, leaving the door open. Anyone who *had* to buy something could simply jot it down on the tablet and leave the money on the counter. Townsfolk marched up to the field like children following the Pied Piper, the village excited about watching Hilbert and Harlin Reese, Yungers, Burkhard, Hinsch, Ramboldt, Benrud, Lensch, Shelstad, Stenlund, their boys tackle this first game. Even though the community knew less about football than the boys, they were *their* boys, and they would shine today . . .

> *Our boys will shine today,*
> *Our boys will shine.*

By noon classes had ended, students had rushed home for lunch, then hurriedly returned to school while Hilbert, John, Joe and the boys dressed in the basement locker room—nervous, agitated, excited. For normally boisterous fellows the locker room was particularly subdued. Guys slipped on sweaty, size ten jock straps—school girls curious about those sizes—shoulder pads, hip pads, pants, socks and rubber-cleated shoes, then held leather helmets in sweaty hands, heads down, sitting on benches, waiting for Coach to release them to the battlefield.

"Boys! You're going to make history today," Coach said, pacing the cramped locker room. "You'll go down in the anals of GHS as the first team to play a football game here."

"Uh, Coach? I believe that's 'annals.' "

"Don't make no mind. It's never been done before. That's why you're the first. Makes sense don't it?" Coach said as the team grew agitated. They didn't want a speech from Coach. They wanted to charge the field to release their pent-up energy. Some of the older boys were feeling as if they had been necking all night and getting blue balls. They needed to get out of the locker room to release that energy, but Coach continued, "This is a great, momentous day for the GHS football team. It'll go down in the anals of GHS."

"Hey, coach, you already said that."

"Today, you can make your parents, your relatives, the village, me, proud. All you need to do is get out there and fight. Now let me hear it from you. Fight! Fight! Fight!"

"FIGHT! F I G H T! F I G H T!"

"I want you to fight hard, to hit hard, to tackle hard, to run hard. You do that, you do what I ask of you, and we'll return to this locker room victorious, winning one, the first in the anals of GHS for the Old Gripper."

"Uh, Coach, that's 'One for the Gipper.'"

"Whatever! Let's go now. Charge that field!" Twenty-seven untested players bounded up the stairs, cleats rat-a-tating like W.W.II machine guns on Guadalcanal. Several tripped on the stairs incurring skinned chins even before the first play, but they soon gathered their composure as the team trotted the long block down to the field, townsfolk anxiously awaiting their arrival under the two-by-four goal post on one end only. (Far-end touchdowns abutting the cornfield were kicked on the near end zone.) They trotted onto the field in sort of purple and white pants and jerseys, sporadic clapping rising from the townsfolk standing on the sidelines. Captain Burkhard gathered the team into a circle to begin calisthenics doing stretching and pushups and squat jumps, running ten-yard bursts, rolling and bumping each other, growling, snarling, farting while charging up their testosterone levels like bulls being released into the corral.

Dodge Center was already on the field warming up in ungodly green uniforms when the GHS team jogged onto the field. Most Wildcats avoided looking at them. The Dodgers had been playing football for ten years and had a big leg up on the Wildcats. But the Wildcats were savage fellows from Belle Creek and Goodhue and Featherstone and Belvidere Townships. Surely, they'd prevail against prissy guys in lime-green uniforms.

The marching band, if you could call it that, formed semi-straight lines in the undulating, uneven end zone preparing to play the National Anthem. A long, uneven, ragged snare drum roll brought players and fans to attention as the band struggled through what was later rumored to be The Star Spangled Banner. Fortunately, the band hadn't rehearsed the entire anthem, so it collapsed by the middle stanza. Fans hoped the football team would be better than the band.

The Wildcats won the toss of a coin—actually a two-sided washer from Jesse's Hardware—electing to kick off to the Dodgers. Arnie Jonas had been practicing kicking for three weeks on the field and at his farmstead, trying to put the pigskin over the pig house instead of through it. Usually, he was successful, out on the farm. The team lined up behind the muscular Jonas. He ran toward the ball, kicked the pigskin so hard he deflated it, the ball skittering to a stop ten yards down field. The stunned Dodgers didn't know what to do. They stopped, appearing as deflated as the pigskin. Arnie had put too much foot into that skin this day. He'd try again. Again the Wildcats lined up, followed Arnie into the kickoff, this time the pigskin tumbling to the Dodger's 35-yard line. The Wildcats were ferocious in pursuing the ball, slamming and tackling the ball carrier before he gained three yards. The boys had begun some kind of a football tradition at GHS.

The GHS defenders were, indeed, ferocious. They loved smashing heads, tackling, grabbing legs and arms and helmets and slamming the Dodgers to the turf. They thought it great fun. After four quick Dodger downs, the Wildcats received the pigskin to see what they could do on offense. Hilbert huddled the team into a circle, called play No. 1 "Buck the line," handed off to fullback Hinsch as he dashed straight ahead into the Dodger defensive line. He was thrown for a two-yard loss, the Wildcats not quite having the hang of blocking yet. Down two, Hilbert handed off to Burkhard off right tackle, again a two-yard loss.

"Come on, guys. Block those sonofabitches," Hilbert shouted in the huddle. "Use your hands if you have to, but open some holes for me. Play No. 3, Off left tackle." Hilbert handed off to Yungers running off left tackle, and suddenly there was daylight where Ramboldt and Benrud had finally blocked the Dodger line letting John pick up nine yards, but short of a first down. Harlin snapped the ball through his bowlegged legs, but too high, the pigskin flying over Arnie's head. It was a mad scramble to the ball, but a Dodger retrieved it before Arnie. Dodge Center's ball on the Wildcat 28-yard line. A groan rose from the sideline, murmured expletives from Coach.

Dodger single wing right, a wing back around the right scooting to the three-yard line, Stenlund finally hog-tying him on the sideline. Down two, Dodger into the line, into the end zone for a touchdown. Extra point no good. Dodger Center 6. Goodhue 0.

I stood on the sideline, just a little seventy-five pound sixth grader, in awe of the entire affair, but knowing little about football. I had read the Sunday Peach section about Golden Gopher games, but had never seen a real game. The Goodhue boys looked and acted tough, but apparently they lacked the polish and finish of a real football team. But everyone cheered them on, nonetheless. Surely, they would prevail and bring pride to the GHS school.

By half time the Dodgers had opened a 20 to 0 lead over the Wildcats as they trudged back to the locker room, the untested marching band taking the torn-up field. As the band struggled to stay in step while executing a company front the length of the field, simultaneously attempting to play a Sousa march, Coach was berating his players in the locker room saying they were wimps and pussy cats and couldn't tackle Dodgers as well as a hog or steer. He said they weren't showing the guts and courage they should. He said they weren't holding up the football tradition of GHS.

"But coach, we don't have a tradition. This is our first game."

"Don't make no matter. We got a half's experience and you aren't holding up half of that tradition. Don't argue with me, now, just get out there and show me what you're made off. Hilbert get that sonofabitchin' ball in the end zone. Let's go."

The Dodgers kicked off to begin the second half. Yungers caught the ball at his 30 and scooted up the sideline all the way to the Dodger's 42-yd line. Great start, I thought pacing the sidelines behind the plank bench.

Reese dropped back on first down to flip a short pass to Sigvard Stenlund on the left side picking up six yards.

Hinsch straight into the line for two.

Reese dropped back to fake a pass, instead flipped the ball to Yungers who headed to the short corner of the field. He zigged and zagged like Paul Giel of later Gopher fame, breaking a tackle here, leaving a Dodger there, until he high-skipped into the end zone for six points. A roar rose from the sideline enveloping the entire town, even though town was only three streets wide. The village was so small that . . .

The folks on Upper and Lower Streets not attending the game knew something big had happened. Dormant dogs asleep near the elevator began barking. Ol' Buck lifted an ear. A flock of pigeons fluttered from the top of the elevator. Cats behind the jail started running. Wildcats had invaded the town.

Arnie kicked off to the now enraged Dodgers for being scored upon who proceeded to run the ball all the way back for a touchdown. Ouch! That hurt. Coach pounded the bench, pounded the water boy, pounded the cheerleaders, knocked over the water jug, kicked helmets and yelled at his defenders. Then the pussy cats, he said, fumbled on first down, quickly giving the pigskin back to the Dodgers. Where was Dodge Center, anyway, I wondered, becoming upset at the mounting score. I knew some about the county, but where was Dodge? Was it in Goodhue County? I wondered as the Wildcats received the spinning, arching kickoff.

Hilbert dropped back to pass on first down, his arm quickly knocked askew, the ball ending up in the arms of a Dodger. Coach was incensed about the "pussy cat" defense. But they dug in like dogs after bones.

Dodger into the line, slammed ferociously, Wildcats growling like wild cats. They were finally as mad as wild cats. They'd had enough of the Dodgers. Play two, around end, Dodger slammed to the ground out of bounds. "Take that you mealy-mouth Dodger."

Down three. Pass, intercepted by Harold Lensch who ran the ball through the defense to the Dodger ten yard line.

"That's more like it," Coach called. "Take it in Hilbert."

Hilbert called for a reverse, handing off to Burkhard around left end, he inturn handing off to Yungers running right for that short end zone again. It worked, completely faking the Dodgers, Yungers skirting into the 99-yard end zone. Score: Dodgers 32, Wildcats 12, Arnie having failed on both extra point attempts. He'd have to spend many nights kicking the pigskin *over* his pig house.

I wanted the team to win badly. The townsfolk wanted them to win, to maintain Coach's tradition! But it wasn't to be this first day of the first game of the first football team of GHS of 1947. They lost 40–12, humbled, heads down trudging back to the stinking locker room. I followed them picking up discarded jerseys, helmets, muddy cleats, just wanting to smell their leather, the sweat of a losing effort from Hilbert and Joe and John and Duane and Harlin and Sigvard and Harold and Junior and Terry. They lost that first day, but they had become my heroes. Someday, I hoped to follow in their footsteps.

C huck G. became my roommate for the final three years, he eventually changing his major from music to theater, thereby abandoning me to struggle with Music Theory II, Music History, Counterpoint, Harmony alone. We remained on the same artistic level, nonetheless, other than his incessant droning of Latin phrases. Chuck loved Latin and he practiced his phrases continuously. Shoot! I had *recited* Latin as an altar boy, but as George O' had so often reminded me at the viners, I didn't *know* what the hell it meant. But I had retorted that God understood Latin, it being the official language of angels, archangels and seconds-in-command. That was good enough. Arriving at St. John's I had known only two languages: English and You Betcha! I struggled through *messieurs*, and *oui* and *le travois* and *amour* in French class, but never became as enamored with French as Chuck did with Latin. *C'est la vie!*

We would rise groggy-eyed, brush our teeth, fight over the lone, grimy sink, cough and spit and fart and piss until rushing to our first class somewhere deep in the slumbering, wakening monastic quadrangle. As he rushed across campus Chuck would shout, *Carpe diem* (Seize the day). I would respond in my best Goodhue County dialect, "See ya later, then." Later, during band rehearsal, he would shout, *Ars longa, vita brevis* (Art is long, life is short). I would respond with, "You betcha," as we tuned up for rehearsal. After dinner I tolerated *In media stat vertus* (Virtue stands in the middle), whatever that meant. Finally, his last words of the day from the lower bunk, *Pox vobiscum* (Peace be with you); my retort *Carpe da carp* (Seize the carp). The only Latin phrase I actually understood was *ad libitum,* shortened to *ad lib,* because that's what the hep cats, the new jazz boppers—Charlie Parker, Dizzy Gillespie, Thelonious Monk—referred to as "at will," free playing, something I was eager to learn on my sax and clarinet.

I could say *ad lib*, but I couldn't do it. To *ad lib* was to play without written notes on a page, something we *never* did back at GHS, other than Noisy Rusch and Jimmy Ryan over in the saxophone section, much to the consternation of Mr Chas Wood. Noisy would get to honking, low and hard like Coleman Hawkins during Dvorak's "Finalé to the New World Symphony," or von Suppé's "Light Cavalry Overture"—Ryan interpreting it as "The Last Supper's Calvary" while accompanying Noisy with subtone, cacophonous growls. Those two couldn't be bored with playing only notes on a page. In spite of Wood's admonitions, they persisted till their graduation day. Chas Wood was never so happy to see the finalé of those two saxophonists.

I played most of the notes on the page then, and now I was playing alto sax in the Moonmisters, still reading notes on the page while Eddie Motzek soloed on trumpet, *ad libitum.* I liked listening to Eddie, his tone luscious, his vibrato wide and even, his high notes bright, stirring. He sounded like Harry James.

The Moonmisters was a student organization, noncredit, so we rehearsed late nights in the band room after the monks had prayed for ten hours and were fast asleep on monastic straw mattresses, no smoking allowed. Ten Moonmisters hacked big band arrangements by Woody Herman, Count Basie, Ralph Flanagan, Stan Kenton, and eventually, Jim Franklin. We used three or four saxes, two trumpets, a trombone, piano, bass and drums to play for Nursing School dances, Benny and Johnny dances, high school homecomings and proms, plus drunken Shriner dances; that is, if they paid us enough money to tolerate their inebriation. The Moonmisters kept me in spending and gas money for the next three years while I improved my skills, even though not *ad libitum,* in spite of Chuck's *Bona fide* (In good faith) encouragement.

The more I played with the Moonmisters the more I loved big band music. I practiced late nights in the Music Hall, wrote awkward, naive arrangements, but eventually lead the band for a couple of years, bobbing my head like Whoopee John. Even then I dreamed about returning to the village to play at the Dreamland Ballroom, a.k.a. Gerken's Hardware on Upper Street, just as I had told Emma Kindseth. I guess it was a hometown thing. I didn't dream about playing at St. Paul's Prom Ballroom or Clear Lake's Surf Ballroom or Sioux Falls' Arco Ballroom in South or North Dakota. I dreamed about returning to the village with a big band in a big blue bus at *my* Dreamland. I wanted a great band so hometown folks could enjoy dancing as they had in the twenties and thirties. Besides, the village could use a dance hall again to complement its beer joints. It could use a smooth, gleaming dancing floor with a revolving, sparkling globe light, a lovely bandstand bedecked in glittering finery, a classy place to dance Friday, Saturday or Sunday nights, a place giving folks something exciting to do in the sequestered village.

Oh, the village had its usual "Lost Swede Town"* activities (*compliments of author Carol Bly, Madison, MN)—church socials, Bridge Clubs, 500 Hundred Clubs, firemen's meetings, Ladies Aid Society, Auxiliary and American Legion Club, Literary Clubs, even a few unsanctioned "Gossip Clubs." These organizations had been popular since the village's first days in 1897 when "Goodhue Station" became "Goodhue." But things began changing in the mid-to-late fifties; in fact, they had begun changing after W.W.II ended in 1945. After the war folks had more money for necessities, even a few non-necessities. GHS wouldn't have started a football team in '43 or '44, the war effort requiring all available monies for guns, ammunition, ships and C-rations. But when Hitler swallowed that pill with Eva B. in his Berlin bunker ending the European war for good, and when Harry Truman dropped the A-bomb on Hiroshima, folks could see their way to buying frivolous items such as football equipment and new cars. Auto designs changed with the renewed availability of steel, becoming sleek, aerodynamic-styled bullets in 1949. The demise of gas rationing, steel rationing and gasoline rationing let folks spread out, drive farther than to Bellechester, Oak Center, White Willow or Ryan, ghost towns that actually weren't there anymore, anyway. They could now drive to Cannon Falls to watch the Cannon River tumble over the dam, recalling the glory days of the Goodhue Mill, the Old Stone Mill, the City Mill, mills making Cannon Falls famous, at least in Goodhue County. They could now drive to White Rock, although they wasn't anything there when they got there besides the bank and remnants of G. O. Miller's General Store. It was a nice drive into the valley, anyway. They could drive through the rolling hills, meandering valleys and deep coulees around Welch to fish alongside the tumbling dam waters. They could drive to Frontenac to gaze at Lake Pepin and the mansions of Col Garrard, his syrupy "southern" opulence of an earlier time still evident, still reeking of Scarlett O'Hara. Villagers could also drive to Red Wing's Skyline Ballroom. Despite the postwar progress, I dreamed it would be nice if Dreamland were once again a ballroom. I dreamed of bringing a big band home after graduation. I dreamed of the lighted marquee over the former Marshall-Wells store: "The Dreamland Ballroom Presents Jimmy Franklin and his Orchestra."

"Yer band playin' tonight, Jimmy?" whiskey-baritone Erv Richter asked shuffling up to the Dreamland front door on Upper Street.

"You bet, Erv. I've put together a great band for your dancing pleasure. How've you been the past several years, anyway? I've been off to college learning how to play saxophone, writing arrangements for my big band, but back home now to open the Dreamland," I said, greeting Erv on the street. He appeared spent, bedraggled, eyes drooping, hat askew, pants tattered as if he had been homeless on the street the past four years. Yet, beneath his bedraggled exterior, I sensed he was still the same ol' Erv I had played clarinet for, nights on the lonesome streets.

"You still play 'Melancholy Baby,' *Jimmy? I always liked that song. You play it again for me?"* he asked, sitting on the curb, feet in the gutter, obviously tired, worn out.

"Sure will, Erv, but I've also written an arrangement for my big band, not just clarinet," I answered, joining him on the curb.

"That's nice, Jimmy, but I like just your clarinet the best. You play 'Melancholy Baby' *for me some night, just you and your clarinet, not such a big band. Big band too loud,"* he said, gazing past the Corner Bar toward the outlying fields, his mind off somewhere recalling earlier, better days.

"I could play it for you on alto sax, Erv. I learned it at college. What do you think?"

"Naw, just clarinet, Jimmy. That's what I like. 'Melancholy Baby' *on clarinet."*

"Okay, Erv, I'll bring my clarinet down some night to play for you, just like I used to do in high school," I said, leaving him at the curb to enter my renovated dream, Dreamland Ballroom. The floor shined like

pure silver, the revolving mirrored-globe worked per-
fectly bouncing light rays around the darkened floor,
deep red upholstered booths lining three sides of the
floor. I had rebuilt the bandstand, raising it two feet so
dancers could better see the band. I had installed
spotlights in the corners to highlight dancers as they
found those old steps they had polished so many years
ago up at the high school or at Oak Center or Belle
Creek, or down in the Hay Creek hollows. I had hung
banners on the proscenium, placed soft-glowing lamps
on each table, and installed a cocktail bar in the corner.
It was ready for the first dance tomorrow night, the
return of the Dreamland Ballroom.

I had assembled and rehearsed a good band with
talented musicians from Rochester and Winona, yet I
was nervous as they warmed up behind the bandstand.
What if this doesn't work, I thought. What if this is a
bust, I wondered, prancing, pacing to make sure every-
thing was in order. I was proud of my musical arrange-
ments, proud of the band, but would the hometown folks
return to a place they abandoned many years ago?
Maybe they didn't dance anymore. Maybe they wouldn't
like my modern arrangements, preferring, instead,
Lawrence Welk or the Six Fat Dutchmen or Whoopee
John or the Polka Dots, for God's sake! I had promoted
the opening gala, heavily, with ads in the Republican
Eagle, _the_ Goodhue County Tribune, _and had even_
taken out a broadcast ad on KDHL. _But would it work?_

By half past eight there were only two couples
sitting in dim-lit booths, strangers, at that. The band
was taking its place on the bandstand, tuning, running
arpeggios, testing embouchures, even playing ad lib
changes. I readied my clarinet and sax, ran through a
few scales and arpeggios myself as the clock reached
8:50, four lone couples waiting for our downbeat.
Damn! This isn't going to work. Folks don't dance

anymore. They now drive to Lake City or Red Wing or Rochester. This was a mistake, I brooded, as 8:55 approached. "Let's tune up, fellows. Need to sound good for the big crowd tonight," I said, sounding a Bb on the piano. "Relax Jim," a sax player said. "They'll come back. We've got a good band. The word will get out, maybe not tonight, but they'll return."

"Is this the way Benny Goodman started?"

"Sure. He was a flop till he hit California. Folks didn't know about him, but he became famous later. We will too," he said, the clock striking 9 o'clock, the band striking into Benny's "Let's Dance," *a new arrangement of mine. The four couples immediately began dancing under the slowly revolving globe, it working even with a recent short circuit that Cy Benda eventually repaired. I relaxed into the music, those old tunes and harmonies enticing me as ever. The couples seemed to be enjoying themselves out on the floor, but maybe they were only anticipating hot sex later in the evening. I didn't know. This would never do. For a second chart we slowed it down, playing* "Stardust" *as the couples danced closer, two more strange couples slipping through the door. By the third arrangement,* "Moten Swing," *the band was loosening up, I was loosening up, even though the floor was sparse. The band could play all night by ourselves; we loved it, but well, I had borrowed considerable money from the Goodhue State Bank to reopen Dreamland. It needed to be a financial success besides a musical pleasure.*

Half past nine and only strangers on the floor. Damn! maybe they've forgotten me. Maybe they've forgotten the little kid who played his heart out for those Bellechester and Belle Creek ruffians. Had they forgotten the kid who murdered the "Clarinet Polka" *at the Goodhue County Artificial Breeder's Association Annual Township Banquet. Even Mother wasn't here. Where was she? Damn! It would be embarrassing if my own mother didn't show up, I thought while kicking off the second set with* "Memories of You." *I started soaring with my clarinet on* "Memories," *closing my eyes, getting into the music, singing on my clarinet when a commotion at the front door suddenly distracted me. Now what? Fifty or more people were storming through the door, shouting, hollering, obviously approaching a state of inebriation, but I didn't care. They were here, flooding the Dreamland: Luverne and Mary Haas, Bill and Laura Mans, Cy and Bessie Benda, Bert and Addie Majerus, Art and Jules Lohman, Julius and Evelyn Ebe, Jean and Les Banidt, Blanche and Lloyd Cook, Dodie and George Gorman, Leone and Casey Ryan, and Mother! bless her Jesus, Mary and Joseph heart. I could hardly remember the melody, I was so excited. They didn't even sit down, instead immediately flooding the dance floor, hugging the bandstand like teenagers at a Frank Sinatra concert.*

"Hi ya, Jim. Glad you came home."

"Good band, Jimmy. Batting a thousand! Just like the old days."

"Didn't think you could do it, Jim, but you did. Dreamland is wonderful."

"Oh, you kid!"

"Not too shabby, Jim. Just like Whoopee John. Play 'Woodchopper's Ball' *for us."*

"Welcome home, kid."

They went on and on, dancing to my best arrangements, drinking Grain Belt and Seven Sevens, talking while dancing, music floating throughout the ballroom, melodies and harmonies and memories being released from long dormant walls, a long dormant ballroom floor where so many years ago bands had played long into the prairie night, folks dancing themselves crazy doing the Lindy-Hop, the Black Bottom, the Charleston, dancing across the county, across Dreamland.

We played for hours, long into the night, folks

enjoying themselves just like the good old days. Finally, one o'clock approached, time for the last dance. I called up "Moonlight Serenade," Glenn Miller's famous closer, our closer with my new arrangement. The saxes began with sweet, lush chords, folks clinging to each other for the last dance, their last high school dance, their last wedding dance, remembering youthful days before the children had arrived, before the Great Depression, before heartaches and good-aches. I stood on the front of the bandstand, sax in hand leading the harmonic saxes, muted trumpets punctuating my arrangement. I didn't want the arrangement to end, the night to end, but there would be more. It was going to be all right. Dreamland was again, dreaming.

As we finished "Moonlight Serenade," the final chord floating ever so slowly past the mirrored globe, folks crowding the bandstand clapping, a lone, disheveled figure pushed its way through the bedecked revelers, limping, shuffling slowly to the bandstand.

"You play 'Melancholy Baby' for me, Jimmy?" Erv asked, leaning precariously on the bandstand's edge, folks backing away from his whiskey-tainted breath and disheveled appearance.

"Sure Erv, we'll play it for you. 'Melancholy Baby' for Erv," I called out to the band.

"Jimmy!" he shouted and slurred. "Just you and your clarinet, like the old days. No band," Erv pleaded, wobbling on spindly legs.

"But, Erv . . . okay, just my clarinet."

I began the verse, soft and low, just my clarinet and Erv, the crowd standing silent, swaying, once again inching toward the bandstand, crowding Erv despite his aroma.

Come sweetheart mine,
Don't sit and pine,
Tell me of the cares that make you feel so blue.

Reaching the chorus, I wasn't in Dreamland any-more, just a high school kid playing for Erv out on the street.

Come to me, my melancholy baby,
Cuddle up and don't be blue,
All your fears are foolish fancy, maybe,
You know, dear that I'm in love with you.

Playing for him had been important then; it was important now. I choked up playing the floating melody now reaching the dusty rafters, lyrical notes merging with bands of earlier times—Rehder's Orchestra, Ben Gorman's Orchestra, "Melancholy Baby" becoming part of Dreamland memories. Erv wobbled and swayed but hung on as I approached the closing chords, descending lower, softer.

Ev'ry cloud must have a silver lining,
Wait until the sun shines through.
Smile my honey dear,
While I kiss away each tear,
Or else I shall be melancholy too.

I finished, letting the last tones linger over the ballroom. Hushed, eerily silent, the crowd mesmerized, not talking, not walking.

"Thanks, Jimmy," Erv whispered, "thanks," a tear running down his reddened cheek. He pushed through the breaching crowd and shuffled out onto his lonesome street.

Well . . . dreaming of the Dreamland became just that, dreaming. While the Moonmisters played "Moonlight in Vermont," "Leap Frog," and "Moonlight Serenade" during my final three years, I kept Dreamland alive. Someday, the good Lord, the abbot, the monks willing, it would happen.

Sophomore year turned into junior, junior into senior with advanced classes, study, exams, chorus and band tours of the Upper Midwest where we evangelized Catholic chants to forlorn North Dakota parishioners. As we carried the Benedictine Rule into the hinterland, the Johnnie family threatened to become a life-long experience for me. Sister Rose eventually stopped sticking cadavers in Duluth, escaped the brutal, bitter Midwest winters by following John Muir's footprints to the sunny West. Tom gained Expert status on his M-1 rifle, then muscled army deuce-and-a-half trucks throughout Germany toting engraved porcelain beer steins to officer's clubs, never actually shooting his rifle, the ghosts of Hitler long having disappeared. Mother and Bill sojourned the country viewing the Black Hills in North or South Dakota, the Grand Canyon, the Golden Gate Bridge, travel experiences Lucy never had with our paltry family finances. Were we poor during the forties and fifties? I don't think so. No worse nor better than anyone else in the village. And Dad rested in St. Columbkill's Cemetery, securing the Franklin family roots, patiently waiting for the rest of us to join him.

Chuck G. continued tossing Latin phrases at me in his basso voice. John worked his engineering slide rule so much that he burned out three, yet I never understood how such an implement worked. Bookie's viner, yes, John's slide rule, no. Bill read western history and eastern philosophy and mystical theology, but "Blue Flame" Bernie never farted on campus again. I wrote four-part harmony in Music Theory and Counterpoint classes, orches-trated inane Mozart sonatas for Concert Band, studied Bach, Beethoven and Brahms for credit, and Stan Kenton for myself. I wrote elementary arrangements for the Moonmisters in the insip-id, boring style of Guy Lombardo, learning the craft by trial and error, mostly error. Besides music classes, I faithfully attended classes in Philosophy, Logic, Ethics, English Literature, Biology, ROTC and Science. I was gaining a humanistic education, a liberal education to coincide with my liberal views that were expanding through readings, lectures and fellow Johnnies' alternate points of view on values I had held sacred. Yet, I never discarded Uncle Dave's or Dennis' or George's or Bookie's village philosophies, only expanded upon them, reading, studying, listening, discussing and contemplating, late nights out behind the darkened monastery. It helped me become more mature, if not wiser, values of which I was in dire need.

As a senior I took a religion class with a visiting professor, a Lutheran arriving unaccompanied from Luther College, Decorah, Iowa. This was an earth-shattering, if not Vatican-shattering event for the late fifties. "Ecumenical" hadn't even been invented yet. But St. John's was a progressive college, despite being Catholic, actually considering academic study of other religions. Of course, it perpetuated Catholicism, even sending Black Robes to Europe where they rode third-class donkeys on mountain top trails seeking secluded monasteries to microfilm centuries-old, decaying manuscripts. Yet, the head priests were also objective, I think. They invited Eastern Orthodox priests to lecture, to celebrate the Eastern Rite Mass. They invited bishops, archbishops and cardinals—no acolytes or incense burners—to campus for seminars, workshops and retreats. Even the famous Trappist monk, Thomas Merton, visited campus the summer of '57 to tell postulant seminarians what they might expect living the life of a monk. I didn't meet him, being back in the village killing those damn little pea lice, but his mystical ghost haunted the campus for many years.

I might have thought about becoming a priest at one time. I think Mother would have been village proud; however, I never worked my way up the Church's hierarchy any farther than acolyte, just a level one Catholic a notch higher than an ordinary pew parishioner. This was similar to progressing no farther than a Boy Scout Tenderfoot tying square knots, learning the semaphore alphabet, lighting fires without matches, never achieving Eagle Scout status. After acolyte one could become a subdeacon, deacon, postulant, seminarian, priest, monsignor, bishop, archbishop, cardinal, pope. That was it. When you reached pope-dom you reached the pinnacle. You couldn't go any farther, alive. Only saints and archangels remained on the hierarchical steps to eternity.

The visiting professor was the Reverend Loren, a grandson of the famous Vilhelm Loren, the epitome of Lutheranism in northern Iowa and southern Minnesota, despite occasional disagreements with Minnesota's Revered Muus, the progenitor of Northfield's St. Olaf's College. I shuffled into the ecclesiastical classroom carrying a ton of apprehension, not sure if I wanted to actually *learn* about Protestants, about Lutheranism. I knew what I knew and I wanted to hold those beliefs sacred. Oh, I was slowly expanding my views of the world's religions and theology and logical logic, but I wasn't ready to become a full-fledged Protestant. But the Reverend Loren surprised me, being an erudite speaker, logical, objective in his point of view, in addition to not *looking* like a Lutheran theological professor. He was handsome with lightly graying, close-cut hair, sharp angular facial features, and he didn't wear a one hundred-year-old, threadbare drab suit as I had anticipated. Instead, he wore casual, pleated brown slacks and an open collared, long sleeve sport shirt. He could have been a movie star. He didn't arrive on our campus defensively, even though he was in *enemy* territory. He hadn't arrived with bodyguards, only with his concordant Bible and theology books.

Loren lectured about the early days of Christianity—Paul's letters to everybody, the catacombs, the lions, the martyrs, the popes, the abuses of the church, the many centuries when the church didn't know if it would become The Church. There had been Roman conquests with sprawling empires, Charlemagne (Roman Emperor 800–814), St. Thomas Aquinas trying to help the cause, and the devastating schism of the Greek Catholics in 1054. The future of The Church was in doubt for centuries. But faith prevailed, Loren lectured. The Church maintained its theological positions, fighting Islam during the First Crusade of 1095, Buddhism and all the other *isms* threatening the one true church.

By the fourth week of the course Reverend Loren had attacked his Martin Luther lectures. Well, things had been going well until this point as we read about the first fourteen centuries of the Roman and Eastern Orthodox Churches, events going well enough with Christianity until those Easterners decided they didn't believe everything the Vicar of Christ enunciated from his Vatican balcony, the Orthos finally cutting loose from Rome in

1054, yet not actually starting a *new* church like Martin was later to do. I anticipated increasing trepidation studying Martin Luther. But Loren remained calm, objective while lecturing that Martin had been a Catholic priest, an Augustinian monk even, something I hadn't realized back in the village. Loren said Martin was from humble Germanic stock, that he had been a Doctor of Philosophy, a professor at Wittenberg University when he started all the brouhaha with the now schism'd-split Roman Church. Loren said Luther wasn't intending to break away from The Church, being only an inquisitive theology professor like the good fathers here at St. John's, he said. Luther only tried to address complex theological issues of the day—the sale of indulgences, getting penance right, reducing the number of sacraments, abolishing priestly celibacy. Loren said Luther might have gone overboard a bit when he nailed his 95 Theses, "On The Sale of Indulgences," to Castle Church's door in 1517—the church janitor extremely unhappy about that—but then Martin had always thought for himself, had always been impetuous as a child, being of humble peasant stock. Martin thought he was only bringing attention to these issues, but the pope didn't see it that way. The pope got downright mad, downright disgusted with Martin. That wasn't any way to treat the Vatican, The Church. The pope whipped out his quill pen, called a red-capped cardinal for parchment, and excommunicated Martin with a swish of his quill, sealing Martin's demise with hot wax. The pope wasn't about to stand for insubordination. Well, Loren said, the pope's UPS (Ultra Pious Subordination) letter surprised Martin, but he stood firm in his beliefs about the need to reform the Romans and their extensive abuses. And as long as he had been excommunicated, no longer having a church, he might as well start one. Luther became Lutheranism, not Martinism. Folks began signing up.

Well, I hadn't thought much about the sacrament of penance other than practicing it faithfully for my many impure thoughts and actions, they being many, nasty, and worthy of extensive soul purging through prayer and flagellation on the exposed streets of the village, according to Fr. Smith. I hadn't pondered there being *seven* sacraments, only taking them for granted and one by one working through Baptism, Confirmation, the Eucharist, penance, someday hoping to gain Matrimony, and finally Extreme Unction before joining Dad in St. Columbkill's Cemetery. I hadn't meditated nights about indulgences, whether one could buy grace to gain grace, as peasants had done in Luther's time. Oh, Mother lit her red and blue votive candles often, as did other parish Ladies of Fervor, slipping a nickel or dime into the container next to the altar. But to me, that was just Catholicism. Mother was beyond buying her way into heaven, although an extra nickel or dime here and there might reduce some temporal punishment. But Martin said those things had gotten out of hand and he was damn mad about it. He'd sure correct those abuses in *his* Church.

As the semester progressed, as I read about Luther's grievances, as I learned about the alleged abuses of The Church, I began reflecting upon this whole issue of religious belief. It was becoming apparent there were more theological beliefs than Catholicism; that Lutheranism wasn't that far removed from Catholicism. Confessing to a priest was an issue with Martin. Adoring the Blessed Virgin Mary was an issue, but the most relevant issue was Jesus Christ himself and Luther hadn't thrown baby Jesus out with the holy water. Protestants believed in Christ. Luther had only been protesting some of the activities of the Roman Church, not Christ. On the other hand, Buddhists believe in the Big Fat Buddha, not Jesus Christ. Islam believes in Allah, their god being brought by messenger Mohammed to somewhere around Mecca. The Jews believe there was a Jesus Christ; they just didn't think he was God, The Unitarians believe in something, but don' know what it is.

For the final exam we were to write an essay on The Church and Luther's impact on Christianity. In my blue book I expounded, as directed, and in a postscript wrote that I might have shown prejudice back in the village—in a personal way rather by out right persecution—but that I understood better now. I would atone for my sins. I said I wasn't ready to become a Lutheran yet, but was glad I had taken the course and had been exposed to Rev. Loren. I hoped, in the future, to work with all faiths for the betterment of God's people. Oh, yes, I also said he was an exemplary professor, hoping for an *A*.

Having passed through Ethics, Church History, Marriage and the Family, Martin Luther, Music Theory, plus ROTC, I was now ready for my final semester. I had been dating Becky for three years, experiencing anxiety with the Church's teaching on sex and life and girls, and well . . . I was confused, but not yet ready to abandon priestly celibacy as Luther professed in one of his 95 Theses. I wasn't ready to nail the St. John's Cathedral door with 95 Reasons Sex and Confession Don't Mix. I wasn't ready to be excommunicated.

Finding resolution between testosterone drives and the Church's teaching on sex before, during or after marriage, was proving to be difficult for every hot-blooded Johnnie, other than the seminarians blessed with celibacy. Late nights, the fellows would lounge in dorm rooms talking about dating and girls, necking and blue balls, "feeling-up" and screwing. There were many different opinions . . .

"The Church says we have to wait until we're married."

"That's bullshit! How the hell you gonna do that?"

"Intercourse before marriage is a mortal sin."

"You mean 'fucking'? "

"Who the hell told you that?"

"How do we find out about a girl, whether we want to marry her, without screwing her first. I want to know what I'm buying."

"I don't think that's what the church is saying. It's saying, respect sex."

"I got a lot of respect for it. I respect it so much it's all I think about."

"What do you say in confession after a date?"

"Me? Hell, I don't go to confession. Just keep it to myself. The Lord gave me a cock and he must figure I'm gonna use it."

"I set boundaries. A little feeling of her tits is okay, letting my hands roam over her body, above the belt, but I guess I draw the line at screwing. I'd have to tell that in confession."

"I don't think we can do anything but talk to girls, light kissing and no French kissing."

"Good luck, Seminarian!"

We never did find resolution to the age-old question of resolving testosterone levels while getting closer to what we wanted to get closer to while simultaneously remaining good Catholic boys. I guess every guy had to make up his own mind. I did.

Becky and I explored our sexuality, Friday nights after a dance or movie, off campus, of course. The classic-looking Becky with deep set dark eyes, pointed chin and high cheekbones, was a cloister-influenced "appropriate" girl, yet over the three years we had dated, she had moved beyond the cloister, beyond the Black Hoods to think for herself. I was still more Church conservative than she, an element causing anxiety in our growing relationship. One spring afternoon, after a day of swimming at a campground picnic with other Bennies and Johnnies, after drinking a keg of beer all day, she lambasted me, accusing me of being a priest. She said I was carrying my celibacy too far. Ouch! That hurt. She said I should just go back and join the seminary if I didn't want to use it. I retorted that it wasn't that I wasn't interested in intercourse; it's just that I didn't want to go to hell for doing it. She laughed a low, rumbling, inebriated laugh, more of a cynical chide than a laugh, vomited on her swim suit and my front seat before releasing a decidedly non-Benedictine phrase . . . "Fuck that!"

"But, Becky! The Church is very distinct on this issue, we . . . ,"

"Fuck the church! Fuck the pope!" she retorted, the last words out of her that night as she suddenly lapsed into a drunken coma. I drove her home, carried her into the house, propped her on the davenport and departed for the Seminary.

Oh, I didn't actually join the Seminary, and Becky later apologized. We eventually kissed more deeply than ever, explored each other more thoroughly, and well . . . she was influencing me on the long, circuitous road to sexual behavior, whether before, during or after marriage. I'd work out the 95 sex theses later. I had more homework to do. It would take some time.

December 1957, one week before Christmas vacation, Fr. Casper banged loud and long on my door. "Phone call for you, Jim. You can take it in my study." I brushed the sleep from my eyes wondering what on earth had happened to be called so late at night.

"Jim! Dick Ryan here. Dad died suddenly tonight. Heart attack," he said into my dumbfounded ears.

"Oh, God! Have mercy on his soul. Sorry to hear that. How's Mother?"

"Pretty upset. We're with her in Red Wing. You coming home?"

"Sure. I'll head right down. Tell Mother I'm on my way," I said before shuffling down the dim, deserted hall to tell Chuck of Bill Ryan's death. I stuffed a bag with dirty laundry, left notes for my professors via Chuck, then fired up the cold, insubordinate Ford. I drove to the village through the bleak night to bury another dad, this time a stepdad. Damn! The somber night and swirling snow mesmerized me as I passed through Elk River, Anoka, the Twin Cites, Cannon Falls to County Road No. 9. This isn't fair, I cried. Mother and Bill had been married only four years, a good second marriage for both. It just wasn't fair, I thought, approaching Belle Creek Township on No. 9.

We properly waked Bill Ryan in his farm home, just as we had done for my real father four years earlier in the village. The undertaker placed Bill's gray casket in the tiny living room surrounded by almost everyone he had known his entire life, at least by those who hadn't preceded him in death. "Ryan" had probably been "O'Ryan" back on the Old Sod and in the early days of this predominately Irish township. The O's were all there: O'Reillys, O'Connors, O'Rourkes, O'Gormans, O'Neills, plus an assortment of forfeited O's, the McNamaras, Ryans, Gadients, Hutchesons, Heaneys and one O'Franklin from St. John's.

Mother almost collapsed during the wake as she had done four years earlier that nasty, rainy November day of '51. Mother didn't like death, having already buried Dad, plus two mothers, a father, several brothers and sisters, brothers- and sisters-in-law, sister Marie Haustein who succumbed to cancer before it was fashionable; Anne Franklin and Jim Franklin departing the county way too soon. Now, Bill, a husband, a friend, a childhood buddy of Thomas B. Franklin. It didn't make sense to me as I steadied her while looking at Bill in his casket. He looked good in his double breasted suit, they said on the couch. He looked so natural with high cheekbones prominent on his chiseled face, they said in the kitchen. He didn't look a day over fifty, the smokers said out by the barn. But he was dead. Dead is dead. No more. Never to come back. But he did look good, I said. Mother brushed his hand, straightened his gray hair, shed a hundred tears as I helped her to the couch.

More folks than I had ever seen at a St. Columbkill's mass stuffed the house toting a bountiful harvest: hotdishes of every size and shape, scalloped potatoes, hams, roast beef, apple pies, cakes, bitter coffee and tangy beer. Irish wakes weren't about to be devoid of beer. It flowed freely. It helped the deceased enter purgatory, if not heaven, they said. It helped those who remained on earth to deal with the departed's departure, they said. Sure and begorra, it was the right thing to do, they said.

Eight o'clock, Father entered the grieving house to say the rosary, slicing his way through mourners toward Bill . . .

"In the name of the Father, and of the Son and of the Holy Ghost . . . ,"

"For the repose of the soul of William C. Ryan . . . ,"

"The Sorrowful Mysteries . . . ,"

"Hail Mary, full of grace . . . ,"

Mother tried to kneel in front of the casket, but she had difficulty, her hands and legs shaking so much she could hardly hold the rosary. I held my rosary with one hand, Mother with the other while Dick and Shorty steadied her on the other side, both sharing the grief of their dad. Eighty-five folks prayed the rosary, beads clicking like locusts attacking Bill's cornfield. Hail Marys to the number of 1850 were intoned to help Bill on his road to heaven.

The atmosphere lightened after the rosary, folks now drinking beer and attacking a heaping table. Mother even relaxed a little, surrounded by so many friends and relatives. They ate ham sandwiches and told stories of Bill, far-fetched stories, too. They reminisced and joshed and said what a good man he was, and he was; how they would miss him, and they would; how things in Belle Creek wouldn't be the same without him, and they wouldn't. Bill Ryan had entered the township sixty-plus years ago, brought three or four children into the land, and buried wife Julia in the deep black soil just up the road. He would now join her.

We put Bill down the next day, several graves downwind from my father. I held one of Mother's arms, Dick Ryan the other as the pall bearers lowered the casket into the hollow vault. Mother cried as much over Bill as she had over Dad. "May his soul and the souls of all the dearly departed rest in peace. Amen," Fr. intoned, mourners huddled like cattle, snow covering the casket.

As Dick escorted Mother to the car, I took a moment to walk to Dad's grave, peering down on the site where Mother, Tom, Rose and I had grieved over only four years ago. Now death had made a house call again. "Well, Dad," I whispered. "Your old friend Bill has come to join you. *Pox vobiscum.*"

Deep snow and ice had encased the campus when I returned for my final semester. Bill's death and Mother's second widowhood had set me back, too, but I needed to refocus my efforts, make the final push toward a May graduation. I wasn't about to let down now.

The Chorus toured Milwaukee and Chicago in February, spreading our Gregorian chanting to audiences who had never heard stoical monk chanting. The Concert Band toured Central Minnesota in the spring bringing Strauss' tone poem, *Death and Transfiguration,* to isolated Germans who would rather have heard two-beat polkas. And the Moonmisters rehearsed monk music, too, Thelonious Monk, late nights in the Music Hall when the real monks slept on straw mattresses, no smoking allowed. We played for hot-and-bothered college dancers during winter weekends, pimple-faced high school teenagers for spring proms. Four years had passed much too quickly, yet I was happy I had chosen music as a major, despite Fr. James' underwhelming initial reception. I had completed my requirements for teacher certification, had student-taught band and chorus at John's Forest Lake High School, although I still didn't see myself as a music educator teaching students like Noisy Rusch and Jimmy Ryan and Kenny Hudson or Gloria and Anita Erickson. On second thought, teaching Gloria and Anita would be a joy. I had been in love with both high school sisters as a sixth grader.

As the vise-gripped winter gradually dropped its death mask, I began considering additional music study—after taking an ROTC-Army tour of duty, that is—possibly at Boston's Berkeley Jazz School. I still dreamed of becoming a professional jazz musician, dreamed of bringing my own big band back to the Dreamland just like Ben Gorman.

Weekends, Becky and I continued exploring our sexuality, continued seeking resolution between burgeoning hormones and the Church's antiquated position concerning proper sexual behavior. We were making progress, but not necessarily in favor of the Church. Chuck had mastered Latin by the fourth year, plus elevating the role of Shakespeare's Shylock to new heights. John had burned out his sixth engineering slide rule, while Bill had decided to enter graduate school at the University of Chicago to study advanced mystical theology, whatever that was. By early May we all realized we were approaching the end of a notable experience.

Saturday night, one week before graduation, the four headed to St. Cloud in the gray Ford, just for old times' sake.

"Bill, you're off to Chicago to study Mystical Theology, you say? What the hell are you going to do with that?" John asked, continuing his four-year chiding as we snaked through the serpentine pine drive that had encased us the past four years.

"Study, write, teach at a university. Maybe return to St. John's as a faculty prof someday," Bill said as I whipped the Ford onto the main highway.

"How about you Chuck?" John inquired. "What are your plans? Become a Latin teacher?" he chided as we drove through the burg of St. Joseph's and the Benny college.

"Possibly, John, but I doubt it. It's just been good for my brain. Makes me think," Chuck said. "I'm thinking of graduate school, like Bill, maybe St. Louis University in theater. Got the army to do first, though."

"What about you Jimmy? Gonna play that saxophone professionally?"

"Sure would like to, John. Maybe a jazz school, but like Chuck and you, we have army duty first."

We drove into St. Cloud, the Ford interior uncharacteristically serene, four fellows apparently realizing this impending commencement was an ending. We had been together four years—friends, musical compatriots, just a quartet in the larger Johnnie family. We had entered green, timid, untested, unlearned, at least I had, but now I could say "mystical theology" as well as "plausible" and "erudite," although I probably wasn't it. We had studied our chosen disciplines, read theology and ethics, English Lit. and World History, plus shuffling hundreds of times under the twin-towered cathedral, through the monastic quadrangle while watching serpentine Black Robes sliding to the monastery's inner sanctum, dedicated men devoting their lives to saving their souls. We had attended classes with first and second year seminarians, none of us four transferring to the Seminary, although each had considered it. But well, that female attraction had just been too strong.

In one week we would receive bachelor's degrees, mine a B.S. instead of a B.A., maybe because of no Latin. Although in the village I had often been chided for slinging B.S., now I could do it officially, "Jim Franklin, B.S." Soon, I would have earned a degree in music education and a brass bar on my shoulder as a second lieutenant. Both would certainly be a big change, but the biggest change wasn't to be the degree I would receive, but what had happened deep inside me these past four years. I had put on new clothes without throwing off the old. I had added new layers. I had gained perspectives on just about everyone and everything, most significantly, a more worldly view of people unlike me, people who hadn't grown up in the village, people with divergent ethnicity, different heritage, differing faiths. I could now look at

Lutherans in a new light, and they me, I hoped.

When Bill Ryan and Mother drove me out of the village on County Rd. No. 9 four years ago; when they abandoned me in front of St. Ben's Hall, I never thought I would get to this point, but I had made it. Bill Ryan didn't: *Ars longa, vita brevis* (Art is long, life is short). In a week I would return to the village, chat with the folks at Heaney & Gorman around the potbellied stove and hold my head high. I hadn't let Dennis Heaney down . . . or myself.

Pox

Chapter 5

Chicken in a basket

Lower Street c. 1920

*Y*OU'RE NEVER A PROPHET IN YOUR OWN HOMETOWN
(SORT-OF MARK 6:4)
    I had been away from the village four academic years, that
B.S. now ensconced securely behind my name, if not on my sleeve.
But when I returned that summer of '58, the B.S. might as well have

been B.C.—"Basket Chicken." After earning a bachelor's degree and ROTC commission, I had six months to kill before reporting for an army tour of duty. No longer killing lice or pitching peas, I was in dire need of cash the day I sauntered into the Lensch & Rusch chicken and egg store.

"How they hangin', Jimmy? Finally let you out of college I see," Noisy hollered from the candling room where he and Harold candled eggs by the hundreds throughout the day, thousands throughout the year. Harold and Noisy received cartons of fresh eggs from farmers' hens, placed each egg in front of a lighted enclosure, inspected it to determine if it was a good egg or a bad egg (like some villagers), then separated them into good and bad cartons (the eggs, that is).

"Hi, Noisy. Yes, they finally let me out. In fact, the Benedictines told me to get the hell out, never come back. Said I should go back down south to live with you Lutherans," I chided, Noisy now setting upon two cartons of fresh eggs to candle.

"I'll bet they did, but even the Lutherans don't want you, Jimmy. What the hell you gonna do with yourself now? Teach that sissified music instead of being a basketball coach like I told you when you left high school."

"I'll probably teach music, but I have to complete my six-month army duty first. I don't report until November, so I'm looking for work until then. I didn't get on with Libby's this summer. Guess they found some new fellows to kill those green lice."

"We've got a job for you, Jim," Harold said as he worked his way through a carton of eggs in the store the two fellows had bought from Naurice Husbyn a few years back. If chickens and eggs were your thing, this was your poultry store. Chicken feed and chicken wire and chicken syrup and chicken photos—Bantams, Rhode Island White, Leghorns, Plymouth Rocks—filled the walls, shelves and floors, and . . . well, the old store had been everything "chicken" since Jim Ryan owned it, then Husbyn, then Lensch & Rusch. The grainy aroma of the store was "chicken" also, but it was a good place to sit on a feed sack and chat with the fellows long into the afternoon. "Our chicken cages and baskets out back need cleaning. How'd you like to clean 'em?" Harold asked as John Stenlund banged through the screen door to buy chicken feed or chicken supplement or maybe just chickens.

To be truthful, I wasn't excited about cleaning chicken cages and baskets caked with months of chicken shit after having become a college graduate. I had just devoted four years to studying world history, logic and illogic, philosophy and religion, music and army. I had read, by candlelight, deep into the monastic night about diverse academic disciplines, expanding my views and philosophies of life beyond the village, but now found myself right back where I had been four years ago. But I needed work. I accepted Harold's offer.

You're never a prophet in your hometown. That's a good aphorism. It keeps one humble, keeps one from getting a big head, keeps one from getting high falutin' ideas, as Mother so often admonished. Regardless of what one does away from the ol' neighborhood, the ol' hometown, folks remember your growing-up years. Oh, they're proud when a fellow or gal goes on to become a high court judge like Gerald Heaney; captains a battleship like Phil Ryan; becomes a lawyer or doctor, successful businessman or business woman, even a teacher. Yet, when those "accomplished" return to the village they're simply Gerald or Phil or Tom or Margaret or Dave or Bob. Those guilty of pride when away from the village quickly receive their comeuppance upon returning. Hometown folks remember you picking your nose in church, wrecking your bicycle near Lohman's Standard Oil, forgetting your lines in the GHS junior class play, forgetting your clarinet solo in the middle, tripping over your graduation gown hem while attempting to act dignified, even pissing on their laps when you were a baby. They remember your miscalculations, your child-hood ways. They remember your long nose, your pimples, your gangly legs, your big boobs, your little boobs, your frequent farting, your failures. But they never *thought* of you as a failure. Their recollections aren't negative; they simply remember you as you were while in their midst, as you will always be regardless of the letters behind your name: M.A. or Ph.D. or Colonel or Major or Captain or J.A.G. or Judge. They let you know they are proud of your accomplishments, but you aren't any better than the fellows and gals who stayed home, on the farm, in the village. And don't you forget it.

Bob and I had been among the first few GHS graduates to enroll in college, not that that was any particular accolade, you understand. Phil Ryan, Class of '44, entered the Naval Academy to play tight end for the Middies; Sigvard Stenlund, Class of '50, entered Rev. Muus' St. Olaf College to study nuclear physics or analytic chemistry after playing loose end on the '47 GHS football team; Jimmy Ryan, Class of '50, matriculated to St. Thomas, but left his tenor sax in the village; George O'Reilly, Class of '51, entered Winona State and became a basketball star downriver from his home court; and Dave Hutcheson, Class of '53, entered St. John's a year before me, preparing for me, the monastic way.

Many GHS graduates before the Class of 1950 returned to the farm to till and plow and thresh and milk and bale hay, continuing the tradition of dad, grandfather, great-grandfather, later buying-out dad to maintain the Norwegian or Swedish or German or Irish or English immigrant-family tradition. Others preferred non-farm jobs—cutting soles at Red Wing Shoe, manufacturing pipe at Red Wing Sewer Pipe, soldering speaker wire at Wipperling's TV & Repair, stocking Campbell's Soup, Tide, and Wheaties at George Diercks' Grocery. Some elected to repair tractors, combines and hay balers at Lodermeier's, earning money for that sparkling new Chevrolet 6 or Ford V-8 with which to date Shirley or Donna or Arlene or Phyllis or Mary Lou lest their mothers think they would become old maids, a millstone, for sure. They raised children to enter GHS so they could, inturn, take over the farm or the shop when the folks retired. A circuitous journey.

But as the college trend of the mid-to-late fifties began, more graduates worked a year or two in the area, later entering college, realizing that just keeping the farm going, just doing what dad had done wasn't necessarily good enough anymore. Good, honorable, but not enough. Continuing one's education at a college wasn't something forties and fifties' GHS teachers—Ray Baty, Suzanne North, Gloria Cree, Enoch Bennett, Gordon Foss, Don Hilling, Bernie Johnson—encouraged graduates to do, although Chas

Wood did encourage me to practice more and go on to college music. I gave it little thought. But classmate Sandbox Bob had startled me shuffling home from high school one day by saying, maybe taunting, that he had decided to enroll at St. Thomas in the fall. Damn! I thought, now Bob has gone and done it again. He's gotten ahead of me once more. But I was cool, simply responding, "Well, that's fine, Bob. Hope you do well, 'course you always do." We parted at the evergreen path near his decaying sandbox just downwind from my dilapidated tree house. But Bob had gotten me to weighing college. I couldn't let him get ahead of me again, I thought, traipsing into the house that day.

Bob had provided intense competition, whether in the sandbox, during our Dixie Cup "telephone" conversations, chatting about movie stars, building model airplanes, memorizing and reciting the *Baltimore Catechism*, even discussing Shakespeare, a name I couldn't even pronounce, much less discuss. Bob had challenged me every day since that first day we trudged to school together, he bragging about his bologna with mustard sandwich being better than my peanut butter and jelly. Geez! Bob even played clarinet alongside me throughout grade school and high school, challenging me with better notes and better seat positions. The only area I got one-upmanship on Sandbox Bob was in sports. But then, he had simply conceded sports to me. I didn't actually beat him on that account. He just wasn't interested, he said, thereby denying me the victory I rightfully deserved. But if Bob was going to college, I would too, I decided, skipping the stairs to my bedroom, looking through the stained window across the yard to his bedroom, wondering where in hell he got the college idea.

Well . . . four years later Robert Roger "Sandbox" O'Reilly graduated from St. Thomas in St. Paul the same day—an hour earlier, ol' one-upmanship Bob—than me from St. John's, two neighborhood tikes who had read "Dick and Jane" together, had practiced the Palmer Writing Method together, had chewed the host with our teeth instead of tongues during First Communion, had received the Holy Ghost during Confirmation, the spirit easily penetrating the holy ceiling of Holy Trinity breaking nary a shingle nor rafter.

I was proud of my B.S. or "B.C." degree, so I didn't mind attacking those imposing chicken cages and baskets Monday morning dressed in Oshkosh-Bigosh bib overalls, blue flannel plaid shirt, three-buckle boots, tattered and pea-stained baseball cap, and a red handkerchief tied across my nose and mouth. I climbed and scraped and cleaned and shoveled and wheel-barrow'd more chicken droppings that week than I had ever imagined existed in the village. I had worked in cages before—Dennis Heaney's freezing Locker cages—but this was a messy cage job. Yet, I didn't complain . . . much. I had my degree. I was back in the village. I would enter Ft. Benning in November leaving six months to work, enjoy the village, love Sharon, play softball with Cueball and Gary Holtz, Bob Madrick, Elroy Schulz, Dallas Diercks, the boys. I would find other work after cleaning these shitty cages. Things were looking up. Not so bad.

By late Friday afternoon I had scraped, scoured and hosed fifty wire cages and baskets before driving to Red Wing, now living with twice-widowed Mother for the summer. I showered quickly before heading out to see Sharon, chicken odor encased in my tender, academic nostrils. Hopping into the Ford, I was clean and tidy on the outside, but needing weeks to rid myself of that caustic odor. This night, speeding toward Sharon's house, I was hopeful her sweet lilac aroma would overwhelm my pungent chicken odor.

Sharon had returned from Iowa U for the summer, I desperately hoping our summer romance would continue before I infiltrated the army in Dixieland. I had dated Becky at college while Sharon dated some brutish Iowa Hawkeye. We were now back home, ready to resume our summer romance.

She skipped down the circuitous sidewalk as I pulled up to the curb, her manner dazzling, fresh as spring water on the Mississippi, sparkling, nubile, like a dancing nymph in the Swan Lake Ballet. I became increasingly excited, certainly more so than when shoveling chicken droppings. But there was no comparison with this "chick," soon to be sitting on my lap and the chicks I had recently dispensed with. She hopped into my car, threw her arms around me before I had even set the parking brake. She placed a heavenly-deep French kiss on me, or in me, taking my breath away. I hoped she couldn't smell or taste chicken on me; if so, she didn't mention it. Quickly, her seductive heat began infiltrating my shirt, my chest, my face, my cheeks, my groin. I returned her embrace with all the gusto I could muster. God! she felt good. Suddenly, I sensed the car backing down the hill, the parking brake not set. I had to break her embrace to brake the car.

"Damn! It's good to see you, Sharon," I said, securing the Ford's rear wheels on the curb.

"You too, Jim, you too," she whispered, again enveloping me in her tender arms while brushing her pink, pointed tongue on my sensitive ear. We tussled until the sun began setting beyond the western bluffs encircling the Red Wing valley, soft rays casting a golden hue upon her face. I had romanced Becky the past three years at college, but we both assumed it ended graduation day, me going my way, Becky her's. Yet, it had been fulfilling for both of us, an "appropriate" college romance, and we had also moved toward resolving our hormonal levels versus the church's dogmatic position on sex—before, during or after marriage. This summer, with Sharon, I hoped for additional research and homework on that subject. I had been hoping she would be cooperative in our mutual study. This day, she was.

Although happy not to be cleaning chicken cages, I was now jobless, needing another for the summer months. I sauntered the streets talking, reconnecting with folks I hadn't seen for a summer or a year. I shuffled to the Goodhue Elevator hoping to see Ray Banidt, but found he had retired, replaced by Gene Jensen in March. I didn't know Jensen, so I bypassed the Elevator, moseying up to the Creamery to see what was happening. I had visited the Creamery often with Dad, he being a milk hauler in the forties, Fritz Shorter manager. Dad dumped eighty-pound milk cans by the hundreds for years, long before anyone thought of "drying" milk. The Creamery had now expanded their facilities with milk-drying equipment, Milo Swenke manager. Milo was cleaning a vat as I sauntered in . . .

"Hi, Jimmy! How the hell you doin'? Haven't seen you in a coon's age, since givin' you a lift couple years ago," he said, his white-capped head deep inside the butter vat.

"Hi, Milo. Good to see you again. I'm doing fine; finally out of college. I even escaped without becoming a priest," I said, inspecting the new drying equipment. "How the heck do you dry milk?" I asked as he continued swabbing the stainless steel vat.

"We take some fat out. Don't actually dry it, you know. It's like drinking a dry martini . . . dry but wet."

"I've learned to drink beer, but haven't gotten the hang of drinking a martini. I'll just take your word for it."

"So, you graduate yet, then?"

"Couple of weeks ago. I'll be around for six months, looking for summer work now, then off to the infantry in November," I said, Milo finally escaping from the butter vat.

"I'd hire you, but don't need help now. Keep my eyes and ears open though. Something'll turn up," he said, retrieving the water hose to wash the vat. "Your dad used to haul milk here, didn't he?"

"Yes, sir. During the thirties and forties. Milk cans, dumping, cleaning, but you have bulk truck tanks now making it easier. Dad enjoyed it many years until the heavy lifting finally got too much for him. He sold out to Toby Buck, then became janitor for Supt. Hubert at the school."

"Well, Jimmy, things changin' all the time. Even Vasa and Bellechester are working with us on this new drying equipment. The business has changed since your dad hauled milk."

"You got that right, Milo, but I have to keep moving. Good to see you again," I said heading out to Upper Street.

The village was still, hushed, nary a dog barking, a screen door squeaking, a baby crying, only the rustle of leaves quaking in a high prairie breeze broke the tomblike silence as I sauntered down the street, my own footsteps adulterating the tranquillity with each crackling step. Being away had been good, my horizons having expanded beyond the coal silo, the Elevator, the Creamery, the old ball park, the lumber yard, water tank hill, Swenson's and Shelstad's cafes, Heaney & Gorman's and Diercks' markets. A wider perspective now extended beyond that invisible perimeter-barrier of this insulated community. Yet, being back was nice, returning to the ol' hometown remained important, even though my splintered family no longer lived here. The sequestered village was still a place where I felt comfortable. And I had learned there are several families in one's life, more than just one's immediate family. I had found a new family at St. John's, what would become life-long friends; the village was itself a "family;" high school classmates were a "family," parishioners, friends, relatives, villagers were "family."

The early June afternoon was unseasonably hot and drowsy as Ol' Buck, the unofficial Black Labrador village mascot, lounged between Ebe's Barber Shop and Gerken's Hardware (formerly Marshall-Wells). Tallgrasses attacking bottle-strewn vacant lots and poking up between sidewalk cracks waved like ripening wheat out on the high prairie. Some things hadn't changed, I thought, patting the relaxing Buck in the afternoon shade, his rich, black fur feeling soft, "welcoming" under my hand. Only two rusty, listing pickups plus one undertaker gray, four-door sedan rested on Upper Street near abandoned hitching posts, the horse carriages and wagons only a memory, the posts remnants of frontier days. This day was too nice for farmers sauntering into town. They were in the fields hoeing and disking and cultivating. And the village was off the beaten path for tourists.

Goodhue has always been a "necessary" town, folks bounding in to buy necessary items—groceries, bolts, propane, gasoline, chicken feed, hog feed. If they didn't have a good reason to come, they didn't. Tourists driving through on a Monday afternoon, a Saturday, a Sunday were unheard of. The only folks who drove as a pastime were Art Haas and Dave Franklin. Art would drive his huge four-holer Buick or Oldsmobile throughout the village for entertainment, taking a relaxed, leisurely break from serving whiskey sours at his bar. Uncle Dave would drive on dusty, gravel roads in the countryside peering over his ever-slipping glasses at waving, endless fields while hunting tiny Minnesota gophers, they even then threatening to overwhelm the state. The village was, indeed, a Carol Bly "Lost Swede Town," on the high prairie of Goodhue County, Minnesota.

Red Wing is a port town, having become a permanent white settlement after the Sioux settled at the base of Barn Bluff long before Daniel Gavin and Samuel Denton arrived on these banks to begin a white settlement. But Red Wing, versus Goodhue, had selected a scenic river location instead of a high, desolate prairie. In the early 1800s Red Wing welcomed explorers, steamboat captains, roustabouts, gamblers, hustlers, whores and suit-be-decked businessmen to build grain elevators, shoe factories, furniture factories, plus merchants—Josephson's Clothing, Johnson & Meyer Clothing, Swanson's & Sons, Ferrin Mortuary, the Corner Drug Store—catering to pioneers seeking restaurants, hotels, opera houses, theaters. But out in the village, "Ya, sure," fellas dawdled in the saloons on Lower Street across the road from the depot, not concerned whether businessmen hopped off the track to start up a mercantile store. They were here. It didn't make any difference to them if anyone else settled. So, Red Wing had a reason for being. Cannon Falls had a reason for being, its Cannon River dams grinding the county's finest wheat. Pine Island had a reason for being, they said, churning its butter to become the cheese capital of the county, even Minnesota. Wanamingo and Kenyon had a reason for being, they said, though I knew little about that part of the county. Both were settlements for Norwegian Lutherans who refused to settle with the Irish and Germans. But Goodhue Village didn't have a reason for being, they said, having neither expansive river scenery like Red Wing, dams like Cannon Falls, overwhelming Norwegians like Wanamingo and Kenyon, nor the New Englanders of Zumbrota. Even Bellechester had been built on a firmer foundation—blue clay—thinking it would become important someday. But the clay and Bellechester both played out. If the truth be told, the county, the state, the world could have gotten along very well without either Bellechester or Goodhue. There were enough settlements in the county already. Had it not been for the Duluth, Red Wing and Southern Railroad stretching tracks through the site in 1889 and building a station in the middle of wheat fields, few immigrant pioneers would have remained or moved here, electing instead to move on to Hay Creek or Vasa. The site would have become a ghost town like White Willow or Ryan or Roscoe, just a dry, lonely post office stop off the main stage route on the way to somewhere else, the site gradually fading into history, the railroad passing it by, maybe in the Belle Creek bottoms. But history had it that the railroad *did* come, helping the meager settlement to begin. There was a reason for the village after all.

I sat on the steps of the hardware store patting Ol' Buck, the laziest dog in the village, so lazy he hadn't noticeably moved during my four-year absence, what with fellows throwing him scraps, Julius keeping him watered. That dog had it made. I watched dust swirls twisting down Upper Street; white, fluffy dandelion snowballs dancing in the light breeze in random directions; butterflies floating lazily in the warm breeze letting it and the stagnant air determine their direction, any direction being good enough. A large, lovely yellow butterfly lit on top of an abandoned hitching post, now a resting place for the butterfly instead of a confining, long-lost horse post of frontier days. Last week's *Goodhue County Tribune* piled up against a snow fence in the alley, the fence staying up all year, folks not seeing the sense of taking it down for only three months. Annoying flies attacked my sweating brow. The town seemed more secluded, more cemetery quiet than I had recalled, but then I realized that *it* had stayed the same. *I* had changed.

St. John's nearest big town, St. Cloud, wasn't big like the Twin Cities, but it did have a pizza parlor, an elegant hotel with granite foyer and shoulder-high, porcelain urinals; a three-story department store; restaurants devoid of linoleum-topped tables serving coffee in porcelain cups instead of two-pound, white, indestructible mugs; menus from which you could order barbecue chicken with chives instead of pork roast and catsup with cottage cheese and cream-style corn; linguine pasta instead of roast beef, broccoli and asparagus instead of Libby's peas, even a tossed salad instead of coleslaw; where by nine o'clock red, white and blue neon lights flickered on Main Street enticing customers into stores and bars, the lights indicating a resemblance of night life; where marquees announced the latest movie in blinking lights. Goodhue owned none of that. The town hadn't seen neon until Mans' and

Benda outlined their Shell Station with red neon tubing about 1949, some townsfolk even upset at such ostentatiousness. Our burg had pockmarked dirt streets until the women of the community finally got up in arms about the dust infiltrating their prairie-plain, dreary parlors, demanding the city council repair the potholes, pave the streets, and install curbs. But this didn't occur until the early fifties.

Shoot! St. Cloud had a highway running through downtown, something our village fathers hadn't thought of when platting the site. Or maybe they had. Maybe they hadn't wanted a highway coming right though town like Red Wing and Zumbrota and Cannon Falls, the traffic disturbing tranquil ambiance with roaring, noxious trucks and speeding autos. Maybe the town fathers hadn't wanted that much activity, after all. Well, they got their wish. Old Highway 58 used to reach the village from about County Rd. No. 6, entering past the old ball diamond and school before exiting eastward on County Rd. 9. New Highway 58 later brushed the eastern town limit, skirting the village, leaving the town's streets just for locals. Out-of-towner cars are and were immediately recognizable, thereby providing the burg with a level of security it obviously desired. That skirting highway also reduced the need for a full-time town marshal in a half-time burg.

Peter Easterly had begun a hotel in the township in 1856. This was rich land, European immigrants soon realized, the soil deep, vibrant, full of untapped ingredients in virgin prairie. Why, some bragged that it was some of the best in Minnesota Territory. After a three-month, seasick, scurvy-filled emigration sail from Sweden or Norway or Germany or Austria or England or Luxembourg, pioneers had been pleased to settle in Minnesota land to begin homesteading, to raise a family. In the 1850s they were seeking security in a new land free of oppression and despair as they had experienced back in the Old Country. To later generations of children in the 1950s, 1960s, 1970s, the village may have been a place to escape *from*, but to their ancestors, it was a place to come *to,* to set down roots in heaven itself.

Drowsiness enveloped me as Ol' Buck, who had scarcely moved since I sat on the stoop, actually rolled over, nary a person on the street seeing his infrequent move. I glanced across the street to read "Sawyer Block" on top of a two-story brick commercial building. But I had lived here, full time, for only eighteen years. At age ten or fifteen I hadn't considered the beginnings of this town, only the town. I had studied World History and Music History the past four years generating an interest in Europe and Asia. Why not my hometown? I began pondering about Sawyer, about Quast, about Anderson and the settlers of this community who arrived long before my unceremonial entrance in 1936, and about those who had paved the way for the community long before getting around to paving the streets. I began talking good ol' country talk to Buck, like Frank O'Gorman talked around the potbellied stove, "dog talk" to Buck, he not much on listening to the King's English . . .

"You know, Ol' Buck, long before you was a pup, this place warn't no place a'tall. It was just a place, that's all. Sioux hunted deer and elk, even bear 'round here. Warn't no whites. Warn't no big dogs like you. Bears et 'em, packs o' wolves too. Latter-day settlers was all back in the Old Country then contemplatin' sailing over here, or living out easterly to the New England states. Don't suppose you know anything about the Civil War between the states, Buck, but long about that time, little before maybe, this countryside started seeing some activity. Oh, not where you is lying now. Shoot! These streets weren't even streets, just tall, bluestem grasses blowing in the breeze, cooling the grasses, sort of like they's doing for you right now. But a couple of fellows got off'n the steamboat down in Frontenac or Red Wing, don't reckon I know which for sure, but they didn't like all that activity, that hustle and bustle along the riverfront—steamboats snorting coal black smoke, steam hissing from escape pipes, calliopes whistling, screaming, roustabouts rolling hundreds of barrels packed with pickles and vinegar and salt pork down the gangplank—sort of like you, Buck, not

wanting too much noise or doin's in the village. Fella named Mann, John, I believe it was, took the stage one day toward Zumbrota. A fellow was riding with him, German cuss by the name of Yergens, I believe, Buck. They'd never liked to make it to Zumbrota. Bumping down that old stage line, bouncing through the hollows of Hay Creek, 'bout where County Rd. No. 4 runs east o' here, they hopped off the stage, pounded a couple of stakes into the ground making their claims right there among the rolling, undulating hills. They's the first white fellows in the area. You listening to me, Buck? They's here long 'fore you littered the place.

Other pioneers followed, soon hearing the soil was deep, rich, good for planting, not having all those stones and rocks like they's had back in Ireland and Sweden or coast of Norway. About time the Confederates fired their guns down at Ft. Sumter, the Governmentals up here surveyed Mann's and Yergen's neighboring settlements into Goodhue Township, naming it for that newspaper editor up in St. Paul, Mr James Goodhue who got his Minnesota Pioneer *newspaper up and going. What you think about that, Buck? You excited yet? I don't suppose you know what a township is, Buck, or how big, or wide or nothing, so I won't bore you with them details.*

Guy named Peter Easterly, from the East, of course, bounded into here just before the Rebs cannon'd Ft. Sumter, settling 'bout a mile and a half east o' where you laying, out toward Bellechester some, Buck, right 'long the stage line. Figured he could make some money, so he built himself a hotel for wearisome stage travelers, even catching the mail for a few years down in a hollow along the stage line. Word soon spread around Red Wing and Frontenac that this was good land, good soil for planting wheat and oats and barley and flax and corn, too, so more homesteaders walked or pulled oxen or rode stagecoaches into the township.

Starting to fill up now, Buck, even some o' your ances-tors began a-comin.

Building soddies and log-hewn cabins, plowing this virgin soil, planting and harvesting took up most of their time, not leaving many hours for anything else. Where you laying, Buck, was just another wheat field in Section 21. Warn't no village here at all. They's a Goodhue Centere out east a spell, and the burg of Elmira tried to get up and going, just a post office along the stage route, but it failed just like some folks and their crops. But most farming was good, Buck, even though folks had to stay home Saturday nights. It'd be some years 'fore folks could traipse to town here for free movies down by the old railroad station. But that depot eventually went up 'bout '89, not for free movies, either, no sir. It went up 'cause the approaching rail-road needed a stopping place 'fore it got to Zumbrota.

We's different up here on the high prairie, Buck. Most other county hamlets started up 'cause of a natural site, often 'long a river for a water mill, like Belvidere Mills and Forest Mills and Cannon Falls, or for protection like Ft. Snelling, whereas—big word for you, Buck—Red Wing and Frontenac and Lake City all wanted a view of the river for their sailboats. The village you laying in, Buck, didn't have none o' them things—no water, no bluffs, no inspiring view, just high lonesome prairie. It's a wonder the town ever took; fact is, wouldn't of hadn't been for ol' Theodore B. Sheldon and his railroad buddies, and I'm not talkin Roosevelt here, Buck.

Couple o' Mayo Bros down in Rochester demand-ed better connections to St. Paul, so they's real interest-ed in a railroad running from Red Wing to Rochester. When ol' T. B. Sheldon heard 'bout that he and his business cronies in Red Wing started laying tracks southways through the hollers of Hay Creek, up into Goodhue Township, not far from where you laying,

Buck. Set up a tenting camp for the workers, and 'fore you knew it, this place began seein' some activity, 'bout as much as today. Now T. B. was mostly a businessman, 'stead of a railman. He was looking to make a buck, Buck, so he bought himself some acres down on Lower Street, 'fore the street was there of course; platted it off, registered it, then built a railroad station and a grain elevator. Place soon became a whistle-stop. He was in business and this old place began booming. Others saw a buck, Buck, so 'fore long, George Uslar put up himself a store, Anderson a hotel, even a Blind Pig showed up in the new whistle-stop 'long 'bout eighteen hundred and eighty-nine. T. B. could have called the site 'Sheldon,' but used the handle 'Goodhue,' instead. Ol' T. B. Sheldon is the father of your village, Buck, and don't you forget it.

Well, Buck. You gettin' tired of hearing all this? Some folks out in the new township weren't much happy about 'Goodhue Station' becoming 'Goodhue,' the township and county already using that handle, so they competed, you might say, fussed to get other whistle-stops going up the tracks at Claybank, down round White Willow. 'Course White Willow isn't there anymore, and Claybank is mostly a memory.

Now, you a dog, Buck, so don't know much about pigs, but we had that blind pig here causing much consternation for teetotalers. Didn't want no blind pig, wet or dry. Folks fought and fought to run that pig out o' town. Did for a while, but that pig was a persistent hog, bout as persistent an' ornery as that wild hog of Dennis Heaney's. Long 'bout eighteen hundred and ninety-three the 'wets' got the best of the 'drys,' Buck. Saloons were here to stay. Them pigs got eyes.

Don't suppose you know what a decade is, Buck. It's a long time for a dog. Anyways, Goodhue Station, as folks called it then, warn't even an official place most of the decade before the turn of the century. Just an unincorporated township burg, not much different from Vasa or Hader or Belle Creek, but we did have that railroad. Folks out in Belle Creek wanted it but didn't get it. Made 'em mad as hell, Buck. They's still mad today about not getting the railroad. The burg looked like it would hang around, looked like it would have a future, 'bout forty years for I crawled to town. Ole Boxrud opened hisself a meat market, and Betcher built a lumber yard east o' the tracks. 'Course you couldn't have a burg without a billiard hall, so Nibbe and Durig took care o' that, and farmers wanted a creamery for their Holsteins, so we got one of them, too. Kid's didn't want to go to school, but folks made 'em walk out to Finney's farm and school, bout a mile west on County Rd. No 9 and 6, the burg itself not doing no schooling yet. Don't suppose you know anything about operas, Buck. Dogs isn't much on operas, but the folks wanted an opera house. Every town had to have an opera house, though 'opera' is an oxymoron. Don't suppose you know want an oxymoron is, either, Buck. You big, but you ain't smart. Anderson's Opera House promoted orchestras and lectures and medicine shows and other acts for locals' entertainment. Began looking like Goodhue Station would hang around the county. The Heaney boys bought out Ole Boxrud, starting a hun-dred-year string of meat cuttin', and soon they's over hundred folks settled here, more than out in Claybank or Ryan or Forest Mills or Hay Creek. But folks got in each other ways sometimes, had a fire one night down on Lower Street by the grain elevators. Took out most of the buildings, Buck, but folks rebuilt. Then the Methodists erected the first village church 'long about eighteen hundred and ninety-five to give thanks for being here, some naysayers thinking giving thanks not appropriate. But I suppose the biggest doin's for Goodhue Station, Buck, was the burg's first newspaper, The Goodhue Enterprise. *You can't have a burg without*

*a newspaper, Buck, even though you don't read. Ol' D.
C. Pierce got 'er up and going and gave the burg what
for, for lots o' years about what folks should and
shouldn't do.*

*But folks here wanted to be proper and official,
Buck. They incorporated themselves in 1897, 'bout fifty
years after John Mann pounded his stakes over in that
northeastern corner of the new township. Now that's a
long time, a lifetime for a dog. The railroad got to be
real successful for the farmers, and folks liked riding
the rails to Red Wing, too, just for a change of pace from
walking and horsebacking and driving carriages. Warn't
so homebound anymore to just the burg. Got themselves a school building, too, and their own district.
Kids didn't have to walk out to Finney's place anymore
up hill both ways. They stayed right in town now to get
learnin from Emily Parker. Yes sir, Buck, the village was
on its way by the time folks flipped their calendars to
1900."*

I was thinking about all that when Uncle Dave walked up with a
carton of hand-packed ice cream from Joe Shelstad's Place.
"Jimmy? What you doin' talkin' to that dog? Ain't workin'?" he
asked, sitting down beside me on the stoop, his long, angular legs
reaching the curb.

"Finished cleaning the chicken cages, Dave. I don't have a
new job yet, so just moseying around the village, talking some to
Buck. Mighty still this afternoon, and Ol' Buck needed petting, and
well . . . ," I said, wiping the sweat from my brow.

"You lookin' for work, then?"

"Yes, sir. Didn't get on with Libby's this summer. I need work
before reporting for duty this fall."

"I've got just the work for you. I'm drivin' bus for the
claypitters. I could have you diggin' clay out at the pits tomorrow,"
Dave said, his ice cream beginning to drip to the sidewalk in the
afternoon heat.

"You mean with Oscar Decker, Erv Richter, Ole, Sigvard and

Hans? Geez, Dave! I'm a young fart. Don't know if I could get along with those old codgers. Damn! I've got a college degree now . . . digging clay?"

"No ifs ands or buts about it. They're good fellows, and the work would do you a heap o' good. Make your dad proud of you. Meet me tomorrow mornin' in front of the Corner Bar and you can begin digging clay. Keep you busy, earn you some dough, too," Dave said, reeling in his legs from the curb to continue his journey home before he didn't have any ice cream left. I hadn't even had a chance to respond. It looked as if I had a job, Clay Digging 101, and a new sobriquet to go with my B.S. and B.C.: "Jim Franklin C.D. Clay Digger."

"Top o' the mornin', Jimmy," Uncle Dave said as I stepped up into his antiquated bus parked catawampus in front of the Corner Bar. "Glad you decided to join us at the Pits today."

"Hi, Uncle Dave. Well, I don't know if I'm a claypitter, but I'm here," I said, my red eyes searching for a seat in the dingy gray W.W.II-vintage Dodge bus, a depressing contraption that must have been lurking around the village since day one, maybe stored in a listing barn. Eight to ten grizzled old farts looked at me through cataract eyes without uttering a word, probably wondering what the hell I was doing on *their* bus. No one scooted over to accommodate me as I worked my way toward the rear, finally finding a seat in the last tattered bench seat. I had recognized Oscar Decker in the first seat, but he was reticent this morning, as usual. I recognized Bump and Tommy Schinnert, both chewing tobacco, spitting out the half-opened windows with more juice splaying the window than passing through. Most other codgers, I had never seen before. I wondered where they had come from. Dave shifted the bus into a grinding, recalcitrant first gear and groaned away from the corner, transmission whining in the early-morning mist.

The sun was just now peeking over the Elevator as Dave drove past Lensch & Rusch's and *my* chicken cages; past Swenson's, Wipperling's TV, Bartlett's Bowling Alley, Taylor's Eat

Shop and out toward the Claypits. I wondered what on earth I was getting myself into, digging clay with a B.S. degree, of all things. But Uncle Dave had procured several jobs for me over the years, taking me under his kinfolk wing after his brother Tom died. Dave looked after me: chatted with me at Heaney & Gorman Saturday nights around the potbellied stove, painted the Standard Oil bulk tanks with me a few years ago, worked at Bookie's pea viners with me, and now had encouraged me to dig clay. I would have to trust his recommendation, once again.

He turned the bus north fighting the oversized, cracked steering wheel just as during the thirties and forties he had fought his ample-ass'd dray horses, sinewy leather reins slapping real horse hide, horseshoes clip-clopping, echoing off slumbering merchant's buildings. Dave had operated the City Dray Line on village streets many years before he became an around-town "supervisor." We entered Highway 58, driving north toward Hay Creek and the Claypits. If the township could claim any natural resource besides deep rich top soil, it was clay. For a geological reason unknown to locals, clay had formed here eons ago, discovered first in Belvidere Township outside Bellechester in 1909. The Bellechester folks had gotten excited then, speculating the discovery would cause their community to boom like San Francisco or Denver, Gold Rush boom towns of earlier years.

The Bellechester clay boom began in 1910, menacing, teeth-baring machines and hand diggers stripping clay from the virgin earth. The digging continued several decades with the Chicago Great Western hauling the malleable earthen resource to Red Wing where manufacturers made elongated sewer pipes and hand-painted pottery dishes. Bellechester even became a two-clay town. Most folks thought one Bellechester enough, but when the railroad laid a spur to haul that clay out, they laid tracks a mile beyond Bellechester Town No. 1, a new Town No. 2 ("Claybank" already taken) subsequently rising near the new tracks. But Bellechester No. 1 wasn't about to move, so two Bellechesters a half mile apart and separated by a no-man's land dotted the landscape. However, Bellechester didn't achieve the prosperity it had hoped for. The clay diggers were mostly migrant fellows, and Bellechester immigrant Luxembourg's and Irish soon realized they preferred farming to digging clay. They chose to *raise* their efforts above ground instead of lowering themselves below it.

The clay finally played out; the railroad company pulled up its tracks, the claypitters left the two towns to the Irish, Luxembourgers and Catholics. Bellechester never developed that vacant half mile between towns. Someone, years later, erected a hand-painted sign there: Bellechester Undeveloped Industrial Park.

Neighboring Goodhue Township had been fortunate to also discover clay in 1922 several miles from the Bellechester find. That's where Dave was driving us today, four miles north of the village. I bounced in the back seat of the dusty bus, coughing from the clay dust covering every torn seat, grimy walls, filthy ceiling, and foul floor. I hacked from the tart, acidic odor oozing from both the bus and the men slouched in front, the bus clanging, banging from every possible spot. My tattered, spring-sprung seat was irritating me, coil springs sticking me in the ass, the bus's springs unbending, unforgiving. But the old farts never once turned around to recognize or speak to me. My lunch bucket fell to the floor spilling two sandwiches into the overwhelming dust. This was not an auspicious beginning, I thought, as Dave turned onto a dirt road. I began thinking that shoveling chicken shit hadn't been so bad.

We hit bottom entering the pit site causing my spine to crack, angular dinosaur-sized drag lines grumbling, vibrating the very earth, looming over a gaping hole the size of Minnesota's Mesabi Iron Range. I had been out here before with general manager Pete Hart; Jack and I had hunted rabbits here Sunday afternoons when the village girls were busy being girls, uninterested in boys, at least us. Older fellows had bragged about necking and screwing here, using the site as a lover's lane when Finney's Woods was already full. Mostly, though, the pits were unfamiliar to me as I stepped down from the bus onto sullen gray earth, the last guy off.

"Have a good mornin', nephew," Dave hollered as he yanked the sprung door shut with a long iron handle. "I'll be back to drive you to lunch over to Mary Moran's."

"But I brought my bologna sandwiches, Dave," I hollered, following the men. "You mean we get lunch?"

"You betcha. Good eatin's too. See you at noon," he hollered, bouncing back over the dusty clay driveway, abandoning me to toothless, reticent men now grabbing long-handled spades and descending into the bowels of the earth like non-Catholics entering Dante's Inferno. I didn't even know what I was supposed to do, so I simply followed them, grabbing a long-handled spade, plodding down a switchback trail one hundred feet into the bowels of Goodhue Township.

Oscar, Karl, Ole, Tommy and Bump trudged slowly downward, spades on hunchbacked shoulders, heads down, chewing and spitting tobacco along the trail, marking it like donkeys pissing on the Grand Canyon trail for a later return. They looked like beaten soldiers returning from Antietam or Bull Run or Gettysburg. I didn't chew tobacco that summer, although I would try Beach Nut leaf tobacco later, just for the flavor and moisture. Reaching the bottom of the yawning hole, each man sauntered off to, apparently, a favorite claim where he began digging rich, deep blue-gray clay from the willing earth, by hand. Entering the site I had noticed drag lines, assuming they dragged buckets through the pit slicing off clay before hoisting it to the surface where it would be loaded onto trucks, then shipped to Red Wing Pottery or Red Wing Sewer Pipe. I assumed incorrectly. That was *not* the procedure. This rich clay was much too precious to be violently extracted from the earth by a shark-tooth drag line. Gritty hands, brawny arms and the hulking shoulders of Oscar, Karl and Tommy and Bump, and wimpy Jimmy Franklin dug this clay. The drag lines only lowered massive steel buckets into the pit to be filled by us diggers, one spade full at a time.

Selecting a digging spot was like searching for a gold strike in a California mountain. It became apparent the fellows each had marked their own claim, not to be tread upon by anyone else, especially a wet-behind-the-ears college kid. As they began spading clay into the huge iron buckets, I trudged to an unclaimed spot, passing Oscar, our eyes momentarily meeting.

I knew Oscar knew me; Oscar knew I knew he knew me. I think he liked me. It's just that he wasn't much of a talker when sober—a rare occurrence—never when inebriated. But he appeared sober this morning as I skirted him in search of a rich vein. When working at Heaney & Gorman during high school, I would deliver groceries on Saturdays to shut-ins, the elderly, and two grumpy old men while driving George's '50 Ford. Oscar lived in a decrepit, ramshackle, sour-wood frame house upwind from St. Peter's German Lutheran Church. "Antiquated," "quaint" would have been a compliment for his house—sour, ghastly, a shit-stinking outhouse out back, spiders and snakes and ghosts every-where inside. I avoided the outhouse at all costs. But I had to deliver groceries to Oscar in wire baskets, meaning I had to enter his kitchen, unload the groceries, then quickly escape. Oscar was rarely home, apparently either at the pits or at a saloon sucking on a day-long, flat beer chased with Seagram's boilermakers. Such was Oscar's life. I had often seen him trudging, unsteadily, up the street wearing his usual bib overalls, flannel shirt in any season, and scabby, square trainman's cap. He would slumber past Emily Parker's, the school, St. Peter's to the then edge of town, being in town but not part of it. He would nod his head toward me, but seldom, if ever, speak. Yet, I sensed he appreciated me delivering his groceries.

I reached the end of the line, selected an area to begin digging, then furiously began attacking the clay, sending the spade into the soft clay like a machine gun, separating it from surrounding sand and dirt, tossing each spade full into the dragline bucket. I worked fast, determined, apparently, to get quickly to the bottom of the township. I felt good, strong, after all, it was nice being outside on a mild early June day, just digging, not thinking about philosophy or religion or mystical theology or harmonic minor scales or Bach Cantatas or four-part harmony, just digging clay in the bowels of Goodhue Township.

I periodically looked up to see how the other fellows were doing. I thought they worked awfully slow, not digging nearly the amount I had that first hour. They trudged with each shovel full, slowly setting the spade into the clay, stepping on it with heavy, tattered, weary boots and hearts before methodically tossing it into the bottomless bucket. God! How do these fellows ever get anything done? Uncle Dave had always said I was a good worker.

Bookie said I had worked hard on the viners. George, Dennis and Dodie said I was a good worker at Heaney & Gorman, most of the time despite being a perennial five-minute latecomer. Oscar and the boys should be working faster, like me.

The morning mist began burning off by quarter of ten, the pit growing hotter as I wiped my brow and drank water from a Thermos bottle. I stopped digging for a minute, looked at the gang digging the blue-gray earth—never stopping, never slowing, never talking, never resting their hot-glowing spades throughout the morning. By the time Uncle Dave appeared at the edge of the cavernous pit, his Model A horn crackling and echoing though the pit, my arms, hands and shoulders were aching, my contribution to the dragline bucket less than Oscar's. Obviously, I was missing something. Obviously, I had a lot to learn about digging clay.

We trudged up the steep serpentine switchback lugging spades on our shoulders like an Alabama chain gang without the striped suits. The men plopped into their seats as I shuffled to the rear, collapsing, aching, hot, thirsty, famished. I didn't notice the coil springs poking through the seat on this trip, nor the hard ride of the bus on my thin, college-ass'd butt. It felt good just to sit after four hours on my feet, to gaze out the dust-encased windows at the passing fields of new Grant Wood corn greening the countryside.

The morning hadn't been what I expected, but then, what *had* I expected? knowing little or nothing about clay or how to retrieve it. I knew Pete Hart was the big boss and that he contracted trucks to haul clay to Red Wing for making pottery plates and sewer pipe. That was all I knew. As we whip-lashed on the swirling, dusty gravel road to lunch, I wondered how clay had been formed here. Why Goodhue Township of all places? What geological oddity had caused this pure, natural resource to form deep beneath our high prairie? I would study that, I decided, as Dave turned off the gravel road up a rutted drive to Mary Moran's Eating and Boarding House just beyond County Rd. No. 9, boarders having long ago disappeared over the horizon. The laconic men stepped off the bus and trudged to the house, their movements deliberate, no wasted energy. I brought up the rear as Uncle Dave parked the bus and joined me.

"How'd the mornin' go, Jimmy?"

"I don't rightly know, Uncle. I found myself starting fast, but then realized it would be a long day, so I slowed down to a steady pace. I'm not used to it, but I'll probably get the hang of it," I said as we reached the wash basins in the entrance. I washed my hands and face, wiped more clay dust on the towel than what I left in the basin before joining Dave and the men at a family-styled, two-by-four table. Mary immediately served roast beef and gravy, boiled potatoes, homemade bread and brussels sprouts, plus milk and coffee. I could hardly begin eating what with so much food being passed. The fellows immediately began eating, heads down, chins almost touching their plates, shoveling in food like shoveling in clay. They remained silent, more interested in eating than talking. Only Dave and I talked.

"It's a lead pipe cinch, Jimmy. First couple of days are the hardest, but your hands, muscles and joints will adjust to that hard row you're a hoe'n'. It's not so bad," Dave said, attacking his heaping plate of roast beef and gravy. Uncles Dave, Jim and Pat, plus Dad were the four Franklin boys raised on the Goodhue-Belle Creek Township line during the 1890s. Great-grandfather David Franklin homesteaded a quarter section set in a long, low dale along a meandering, rippling stream in the northwestern corner of Goodhue Township. Here, he raised four boys plus Anne, Cecelia and Helen. They tilled the rich soil, sowed wheat, barely, oats and flax, milked cows, raised chickens, sold eggs, attended mass at St. Columbkill's, and lumbered up the hill to read *McGuffey Readers* at District 107's one-room school, a stone's throw across the road from the minuscule Swedish Evangelical Lutheran Church, established 1864. They did all this while deferring to Catherine Franklin, the matriarch of the settlement.

Dad later shipped off to Europe to battle the Kaiser in World War I; Jim got his own farm down the road near St. Columbkill's; Uncle Dave decided he preferred living in the village to an extended farm life; Cecelia married into the Belle Creek O'Neill clan; Anne married Bill McWaters and moved to Zumbrota, while Helen headed to Grand Rapids, Michigan, leaving only bachelor Uncle Patrick and grandmother Catherine on the farm after grandfather David died ten years before I entered the world and township.

"Gimme the bread, Jimmy. I've worked up a powerful hunger this mornin'," Dave said, the others staring straight into their food, taciturn, only the sound of smacking lips disturbing the table.

"What did you do after dropping us off?"

"Went to town to buy fixins for Mary, then hauled a few things for Pete, then . . . well, I was busy."

"You ever dig clay when you aren't busy, Dave?"

"Don't have time for that. I'm a supervisor, you know, Jimmy. I leave the diggin' to Oscar and Karl, Ole and you," he said, now attacking a huge slice of apple pie.

The food tasted wonderful. I ate heartily having generated a huge appetite throughout the morning. The fellows finished their meals, then left the table to go outside and sit under a sweeping oak tree for a smoke or a chew or just to sit. Dave and I finished our dessert, thanked Mary, then joined the men. Before long I had dozed off in the warm afternoon.

Dave shook me awake saying it was time to head back to the pits for the afternoon, something I didn't want to hear at that moment. I joined the fellows shuffling slowly toward the bus, again selecting my rear seat. Bouncing back to the pits on a heavy stomach, I wondered why Oscar and the fellows didn't talk, why they didn't share their lives, their concerns with each other. Maybe they were all talked out. Maybe their lives were just this: digging, eating, digging, drinking, sleeping, digging. Life had to be more than that, I thought while gazing at the passing fields. I had gone to college to improve myself, to develop a profession, which I now had. I had my entire professional life in front of me, but what did these fellows have? Had they professions years ago? Where had Oscar come from? What had he done? I didn't know anything about him, other than he dug clay, drank cases of Grain Belt, ate Heaney's pork chops and roast beef, and trudged home lugging long-necked bottles in brown bags. What had Karl been? Where was he from? Did he have relatives? How did these fellows end up on the short end of a long spade, day after day, digging clay? What had happened to their minds, their intelligence, their motivation,

I wondered as we bounced back to the gaping pit. Too soon, I was back at my claim, digging the afternoon away, awaiting Dave's five o'clock return.

The afternoon heated up in the cavernous hole, but the fellows continued plodding at the same speed, indifferent to the heat. I had adjusted my digging pace to theirs, realizing that a slow, steady pace was more productive than rushing. By three o'clock I was tired, but at peace in the pit. I had begun observing the various colored veins in the clay: greens, grays, blue streaks, even periodic reds. I had noticed various veins running through the pit, wondering how this material had been formed, what acids or ingredients or sea crustaceans or fossils, millions of years ago when this land had been crushed by the menacing Arctic glacier, had caused these veins to be compressed into clay, in Goodhue Township, of all places.

John Paul discovered this clay in 1862 only a couple of miles down the road from where first-township homesteader John Mann settled. J. P. was a potter throwing jugs and pots and bowls and crocks for homesteaders. He knew this was quality clay, so he set up a small potter's studio near the road and began turning pots in his wood-stocked kiln. Neighbors bought his innumerable pots, yet after ten years, John Paul tired of the effort and moved, out of the county even, leaving the deep blue clay for others to turn. Red Wing Stoneware folks purchased the land, finding the clay to be of excellent quality for dinner plates and pots. But as with many natural resources, the quality began playing out, deteriorating, not good enough for the pot shops, but good enough for sewer pipe.

Almost one hundred years after John Paul discovered the clay, I found myself deep in his pit digging what Paul eventually abandoned. I dug throughout the afternoon, daydreaming about clay, about the college I had just left, about Sharon's nubile body and when I would see more of it. Suddenly, a loud, shrieking steam whistle startled me. The boys froze, shovels suspended in mid air, and began straggling up the switchback trail. I followed. The first day at the pits had ended.

"Not bad, youngun," Oscar muttered as I reached the spade bin. I was stunned. Oscar talked.

"Yes, sir, Oscar. I made one entire day. How many years you been digging?"

"Twenty-five."

"Twenty-five years in this pit. Geez! That's a long time."

"Ain't so bad," he said, walking toward the bus, conversation ended.

I followed the chain gang to the bus, slumped into my rear seat for the joyful ride back to the village. I felt tired but satisfied. I began realizing there were many circuitous routes to an education, many roads toward living one's life. These men were satisfied having worked a good day, having supported themselves another day instead of living on county welfare or at the poor house. A day digging clay was, for them, as good as a day of prayer by the St. John's monks. By the time Dave screeched to a stop in front of the Corner Bar, brakes burning, screeching for two blocks, irritating Ol' Buck's peaceful repose, I had gained a new perspective on my colleagues. Oscar, Karl, and Ole nodded slightly in my direction as they stepped from the bus, an indication I wasn't so bad. I had gained a parcel of acceptance.

I stepped onto the bus the next morning and for another month of mornings, hand digging at the pit before Bert Majerus hired me to help him lay sewer pipe, unplug stuffed toilets, solder copper tubing, and deliver sulfur-smelling propane tanks to the county's Old Folks Home. I hadn't had highfalutin' ideas when digging clay. I sure didn't have any now. Although I had often seen them on the streets before, I had now gained a new appreciation for the Clay Diggers of Goodhue Township. Late Friday afternoon, my last day at the pits, I jumped from the bus, nodded to the boys, then skipped to the grassy area between Ebe's Barber Shop and Gerken's Hardware, heading toward Swenson's for a soda. Ol' Buck was ensconced in his usual spot under the eave of the barber shop wearing himself out panting all day. I reached down to pet him saying I'd be back in a few moments with his water after getting a soda. He rolled his eyes toward me in semi-recognition, no other discernible movement.

"Your kind caused lots o' consternation 'bout 1905, Buck. Dogs running 'round the village like crazy. Some o' your ancestors might o' been in those packs. Horses too. Folks had their own horses, and the Livery Barn rented 'em out, too. And you like our village today, take things for granted? Warn't always so. First villagers built wooden sidewalks, dug cisterns and wells and cesspools and put up gas lamps, all the things you take for granted, Buck, though you don't use most yourself. No, dog! Starting up a village warn't all that easy. Lots of 'em failed. Just ask the folks at Burr Oak and Eagle Mills and Spencer and Ryan and White Willow. Some villagers thought this place just a big farm yard. They wanted to keep cattle in town out behind their lean-tos, let 'em run free, got mighty uppity when scolded for doing so. They's in the city now, Buck, but they warn't citified.

This is a farming town, Buck. Warn't for the farmers, the railroad never o' come through here. Farmers meant grain and grain meant elevators, 'bout four of 'em 'longside the tracks early on. Homesteaders out in Belle Creek, Belvidere, Featherstone, some Hay Creek, threshed wheat until they almost burned out the soil, that and those chinch bugs that epedemic'd the wheat crop 'fore the turn of the century. But warn't long 'fore non-farmers got in the act, folks like Willis and Charles Sawyer startin' up the City Bank, and G. O. Miller out there in White Rock put up telephone lines, and gettin' a permanent post office with regular mail, and you know what, Ol' Buck? You warn't the first 'Ol' Buck' in town. Hate to hurt your feelin's, but Will Heaney had a horse called Ol' Buck long 'fore you came about. Now don't go feeling bad about that. You still the town's mascot, even though you is lazy as the day is long.

Page 224:

Warn't long 'fore the whistle-stop attracted folks who wanted to service farmers and townsfolk. They got doctors Sawyer, Gates, and Featherstone, general stores from J. N. Banitt, John Quast and John Meyer, the Goodhue Cash Store, too. 'Course they had undertakers and coffin makers even before Ole Haga, and hardware stores, plus Pete Nei and Anton Rosener and Bill Huebner blacksmith shops. Hotels was popular, Buck, what with folks getting off the train for a night or two—Headquarters Hotel right down on Lower Street, and the Merchants Hotel on Upper. Heaney Bros even ran the White House Boarding House, and horses got stabled at the Goodhue Livery Barn while folks ate fixin's at Schinnert's Restaurant & Confectionery. And Buck, you could even get your picture taken at Frank Sjoblom's Studio.

Once the village got to going, folks found time to play in the village Cornet Band, played basketball and baseball, even some tennis when the balls warn't soggy. They organized literary societies and thespians and magic pictures and steroptical slide shows. 'Course they loved dancing, Buck, to Ben Gorman's Orchestra or Rehder's Orchestra, though you ain't much for dancing. Townsfolk started having a grand old time out here on the high prairie next to the railroad tracks."

B C. Majerus hired me as a "go-pher" at Majerus Gas & Appliance, an extremely big name for a small town. He might have named it Bert's Gas, but Addie didn't think that appropriate. For some unknown reason village men, especially, were known by their initials instead of first names, it maybe an ostentatious attempt at formality in a community lacking formality. Bert was "B. C.," so I called him that, too, as I began learning his plumbing and gas trade. I had previously learned basic electricity from Cy Benda, raw woodworking from Pete Hart—nights in his woodworking shop behind the house—and I already knew how to cut and package pork chops, steaks and roasts, stock grocery shelves and trim hamburger meat from years at Heaney & Gorman. B. C. would now teach me about the plumbing trade, gaining skills I would later use when owning several homes. But he didn't demand all my time that summer. There was time for summer softball, baseball . . . and Sharon.

Sharon and I shared an intense interest in classical and jazz music, listening to various jazz artists: England's Ted Heath, Kansas City's Count Basie and Milwaukee's Woody Herman, plus classical composers Respighi, Bach and Tchaikovsky. We grooved to singers Tony Bennett and Frank Sinatra, romancing nights in her cozy home or along Levee Park, up on the Memorial Park bluffs or at the beaches of Frontenac's Lake Pepin. I would set sewer pipe with B. C. during the day, then shower at Mother's Burnside house before rushing off to meet Sharon, later dining at a restaurant. Mother was away most of the summer visiting Rose at the foot of Rocky Mountain National Park. I had the house and Sharon to myself.

Achieving sexual maternity . . . er, I mean maturity, had been a long, arduous journey since my early days in the village—grade school to high school to St. John's, then back to the village. Growing up Catholic, we Catechists had been bombarded with the strict teachings of the "One and only Church" regarding sexual activities or any other theological impediment. I had faithfully believed the Church's dogmas and Fr. Smith's reiteration of them. I knew and believed sex outside of marriage was wrong—venial or mortal sins depending on the depth of intimate activity—having and enjoying impure thoughts, which I frequently had and did; looking at Eddie's girlie magazines, which I frequently did; engaging in self-abuse, which, like all village boys, I frequently did; engaging in intercourse (an ostentatious word the GHS locker room fellows never used, they preferring "fucking," "screwing," or "balling" to "intercourse"), which I hadn't in high school, but was anxiously anticipating.

Mother never had that "talk" with me about sex, the word "sex" itself never being uttered in our forties' home. The Franklin and Haustein womenfolk would sit around the kitchen table slurping coffee, chomping angel food cake, chatting of women things, men out on the porch in rotting rocking chairs smoking dry Harvester cigars, picking their noses and scratching their balls. "She's 'pg' you know," I would hear passing the table on the way to the frige. I knew early on that "pg" meant pregnant, but had little idea of how one actually got there. I had had light experimentation when dating during high school, but was mostly fearful of extended consequences, secular or eternal. Enjoyment of a sexual act was unheard of in our parish; that is, until they published "The Kinsey Report."

When the *St. Paul Pioneer Press*—the village's namesake, James Goodhue, first publisher—began excerpting the Kinsey Report, every red-blooded guy in town began reading more than the sports section. The Kinsey Report revealed what men and women throughout the country were actually doing behind closed doors, behind pulled curtains and drawn shades on Main Street, up in the neighborhoods. The University of Indiana's Professor Kinsey reported that married couples engaged in intercourse three and a half times per week, on average, whatever a half time was, and that seventy-one percent actually enjoyed it, for heaven's sake! The Catholic Church had never, absolutely never, stated nor implied that sex might be enjoyed. The Church said sex was for the procreation of the family, pleasure be damned! And now Kinsey had released his data by surveying 20,000 people. Wow! That's as many as forty Goodhues, we thought.

"What are you reading there, Jimmy?" George Gorman asked at Swenson's Cafe during an afternoon break from the grocery store.

"Oh, just baseball scores. Sort of interested in the White Sox this year," I said, quickly flipping the page to Sports.

"Thought you might be reading the Kinsey Report."

"Oh, no. Shoot! I'm not interested in that," I said, quickly finishing my Nesbitt's before scooting back to Heaney & Gorman for the afternoon, the Kinsey section on "Frequency of Intercourse," frustratingly unread this day.

Folks also talked in hushed tones about the Rhythm Method, a concept difficult to understand for those of us who hadn't had the "pleasure" of intercourse yet. My rhythm method had been limited to musical three-four or four-four on my clarinet, and I had plenty of experience in that. Sexual rhythm was incomprehensible.

The guys in the locker room had bragged about "making out," and "balling," and "getting some," but we didn't believe most of the braggarts. What could a guy believe? Catholic boys feared confession. Oh, we sought sex, but didn't want to go to confession and hell for having found it. We envied the Protestant fellows who only had to confess directly to God, never having to face the taunting and daunting Fr. Smith face-to-face, or face-to-black curtain.

Throughout grade- and high school we assembled bits and pieces of the puzzle, fleeting opportunities for experimentation and lab work presenting themselves during body changes, attitude changes. New perspectives and interpretations of Church sex slowly emerged as college dorm mates countered with more than our local parish's perspective, they offering opposing points of view as I moved through the obstacle course of balancing churchly, moral positions with hormonal, testosteronal demands. Often, they didn't meet, but I persisted, nonetheless.

Sex before, during or after marriage remained an uncertain concept that summer. St. John's prof Fr. Coleman Barry had stated the Church's position in his Marriage and Family course (interpreted, "If he wants to do it, you gotta do it."), and I had no idea of sex after marriage, not having even experienced sex before marriage.

College sweetheart Becky had thought me too priestly, too bound to the pope's cassock strings, too chained to his rosary. She had wanted me to be more left-winged liberal, more like Hubert Humphrey or Gene McCarthy, Gene a Johnnie alum. And Sharon had taunted me with nude *Playboy* photos while lounging on her living room floor, she smiling and blowing in my ear as I tried to nonchalantly look at the photos, an effort comparable to attempting to read books outdoors with mosquitoes attacking your face. Yet, she had stopped my wimpy advances after taunting me, leaving me to wonder how all this worked. I had to learn about sex and women at the same time, for God's sake!

Seeing Sharon most nights during that summer, I had been getting closer and closer to her—hours spent in deep embraces and explorations, hearts beating faster, breath growing hotter, hotter even than her hot-buttered popcorn—but not taking the final step over the precipice into the unknown valley. We listened to my Ford radio, danced in her living room to Frank Sinatra, Perry Como and Antonio Benedito, the Four Freshmen. We lounged on blankets at Frontenac's Lake Pepin beach, late nights with the white-capped surf slapping the sandy shore and our feet, the radio's music enveloping us, romancing us as the moon bounced off rippling waves. I liked Sharon, maybe even loved her that summer. I would be reporting to the army in November, Sharon to the Twin Cities, but that was a long way off those hot, sultry summer nights. I didn't know how the summer would end between us.

Fourth of July, a sultry weekend, we had joined several other couples from the village and Red Wing for swimming, a cookout, partying on the expansive beaches of mysterious Lake Pepin. Elroy Schulz, Dallas Diercks, Bob Madrick, Dale Bremer, Darrell and Dale Jonas, brother Tom were there with girlfriends enjoying the youthful camaraderie. The Grain Belt keg had floated in the cove all day, rising higher on the surf as the afternoon and evening wore on. Sharon had worn a modest two-piece bathing suit that day as we repeatedly dove from the dock in the secluded cove above the Methodist Campus. The beer had caused everyone to become increasingly silly, garrulous, inhibitions becoming as loose as our mouths and Sharon's two-piece halter straps. She had been show-ing ever more cleavage throughout the afternoon, and as moon-beams bounced off the sapphire lake, all elements generated an increased interest on my part, to say the least. She would throw her slim arms around me, place a deep French kiss while rubbing her wet, clinging body into mine, causing every part of me to tingle and throb. Sharon was getting ever closer, the Church's teachings, farther away.

Couples began peeling away, some into the bushes, some into cars parked on the beach. Soon, Sharon and I found ourselves alone on the still hot, pebbled beach. She slurred nonsensical words into my ear, I into hers. She felt very good, round, soft, even though she smelled of burnt sun, scorched sand, and a bit fishy. But, I didn't mind. I smelled the same. We embraced and fondled each other in exotic places on the secluded shores of Lake Pepin, the beach now devoid of the day's raucous, inebriated gesticulations, empty Grain Belt kegs floating like freed buoys. "Let's go to my place," she said, suddenly springing from the blanket, kicking sand into my face.

"You don't have to say that again," I retorted, gathering our gear and rushing to the Ford. We spun sand from the beach racing toward College Avenue, wet, sandy, sunburned and slightly tipsy. In the Ford she brushed her wet, sea-weed hair, then laid an icy Lake Pepin hand on my thigh, her halter top drooping lower than it had all day. I didn't know where this night was heading and I was having difficulty keeping my eyes on the road through Wacouta, but . . . well, as the locker room boys so often said, I was mighty horny.

We reached her house and dragged our picnic gear into the kitchen. Sharon heading immediately for the bathroom to clean up. I would follow when she finished. I passed the time fetching a Grain Belt from the frige, combing my hair, glancing at the *Daily Republican Eagle's* obituaries for anyone I might have known. Her parents had been away most of the summer, cabining up north. We had this night and the house to ourselves as we had had most of the summer. Sipping a Grain Belt I didn't need after a hot day of kegging on the beach, I wondered how the remainder of the evening would proceed. Was I ready to make a move? Had I resolved The Church's issues with my personal, male testosterone issues. I hadn't, to date, been concerned with sex during or after marriage, but was struggling with sex before marriage, which was where I was halfway through my Grain Belt when she emerged wrapped in a fluffy, brilliant white towel covering some of her, her exposed body parts pink, hot, her hair wet and shiny, her face fresh, vibrant. "Your turn," she said, laying a fresh, wet kiss on me. I reached for her towel, but she intercepted my pass like a Zumbrota basketball guard.

By the time I emerged from the shower, Sharon had lit several candles in the living room, had turned off lights, and placed

Tchaikovsky's *Swan Lake Ballet* on the hi-fi. She was leaning on the fireplace mantle as I approached, Grain Belt in hand, Tchaikovsky enveloping us. We stood at the mantle, swaying, watching the dancing candles, my mind recalling similar flickering nights in my village tree house with Sandbox Bob, Larry O', Jack O', Lee J. We began embracing, responding to Tchaikovsky's sweet, syrupy romantic ballet music, Peter Ilich drawing us into his romanticism, drawing us into the night.

By serendipity or planning, Sharon's towel suddenly fell to the floor. She was nude . . . and smiling. She stepped back, pirouetted in the flickering candle light and preened like a Diaghilev ballerina peacock, this ballerina gorgeous, voluptuous, *au naturel*, now dancing through the living room like a *Swan Lake* nymph. But I wasn't thinking as much about *Swan Lake* as about Sharon. This night wasn't for looking at *Playboy* women. Directly in front of me, dancing, uninhibited and unembarrassed, was Sharon relishing her freedom, her nudity, sharing with me her golden, glowing skin now flickering in the room's soft light, her rounded, caressing shoulders, her nubile breasts, full, pink, pointed; her slender waist and lovely hips beckoned me like a siren on the shores of Lake Pepin. I inched closer but she taunted me with a pirouette, a possible *pas des deux* or two, dancing forward, backwards, sideways, executing flawless arabesques and pirouettes while I pursued her like an awkward gander with my own stumbling, not-so-grand *jetés*. She was marvelous dancing on the davenport, the end tables, the gleaming oak dining room table, pirouetting in the dim candle light of the hallway. I gave up chasing her, breathless, choosing to sit in an overstuffed chair caught up in her nubile dance of the nymphs, caught up in Tchaikovsky's sentimental romantic music, but more importantly, Sharon's seductive dance. She approached bending low, letting her full, melon breasts float freely, impulsively jumping high into the air, dancing on tip-toes, dancing evocatively, body undulating simultaneously in several directions. I reached for her, too late, as she danced toward the staircase, to the top of the landing, then slid down, legs straddling the banister. God! What a spectacle. Tchaikovsky's music grew louder, exploding in my ears, or was it just my heart.

Sharon's dance was affecting every part of my body, parts I didn't even know I had. I could hardly sit in the chair, wanting to be more than a spectator to this event as she again, seductively, danced toward me to sit on my lap, yet not allowing me to touch her. She was in her ballet trance, writhing, responding to Tchaikovsky.

Although enjoying her dance, I wanted Tchaikovsky's ballet to reach its climax, to hold her in my arms. The finalé exploded in my ears as she suddenly jumped out of my lap toward the stairs, up to the balcony, out and above the columned porch. She even danced outside in the moonlight! What will the neighbors think? Stretching and pirouetting and arabesquing and thrusting her arms and pink breasts and hips to the moonlight, I stumbled up the stairs, caught her, turned her back into the house, she again sliding down the banister, legs spread-eagled, How does she do that? as *Swan Lake* came to a blaring, rousing climax, Sharon collapsing on the floor like Diaghlev's Dying Swan, her long, white neck undulating in deep gasps, she unaware of my presence. I sat in the chair gasping for breath myself, although I had only been the dancee instead of the dancer. After several minutes Sharon slowly returned to reality. I stepped over her prone body to the hi-fi, replacing Tchaikovsky with Sinatra.

> *Did you say I've got a lot to learn?*
> *Well, don't think I'm trying not to learn,*
> *Since this is the perfect spot to learn,*
> *Teach me tonight.*

Slowly, Sharon looked up and focused her eyes before joining me in the overstuffed chair, her nudity now almost common, oh so *naturel*. She nestled in my arms as Frank began sinning . . . er, singing *Teach me tonight* . . .

> *One thing isn't very clear my love,*
> *Should the teacher be so near my love,*
> *Graduation's almost here my love,*
> *Teach me tonight.*

My swimming suit somehow found its way to the floor, two now nude instead of only one, I no longer trying to resolve the Church and my hormones.

"Nice dancing, Sharon," I whispered while biting her ear.

"You liked it?"

"Are you kidding? But how do you do that spread-eagle banister thing?" I said, holding her even more closely, if that were possible. "I particularly liked that."

"Practice, Jim. Late nights, late nights, waiting for you."

When somebody needs you,
It's no good unless she needs you,
All the way . . .

This night was beyond analyzing. Sharon's powers had overwhelmed me. She was singing her siren's song. I gathered her in my arms, gathered her sweet smell, her ambiance, her countenance into my total being. It had been a long, circuitous journey since those eighth grade nights in the swaying, listing, lonesome village tree house gazing at Eddie's girlie magazines. But tonight, Sharon and I danced *Swan Lake* together.

Who knows where the road will lead us,
Only a fool would say,
But if you let me love you,
It's for sure I'm gonna love you,
All the way,
All the way.

The summer of '58 became a potpourri of cleaning chicken cages for Lensch & Rusch, digging clay with Oscar, and plumbing with B. C. As July's humidity began attacking, enveloping the village, I was glad to be free of the depressed, hot, depressing clay pits, although B. C. and I got ourselves into some hot corners later on. I sweated alongside him digging trenches at Donnie Ryan's Belle Creek farmstead, at one of the innumerable Majerus Bellechester homes installing commodes and bathroom fixtures, at Donald O'Reilly's new home in the village where we plumbed kitchen appliances, bath and basement fixtures. We plumbed Reinhold Schulz' new home on water tank hill and Shug Ryan's Belle Creek farm, setting submersible pumps into his "damnable" well as B. C. so often uttered. B. C. taught me how to set grainy rope into sewer pipe joints, heat lead bricks to secure the joints, solder copper tubing for a perfect, leak-less seal without burning my hands with hot solder. He taught me how to seal commodes and faucets with caulking . . . well, just about everything in the plumbing business. I liked learning, too, because although I wasn't intending to become a plumber, electrician or meat cutter the rest of my life, I figured I would eventually own a house. These skills would come in handy, as they certainly did.

But simply working alongside B. C. was more important and enjoyable than even learning plumbing skills. B. C.—portly, high-forehead, five-by-eight stature—was one of the village's towering characters taking his rightful idiosyncratic place alongside Dave Franklin, Cy Benda, Oscar Decker, Red Ryan and Erv Richter. I had known B. C. forever, as he and Addie had been friends with Dad and Mother. They played Bridge and Five Hundred with Laura and Bill Mans, Bessie and Cy Benda, Leone and Casey Ryan, Mary and Luverne Haas, smoking cartons of Pall Malls and Chesterfields, drinking Grain Belt, laughing, joshing and having a "hell of a time," while biding four spades or a small heart slam. B. C. and Addie attended Holy Trinity, too, seeing me tripping over my cassock and spilling holy water innumerable times . . .

"How come you didn't become a priest at St. John's, Jimmy?" B. C. asked as we sweated copper tubing in Donald O'Reilly's basement. "You were a fair-to-middlin' altar boy for Fr. Smitty. Thought you might hang with it."

"Thought about it, B. C., but finally figured I couldn't handle the chastity requirement," I said, twisting copper-angled joints in place for soldering.

"Hell! That don't make a hell's bunch o' difference anymore. Priests becomin' more liberal than Minnesota Democrats. You probably could've been a priest and still got some action on the side," he said while sanding a copper tubing end with an emery cloth.

"But that would have been defeating the purpose of becoming a priest, B. C.," I said, centering flamed heat on a joint. "Priests and monks at St. John's dedicate their lives to God just for guys like you and me."

"Shoot! I do my prayin' myself. Your St. John's monks don't pray for *me*," B. C. snarled while sliding into a tight corner to set another ninety-degree joint.

"Oh yes, they do. They pray for everybody in the world, including folks in the village, even non-Catholics. You got too many sins, B. C., to gain purgatory or heaven all by yourself," I chided while retrieving more solder from his overflowing tool box, as we set hot and cold water tubing throughout the basement.

"Tarnation, you got that bass ackwards, Jimmy. I've been living a good life, faithful to the wife, few brews now an' then. The biggest thing the Lord'll take me to task for is cussin', I suppose. My exploration words just seem to pop out when a damnable joint won't fit, when these detestable fittings prove to be consternatious. Cussin' words help gettin' a joint into place, but I figure the Lord'll understand I was only lookin' for help while doin' my job. Hand me another angle joint there, Jimmy. We got to get this sonofa-bitchin' job done 'fore the day's kaput," B. C. said, squeezing his developing paunch into a tight corner.

"Lot's of guys in the village swear, B. C., but Dad didn't, at least when I was around."

"Your dad was a good man, Jimmy. Nope, he didn't cuss like me and Vern Haas. Between the two of us, we get enough swearin' in for the whole village, but there's worse things, like whoring around with women you oughten not to with, comin' home drunk ever night. You got a girl, Jimmy?"

"In Red Wing, a summer romance thing. Had a girl at college, but well, its probably over, me not being ready for the marriage thing yet, and she thinking I should be a priest."

"This Red Wing girl? You making out with her? More solder here, Jimmy."

"She's awfully nice, and we get in some good necking and

petting, but well . . . a guy's got to be careful, you know. Got to have the right rhythm and all that. Here's your solder, B. C."

"Help me get this damnable pipe in place. The sonofabitch doesn't want to go where it's suppose to. Put some English on that pipe, Jimmy. Get the fucker in there!" We pushed and scraped and bent pipe until it fit into the corner below the commode. "Damn, I didn't think we'd get 'er in, but see, those cussin' words helped." B. C. said he'd never practiced the Rhythm Method, it being too much counting and figuring. "You screwin' your Red Wing girl, Jimmy?"

"Uh . . . well, that's sort of personal, B. C. I . . . ah . . . we've come close a few times. She likes to dance to ballet music, so the other night she . . . well . . . executed a *pas de deux* or two, and an arabesque."

"Hell! Jimmy, don't know what you're talkin' about, 'pay for two?' but you're only young once. Go for it. Now, let's pack up and get back to town, if we can navigate that damn County Rd. No. 9. Why, they ought to plow it up and put the sonofabitch in Soil Bank. 'Taint much of a road. We're finished here for today; besides, you got a softball game tonight, ain't you?"

"Yessir, playing in the Zumbrota league. Game at seven."

"Let's get the hell out of here, then. We've done about as much damage to this place as we can for one day."

Carl "Cueball" Holst had been organizing softball teams in the village for several years, usually playing in the Zumbrota League, nights out behind their antiquated high school. That league, as well as the village baseball team, provided opportunities for would-be major leaguers to dream their dreams on the local level. Carl had played basketball for GHS in 1949, '50 and '51 with George O'Reilly, Hal Peper, Lyle Rusch, Tom Franklin, Harvey Opsahl and John Reese. Carl's basketball shot was unique in the county, perhaps Minnesota. His shot was as flat as a three-day-old Grain Belt. You see, Carl had converted his Dad's hay mow west of the village on County Rd. No. 9 into a basketball court where he would practice all hours of the night, fellows then joining him Sunday afternoons for dusty, hay-seed games above the milking parlor. But the hay mow rafters hung precariously low for getting off a real basketball shot. When the village fellows joined him, we were at a decided disadvantage, our shots bouncing off the low-slung rafters, chickens and wayward cats scurrying for safety. But Carl had adjusted his flat-as-a-crewcut-nonexistent-arch shot to the low rafters, creating one with absolutely no arch, impossible said the GHS physics teacher, but then, what did he know. Teams from Zumbrota, West Concord, Dodge Center and Pine Island couldn't believe it. They would have Carl tied up in the corner, never assuming he would actually get off a shot. Carl would release that ball toward the basket—his shot the antithesis of Lefty O's 1944 high-arching shot that had won the District Tournament—hit the back of the rim hard like Carl's cows slamming into milking parlor stanchions, the ball finally dropping through the net for two points.

Monday morning physics class: "Carl, your shot is not possible. According to the laws of physics there is no way you can send a projectile, a basketball in your case, into a downward-displaced net without an arch. The moon revolves around the earth; the earth revolves around the sun; everything depends on the law of gravity. Without an arch to your shot, the ball, theoretically, should only continue in a straight line. The ball will miss the basket. Physics Rule Number 33: No straight projectile can enter a basket without a minimal deflection of projectile displacement."

"Whatever! You ever come to the games, Teach? Blows your theory all to hell," Carl answered, his extensive, seemingly dis-jointed frame slumping in the chair. He paid no attention to the physics teacher or his textbook. Carl had developed his shot through trial and error, not physics' laws. There wasn't another shot like it in the county, maybe even Minnesota. Opposing guards would raise their arms and hands to guard his shot, but Carl would simply shoot between their arms, right over their heads. Two points for Cueball!

With his basketball success, Carl wanted to keep playing ball after high school, even though no teams offered to pay him for his flat shot. Instead, he turned to softball, organizing and managing the village team in the summer league. Summer of '58 Schulz

Transfer sponsored the team, Big "E" Schulz and Big "D" Dallas Diercks, Gary Holtz, Bob Madrick and Jimmy Franklin making up the team—Eddie Feiner's All Stars we weren't, but Village Boys of Summer, nevertheless, playing out our youthful dreams.

Big "E" and Big "D" had both been forces to contend with at GHS, Schulz at 6 ft. 3, 225 pounds had been a reserve on the famous 1944 team fielding local stars Phil Ryan, Gene Haas, Gerald "Lefty" O'Reilly, Dick Eyestone, Burt Eppen, Toby Buck, Willard Eppen, Hank Bartel, and Billy Schulz. Big "D" at 6 ft. 4, towered over us 5 ft. 10 guards and most of the league's centers. El and Dallas could certainly play ball, Schulz swinging his 36-inch bat for deep centerfield fences (Our town was so small that when that ball cleared centerfield, it cleared town!), Diercks smashed home runs and triples like Mickey Mantle. I would tag along with those fellows trying to pick up hints and tricks, sometimes even their girls, rarely getting lucky with a Texas League wimpy single to short right field. Bob Madrick, a muscular Illinois transplant to Red Wing and the village, could stroke a long ball, left handed even. Carl pitched, brother Gary covered shortstop or third base as we battled fellows we had battled in high school, not playing any longer for the glory of ol' GHS, only for ourselves and our girlfriends who sat in rickety, plank stands cheering our misadventures, impatiently waiting to head back to the village for a few beers at George's Corner Bar.

Sharon would drive out from Red Wing, so I could show off for her, my attempts usually failing from trying too hard. I was a better ball player *without* a girlfriend, but then, times were a-changing. Playing ball wasn't the *only* important thing anymore.

Whether victorious or not the team would head back to the village, congregating at George Lucman's for postgame analysis and fellowship, storming in loudly, tramping on the floor in muddy cleats while tossing bats, hats, gloves and shoes on bar stools and bar, thereby shaking the drowsy, regular patrons out of their melancholic reveries—toothless old farts with nowhere to be but the bar, their hang-dog heads rising slowly like a windowsill drinking bird. They squinted through glazed eyes, their ever-present boilermakers at the ready wondering who in hell was invading *their* torpid reserve. Sharon would snuggle against me in the antiquated wooden booths lining the wall as postgame analysis quickly began, dry throats being eased with long, tall, cool bottles of Grain Belt, Schlitz, Blatz . . .

"You sure fucked up that double play, Franklin."

"Nice catch on the foul line, Madrick."

"Where in hell did you get that throw, Cueball?"

"Hell of a smack, Schulz."

"Next, time, try to actually catch the ball, Gary."

"How in hell did you manage a double, Franklin?"

"Shit! We would have won the game if Cueball hadn't given up fifteen runs."

"Wait till next game."

As the beer flowed, as the Seagram's boilermakers slid down parched throats, our hits became longer, catches more dazzling, errors less significant, images and fantasies larger. The women enjoyed our postgame antics as much as the game, Sharon sliding in closer after two or three beers despite my odious locker room odor.

"Hell, Franklin, you should have slid into second as neatly as Sharon is now."

"At least I slid, Bob. You were afraid of getting a scab on your white ass."

Sunday afternoons, the town baseball team played down in the oppressing hollows of Mazeppa along the meandering Zumbro River, or along the steaming Wabasha riverfront under the Mississippi high bridge. The team members of my childhood—Vaughn Bein, the Lodermeier brothers, Jerry, Norb, Ed, Leonard—now retired from the game, bones, joints, ligaments and eyes too tired to run around a dusty, dry baseball diamond. But they still came to the ol' diamond to watch us, to remember their days when Vaughn David raced to first faster than Mickey Mantle, when Lefty O' scooped every ball screaming down the first base line, El Schulz driving towering balls over the left field gravel road, the defending fielder sliding in the gravel tearing tender skin from arms and hands—"Who the hell is that guy?"—Billy Schulz firing fast balls from the pocked pitching mound, balls often bypassing the catcher, horsehide slicing through the nonexistent chicken wire back-stop behind Blanche Barry's house. But that summer was, for the GHS classes of '53 '54, '55 and '56, a time to play out our fantasies, a time to become as big on the field as we were in our minds. It was important to play well, to beat Mazeppa, Wabasha, Pine Island, Bellechester. Big "D" even played for the Red Wing Aces a couple of seasons, tried out with Bill Rigney's Minnesota Twins too, but then settled for just Sunday afternoons at the ol' ball diamond on the edge of town. Just as well, we thought. We needed Big "D" to anchor the team.

July's heat and humidity gradually yielded to a warm, golden fall in the village and countryside, some would say the best time of year. But then they were folks living entire lives here, folks knowing little or nothing about other climates in Arizona, Florida or Southern California. These were hearty folks descended from hearty ancestors: Eppen, Haas, Barry, Johnson, Buck, Rosener, Anderson, Wipperling, Erickson. Grandfathers and great-grandfathers had immigrated from Norway, Sweden, England, Ireland, Germany, Austria, homesteading this township, this county in the 1850s and 60s after sailing treacherous seas for months on rolling, rat-infested ships. They became seasick, fighting scurvy, arriving emaciated, some dying before even arriving in Goodhue County. In the village you could talk about the weather, but you couldn't complain about it. No sir, for succeeding generations, complaining was not appropriate.

A late Sunday afternoon, the ball season over, I found myself sauntering alone through the deserted streets to sit near Ol' Buck again . . .

"Aren't only two rusting pickups on the street today, Buck, but that's 'bout two more than you'd a seen on Upper Street 'bout 1905. Horses is what villagers trusted then, not these new-fangled contraptions with harsh, smoking engines. Yet villagers started buying 'em 'cause they didn't have to strap 'em to a hitchin' post and feed 'em hay. I told you, couple days ago, starting up a village warn't an easy task, then. In the

teen years, the village finally erected that big water tank up on water tank hill providing running water to houses that could afford it. And they got more cemented streets that didn't actually go anywhere, and they eventually got electric lights, too. It was starting to look like a real town, Buck, looking like it was gonna stay around and not wither away like Claybank up the tracks there some.

See that clock hanging from the bank, Buck? First National hung it 'bout 1914. Been there ever since, though it didn't always tell good time. Folks liked the clock anyway, made 'em feel important. Later on they depended mostly on the noon and six o'clock fire siren anyway, the one Central fired up from Miller's Telephone Exchange above the bank. Warn't no need in the village for exact time. Well, mercantile folks saw opportunities, so they began hanging out shingles 'round the square here where you laying lazy all day, Buck. Lots o' changes over the years, though—starting up, buying, selling, exchanging, failing, fires, moving on to someplace more exciting. George Diercks started clerking in Banitt's store, but tired hisself out working for someone else. Bought 'em out. Herman Diercks got an early start on Lower Street, and Eppen & Ryan mercantile'd few years before selling out. My neighbor up the street, Ole Haga, bounced into the village to undertake, sell caskets and furniture. Buried lots o' pioneers here, even built my dad's casket 'fore buryin' him. Those automobiles were as persistent as flies, so 'fore long the village had garages to fix 'em 'cause they was always breaking down, Buck. Cavanaugh guy opened City Garage, and the village's master mechanic, John Yungers, fiddled at the Goodhue Garage before starting his own shop. And Henry Diercks worked a machine shop, too. 'Course Uncle Dave depended just on big-rumped work horses for his City Dray Line for lots o' years.

Things in the village slowed a bit during the first

war when folks got mighty sick, some dying with the big influenza outbreak. But by the beginning of the Jazz Age—you ain't much for music, are you Buck?—townsfolk were ready to kick up their heels, shake some of the dust off their new buckled shoes. That blind pig showed up again, what with prohibition and all, but folks came to the burg even though Highway 58 warn't where it is now. The village warn't like Chicago where all roads lead to it, Buck. You had to come here on purpose; you didn't just happen through. By the time Louis Armstrong and Bix Biederbecke and Paul Whiteman began blowing blue notes in Chicago and New York, George Mann and Eles Wseneing and William Hennings and G. B. Johns and H. E. Finney and Ole Carlson and Tom O'Reilly and Willard O'Reilly and D. W. O'Reilly and H. Swanson and Peterson and F. Fredrickson and W. Mehrkens and D. Kelly, Tom and Will Heaney and Wm Voth and Martin Vomhof and Wm Holst and Hein Matthees and Emma Thomforde had all settled their quarter sections or so out along County Rd. No. 9 just beyond the village limits. Grandfather David Franklin homesteaded out on the township line, Buck, figuring County Rd. No. 9 would get too busy for him. He set down in the same section as the Swedish Lutheran church, Section 18. Folks planted roots for several generations, kids later trekking to the high school in the village's old clapboard, wood-frame building long before we got the new brick school same year I popped into the village. They came to get learnin', Buck, some to raise hell. Some farmed here even before the railroad came through, but the Chicago Great Western helped 'em ship grains and livestock to distant markets. Belle Creek's still mad about not getting that railroad. They got the Irish O's instead.

Twenties were good years in the village, Buck, 'fore the stock market failed, that is, 'fore the Great Depression of the thirties. Lloyd Cook took over the newspaper then rehandled it the Goodhue County Tribune *and John Richter opened a merchandise store, and Arnold Stemman gave the Heaneys competition in the meat business, and Ryan and Nei Implement brought in McCormick-Deering farm machinery, and Jim Ryan began cracking eggs in his hatchery, and Art Lohman pumped oil and gas at Standard Oil over there, and Mrs George Johnson delivered milk to villagers from the back of a horse-drawn wagon, and Heinie Swenson became sole proprietor of the cafe. Now, you interested, 'cause I'm talking about Heinie, Buck?"*

Buck rolled a lazy eye toward me when I said his name, readjusted his position ever so lightly before I continued . . .

"Now, you might be thinking that the village had no music before Chas Wood bounced into the village in '47, but you'd be wrong about that, Buck. Germans and Scandinavians and Irish clans brought their music with 'em to the new country. They might not o' cared much for ol' Wagner and Mozart or that Beethoven fellow, but they liked their folk music, specially with accordions, Buck. How do you think all these old-time bands got to be in Minnesota—Whoopee John, Art Fitch's Polka Dots, the Kufus Brothers, the Six Fat Dutchmen? Did you ever think about that? Settlers had brass bands, cornets mostly without my clarinet and saxophone, early as turn of the century. Used to play for horse races and socials and doin's, just about ever place you could think of, Buck, if you were a-thinkin' dog. George Diercks played music, Fred Eppen too. Shoot! By the time the Great Depression kicked in, thirty-forty folks honked in a local band, sort of emulating John Phillip Sousa, but I don't suppose you a heard of Sousa. Townsfolk had, though. Why, Marldine Richter got his start, and Fred Vieths and Ole Haga even, when Ole wasn't embalming. And Frank O'Gorman, too, when he warn't lawyering, and Ben Gorman. Even Elmer

Bremer banged a paradiddle now and then. Marldine directed the village Concert Band in the early thirties, then the school board tapped him the same year I arrived in the village. Asked Marldine to start up a school band after school when he wasn't selling groceries. Said he would. He did.

Well, Buck, I arrived in a bad decade, folks not having three cents for a stamp, lots not even able to hook up to the new village sewer system. They still used, sometimes preferred, outhouses out back. Me too, and let me tell you, Buck, those hard, shiny pages of the Montgomery Ward catalog where mighty cold on my butt 'long 'bout January. But I was happy to be here, anyway . . . good place as any. Coulda been worse. I warn't much more than a toddler when the village got a drugstore and W. Sawyer took over the Goodhue State Bank—owning, not robing it—and Marldine Richter managed Sundberg Grocery when not practicing his clarinet or teaching the school band, and Mans & Benda opened their new gas station and my old friend Sidney Berg began soling shoes right there.

Yes sir, Buck, the village was on its way but the biggest deal was, when after considerable consternation (which the village had a reputation for in neighboring newspapers), and FDR's WPA help, we got ourselves a new two-story brick school with inside toilets and a real gymnasium just in time to begin my schoolin'. Folks said they weren't gonna send their children to Red Wing's high school. They was obstinate. They'd build a new building and by golly they did. Became the biggest deal in town, Buck; in fact, it was a heckuva deal. Warn't long 'fore Supt. Hubert replaced Supt. Eyestone and said we should have a football team, and Chas Wood built us a band, and custodian Lou Schinnert died and my dad replaced him, and we got school lunches serving warm milk and dry graham crackers, and Karl Tomfohr coached the boys of '44 to the state championship, well not exactly, but they went a long way, those boys, and the village wanted the rural one-room schools to join 'em in their new school but the township folks weren't ready for that in '49. It'd take some time, Buck, but the village warn't going any place. It'd been around sixty years already. It'd wait.

Down the street there, John Angus took to buying wheat and oats at the Elevator, and Fritz Shorter took to buying milk and churning butter at the Creamery, and Don Center took to making dollar bills at the Goodhue State Bank, and A. B. Overby telegraphed to the world from the railroad station, and Heaney's Market burned to the ground in '45, and Marshall-Wells Hardware opened in '47, and Art Eppen sold new ice-less refrigerators after the war, and Eddie Rosener pounded his anvil while singing Il Travatore arias, and the four Wisconsin horsemen, the Lodermeier Bros, rode into town on identical orange Allis Chalmers tractors to take over the town some years later, and John Berlinski became the new barman at the Corner Bar just across the street from where you is loungin', Buck, but you needn't get up to look. Just take my word for it.

The village, being out of the Great Depression now, organized festivals and parades and doin's on Memorial Day and the Fourth of July when Tommy O'Reilly and Karen Haas won blue ribbons for deco-rating their fat-wheel bikes, and thing's going pretty darn well in the village until Hitler unleashed his panzers and bombers a long, long way from the village, somewhere beyond Hader we heard later.

The village sent Doughboys to W.W.I and they sent GI's to W.W.II, Buck. Folks pitched in to defeat Hitler, though Hitler'd probably never heard of Goodhue. The Township did its part with rationing and bond drives and liberty drives and victory gardens and driving slower and not driving at all and writing letters to service men and sending its own home-grown boys to the war effort: LeVerne Diercks and Vince Goodsell and Charles O'Gorman, three of the first to leave our insulated village. Well, Buck, most GI's came home. Some didn't, though. They honored 'em in that big village celebration of '47.

Then I got myself into high school, finally, a hundred of us congregatin' in the second floor Assembly Hall with Super Hubert staring us down like a Master Sergeant. The rural districts had all abandoned their one-room schools, Girls and Boys outhouses too, their grammar texts, their McGuffey Readers, so though we were an all-white, all Christian school, we did have some diverse elements, like unruly students from Belvidere and Bellechester and Belvidere Mills and parts of Hay Creek and Featherstone and Belle Creek Townships, students who didn't know how to act in a village. After school, students hung out at Swenson's and Joe Shelstad's Place and Elsie's Cafe and Bartlett's Bowling Alley and they attended Luther League and 4-H and Holy Trinity catechism. Senator Edward Thye bored us to tears graduation night of '54 and we drove to the Wisconsin Island to roller skate, and I played my clarinet for Erv Richter one last waltz right across the street from where you sprawled out Buck, 'fore I shuffled out of the village to college, and . . . ,"

But Buck had suddenly gotten up from his prone position and began dog trackin' down the street around the corner of the Corner Bar toward the creamery. I was stunned seeing Buck move so rapidly. Apparently, he had gotten tired of hearing about the village. Apparently, he had gotten more information than he wanted.

"Well, Buck, that about brings you up to date. See you around, ol' friend."

By mid August I was working my fourth job now painting bleached midwestern, two-story clapboard houses and parched Gambrel-hipped barns instead of sweating copper joints with B. C. His new house business had come to a screeching halt, so I had found myself out on the deserted, unemployed street again, eating nightly supper with bachelors at Taylor's' Eat Shop while waiting for the U.S. Army to make an officer and gentleman out of me down in Georgia. I swabbed inch-deep, cracked barn siding out in the townships, slopping red paint on sponge-like planking, village homes, too, with Sherwin-Williams best white paint. And I succeeded in infuriating the village's German Lutherans, thereby denying me any hope of closing the theological gap between village Catholics and Lutherans.

Oh, the event began innocently enough when I acquired a job painting St. Peter's Lutheran on the western edge of the village—the village so small that the western edge was only three blocks from the eastern edge. That in itself was surprising—hiring a Catholic to paint a Lutheran church—but the Lutheran painters were busy and the church needed painting to cover up untold sins. I was their third or fourth choice, Catholic, but available.

The initial painting had gone well enough, white paint flowing smoothly, evenly on the outside walls and back. I had been especially careful while trimming the Gothic-shaped windows. I even traipsed inside a couple of times, wondering what on earth it was they did in here, Sundays, the inside devoid of Catholic medieval accouterments—holy water fonts, holy pictures, stations of the cross, Blessed Virgin Mary and St. Joseph statues. For two weeks I had been hoisting extension ladders, climbing, scraping and painting with ladders and scaffolding borrowed from a real painter, the retired Casey Ryan, until it was time to attack the soaring, high steeple looming above a towering peaked, smooth, moss-covered, shingled roof.

Preparing to scale the steeple like a latter-day rock climber, I had nailed two-by-four boards to the steep roof—fortunately not to the front "Wittenberg" doors—to mount the steeple. I straddled the roof peak, balancing precariously. Again, things went well, for a couple of days. I was gaining on Mount Sinai. It was on the final day that all hell broke loose, not on the front doors, but on the roof.

I had finally finished painting the precarious steeple and was gingerly straddling the peaked roof preparing to descend, this while holding a half full can of white paint in one hand, paint brushes in the other. I made a mistake—Uncle Dave would later absolve me of any official sin, but then he was Catholic, too—that went down in the annals of St. Peter's, forever sealing my fate with that faith.

My arms and legs were aching from climbing and swabbing paint. I wanted to descend quickly. Instead of proceeding cautiously, this being the last day, I decided to sit on my butt while holding the paint and brushes at shoulder level. I would simply slide from one two-by-four to the next, my boot heels stopping me at each board until reaching the eaves and the ladder. I sat on the peak in preparation, momentarily viewing the village from this high site. So far, so good. I slid to the first board, stopped, breathed deeply, then headed for the second. But my hells . . . er . . . heels, didn't catch the second board, slipping instead to the third, over that, my momentum now increasing, heading for a 30-foot drop. I was concerned about my welfare, my soul, my life. The brushes went flying, but most significantly, the paint went flying, splaying white paint the breadth of the shingled roof, marring it, scarring it, a sin of such magnitude that it remained there years for all to see.

"It was that little sonofabitching Catholic Franklin boy who did this, on purpose, I might add. That's what those Benedictines taught him at St. John's."

I had only one more board to stop me before flying off the roof and into eternity. Jesus, Mary, and Joseph, my feet caught the metal eave halting my downward thrust and saving Mother the expense of a St. Columbkill's funeral. I had escaped eternity, but not the eternal wrath and damnation of the Lutherans. I climbed down the ladder on uncertain legs, collected my paint supplies, and drove out of the church's lot, but not out of their memories. I was forever damned by that congregation.

Mea Culpa.

By Thanksgiving snow flurries had again returned to the village, encapsulating it for the next six months just as winter had been doing long before white Europeans homesteaded this territory, long before T. B. Sheldon brought his railroad through here. This secluded burg out on the high prairie had endured blizzards, devastating fires, hostile attacks, wind storms, locust plagues, droughts, Democrats, Republicans, Lutherans and Catholics. It wasn't likely another hard winter would see its demise.

But from a later, thirty-year perspective, my personal presence in the village was beginning to wane that late fall of '58 as I packed my bags to become an infantry officer, infiltrating the South like General Sherman invading Atlanta, or as the locker boys of the village often said, "Like shit through a fan!" I couldn't foresee, then, that although I would be absent for long periods during ensuing years, the village attachment would remain, in spite of the Lutheran's hopes, desires and prayers.

Chapter 6

Gold star mothers

Boys of Goodhue County

A NARROW BOUNDARY SHIELDED MY FIRST 17 YEARS as I traveled mostly to settlements at White Rock, Cannon Falls, Pine Island, Welch, Vasa, Hay Creek, Red Wing, less often to Kenyon and Wanamingo in the western townships. Periodically, I visited Wabasha County hamlets at Oak Center, Zumbro

Falls, Mazeppa and Lake City before breaking out of southeastern Minnesota to central Minnesota's St. John's where, with music groups, I later toured desolate Dakota buffalo country devoid of horizons. Notwithstanding my limited horizons, I was little different from friends. The people, the values and beliefs I had been indoctrinated with were exclusively of the Upper Midwest White European Immigrant Ilk (UMWEI). During the forties and fifties, Irish, Swedish, Norwegian, English or German ancestry was the extent of my known diversity. Oriental, Asian, African-American were unheard of unless we entered inner city Minneapolis or St. Paul, staying on well-traveled Summit or Hennepin Avenues if we did.

November 20, 1958, I left my known Upper Midwest to begin Basic Officers Training (BOT) at Ft. Benning, Georgia's Officers Candidate School (OCS), sort of an updated "ninety-day wonder" elementary school. I subsequently entered a region devoid of my upbringing, a region holding and expressing different community values, different religious beliefs, different ethnic diversity. I was both excited, eager and naive about what I would encounter, yet the Ford purred smoothly past the Bellechester turnoff, Zumbrota's Blue Goose Tavern, the Wagon Wheel—deep-fried french fries filtering the autumn air—onto Highway 52 past Pine Island's Cheese Mart, Oronoco's bluegill-filled blue lakes, Rochester's enveloping medical clinics, and southward toward the Old South. I was leaving the known, venturing into the unknown.

I had never entered Iowa prior to that trip, the first night spent in Sharon's Iowa City. I thought I was *in* the South simply because Iowa City was south of the village. Little did I know then that years later I would attend the University of Iowa, get married, and sire two Iowa City-born and U of I children. This night at the Jefferson Hotel, I felt far-removed from the village, attacking the land of Hawkeyes instead of Gophers. But I didn't dally as Ft. Benning awaited my arrival.

The next day I headed south into Missouri, skirting the meandering Mississippi River through Cape Giradeau, spending the night in Paducah, Kentucky, certainly out of the Upper Midwest now. I had begun noticing a non-Minnesota dialect the last hundred miles among gas station attendants, waitresses, and bar tenders. Farther south the dialect and drawls themselves went south, lower, longer, slower.

I shuffled into a bar nestled under the angular high bridge in Paducah, Kentucky, a "Colonel Sanders" good ol' boy sauntering up ever so slowly. "What'll it be, Mr?" Without even realizing I was in Paducah instead of the Corner Bar, I ordered a Grain Belt.

"A what?" Colonel Sanders asked.

"Don't you have Grain Belt here?"

"Not only don't we have it, we don't even know what it is," he said, impatiently wiping the bar with a gray rag. "You must not live in these here parts. Where're you from, fellow?"

"Minnesota."

"That explains everythin'. Y'all in Kentucky, Yankee, and we don't got no Grain Belt. How 'bout somethin' else?"

"You have Hamm's?"

"No hams, just burgers with southern fries. Try again."

"Just make it a Miller High Life, then. You have that?" I asked, sheepishly trying not to make a fool of myself.

"Miller High Life, right." Geez! I thought, only two days out of the village and already I had made my first faux pas. How many more would there be in the next six months.

I had enrolled in the Reserve Officers Training Program (ROTC) at St. John's to fulfill my military duty. It was either that or wait to be drafted. I opted for second lieutenant bars upon graduation. Studying military science, an oxymoron if there ever was one, was all right, though. Over-the-hill W.W.II and Korean vets: beer-bellied sergeants and monotone, uninspiring colonels lectured us in war-remnant steel Quonset huts out behind the monastery about M-1 rifles, artillery pieces, regiments, battalions, divisions, platoons, squads, the chain of command, the commander and chief, saluting, shining black boots, map reading, right shoulder arms by-the-numbers, escape and evasion, and WACS. We read inane, boring, brown-covered military manuals with stenciled titles, executed close-order drill maneuvers in the armory, and attended summer camp for novice, pre-soldiers at Ft. Riley, Kansas, where we fought more chiggers and mosquitoes than Aggressors. If Aggressors were Kansas chiggers and Minnesota mosquitoes, there would be no more war. We crawled on tender, academic white bellies through dry, red Kansas dirt sucking up little red chigger devils until they bit every pore on our ankles, legs, bellies, chest, arm pits and asses. But we were soldiers ... well, not real soldiers; rather, getting-ready-to-be-real soldiers. But for reading the military manuals (U.S. Army C143285769–102–967), shooting guns, firing bazookas, firing mortars, tossing live grenades at straw-filled "gooks," saluting, learning not to say "sir" to sergeants, the big brass would award us with little brass bars on SJU's graduation day, as well as our Military Occupation Specialty (MOS), officially making us Officers and Gentlemen (by an act of Congress), and unofficial Benedictine monks (BM) like Brother Leo. I particularly appreciated the "gentleman" award, never having officially been one, also becoming an unofficial monk.

I sat at the curved, forlorn bar in downtown Paducah drinking a Miller Beer, wondering how I would tolerate active military duty. I was mildly apprehensive about the next six months, but that was only because it would be a new experience in a new land. I thought it would be all right, not having anything against the army. After all Dad, Private Thomas B. Franklin, had seen action in W.W.I when General Pershing pulled him off the Franklin farm—146.12 acres, Section 18, Goodhue Township, 111 North, Range 15 of the 5th Principal Meridian, Goodhue County, Minnesota; neighbors John Bremer, J. A. Peterson's Box Elder Farm, C. D. Fors, J. C. Johnson, D. F. Larson, Andrew Newman, and the Evangelical Lutheran Church. Grandfather Franklin had sired sons Tom, Dave, Pat and Jim. General Pershing said three were enough to run a farm. Grandfather could give up one, so Dad became a Doughboy fighting Huns in France at Verdun and Somme with other Goodhue Township men: Earl Ahern, John Diercks and Dwight Erickson. He sailed to France in 1918 on an oil-leaking listing freighter, and was subsequently assigned to an infantry squad to shoot real bullets at real Germans instead of deer in the cornfields or gophers on the township's dusty roads just beyond the tree-in-the-middle-of-the-road. Yet, Dad talked little about it—only one significant episode—keeping most of the war inside for his fifty-eight years. Invading Ft. Benning, I was only following in his infantryman's labored, dog-faced footsteps.

The beer slid down easily even if it wasn't a Grain Belt or Hamm's. I ordered a second as two southern belles—obvious, as they weren't talking Minnesotan, "Ya, you betcha . . .Ya, sure, that's fer darn sure, then . . .You got that right, hon"—entered, sitting in a booth and immediately plugging the jukebox with southern redneck music. I wondered about them as I watched cars crossing the Ohio River high bridge, wondered about life here so far from the village. I pondered these folks living, growing up, never knowing there was a Goodhue County.

Villagers defended their perimeter-barrier as fiercely as Huns had at the Hindenburg Line Dad fought at, the village barrier causing my friends to lead sheltered, protected lives. Television hadn't arrived in the burg until 1949 and then only at Arts' Bar, off limits to teenagers. Tomfohr's International Harvester store got one—plopped it right between two blazing red tractors—eventually selling them to unsuspecting locals saying TV was the wave of the future to folks whose future was already obvious. The Corner Bar hung a set on a two-by-four near the Seagram's Seven and Hamm's Bear signs; Shelstad's and Swenson's Cafes finally got sets so customers could watch snow-filled screens while chomping on greasy burgers. Television broadcasting had extreme difficulty breaking through the village's perimeter-barrier, though. And it was a long time coming to households, the Franklins not getting TV until 1953. Before that we knew what happened inside the perimeter, little about people or places outside. We had been secure, cozy in our UMWEI.

Villagers traveled little in the thirties, forties and early fifties, gasoline not especially high priced, but leisure driving thought to be frivolous. Detroit designed basic cars for driving to town for groceries, feed and feed supplements, bolts, nails, aspirin, feminine napkins at Eddie's Drugstore, not for gallivanting around the county or state, much less the country. News from the East, the West, the South reached us slowly, if at all. Oh, we read the *Daily Republican Eagle*, the *Minneapolis Tribune*, James Goodhue's *St.*

Paul Pioneer Press. Villagers weren't illiterate, by any means. It's just that we knew mostly our own. We didn't know folks from other places and many villagers felt that was just fine. Villagers were doing all right just they way they were.

But a tiny hole in the perimeter released me to four years at St. John's, opening my eyes and mind to views other than villagers, other than mine, even though most Johnnies were White European Catholic (WEC) offering little more diversity than townsfolk. St. John's did accept a handful of token African Americans from the Bahama Islands, not inner city St. Paul. The campus sported no Jews, Buddhists nor Islamites. Diversity awareness came primarily from reading, study, lectures, rather than real life.

Sipping my Miller's while eavesdropping on the two giggling women, I pondered the impending changes in my life, suspecting I would encounter considerably more diversity at Ft. Benning, maybe even regional or religious persecution. I ordered a third brew, "Another Miller's here."

"Where you from, Mr? Don't sound nor look like you from our parts. Kind of nasal in the nose, I'd say. Sound like a Yankee to me."

"Yankee?"

"Damn Yankee, in fact. We whipped yo asses in the war; should've kept right on attackin' all the ways to Canada, if you ask me."

"What war are you talking about?"

"The civilian war. What other war was there?" he snarled, popping the cap off a fresh Miller's and slamming it onto the bar, the sound like a musket shot echoing through the bar.

"Well, my Dad was in W.W.I, and lots of men in my village fought in W.W.II, and fellows fought in the Korean Conflict, too."

"Hell, those were measly skirmishes. I'm talking real war here, the Civil War, Confederates vs. Yankees, North vs. South. Didn't you study nothin' in school?" he said, pushing the fresh beer toward me while looking me in the eye as if he wanted to *start* a war.

"Sure, but well, the Civil War has been over for over one hundred years. Up north we've been fighting Lutherans more than

Confederates. You a Confederate?" I asked, suddenly aware of what I was asking. Must be the third beer.

"You got that right, Yank. Stars and bars and proud of it. Confederate to the core," he said, sidling down the bar to fix a couple of mint juleps for the booth ladies. Wow! I thought. I hadn't anticipated this. I hardly remembered anything about the Civil War. When had we studied that; eighth grade, sixth grade? I had forgotten everything I knew about it, recalling only that it had happened and we northerners . . . er "Yankees," had won. For me a Yankee was a New Englander, not a Minnesotan. I had never thought of myself as one, but this bartender did, and maybe those ladies in the booth did, too. I suddenly wondered if I *looked* Yankee. What does a Yankee look like? I had no idea, but I'd probably find out.

I was only in Kentucky, not even the Deep South yet, but was beginning to feel *I* was now one of the diversified, a minority in a major land. It felt odd. I had never been singled out, just one of the guys or gals at GHS, an Irish Catholic White Democrat (ICWD). But I wasn't to this bartender and probably not to the booth ladies. Were they laughing at my Yankee looks, whatever they were? Were they picking up on my Yankee dialect? Is that why they were snickering as I walked past their booth to my Ford? Damn! I thought. I'm a long way out of the village.

The next day I actually entered the Deep South—Alabama, Mississippi, finally Georgia . . . "Y'all ain't from around here, is you?" the cute, young, blond-trussed waitress exclaimed when I asked for a breakfast menu. "You want some hominy grits, hon?" she said, her prodigious cleavage distracting me from reading the menu. "Eggs and what?" I asked, almost saying "'horny" instead of "hominy."

"Sure, hon. Don't you know what hominy's is? Well, I'll sure enough fetch you some, then. You just sit there sweet as a bun-like an' I'll bring you a sweet breakfast with a side o' grits," she said, toddling to the grill, her dress tight in all the right places, southern-like. I glanced around the diner wondering if others were looking at me, as if I had a boil on my nose, as if I were wearing a sign "Yankee Here." But folks just sipped coffee, read the newspapers while my eyes kept following the cute waitress as she slid effort-lessly along the counter serving hominy grits and eggs and southern fries, pouring coffee to beagle-eyed truckers. But, I thought, if all southern gals were as cute and nicely shaped as she, I could forgive their Yankee taunts and slow, southern drawls, y'all.

"Where're you headin' mostly, hon?" she asked, setting my plate in front of me while bending low, distracting me from testing the hominy.

"Ft. Benning, Georgia for army training. Got to report in a few days. Just passing through, ma'am," I said, attacking my eggs and grits.

"Ooooh! That's mighty fine, hon. Big man like you got to protect us fair belles," she said, her body moving simultaneously in several directions while serving men lingering at the counter, they too enticed by her sweet cleavage. The eggs were tasty, but I didn't know what to think about the grits, they not emitting much flavor, I thought reaching for the Tabasco sauce. I would much prefer home fried potatoes at Swenson's Cafe, but then, I wasn't at Swenson's. I was at a whistle-stop somewhere in the hills of Georgia eating southern fried eggs and hominy grits, gazing at a luscious blond-haired waitress showing me more cleavage than I'd ever seen in the village. And she talked cute, too. Maybe there was something to this southern thing, I thought.

I finished my eggs and grits, left a bigger tit . . . er, tip than normal for the cutie, waved as she flashed bright teeth and a full-lipped, wet, sensuous smile. I'd remember her while entering Georgia and pulling up to the gates of Ft. Benning. At the last pissing stop I had changed into my uniform according to official orders (U.S.A. 5869403–5–79856–383726RN), stating to report for duty in full dress uniform. As I pulled up to the guard's gate an MP corporal or buck sergeant with one chevron clipped off a smart, crisp salute, embarrassing me as I forgot I was actually an officer. I said I was reporting for duty.

"Yessir, sir," the corporal or private or sergeant barked. "Take a right on General Eisenhower Way, then a left on General Pershing Boulevard to Fort Headquarters. Report to the Officer of the Day. And have a good day, sir," he said, clipping off another razor-edged salute. I managed a wimpy ROTC salute in return before driving into the military compound for two months of training to see if the army could actually make a real-life officer and gentleman out of me instead of just a paper one.

That regional diversity showed up immediately in the barracks while I unpacked my duffel bag into a footlocker at a double-decked bunk, hundreds of bunks lined up in an open, second floor hanger-sized barracks. My bunkmate, Jedidiah Robert Lee, was a great-great-grandson of *the* Robert E. Lee, for heaven's sake! And the other voices I heard were obviously from places beyond the village. I heard a Georgian talking about his girlfriend, "She might can do it," he said, apparently talking about screwing; a Louisianian bragging about eating jambalaya and gumbo soup; a Texan boasting about long horns and long dongs. I heard New England twangs and New York nasal noses . . . well, about everything except *normal* Upper Midwestern. There were non-Catholics, too, from Bob Jones University, Oklahoma Baptist University, Texas Southern University, Southern Methodist, The University of the South for Ever-Loving Non-Catholic Evangelicals, plus the U of Texas, A & M, M & M, Rice, Grain, Tennessee, Alabama. Why, it was overwhelming, the differences between their backgrounds and mine. What we did have in common was our green-behind-the-ears second lieutenant brass bars, this untested and untried regiment fated together for the next two months while growling captains and majors and colonels and sergeants beat us into military submission instead of civilian life.

"Where y'all from?" Jedidiah R. Lee, Tennessee, my lower bunkmate, asked while emptying a duffel bag on his bunk. I knew he had spoken, yet I didn't understand his drawl.

"Where y'all from, I say again?"

"I didn't know you were speaking to me, Jedidiah. Minnesota, up north," I said, spilling my bag on the upper bunk.

"I know where Minnesota is, Yankee. Y'all north of the Mason-Dixon line."

"Just where is that line, Jedidiah?"

"Divides Maryland from Pennsylvania, the Yankees from the

Confederates, the South from the North, me from you. Big line, strong line, and don' you forget it."

Jedidiah was six-foot-five, red-haired, angular, strong as Goliath and a chewer of Bull Durham tobacco. I was hoping he wouldn't begin beating on me for being a Yankee. "Oh! Where are you from, Jedidiah?"

"Possum Hollow, Tennessee, up on the Georgia border and mighty proud of it. Never thought I'd a be bunkin' with no damn Yankee," he said, slapping me on the back, "but you don't look so bad. I got time to straighten you out."

"Thanks. And, well, we got to bunk together for eight weeks, becoming officers and all. I'm glad to meet you. We've got a lot to learn about this army business."

"You ain't jus whistlin' 'Dixie,' Yank. Y'all *in* Dixie!"

For the next two months we played little tin soldiers just as my childhood chums had done in the village, but now marching through Georgia instead of Minnesota. The reveille bugle sounded at five o'clock for calisthenics followed by breakfast—"How do you like your eggs?"— in the mess hall. We jumped into deuce-and-a-half trucks, M-1 rifles slung over our backs, bouncing to Ft. Benning's farthest outpost where we endured endless field lectures on map reading, defensive perimeter positions, enemy attacks, firing bazookas, firing mortars, firing artillery shells, integrating infantry with mechanized tanks, plus spit-shining boots, polishing brass buckles, and making cots you could bounce a dime off. We ran and sweated and studied and listened and saluted, arms, legs, bodies becoming taut, military, slowly replacing soft civilian bodies and attitudes with military tough, shit talk! and manners. We hiked twenty miles strengthening legs, feet, minds. We were officers in training, yes sir, sir! Yet, officers without commands. That would come later in a far off Alaska, Hawaii, Texas, Oklahoma, Kansas, Missouri at a Ft. Sill, Ft. Riley, Ft. Leonard Wood post.

The army threw everything at us they could, including live machine gun rounds as we crawled beneath barbed wired emplacements, racing, red hot bullets zinging above our heads, officers shouting at us to keep heads and asses down, as if we didn't already know that. They rolled out their biggest guns, biggest shells,

Gold star mothers

259

biggest tanks, and biggest mouths as we sat in field bleachers watching war games unfolding a thousand yards downrange. "Someday," they growled, "you men will be commanding battles like this." "Someday," they growled, "you'll be expected to command a skirmish or battle in a far off country." "Someday," they groaned, "you'll actually become officers instead of lily white college boys."

Georgia days, even in November, were fiery, endless while sitting on hard-ass'd, sun-bleached plank bleachers. One such day, while listing to a colonel drone on about artillery attacks in support of infantry ground troops, I began drowsing off, chin dipping toward my olive drab fatigues. I began daydreaming about rubber gun wars (RGWII) back in the village . . .

> *"What we need, Jack, is heavy artillery to support our infantry squads against the Lutherans," I said one lazy, drowsy afternoon in 1947 at Jack O'Reilly's house. "We're still using the same oak stock guns John Yungers designed a couple of years ago. They're okay for close-in fighting, but we're having a hard time routing the Lutherans from their stronghold behind St. Peter's Lutheran."*
>
> *"What're we gonna do about it, Jimmy? These guns are all we have. They're good enough," Jack said, growing impatient with my idea. We'd been skirmishing against the Lutherans for two summers throughout the village, firing inner-tube-strength rubbers from distances of ten- to thirty-feet, sometimes winning a skirmish, sometimes losing. But John Yungers, Harold Lensch, Noisy Rusch, Fritz Schulz, Frederick Rusch were smart and talented, even if they were Lutherans. They kept making stronger, longer-barreled guns that would smack and bruise a guy at twenty-feet. We Catholic Crusaders needed to devise a more powerful weapon. I'd been thinking about it, nights in my tree house.*
>
> *"Jack, now listen to me once more. If we just*

expand on the inner tube idea, we could make an artillery piece to bomb them. Why don't we go to work on it? Might help us in the next Lutheran battle."

"Oh, all right Jimmy, but tomorrow. I don't want to start today."

That night, as I sat alone and cross-legged in my swaying tree house, the wind blowing lightly from water tank hill, I figured I could cut an inner tube lengthwise instead of crosswise, thereby obtaining a longer rubber. I could build a wooden stand and projector from lumber I'd find behind Streater's Lumber, get heavy duty clamps from Jesse's Hardware and other needed stuff from B. C. Majerus' Gas & Appliance & Sometime Hardware Store. Then I had a brilliant idea. I'd buy white flour from Heaney & Gorman, fill brown paper lunch bags and use them as artillery shells. If packaged properly in the rubber sling, I'd have an artillery piece just like in Dad's W.W.I Pershing Army. Planning the mortar piece, I fell asleep dreaming of a successful conquest against the Lutherans.

Next morning I hustled out of the house after two bowls of Wheaties and three slices of Wonder Bread toast, then scurried down to Jack's to tell him of my plan. He was more encouraging this morning, so we ambled to Streater's for wood, Jesse's for bolts, B. C's for clamps, then to my house to build the mortar piece. We sawed and cut, stretched rubber and bolted until the thing at least looked like a mortar. We persisted throughout the afternoon until it sort-of functioned like an artillery piece as we slingshot progressively larger stones thirty to forty feet out beyond the tree house and pine trees. Next day we would try the flour bomb.

"I need five pounds of white flour, Dennis," I said, plopping two dollars on the counter at Heaney & Gormans' Market.

"Gonna bake a cake, Jimmy?"

"*Naw, Jack and me are making a mortar gun to bomb the Lutherans.*"

"*Bomb the Lutherans? What have they done now?*" Dennis said, actually getting the flour for me.

"*Just a friendly battle, Dennis. Nothing serious, but, well . . . it's time they got their comeuppance, what with Luther nailing his 95 Theses to Wittenberg's doors. Jack and me figure it's time to nail 'em back.*"

"*How do you know about all that?*"

"*Father Smith talks about it all the time in catechism class. We're gonna beat the Lutherans into hell with our new mortar,*" I said, grabbing the flour and rushing out the front door, almost knocking Emma Kindseth and her ever-present purse into the gutter.

We experimented with the mortar for two days trying different sizes and loads, even draining Mother's dozen eggs, filling them with flour to use as flour bombs, but they always broke before getting launched. Boy! It would be great bombing the Lutherans at their headquarters compound. They'd never expect an artillery attack, Jack and I thought as we fine-tuned the mortar, ending the test day covered with white flour ourselves.

By the end of the week we could fire a flour bomb twenty yards, splashing and spreading flour near our target but not yet on it. We had work to do, but soon we'd be firing at Lutherans.

"*Ain't seen much of you whimpering Catholics lately,*" John Yungers said a couple of days later in front of the Goodhue Tribune *office on Lower Street.*

"*Hi, John. We've been busy, but we haven't been whimpering. You must have us mixed up with the Methodists.*"

"*Methodists, shit! I know and smell a fishy mackerel snappin' Catholic when I see one, and you're one. Why, I ought to smack you right now, but guess I'll wait to use my new long-range rubber gun on you. You Catholic altar boys show up Saturday morning and we'll have ourselves a battle," John said, huffing and puffing toward Bartlett's Bowling Alley.*

I was excited. This is just what we wanted—a challenge to try out our new artillery piece. I rushed up to Jack's house by the old ball diamond and excitedly told him about the pending RGWII challenge in two days. Yungers and his band of Evangelical Lutherans had laid down the challenge. The Catholic Crusaders would be there to meet it, that was for dern sure.

For the next two days Jack and I fined-tuned the mortar, strolling down the rusted railroad tracks a couple of miles to Claybank for secret test firing. We didn't want to divulge our secret gun. The mortar wasn't perfect, as we often returned home covered with white flour instead of the intended target, but we were getting closer; besides, we were running out of money to buy flour. We only had one more day for test firing, and we had to increase our accuracy.

Jedidiah elbowed me in the ribs to wake me as a snappy captain marched in front of the bleachers slapping his swagger stick (idiot stick to the noncoms), eyes burrowing in, searching to seek and destroy sleeping second louies. I came to, to hear the droning colonel . . . "Now lieutenants, the best means of accurately firing an artillery piece one thousand yards or more is to utilize the Bracket Method rather than a helter-skelter shooting tactic. You'll notice, to your immediate front a 105 mm, M–101A1, 8.5 foot, 4,978 pound, split-tail carriage howitzer with a sustainable rate of fire at three rounds per minute, range 12,315 yards. We will fire at that white refrigerator target downrange 2,000 yards. It's unlikely the forward observer can call in directions to hit it on the first round, but he'll certainly do so by the third round. His method, men . . . bracketing. Fire one when ready!"

B O O M!

A projectile zipped from the howitzer screaming toward the

white target 2000 yards downrange, but landed a hundred yards high of the target on the mountain side. "Now, if you'll properly observe, the gunner will make an adjustment to land the second round short of the target. Fire two when ready."

B O O M!

A second shell screamed downrange as our ears rang from the backfire. The projectile landed 100 yards short of the target, all second louies observing carefully in U.S. standard-issue binoculars. "Now gentlemen, and I use that term lightly, the forward observer, whom you cannot detect, will divide the divergence between the first shell and the second shell. He has bracketed his target. The third shell will blow that refrigerator all to hell. Fire three rounds for effect."

B O O M!...B O O M!...B O O M!

Three consecutive shells screamed toward the target. As we anticipated, direct hits blew that discarded General Electric W.W.II-era refrig all to hell, just as the colonel predicted. After the target had been defrosted, the colonel began a long harangue about firepower and artillery maintenance, even though I was infantry and not artillery. I'd be shooting M-1 rifles, not howitzers. I got drowsy again, daydreaming . . .

Skipping with Jack along the Chicago Great Western tracks past the landmark white-washed coal silo toward Claybank, I excitedly talked about our last day of range testing. "You know, Jack, I'll bet if we bracketed our shells on the target, we might improve our accuracy. It just makes sense that we'll never hit the target with one bag of flour, we might with the second, but we surely could with a third. Let's fire the first shot long, the second short, then the third should be right on," I said as we toted our mortar, secretly covered with a gunny sack from the Elevator, to Claybank for final testing.

"You think that'll work, Jimmy?"

"I don't know, but let's give her a try. Those Lutherans will be loaded for bear tomorrow morning. We got to get this thing working."

We hopped and skipped the rails and creosoted ties toward Claybank, lugging our mortar but enjoying the balmy day—sun shinning brightly, humidity low, corn and beans high, fields emerald-green—as the passing days moved through the summer. Jack, Lee, Bob, Larry, Tommy O'Reilly and other Boy Scouts had trekked these rusted, undulating Dinky rails often, hiking to Claybank for scout outings where we rubbed sticks together hoping to light a fire, but deferring to farmer's matches when the sticks usually failed. Jimmy Ryan owned every piece of Boy Scout equipment there was, but most of the boys only owned a Boy Scout cap, a small knife, canteen, and maybe a mess kit. Yet, we were pioneers marching beyond the village's borders to Claybank, Bellechester, Finney's Woods, even to White Willow, which wasn't there anymore, one of the innumerable ghost towns of the county.

"Now, Jack, you set the target about twenty yards downrange, and I'll set up the mortar." Jack rushed off to place the target—his mother's discarded, veiled Easter hat—at least he said it was discarded, while I adjusted the mortar and filled brown paper lunch bags with flour. This had to work. I was sort of confident it would with my new bracketing, firing operative.

"All right, Jack, let's fire this one about five yards long of the target. Fire one when ready."

We released the clothespin catch catapulting the flour bag toward the veiled Easter hat. It landed five yards long splaying the sullen Claybank clay with white flour. "Great round! Jack. Load round two. Let's fire the second round five yards short of the hat, then mark it on the mortar board with a pencil. Fire round two, when ready."

The bag floated toward the veiled hat landing three yards short, again splaying white flour on the sullen clay. "I think we've got it, Jack. Lock and load round three. Fire when ready." We released the taut rubber, the brown bag lofted toward Easter, Jack and I excited, anxious, desperate. The bomb seemed to linger a long time in the cerulean sky; maybe we had more arching trajectory on it than the other rounds. It wanted to hang over Claybank instead of landing on Claybank. But finally, it descended, hopefully toward the hat. It did, smacked directly on it obliterating the black veil with white flour. We were ready for the Lutherans (RGWII) tomorrow morning in the village.

The Crusaders gathered at the former Catholic Church basement hole at 0800 hours. Jack O', Bob O', Larry O', Lee J—was he Catholic or a spy?—George O', Pat O', Tom O', even brother Tom checked camouflaged gear, tightened belts, tied baling twine around pant legs, blackened faces with burnt cork. The fellows adjusted short, medium and long-range rubber guns as Jack and I brought out the mortar for the first time.

"What the hell is that?" Larry O' asked.

"Our new mortar. We're gonna blast five more sacraments into the Lutherans with this thing," I said, adjusting the heavy rubber on the awkward-looking Rube Goldberg contraption.

"Hell! That thing'll never work," brother Tom snarled, often the skeptic concerning my inventions. "You guys are jerks for thinking it will."

"Does. Jack and I test-fired it this week," I retorted while filling the paper bags with flour.

"Well, let's synchronize our watches," Jack said, pulling out a pocket watch, obviously his dad's.

"But I don't have a watch," Lee whined.

"Well, just pretend then," Jack snapped. "Ready, synchronize at 0815. Mark!"

We departed from the deep church basement dirt hole deploying through the weeds and underbrush, up the street marching toward St. Peter's Lutheran on the quiet western front. A light morning mist hung over the village as we darted like real GIs toward the school and cover before making our final assault. The squads with rifles moved out as point squads while Jack and I brought up the heavy artillery in the rear. We reconnoitered near the school swings and teeter-totter. "Alpha Omega squad, you guys begin a right-flanking action, then bring up the end. Beatitude squad, you blessed fellows execute a left-flanking movement. Jimmy and I'll bring up the rear with the mortar. It's 0817. We attack at 0830. Move out!" Jack commanded as the squads began creeping, crawling through back yard weeds and thistles, darting from tree to tree, alley to alley, garage to garage, outhouse to outhouse, under '46 Fords and '47 Plymouths, even a couple of Model Ts, past Hank Befort's moving ever closer to the Lutheran headquarters behind St. Peter's near a copse of trees. Jack and I hoped that if our point squads were detected, they'd offer cover for our heavy artillery. We moved toward St. Peter's lugging our mortar under the cover of spreading elms, weeping willow trees, odoriferous outhouses, lean-to garages, unmown back yards, Maytag-washed Long-Johns blowing in the breeze like regimental flags. Twenty yards from the church we slid into a ravine running from Oscar Decker's shack to the church, a good place to set up our mortar.

We heard the Lutherans talking excitedly about what they were going to do to the irreverent, domineering Catholics, those fishy, mackerel-snapping Doughboys who believe in seven sacraments instead of two, whimpering fellows who recite their sins to priests instead of directly to God; fellows who constantly badmouth Martin Luther for breaking away from the Romans to start his own church, Martin refusing to accept paid indulgences as a way into heaven.

Jack and I set up the mortar in the ravine, undetected, but within hearing range of the Lutherans. They were deploying their Evangelical Squad, and their Missouri Synod Squad to a perimeter barrier to ward off any surprise attack, which they were soon going to get.

Alpha Omega Squad under the command of Sergeant George O' released a banshee yell and stormed the right flank of the Lutheran's perimeter. Simultaneously, brother Tom commanding Beta Omega Squad sliced in from the left flank, surprising the Lutherans, now scattering to defend their church, their faith, their pride. Alpha and Beta fired long range rubbers at John Yungers, Harold Lensch, Lyle Rusch, Dale Jonas, Bill Center, Richard Cook, Frederick Rusch, Junior Lunde. Rubber filled the air around the church, some landing as direct hits, others skittering in the grass or echoing off the white-washed church like broken rosary beads. Lutherans began sticking up their heads to see what was happening and to fire back. It was time for us to unload the heavy artillery.

"Lock and load round one. Fire when ready," I hollered as Jack released the first round, it landing long, but within the compound, startling and distracting the Lutherans, nevertheless.

"Lock and load round two. Fire when ready," this round falling short of the barrier.

"Lock and load round three. Fire when ready," this round slowly arching toward the church like Lefty O's famous basketball shot in the '44 district tournament. Lutherans suddenly froze in place, stopped firing to see what in the hell was approaching their church position. Our Alpha Squad even halted, Beta Squad too, while the brown bag continued arching through a beautiful trajectory, then descended toward the church. The Lutherans froze, not firing, wondering what was happening. The projectile looked like a ghost, but they didn't believe in the Holy Ghost, either. The bag landed directly on John Yungers' head, splaying flour over him and every other Evangelist in the compound. They stood dumbfounded, whitened from head to toe. Yungers,

Lensch, Rusch, Schulz laid down their rubber guns and
trudged home, dejected, past the victorious Crusaders.
*   This day, this battle of RGWII, the Catholics were*
victorious. Our mortar had turned the tide. But the
Lutherans would return. They always did. They'd not
give up. They'd be back, firing taunts at us just as they
had been doing since Martin's first attack. The battle
would rage on.

> For you'll wear a wooden jacket
> After Heinie gets your bracket
> And you'll never see your sweetheart anymore!

A sharp Jedidiah elbow to my rib cage awakened me from my
daydreaming. The droning colonel was finishing his monologue
on artillery firing and piece maintenance . . . "And now gentlemen,
and I use that term lightly, I'll select three second louies to
demonstrate their artillery firing ability on what you have learned
from my discourse this afternoon. Only three of five hundred
encamped here will fire today." He pointed a long, hard finger:
"That lieutenant in the first row, a second there from row three, a
third, you, lieutenant, row four who has been sleeping throughout
my entire lecture." Jedidiah poked me again indicating that the Full
Bird was speaking directly to me. I stood, unsteadily, and came to
attention attempting a wimpy salute. Colonel Full Bird nodded his
head as I made my way down the bleachers toward the imposing
colonel, three second louies "volunteering" to demonstrate newly-
acquired artillery firing skills.

        Louie I, a short, Napoleon-sized New Jersey runt, was first
up, but highly unsuccessful in spite of his braggart mouth, his
bracketing shots long, short, his final shell missing the marker by
five hundred yards, an "artillery bull" in military jargon. He
slumped to the rear of the line. The white refrig stood.

        Louie II, a tall, gangly fellow looking as if he'd just escaped
the deep hills and hollows of Appalachia was second up. His first
round was long, his second short—by the book—but his third
missed three hundred yards to the right, another bull, the colonel

strutting, slapping his idiot stick on his crisp, starched khakis, smirking, his full-shoulder birds cawing, taunting.

Second Louie III, me, a medium-built, white-European-fourth-generation-immigrant, was the final victim. Colonel Bird snarled and hissed through his long teeth, a low guttural sound escaping from his deep military throat. "Nobody sleeps through my lectures, lieutenant." He knew he had me, a slouching recruit who had slept through his entire discourse. I lifted olive-drab binoculars from my hip strap, called for the first round to be long, it landing three hundred yards above the refrig on the distant mountain. Colonel Bird flashed white, shark-fanged, gleaming teeth in a tight snarl. I adjusted my range and called for the second round to fall short by three hundred yards down the mountain below the refrig. Big Bird coughed, cawed low, long, hands making a tight fist against his khakis. I calculated rapidly, called for round three, the round sizzling toward the target, the sonofabitch smacking that refrig all to hell! Big Bird cawed . . . "Lieutenant! You've fired an artillery piece before?" he demanded without asking, placing his curved beak directly in front of my beak.

"Yes, sir!"

"You've been in the military before?"

"No, sir!"

"Well, then, Second Lieutenant Franklin, just where in the hell did you fire an artillery piece?"

"The village, sir. Against the Lutherans, S I R!"

"The Lutherans?"

"Yes, S I R. Blew them all to hell, just like that refrig."

"I see, lieutenant . . . Dismissed!"

Big Bird's wings had been clipped.

Weeks passed, arms, legs, minds becoming more taut, more military as the officer cadre drew us out of academic behavior into military behavior. I qualified "Expert" on the M-1 rifle, of all things, not being a natural-born hunter in the village. Yet, on the firing line I learned to squeeze the trigger softly—like testing Heaney's margarine—instead of jerking it, thereby scoring enough bulls-eyes to avoid Maggie's Drawers, wherever Maggie and her drawers were. I tacked that Expert bar to my fatigues, it devoid of any battle ribbons.

We tossed live grenades at dirt bunkers, charged Aggressor hill emplacements while firing live ammo during scary night maneuvers—"If this is scary, what the hell is war like?"—rode deuce-and-a-halfs across Ft. Benning's sprawling red-earth camp, and learned to deposit our "Officer and a Gentlemen" calling cards when invited to a social gathering at the Officer's Club. The guys in the barracks continued razzing me about "bombing Lutherans," but it was now good-natured chiding; besides, many were fundamentalists, of the Southern Baptist ilk who thought Lutherans liberal concerning Bible interpretations. By week eight we were short-timers and ready for final graduation exercises—escape and evasion. If we passed that, they said, we would become real instead of paper officers.

We had heard about escape and evasion exercises since day one, much of our training leading up to it. It was the final test at OCS. If we successfully completed the test, we would become full-fledged, honored officers, not of the elite Ranger status next door, but "good-enough" officers for infantry, artillery, engineers, quartermaster corps, Vatican Guards, White House Guards . . . well, maybe not the White House.

We devoted most of Saturday afternoon to prepping in our barracks for E & E maneuvers to begin at 1800 hours and lasting throughout the night or whenever we completed the course. We were to be driven fifteen miles north of the compound and dumped from deuce-and-a-halfs on the starting line like 10k runners before a race. A live rifle round would shoot us into the vast boondocks of deepest Georgia.

"Your mission, sirs, is to run the course and return to camp by 0600. Good luck."

BANG!

We set off, gung ho, a hauling ass battalion of not-so-longer-green second louies invading the wilderness burdened with M-1 rifles strung across backs, canteens and mess kits banging hips, field ration packs strapped to web belts in the event we finished before the anticipated twelve-hour allotment. Jedidiah and I set off together, his leading-long legs setting a vigorous pace, but not running like others into the wild land. Planning, nights on our bunks, Jed and I hadn't thought running a good plan. We would use our heads instead of our brawn. Fifteen miles through a rugged wilderness filled with snakes, bears, hills, mountains, ravines, mosquitoes, chiggers, Aggressors, Confederates, and Southern Baptists would surely test our mettle. We had planned a tactic of steady progress—brisk, fast-paced, but not running.

Infantry crowded the first five hundred yards which yielded an easy terrain. Guys were laughing, excited, boasting and bragging about coming in first. We had compasses, maps, bowie knives and field rations. What more could we want? We had studied compass reading and terrain map reading; besides, we were officers preparing to lead others into battle someday—The Infantry motto: "Follow Me!" It would be a piece of cake.

The golden Georgia sun was on my mind as Jed and I continued a brisk pace through the flat, open terrain beyond the starting line, me mostly trying to keep up with stilt-legged Jed used to hiking through the Tennessee mountains while possum hunting. The pine trees were releasing a fragrant, scintillating aroma, the green bushes soft, welcoming as we passed magnolia trees, sans Scarlett O'Hara. Five hundred men in excellent physical condition after seven weeks of grueling marching and calisthenics, had toughened bodies and minds, on our way to the finish line by 0600.

We continued a brisk pace, without running, yet taking advantage of the existing daylight. We only drank from canteens *on* the hike, not stopping to drink nor eat field rations. We hiked two hours before the sun dipped behind the western hills deep in the heart of Georgia, if not Texas.

By 2030 the sun had set; we found ourselves alone, isolated, the other 498 OCS officers having dispersed in various directions, some in large groups, squads, even guys choosing to go it alone, seeking chosen routes to the finish line. I was happy I had Jed as a companion and guide, his Tennessee mountain hiking a definite tactical benefit to a high, open-prairie guy, even though he was a Johnny Reb. At 2100 hours we rested, sitting under a pine tree eating a small portion of field rations, drinking water, studying maps. We were on course and on pace, just as we had projected. This escape and evasion test wasn't as bad as the rumors, I thought. Why, this wasn't any harder than hiking with the Boy Scout Troop to Claybank or Bellechester or out County Rd. No 9 Sunday afternoons. Jedidiah and I would surely be in by 0600.

When the stars fell on Alabama, the sun and temperature fell beyond Atlanta in the Georgia night. We got moving again, following Reb Ridge into a long, meandering valley, the under-brush now thicker, heavier, the terrain increasingly demanding. The night was moonless, map-related landmarks disappearing, terrain unknown. At the bottom of a long decline we came to a gaping ravine covered with heavy, thick, menacing and thorny bushes, almost trees, the likes of which I had never encountered back in the township. We had to help each other crossing the ravine, Jed going first, then me handing his rifle to pull me up the far side into the thorns. After traversing the steep ravine we rested for a few moments before continuing, the moon gone, the night dark, lonesome wolf howls piercing the brisk night, growling bears and slinking, hissing twenty-foot pythons looming in the night.

The far side of the ravine proved to be extremely difficult with dense thorn bushes being almost impossible to traverse. My rifle kept getting hung up in the burrs regardless of the direction I moved. Thorns caught my fatigues, boots, rifle strap, canteen strap. Our forward progress diminished to fifty yards in the next hour, and we couldn't even tell if we were heading in the right direction. "Damn, Jed, this is gettin' to be a sonofabitch," I said, trying to release myself from the thorns. "Jed. You there? . . . Jed! Report in, front and center!" I hollered, trying to release myself from the tentacles of a thorny tree. Jed didn't answer, only the whine of an increasingly cold wind whipped the rattling thorns like an Aggressor's machine gun. I retrieved my flashlight and swept it through a 360-degree arc. No Jed. I was alone in the middle of Georgia, just my compass, my map, my rifle, my wits. I prayed they'd be working. I stopped struggling with the thorns for a moment to gather myself and reconnoiter the situation as the officer cadre had taught us. I don't know if I was scared, concerned maybe. I needed a couple of minutes to think, plan and determine my next course of action, here, alone in Aggressor territory . . .

D ad had found himself alone on the battlefields of Chateau-Theirry and the Somme toward the end of W.W.I, deep in a corpse-filled, muddy trench in the Trench War of Europe. It's the only event he ever spoke about, Dad being more reticent than me. He had been slithering through the scarred, treeless, bombed-out fields stepping over dead horses, corpses of both GIs and Huns, trudging forward to somewhere, nowhere. Artillery shells flashed beyond the perimeter as the week-long rain continued, but he said it hadn't really made any difference anymore. How wet could a guy get? He too had gotten separated from his squad, finding himself alone in a water-filled trench wondering where in the hell his squad was, where the enemy was. He cocked his rifle and pointed it toward Germany waiting to see the swarthy eyes of the enemy, waiting to be killed himself, his body shipped back to St. Columbkill's Cemetery in a pine box. He said that, despite his best efforts, he fell asleep, unable to pass the night awake. He awoke to a bright morning sun and an eternal silence covering the battlefield like a fog; it was deathly quiet on the Western Front. He dragged himself from the water-filled trench and began trudging to somewhere, anywhere—carcasses, corpses, burning wagons, disjointed artillery pieces scattered everywhere, the scene, hell itself, he said. He trudged on, seeing no one, only black, curling smoke, smelling the stench of the dead. He dragged his rifle through the mud, his leggings, boots, nothing but mud until reaching an officer riding an emaciated horse. Dad dragged himself to the officer and horse, tried to salute—the officer, not the horse—but failed. The officer reached down and put his hand on Dad's shoulder. He said the war was over. Germany had surrendered during the night, about the time Dad fell asleep in the trench. Dad was not an overtly emotional man, but he said he cried at that moment upon hearing the war was over and that he would be able to return to his Goodhue Township farm.

Like Dad, I didn't realize I had dozed off, apparently more fatigued than I had thought. I snapped awake thinking about Dad's lonely night on the French battlefield. Surely, if he could get through that night, I could get through this night. He was fighting a real enemy. I'm only fighting a simulated enemy, Aggressors, although rumor has it that, if caught, they fill your rifle and shorts with sand and demand you sit in the cold for hours without food or water, taunting you about being a Yankee, a Christian and for saying "You betcha" one too many times. I wanted to return to my warm, safe bunk, not become a prisoner of war deep in the heart of Georgia. I wanted to come back, alive . . .

During W.W.II in the village and surrounding townships, some GIs didn't come back, alive. Goodhue County paid its dues to the war effort with the lives of its men and women.

When the GIs were fighting in France, Germany and the Pacific Islands, I was an elementary student, but I knew about the war; I couldn't escape it. Rambling around the village, I'd noticed military stars in some home windows indicating that house, that family, had a service man or service woman on active duty. They were stars of pride, honor, letting the village know their contribution to the war effort, sort of like a Blessed Virgin lawn statue indicating a son in the priesthood, a daughter in the sisterhood. The village planted Victory Gardens, collected read and unread *Goodhue Tribunes*, rationed gasoline—"A" stickers for restricted, "X" for unrestricted, "B" stickers for doctors and ministers—nylon stockings, although that didn't affect me, and chocolate chip cookies that did affect me. Many items and goods were rationed, especially steel which went into building USS Iowa-class battleships, Sherman tanks, fighter planes and B-29 bombers. Cars and trucks sported rough, two-by-four bumpers instead of steel bumpers, and hard rubber tires instead of soft, pliable tires. The war effort demanded effort, even a boy's who couldn't buy Hershey Bars at Swenson's Cafe or Joe's Place, because chocolate was needed for the GIs.

Mother and Dad periodically dropped us at the Chief Theater in Red Wing where Movietone News updated us on the war effort before the main feature: *The Sands of Iwo Jima, Guadalcanal, Victory at Sea.*

On a sweltering day in 1942 while walking home from second grade, I passed the Schafer house, as usual, this time surprised to see a black banner covering their military window star. I didn't know what the black banner meant, but asked Mother as I rushed in the back door for my usual after-school peanut butter and jelly sandwich. She set me on her lap in the parlor and said that Will Schafer had been killed in the war. The black banner over the star was an indication and recognition of his death. I didn't know what to think about that. I didn't know Will personally, but I'd seen the family mowing lawns and tending their Victory Garden. They had a dead soldier? How could that be? The war was only for the effort of collecting cans and bottles and newspapers and rationing things. It wasn't for dead soldiers. When my childhood buddies played war in the church hole or around Streater's Lumber Yard or the village dump, we were only "dead" for five minutes, not forever. Geez! I rushed outside with my sandwich and sat under the apple tree, perplexed, realizing for the first time, that the war effort really was an effort.

Before W.W.II ended other black banners graced gleaming-white military stars in the village and townships: Charles O'Gorman, Willis Schafer, Sidney Bodelson, Russell Ryan, Ernest Diercks, Richard Musty, Joseph Redding, Marshall Haas all gave their lives so I could eat my after-school sandwich, in peace, under the apple tree. For the next couple of years, until the final surrender, I walked passed military-star houses with trepidation, fearful that another black banner would appear.

Jedidiah was nowhere to be found. I hoped he hadn't gone AWOL after all our planning. I hitched up my fatigues, retrieved my map and rifle, then headed for Bloody Ridge, determined not to disappoint the folks back home, even though I wasn't in a real war. This was for Willis, Richard, Joseph, Marshall, Russell, Sidney and Charles, a small token of appreciation for my peanut butter sandwiches.

I hiked a steady pace, finally released from the thorny bushes. I checked my map frequently to maintain my chosen course, attempting to read terrain landmarks in the night much as Mark Twain had done while piloting steamboats past Frontenac and Red Wing on moonlit nights. I hiked steadily, the terrain difficult, some thorns, but not as bad as the thorns in my side. By 2400 hours I had made good progress toward what I hoped was the finish line, if I didn't get lost.

When meandering outside the village, my buddies and I never got lost, because we could always see the water tower up on Cranson Heights, or the towering coal silo near the highway, it looking more like a later-day ballistic missile than a coal silo. The village was set on a high prairie, not in deep hollows like Hay Creek, Wacouta, or along the Belle Creek in Belle Creek Township. The village's site hadn't been chosen for its natural beauty. No sir, you got that right. It had been selected because of its deep, rich wheat fields. The burg stood high on a breezy prairie, just right for little guys playing soldiers.

Surprisingly, I was alone in the night, not encountering other fellows. I wondered about that, wondered if I had diverted so far off course that I would never get back to my bunk. Climbing over a high rise, voices in the ravine startled me. I immediately fell to a prone position and pulled my rifle to a firing position, listening . . . an Aggressor Camp. They had captured two prisoners. I could see my buddies in the fire's flames, the warm fire I wanted to sit by. The Aggressors were shouting, "Yankee," "*Bab*tist," "Norther'" "Christian," even "Midwesterner." I crawled off the stony ridge not wanting to hear those taunts. I skirted the ridge around the Aggressor Camp, feeling more secure in my tactical maneuver.

By 0200 I had made excellent progress, according to my map, but still had difficulty locating guiding landmarks. I approached a clearing, a path obstructing my course. I hid in the bushes observing actions around me. It was an open field of fifty yards, not as big as the Gettysburg field the Minnesota 1st Regiment defended, yet I had to cross it, undetected. I made a rush for it, hit the road running, banging, rushing when the sky exploded. I had tripped a flare, it shooting into the ebony sky. Startled, foolish, I ran backwards instead of forwards, running one hundred yards before collapsing into a depression, expecting Aggressors to hurtle on top of me. But while catching my breath, I realized I hadn't been detected. I wasn't in the hands of the Aggressors. Yet, like Dad in France, I was alone on the moon-less battlefield, hoping for an armistice by morning.

After recuperating about five minutes, I executed a flanking movement around that open area, this time successfully circumventing trip flares. By 0400 hours I was tired, cold, hungry. I stood on a high ridge above a deep ravine, the far side according to my calculations, the finish line. I had two hours, plenty of time, if I avoided capture, to traverse down the ridge, wade the river, climb the far embankment, then march triumphantly into camp. I decided to rest for five minutes before making that final thrust, pondering this entire military thing . . .

I had been a boy during W.W.II when George Gorman, Gerald "Lefty" O'Reilly, LeVerne Diercks, Vince Goodsell, Maynard Haas, John Ryan, John McNamara, Jim O'Reilly, John Moran and seven Matthees Bros: Herbert, Herman, Henry, Harold, Norb, John, Rudy served and returned home; when Richard Musty, Willis Schafer, Charles O'Gorman, Joseph Redding, Sidney Bodelson, Ernest Diercks, Russell Ryan, Marshall Haas served and didn't return home. I was too young for the Korean Conflict, but was now training to be an officer in the event of another war, which hopefully wouldn't happen. Practicing for war was one thing, being in one, another.

During W.W.II the deaths of the Sullivan Brothers of Waterloo, Iowa, stunned the nation, five brothers serving on the same navy ship, the USS Juneau, torpedoed November 13, 1942, in the inky waters of Iron Bottom Bay during the Battle of Guadalcanal. Five brothers went to the bottom of the Bay along with 682 other navy officers and enlisted men. Five military stars from one household, five black banners covering those stars appeared on the streets of hapless, dreary Waterloo. Hollywood made a movie about the Sullivan Bros who came home in pine boxes.

The village had had the Matthees brothers, seven who served

simultaneously in the war, not on the same ship, not in the same infantry squad, but they returned home. Our village "Sullivans." After the Sullivan debacle the navy never permitted siblings to serve on the same ship, the same aircraft again. But it had taken five deaths to make that rule. The village and county were proud of our Matthees Bros contribution, our hometown heroes.

During the forties Dad, Tom and I would sit in the kitchen listening to the Minneapolis Lakers basketball team dueling the Ft. Wayne Indians or Rochester Royals before Cedric Adams' WCCO 10 o'clock news. Dad said Stalin wasn't to be trusted, but FDR and Churchill were. He hoped something good would come from the Yalta Conference with those three. Stalin looked fierce in newspaper photos, but FDR and Churchill could've been village men sitting around the potbellied stove at Heaney & Gorman. Frank O'Gorman and Churchill would've gotten along just fine.

On a bright Saturday morning, while playing outside our house just kicking stones and climbing sticky pine trees, Mother caught me by the arm and set me on the stoop. She never did like me climbing those pines, getting sap on my pants. I was in trouble again, I thought. But, instead, she said that President FDR had died. I wondered if they placed a black banner on his White House Star. She said she didn't know, but that Harry Truman was now president. I didn't know Harry Truman from Harry Holst, but I figured he'd be as good a president as anybody, being a midwesterner, Mother said. I hugged my Teddy Bear as Mother left me alone on the stoop. FDR wasn't a villager, but I felt sad anyway.

After some R & R, I was ready to make my final march through Georgia. I stood, shook out my aching legs and arms, conducted a final reconnaissance of the area, then headed down Heartbreak Ridge into the ravine, avoiding roads, trails and open areas, hoping Jedidiah was heading home also. The stump into the ravine went smoothly, but crossing the sandy creek and hiking up the far hill exhausted me. No Aggressors appeared. As I approached what I hoped was the final summit, the finish line on the far side of the ridge, I crawled toward the peak. The finish line appeared in the distance, but two hundred yards ahead of it, between the line and me, jeeps and deuce-and-a-halfs displaying red Aggressor insignia blocked my way. I would have to circumvent them to reach the line. 0500. My ass was draggin'. I wanted to make a thrust straight through the Aggressors line to the finish, just like the Wildcats through the Dodgers, but couldn't risk it. I would have to execute a flanking movement, recalling our RGWWII flanking maneuvers at the Lutheran Church.

I backtracked twenty yards below the ridge, followed the ridge into a gulch, across another burbling creek until I was within one hundred yards of the finish line, freedom on one side, imprisonment and taunting on the other. I cautiously approached, skipping behind magnolia trees just as Jack and I had approached the village Lutherans, this time, though, nasty Aggressors smoking broad-leaf cigarettes near their vehicles, anxiously waiting for green second louies to make a mistake. Seventy-five yards and I hadn't been detected. I dropped to my knees and crept behind bushes, rocks, trees. At fifty yards I heard the Aggressors joshing, swearing. I smelled their smoke. At twenty-five yards, I could see the finish line, smell coffee brewing beyond it—freedom, safety, only open ground between the finish line and me. I hid behind a tree gathering myself for a final thrust to safety. I had always been fast dribbling a basketball or running the bases at the ol' diamond, outrunning the taunting Terry Shelstad, Harold Lensch, Noisy Rusch, or escaping their icy snowballs, but was I fast enough for this? I hoped so. "Jesus, Mary, and Joseph, watch over me and here I go." I burst from behind the tree, canteen, rifle banging my legs, hips, my helmet falling off. The startled Aggressors rushed after me, tossing cigarettes to the ground. Ten yards to a touchdown. I heard and felt heavy boots tramping, labored breathing, swearing, "Catch the sonofabitch!" At five yards I felt a hand on my backpack. Now or never, I thought. One step, two and a skip. I dove toward the finish line like John Yungers and Joe Burkhard diving for the GHS goal line in '47. I was a long time in the air, suspended forever it seemed, catapulted off the red, stinging, thorny Georgia dirt. But as with Lefty O's famous final shot, his ball finally dropping through the net for the win, I too returned to earth, on the far side of the finish line. Home. Free. Safe at 0545!

Jedidiah straggled in a couple of hours later, bedraggled, torn, ripped with thorns, looking as if he had been crucified, but having eventually evaded and escaped the Aggressors. He was happy to see me, I him. Confederate Jedidiah R. Lee and Yankee James L. Franklin, far apart in background and homes, were this night, comrades.

Two days later the OCS recruits marched across the parade grounds in dress blue uniforms to accept an OCS/BOT medal pinned to our coats for having successfully completed the course. I would be marching off to Ft. Leonard Wood, MO to train Basic Recruits to march, in-step, the manual of arms drill, the nomenclature of an M-1, and to run the infiltration course, keeping their heads down, of course, as if I needed to tell them. Jedidiah was shipping out to Ft. Still to fire 105 mm howitzers at barren rocks on the Oklahoma llano. I shook his hand, he mine as we marched, two abreast, to the reviewing stand. As I approached Big Bird on the stand, I recalled a similar march back at GHS when graduating with the Class of 1954, they too having successfully completed twelve years of education. As I reached Big Bird, he announced, "Lt. James L. Franklin has successfully completed the courses at OCS/BOT. Congratulations, Lt. Franklin!" he shouted into the public address system. Then, while passing him, he said in a lower, off mic, gravely voice, "Franklin, I'm Lutheran, but that was one hell of an artillery shot anyway. Congratulations."

"Thank you, SIR!"

Big Bird had flown.

Chapter 7

Musical mentors

The Moonmisters of St. John's U

MY PERSONAL "WAR" REACHED AN ARMISTICE after serving as a basic training officer at Ft. Leonard Wood. That completed, it was time to follow another "Wood," this time Charles, my GHS musical maestro mentor. The time had come to put into practice my musical training extending from grade school through high school and St. John's. I had never planned to *teach* music even though preparing for it. A cloverleaf bird encouraged me to re-up for a longer term before mustering out, but I dropped my M-1 rifle at the guard's gate, picked up my clarinet and sax and began marching to a new beat.

Musicians don't choose a career as much as they are chosen. Music chose me early on even though the village offered little in the way of musical experiences. The forties were W.W.II and postwar years, music technology greatly lacking until after the battles of Guadalcanal and The Bulge. Even then there was always that old nemesis, money, usually having only enough for the basics, plus maybe a burger, fries and malt at Swenson's or Shelstad's. Few villagers owned phonographs or had the money to feed them 45 or LP records. Radio, scratchy a. m. only, was limited to KDHL out of Faribault broadcasting mostly old-time music, hog and beef futures, tips from Heloise, western (hillbilly), pop music by Pat Boone, Perry Como, Eddie Fisher (not the village's), Frank Sinatra and the Andrew Sisters. The Twin Cities' WCCO station broadcast Cedric Adams' ten o'clock news and the Minneapolis Laker games. I could sometimes pull in big bands from Del Rio, Texas, Chicago or clear channel Kansas City stations late, starry nights up in my bedroom if the old Crosley radio wasn't too cantankerous. Broadcast waves struggled to reach the sequestered village, the crackling, static noises obstructed by the village's invisible barrier. The village was in a "Bermuda Triangle" long before we had even heard of Bermuda. I strung extra lengths of copper wire from my bedroom to the apple tree much to the bewilderment of neighbor Clara Hennings who wondered what on earth I was doing now, but it improved the reception, somewhat. My Johnson-Smith catalog crystal radio proved worthless for anything other than static.

I knew nothing about the theory of music then, only that I responded to its melodies and harmonies. Music did something to me, grabbed me like Catholicism, like the Democratic Farm Labor Party. But classical music was unheard of in the village, the symphonies and sonatas of Beethoven, Berlioz, Bach, Brahms, Mozart and Haydn deflected by that barrier just beyond the soaring coal silo, the peaked Elevator, the weeping pines of Evergreen Cemetery. It was as effective in keeping classical composers out as non-white diversity or non-Christian faiths in.

Yet, inside the barricade Ben Gorman, Marldine Richter, Lucretia and Frank O'Gorman, Fred and Frieda Vieths had sought music to round out their lives, inturn exposing villagers to music other than corny polkas, bouncy old-time waltzes, inane mazurkas and schottisches. By the time I succumbed to first grade in '41, Marldine had started an in-school band out of school. He collected unmanageable used metal clarinets, frozen-piston cornets, sticky slide trombones, dented tubas, torn snare drums, and musty C-melody saxophones from Elmer Bremer, John Nei, Fred Vieths, Carl Rosener, John Stenlund, Ben Gorman, Ole Haga, villagers who had played in The Goodhue Concert Band during the twenties. Richter asked them to tote antique and dormant attic instruments to the school, because he was going to start a band for the village children, a real band for real folks right here in River City, though we didn't have a river. Children honked and tooted, plunked and banged, blew and farted on those instruments for five or six years, Marldine doing the best he could with the limited talent while simultaneously holding down a grocery job. The band eventually presented concerts in the park, at the old ball diamond, and Wednesday nights on a rubber-wheeled hay rack on Lower Street near the railroad depot. And they marched, route-step, for the Fourth of July parade until Marldine grew tired from the exertion of teaching music to unmusical people. Yet, he had planted a musical seed in the community, and with school superintendent Eyestone. Some folks said it was time the school had a real, full-time music teacher. They got one, sort of, along about '48 in Charles Wood. This is how it happened . . .

Chas Wood hummed toward the village in his Gatsby-era roadster down County Rd. No. 9 hoping to teach instrumental and choral music to musical hicks in the sticks. Top down, he zoomed out of Hamline College into the hinterland, hell bent on bringing Mozart, Beethoven, even Palestrina to folks who couldn't spell "Beethoven," couldn't pronounce "Mozart," and didn't give a damn if they couldn't. There were cows to milk, corn to cultivate, hay to bale, lawns to mow. Approaching No. 6 while singing an aria from the *Student Prince,* he felt happy, excited, but the Deliverance Boys were waiting for him at the village perimeter just beyond Evergreen Cemetery. "Woods? That what they call you up in Minnyapolis? Chas Woods is it, then?" burly Claybanker snarled as he and five other bearded, toothless men wearing bib overalls and seed caps stopped Wood's car at a two-by-four road blockade, pitch forks and axes slung over hulking shoulders. Wood brushed back his long hair, straightened his painted Windsor knot before speaking, "Well, not quite correct, men. The name is 'Wood,' not 'Woods.' I am the new music teacher for the Goodhue Schools. Are you gentlemen the welcoming committee?" Wood said, thrusting a trembling hand out the window.

"Ya, you could say that. Ya sure, we're the welcoming committee, ain't that right, fellas. Only thing is, Wood*sss*, we're not welcomin' you nor yer silly music. We're the 'get-your-ass-out-of-town committee,' ain't that right fellows? Turn 'round right now and take your silly, prissy music back to the Cities, then. Ain't got time for music here. Now skat!" burly Claybanker, caked clay sticking to his tattered Red Wing boots, said as he placed two meaty hands on Wood's door and stuck his bearded face two inches from the sartorial Wood.

"But I have a contract, Mr?"

"Don't need no name, Woods. Just head for them there woods back up there by Finney's spread."

Wood gasped for air on the dry, dusty road trying to buy some time. "I must see Mr Eyestone to inform him of this peculiar development. Does he know you gentlemen are the 'welcoming' committee?"

"Don't and don't need to. Like to run him out of town too, him wantin' to teach our kinfolk music. We'uns an' kids got more important things to do. You just turn your jalopy 'round now and scoot back to Minnyapolis," Claybanker said as Bellecreeker, Belviderian, Featherstonian and Villager strode menacingly toward the roadster convertible, pitchforks now *off* their shoulders. Wood had prepared himself to teach music, not deal with the Hatfields and the McCoys. He needed to think, prestissimo!

"Men, I am sure there has been a misunderstanding. Maybe I've got the wrong town. This is Goodview, isn't it?" he said, wishing he had a drink of water.

"Hear that fellows! He thinks he's in Goodview. Hey, Woods, you ain't all bad. This here's Goodhue, don'tcha know. You got the wrong town. Hell guys! Let's let him through. He ain't teachin' in Goodhue, after all. He's headin' to Goodview down by Wynona." Claybanker reached into the window, slapped Wood on the back almost knocking his tenor voice into a baritone. The men pulled the barricade down letting Wood pass through Evergreen Cemetery instead of being buried there. He hightailed it to Superintendent Hubert's office, parking behind the boiler room to hide from the welcoming committee.

Well, things settled down. Wood stayed to build a band on the heels of Richter, teaching farm ruffians, corn-fed girls and village hayseeds like me something about music, even though we were reluctant learners. He shared his enthusiasm for music with the children. The Concert Band got pretty good at playing von Suppe's "Light Cavalry Overture," Karl King marches and easier Sousa marches, plus Hal Leonard pop tunes which I particularly liked. We strained our nuts and vocal cords in Boys Chorus, while the Girls Chorus put the boys to shame. The Mixed Chorus sometimes became a farce with bass guys in the back row goosing tenors in front, even grabbing girls' derrieres. Wood certainly had his hands full in Goodview . . . er, Goodhue. The Girls Trio and Girls Triple Trio sang for hotdish banquets in the outlying township halls and well, even those old farts, the "welcoming committee" from Claybank, Belvidere, Belle Creek, Featherstone and the Village eventually attended concerts, proud as punch with their "talented," musical children.

"You ain't half bad, Woods, just all bad. That's a joke, boy. That's a joke."

I thought a lot about Chas Wood my first weeks, months, years of teaching band and chorus out in windy, forsaken western Minnesota before escaping to northeastern Iowa's glorious Mississippi River country. College hadn't fully prepared me for teaching band, chorus and general music to children. Oh, I hadn't been "greeted" with a welcoming committee like Wood, yet there were some rough roads lined with recalcitrant students, pushy parents and impatient administrators along the route. Infusing musicality into unmusical children was no easy task, I was soon to find. But like Wood, I wanted to share my love of music with students, with parents, with the community. I would have to make that road smoother.

Like Wood, I didn't walk into a developed music program—a band with a full, talented instrumentation, a choir with balanced sopranos, altos, tenors, basses, quality abounding. I would need to prove my mettle if I were to succeed and enjoy this business of music education, if it were to become something more than an avocation. I would also learn about my teaching skills and myself. Playing clarinet and saxophone at GHS and St. John's wasn't the same as teaching clarinet and saxophone to public school students. For the next several months, maybe years, I would be uncertain about my teaching methods, uncertain they would produce the students I envisioned. Chas Wood had taught village classmates Sandbox Bob, Bettie Lunde, Mary Benda, Janice Cook, Brona Bartlett and me foot beating, fingerings, embouchures, melodies, scales and arpeggios in the dank basement lunchroom of the Goodhue School. Now, I was doing the same, teaching scales and fundamentals anywhere, anyplace I could find: lunch rooms, boiler rooms, gymnasium, even locker rooms on occasion. The site wasn't important. The music was.

"Band! 'Activity March' just isn't this hard. Now bear down—count, beat your feet, think, work together like an infantry platoon. Let's see if we can get past the first eight measures," I said for the fifth time during rehearsal. I was conducting, beating time, perspiring in the sultry, late August band room, but like a drowning man, getting nowhere. They just weren't getting it. Most of my bedraggled McGregor, Iowa students couldn't play the simple music in front of them, "Activity March," *Bennett Band Book Number One,* the same book Chas Wood used after he escaped that welcoming committee. I thought it a basic, easy march to begin with in McGregor just as Wood had done in the village, but, it wasn't working. I believe my first high school band was actually worse than the GHS Band of '45 Wood inherited from Marldine Richter, if that were possible. The McGregor students failed repeatedly, unable to count rhythms, to finger accurately, to blow anything other than farts. We devoted all of week one and week two to "Activity March," and yet, by Friday of week two, we still were unable to get from the beginning to the ending without falling apart in discordant chaos. Two weeks on the same easy march. Teaching music was going to be a challenge, I thought, weary, shuffling down-headed from school that late Friday afternoon. Discouraged, I was looking forward to recuperating along the lazy Mississippi River during the weekend. Pete intercepted me in the parking lot.

"How's it going, Jim?" the veteran basketball coach, said as we plopped on listing stools at a riverside saloon in Prairie du Chien just across the Mississippi River from McGregor. We sipped beers, chomped on aged cheese and wheat crackers. The genial Pete had invited Dale and me, another new teacher, to join him for social camaraderie after school, after the week. We readily accepted.

"I don't know, Pete. Teaching the kids music is more difficult than I anticipated. The band can't play anything. They're terrible," I said, sipping on an Old Style.

"Of course they can't. That's why we *hired* you," he said, spinning his bar stool toward me. "You got to teach them. Your predecessor didn't teach anything, just messed around smoking cigarettes in the boiler room drinking coffee all day, let the band go to hell. You got your work cut out for you. Just hang in there, though. It'll get better. Hell! I've been teaching for twenty years— good teams, bad teams, good students, bad students. It'll come together if you stay with it."

"If you say so, Pete, but I've got my druthers after these first two weeks. I don't see how I'll ever make a band out of these students, plus I've only got twenty-one in band. That's hardly a band, more like a triple quartet. And the choir! Shoot, I've never heard such terrible, out-of-tune, strident voices. Worse than the Holy Trinity congregation."

"The what congregation?"

"Holy Trinity, back in my Minnesota village. They were loud and harsh, but pious," I said, finishing beer one and reaching for beer two.

"How about you Dale? How are your eighth graders?" I asked, he too a new teacher to the district.

"About the same as your band students, Jim. They don't know how to study, are raucous, unbehaving. I've been teaching in central Iowa for ten years, but my first year here will be a challenge. I guess we're in this together," Dale said, executing the Florence-Taylor-Eat-Shop-boarding-house reach for cheddar cheese, crackers and sardines at Sue Z's Bar down by the levee in Prairie du Chien. I passed on the sardines, never liking those salty Norwegian things.

The lovely fall weekend along the soaring river bluffs passed much too quickly. "Choir, try to sing your parts rather than shouting them. More softly. Listen to your voices. Blend them with the rest of the choir. Now, let's take it from the top of this Mozart piece. Try harder now . . . pitches . . . and a-one and a-two and a-three . . ." Individual voices and choral blend were excruciating. I could hardly believe my ears, and I was proud of my ears. Damn! This is *worse* than Holy Trinity, I thought, stopping again and again, pounding pitches from the piano. "Now sopranos, here is your starting note . . . pitch . . . altos . . . tenors . . . basses. All together now . . ." Crunch! The sound of the Mormon Tabernacle Choir in reverse.

"Do we have to sing Mozart, Teach? How about something more modern. We don't like Mozart."

"Young man, my name is Mr Franklin, not Teach, and Mozart

is good for you. We will persist with Mozart . . . pitches . . . from the top." The choir was wearing me out as we entered week three, and the band still hadn't succeeded in finishing "Activity March." At the end of week three, I trudged home to sleep, to spend the weekend reevaluating this music education thing. Three weeks of conducting, directing, counting, beating and haranguing had produced nothing. I was getting nowhere. Something would need to change if I were going to make it, if the students were going to make it. Where was Chas Wood when I needed him?

I didn't join Pete and Dale for the weekend at Sue Z's Bar, electing instead to spend the time alone, pondering, evaluating what the problems were, and what I was going to do about them. I hiked along the McGregor levee enjoying the warmth of the descending fall sun, the golden, blazing leaves turning vibrant colors on the high bluffs, leaves, dancing along the upper Mississippi. This was a beautiful site, a pocket city 150 miles downriver from Red Wing. I enjoyed the hike, liked living here, a cozy burg like my village. It felt good and the folks on Main Street were friendly, merchants at the grocery store, the cafe, the hotel, accommodating. It felt like home. If only I could make progress with the students.

I mused about Chas Wood entering Goodhue with a similar experience, trying to teach music to rough-hewn village and farm ruffians, fellows who would rather wrestle a bull than a Mozart melody, tittering girls who would rather put their lips on a farm boy's red mouth than a Bach or Mozart two-part harmonic theme, tenors who where embarrassed to be even seen in chorus—"You guys ain't got any balls singin' that sissified music,"—singing, music participation not the manly thing to do, football, basketball, baseball the sports real guys did. Chas Wood hoped to teach music in the village, but first he had to teach attitude. He felt it was important. He persisted.

After hiking several miles along the river's shoreline under towering bluffs, thinking about Wood's first year, I realized I was facing a similar situation. Yes, my students were musically untrained, but also behaviorally untrained. I had arrived here teaching at *my* musical level instead of *theirs*. I was ten steps ahead of their game. I would need to back down, find their level and work from there. Reaching the undulating docks at the foot of Main Street, I realized I would need to start with beat one, page one, day one, just like mentor Chas Wood.

Rejuvenated, I bounced into school Monday morning. The superintendent approached me in the hallway. "Jim, our band traditionally marches in the county-wide All Vets Day parade in November. We'll expect you to have the McGregor Band ready," he said while simultaneously directing rampaging students scooting through the hallway like agitated cattle.

"March? We can't even play sitting down. We certainly can't march and play at the same time," I said, startled by this new development. I had returned from the weekend prepared to teach whole, half, quarter and eighth notes, not . . . right, left, horns up, horns down, forward march! "We won't be able to participate this year. Give us a year to get ready," I said, heading toward the band room.

"But the American Legion expects the band to march with them. They'll be upset if you don't participate."

"And they'll be upset if we do. We can't even keep a beat yet. We can't get through 'Activity March' sitting down much less standing up. We'd fall apart, upsetting the American Legion, the band, and me. We need time," I exclaimed. "Explain it to them. We'll be ready next year."

The super was not happy. He would like to have fired me on the spot, but then, what would he have done with the band and choir students. At least ten applicants had turned down the job before I signed on. He persisted, though, not accepting my answer for several weeks. And the American Legion *was* unhappy with my decision, as the super had predicted. They let me know about it, firing broadsides as I sauntered Main Street, adjusting their bracketing artillery, me the target. But I stuck to *my* guns. We didn't march that year. Instead, we practiced counting and fingering and whole notes and quarter notes and breathing and posture and breath support and attitude. We didn't march. That would come next year.

Making *most* current musicians unhappy, I reverted to basics, fundamentals, just like basic training at Ft. Leonard Wood. I returned to book one, page one and began teaching fundamentals to every student: rhythmic understanding, counting, foot beating, feeling the beat, feeling the pulse, scales, arpeggios, brass lip slurs, tone control, breath support, plus practice, practice, practice. I demanded daily practice until we began making slow progress. In full band rehearsals I stopped conducting and began teaching. This band wasn't ready to be conducted. After six weeks we finally reached the end of "Activity March." The students were elated, smiles breaking out, clarinets and flutes and trumpets and slide trombones honking in jubilation. Four weeks of excruciating effort, but for the first time, they were proud of themselves. Oh! we didn't *sound* good, but we hadn't faltered, either. Sounding better, like a real band, would come later.

In choir I put Mozart back into his eighteenth century box, then pulled out Stephen Foster melodies and the *Golden Song Book*. We too retreated to the basics of matching pitches with the piano, singing up with life, down with energy, developing breath support with tummy exercises and trying to sing without straining vocal cords. Mozart would have to wait. Progress was extremely slow, but there was some. That too was something to be happy about. We were gradually catching Holy Trinity.

As the weeks passed I realized I was teaching the same values I had acquired back in the village, values I had taken for granted. My students needed discipline just as I had gotten at Heaney & Gorman when sacking potatoes—best potatoes for Catholics, "holy" potatoes for Lutherans—trimming meat, and stomping fifteen-foot wool sacks. My students needed good examples just as I had received from Dennis Heaney, George and Dodie Gorman, Uncle Dave and the rest of the Franklins, Pat Rowles and Bill Mans and B. C. Majerus and Cy Benda, even Fr. Smith. These students needed patience just as I had gotten from my mother and her Red Wing Haustein kinfolk. These students needed prodding just as I had gotten from about everyone in the village, particularly when I was "off-track" in school or church, even on the street. As a teacher I was simply transferring values from one village to another, Goodhue village to McGregor village. It would work.

"Will you be giving a Christmas concert, Jim?" The persistent super asked during a mid November lunch period.

"Christmas concert? Can we make a concert out of one march?" I asked while chomping on a slurpy Sloppy Jo sandwich.

"Surely you can play more than one song by now, can't you?" he asked, pressing again just as he had with the All Vets parade.

"We can play many songs, but we can only get through one!" I said, reaching for my lukewarm milk.

"Well, the community would surely like to see what you've been doing in the band room," he said, reaching for the ketchup bottle to aerate his Sloppy Jo. "They would appreciate a Christmas concert. See what you can do," he said, rising from the table and heading back to his office without letting me respond. How on earth could I present a Christmas concert with my measly . . . er . . . improving musicians. I would have to figure that one out.

It was obvious the band couldn't present a full concert, nor the choir, but maybe I could present a program if both could learn a few Christmas songs. Maybe these villagers weren't any more musically astute than the Goodhue villagers were in '45. I began realizing my job involved more than teaching students. I also needed to teach musical values to the community.

Besides directing the choir and band, I also taught grade school music and junior high general music. I was *the* music teacher in the tiny school system, a not uncommon assignment in the early sixties. After the super again challenged me, I decided to pull out the stops, use my resources, call up my reserves. I began teaching unison Christmas carols to the grade children, two-part harmony carols to seventh and eighth graders, three- and four part harmony carols and hymns to the high schoolers, and whatever we could get by with or through with the twenty-one piece Concert Band. We honked and strained and shouted and beat and clanged and sang off key and out of tune and out of time and out of breath for three weeks before Christmas vacation while I ingested an increasing number of Rolaids for a churning stomach. This was to be my first concert in the village. Their progress didn't please me. I needed more time. Did Chas Wood go through this? In college I had sung four-part, harmonized Gregorian chant, played "Death and Transfiguration" in Concert Band. Now, I was hoping to get these students through the most basic carols and marches. God! I thought, I didn't think teaching music would be *this* difficult. I wondered what Brother Leo was doing.

The grade school children shouted more than sang, but we could get through "Oh, Come All Yee Faithful" and "Silent Night" and "Rudolph The Red Nose Reindeer." The seventh and eighth graders reluctantly sang "The Night before Christmas" and "Little Town of Bethlehem," while the Mixed Chorus attempted to harmonize "Bethlehem," even a Bach choral. But preparing the Concert Band was a quandary, because there wasn't anything Christmas about "Activity March" unless I changed its name to "Actively Marching Through Bethlehem." We struggled through a watered-down Christmas medley but couldn't play "Sleigh Ride," it being in a terrible, orchestral key for band, most keys being terrible, for that matter. But finally, with the elementary children, the junior high brats, the high school Mixed Choir, the discordant twenty-one piece Concert Band, I put together forty-five minutes of music . . . well . . . attempted music.

By the evening of the concert—tomorrow, followed by Christmas vacation, thank God!–I had commandeered 200 students into the Christmas pageant. Janitors erected hard, splintered wooden bleachers on the gym floor to seat the grade school children while the junior high choir, high school choir and band where placed throughout the gymnasium. I had developed an imprisoned, parental audience. The program was to begin with the elementary children singing carols, 200 wild children dressed in white blouses or shirts, excited, agitated, hyper looked more at mother, father, grandma and grandpa than at me. In front of the bleachers, I gave them final instructions before performing.

"Now, when I say 'start,' I'll give you a downbeat for "Little Town of Bethlehem," but when I said 'start,' half the group began singing. Somehow I stopped them, turned to the audience in embarrassment and apology, but they just laughed, even began applauding. Precisely at half past seven the pianist sounded a "good" starting pitch, this after two wrong pitches. This time I kept my mouth shut and gave a downbeat into "Little Town of Bethlehem." They sang with gusto, shouting and hollering more than singing, but they had known the song since birth. I really hadn't taught them as much as fired the starting gun. Once started there was no stopping them. Moms and dads loved them, though, applauding with gusto as we sang three more carols. The children stood, on command, and bowed to the applause of family and friends. They were the brightest Christmas star in their mothers' eyes.

The junior high choristers were more reserved, thinking this entire escapade beneath them. They grunted their carols rather than attempting melodic, lyrical singing in the spirit of Christmas. It was more of a tragic Lenten effort, but we got through "What Child is This?" and "Joy to the World," lacking the joy, before they gratefully sat down on the bleachers without recognizing the applause from their families, this entire concert corny, not cool to seventh and eighth graders. I breathed a sigh of relief. Now, if they would only remain silent while the high school choir and band performed.

The high school Mixed Choir was visibly apprehensive and unsure of themselves. I stepped in front, gained most of their attentions, called for the beginning pitches from the pianist and gave a downbeat to a Christmas hymn, or so I thought. The piano pitches were there. My downbeat was there. The choir wasn't. Performance fear, en masse, seized them. Mouths moved, throats tried to release pitches, but silence enveloped the auditorium. I slowly dropped my conducting arms, the pianist stopped accompanying, the audience stopped breathing. I considered turning to offer an explanation. I refrained. Through silent mouth language, I encouraged the choir to relax, breathe deeply while offering a thumbs-up gesture.

Pitches. Downbeat. This time almost inaudible notes emanated from timorous throats, almost a whisper, but I felt they would grow stronger. By the end of the hymn I heard so-so melodies and some lyrics. The second selection, a carol, was stronger; the third, their best, although our harmonization, pitch and overall choral quality lacked finesse. We had a long way to go. But significant applause and foot stomping accompanied the end of their selections, startling the choir, starling me. We weren't good, but . . . these were *their* kids. They weren't so bad. We had a lot of time to get better.

Now for the band, my biggest worry. Voices could falter sounding harsh, off pitch, and keep going. But instrumental fingers and lips might falter, totally. That would be embarrassing. I gave the downbeat to twenty-one band members for the Christmas Medley—"Rudolph, Jingle Bells, Sleigh Ride, Sleigh Sliding,"– a simple arrangement of classic Christmas carols, but a challenge for this band, nevertheless. "Jingle Bells" went well enough, but troubles erupted with "Sleigh Ride," the clarinets and flutes getting at odds with each other, the bass drummer looking at his girlfriend in the audience rather than at me, thereby seriously attempting to divert the band into three-four meter instead of four-four; a trombonist lost her slide, it skittering under the band into the saxophone section, and the snare drummer banged like a Civil War drummer marching through Gettysburg. We certainly weren't musical; neither had we fallen apart, broken ranks nor retreated.

For the final selection I stood in the middle of three hundred grade, junior and senior high school students to conduct "Silent Night," asking the audience to join in. The lights of the gymnasium were too bright for a silent night, but it was the best we could do. I didn't say 'start' to the children this time, instead, stood for a moment until all eyes were on me, then gave the downbeat and introduction to the band. The children, especially elementary, sang with gusto, the junior high with apprehension, the high school affirmatively . . .

> *Silent night! Holy night!*
> *All is calm, all is bright,*

Even the band suddenly sounded better, or it might just have been the spirit of the moment. I turned around to encourage moms and pops to join us, emotion in their faces, ever some tears in their eyes.

Round yon Virgin Mother and child!
Holy infant so tender and mild,
Sleep in heavenly peace,
Sleep in heavenly peace.

It ended. A hush fell over the children. Slowly, I lowered my hands as applause grew from the audience, gradually enveloping the songsters as the children began applauding themselves. I don't know if we did the baby Jesus justice or harm, but it had been a silent, holy night . . . and it was over.

W ith the first concert under my belt, I was happy leaving my adopted village, returning to my boyhood village even if it was father north. I loved the winding drive up along the Mississippi River to Red Wing before heading out onto the high prairie. I would drive that route many years while returning to visit Mother, now widowed twice and not particularly interested in seeking a third husband. In fact, I mentioned to her one day that she might consider not getting married again, because her children wouldn't be able to afford two cemetery plots for an extended headstone, her name already excessively long: Lucille Anne Haustein-Franklin-Ryan. Adding a third husband's name would be too expensive. She didn't see the humor in my comment, but was kind to me nonetheless, praying for me under her breath: "Jesus Mary and Joseph," just as she had done during my adventures in the village.

Several high school classmates lived in the village or returned periodically then: Bob began teaching in Preston and never escaped, forty years in the same town; brother Mick O' began teaching in western Minnesota; Larry O' migrated to the Twin Cities; Dave Hutcheson become a colonel or general in the U.S. Army; Jack O' entered teaching; Big "D" Diercks worked for U.S. Gypsum in Red Wing for several years before realizing that was a dead end, subsequently returning to college then graduating to count wieners for Oscar Mayer, not on the assembly line, but as an accountant. And Big "E" Schulz, along with his brother Billy, attempted to become the county's largest trucking firm, or at least Goodhue's, which they did until Elroy finally tired of pushing 18 wheelers across winding county roads. He returned to college, entering the field of education. Fellow Johnnie Tom O'Reilly escaped the Benedictine monastery to marry Gayle Banidt and teach in the Twin Cities, as did their classmate Frederick Rusch (teach, that is). Patricia Ryan married one of the horde of Minnesota Carlsons, escaping the village to the Twin Cities, while Al Jean Majerus, Yvonne Befort, Cathy Benda, Jane Drenckhahn, Karen Haas, Isabel Man and "Smoky" Shelstad returned home for holiday dinners.

Some stayed around the village throughout the sixties, pals to visit while home, to sip a few beers with at the Corner- or Art's Bar, maybe drive to Edgewater or Mary's on the Wisconsin island to see what or who was new in the crop of Minnesota or Wisconsin girls. I had lost contact with Sharon as well as Becky. Doris was long gone to somewhere beyond the county's horizon, and I was only slowly breaking in with Iowa corn-fed girls.

Mother and I joined the Belle Creek Ryans for Christmas Day dinner and festivities, the house getting smaller as more and more children filled its spaces. Dick's seven children, Tom's six, plus an assortment of Belle Creekers with nowhere to be on Christmas Day filled the small farm house to overflowing. There were hams and turkeys, coffee and hot toddies for everyone. We ate the required two full meals during the day, played Euchre, drank beer and told far-fetched stories. Dick milked forty Holsteins before the final supper. Later, Tom discussed distributing Budweiser tall-neck, 12-ounce bottles to saloons and dives from Welch to South St. Paul, while the kitchen ladies chatted about cross-stitching, angel food cakes, favorite hotdish recipes—round steak, tater tots garnished with La Choy oriental noodles seemingly the most popular—and who in St. Columbkill's parish was pg, which was just about every woman.

Attending St. Columbkill's for Christmas Mass before arriving at the farm was like entering a nursery. There were more crying babies than incense, and there was plenty of incense; more bawling babies than sacraments, and we had five more than the Lutherans;

more screaming one-year-olds than saints, and we had tons of saints. Yet, farmstead mothers toted their offspring to church, hordes larger even than the Mormons of Utah. To have five or six or seven children tagging on mother's skirt up the aisle, plus a bulging tummy baking number eight was next to godliness itself. "Blessed are they who bring their young ones into the world, for you shall be blessed in the eyes of the Lord and around the kitchen tables of the township."

But I had difficulty concentrating on the mass that Christmas Day. I wasn't a father yet, one of *them* yet, so my patience was retreating by the Agnus Dei. But Father-what's-his-name plowed right on through the cacophony just as his congregation plowed the resistant soil surrounding the church and cemetery. He appeared indifferent to the wailing, the screaming, the bawling, the shriek-ing of children: O'Reillys, Gadients, McNamaras, Ryans, O'Connors, O'Gormans, O'Rourkes, O'Neills. By the time we had praised the new baby, Jesus that is; by the time Fr. had intoned *Ita Missa Est* (the mass is ended, go in peace), I was, indeed, happy the mass had ended, ready to escape into the bitter-cold Minnesota air. The wind screaming in from beyond the cemetery, folks didn't linger on the front steps to chat as they normally did, to catch up with the past week's hog and beef prices, milk production, egg production, births and deaths. Most walked directly to their cars and trucks; besides, that Christmas ham or turkey needed to get into the oven.

"How's the music teaching going, Jim?" Dick asked as we men retired to the living room after the noon dinner.

"Just finished my first concert a couple of nights ago, but it's too soon to tell. It's difficult teaching music to unmusical students. It'll take some getting used to, that's for sure," I said, settling into an overstuffed chair, my stomach likewise.

"I'll bet you'll do just fine, you being such a hot shot clarinetist. Playing in a big band?"

"With a few area high school band directors. We've got a nine-piece group called the Music Maestros. We play for high school dances, Elk Lodges, Shriner dances, mostly. But it's fun and I'm still hoping to front a big band of my own someday, you know, to bring back to the Dreamland," I said, sinking farther into the chair, becoming drowsy on a full ham and turkey dinner stomach. Light snow fluttered on the lawn, accumulating on the open-lathe corn shed, the red brick silo, the tidy white barn, the tractor and hay baler parked by the machine shed. This setting was much different from my Iowa village, but I liked coming here, the farmstead of stepfather Bill now in the hands of son Dick, later to be passed on to son John, and on and on through the generations.

Though a villager, most of my kindred Franklins were farmers. We often visited at Cis (Franklin) O'Neill's place across the back forty from the W. C. Ryan's, at Uncle Jim Franklin's farm, Grandmother Catherine's and Uncle Patrick's farm on the township line—the homeplace—before they moved in the late forties to Red Wing to enjoy a non agrarian life. Mother's Haustein clan had long ago abandoned their Wells Creek farm in Florence Township, preferring urban Red Wing. Yet, I managed to get some farm work during high school and college summers, windrowing hay for Frederick Benitt east of town, baling hay for the Bucks west of town while avoiding the milking parlor. I never got the hang of pulling tits. Only later would I become interested in that.

Nevertheless, the bucolic environment fascinated me whether riding with Dad in his milk truck early misty mornings through Belvidere Township, bouncing down County Rd. No. 9 Sunday afternoons with Uncle Dave, hiking from our sleepy village to Finney's Woods, skipping along grass-strewn, decaying railroad tracks to Claybank, or tromping across undulating fields toward the Claypits. Any direction brought farm land, the village an oasis among immeasurable tilled fields. Traipsing beyond that village barrier, we encountered mile upon mile of wheat, barley, flax, oats, corn, dairy cows, periodic Norwegian or Swedish Lutheran church spires punctuating endless crops, their spires emerging like German U-boat periscopes on the Atlantic. Years later I would visit Alcatraz Prison in the San Francisco Bay, built to deter prisoners such as Al Capone, Machine Gun Kelly and Robert Stroud "The Birdman," from escaping across the cold, shark-infested bay waters. Our village, in the thirties and forties, was isolated like Alcatraz, not surrounded by shark-infested waters, but by to-the-horizon flowing fields, an ocean mirage. We could walk out of the village, but unbounded fields would consume us. The farmsteads, the fields, the untold high prairies were as much a deterrent to escaping the village as the deep waters of Alcatraz.

But we weren't trying to escape then. That would come later. The village provided about everything we needed or wanted. Oh, we hadn't a Woolworth's "Dime" Store. We hadn't an A & W drive-in. We hadn't an inside movie theater. We didn't even have a soda fountain where we could order carbonated cherry cokes or chocolate floats. But we didn't mind. We had other things . . .

The village had the sounds of barking, wailing dogs when the jail-top siren whined "noon" and "six o'clock," and for an occasional fire. It had the whooshing sound of the Goodhue Elevator siphoning barley, wheat and flax up long metal tubes into the storage silos. It had the squealing sound of Dennis Heaney's hogs as Bump Schinnert sliced their throats in the slaughter house, ruby red blood seeping, gurgling into the drain. It had the blatting sound of Dennis' steers as he or Bump slammed them with a hammer, a ton of beef slumping to the floor to later become roasts, tenderloins and steaks. Townsfolk were accustomed to those sounds. We heard Luverne Haas cussing in the bays of Mans & Benda's Station. We heard B. C. Majerus cussing as he skinned a hand installing a plumbing joint. We heard the Sunday morning peal of St. Luke's English Lutheran, the chiming of the Methodist Church carillon, the tolling of St. Peter's, sonorous bells and chimes calling the faithful to service, to God. Holy Trinity had neither a chime nor bell tower, but the Romans knew where to find the church, nevertheless. We heard the squeaking of the school's swings and teeter-totters, the rusty-nail scraping of my tree house when the wind blew in from water tank hill, the grinding machinery of Lodermeier's Garage, the high-pitched whine of Julius Ebe's hair cutter. We relished the pitter-patter of a summer's rain pelting tin roofs, of grandfather Schulz' Model T sputtering to a start, or a stop. We enjoyed the sounds of silence, inevitable stillness undulating in inaudible waves through the pines of Evergreen Cemetery on lazy, hot, drowsy, butterfly-filled Sunday afternoons out on the high prairie.

We didn't have the scintillating aromas of Red Wing's Allen Bakery, nor the grainy, musty odor of its flour mills, nor the blood-hide odor of its tanning factories, nor the freshness of Frontenac's rushing sapphire Mississippi waters. We had our own aromas—the smell of Florence Taylor's oven-baked roast beef, cabbage and sauerkraut dinners; the manure odor of outlying feed lots, farm-yard odors enveloping the village when the wind was right, a thick, misty odor covering the village like W.W.I German nerve gas. We raised our nostrils when Heaney & Gorman slaughtered cattle on Mondays, when gasoline trucks filled bulk tanks at Standard Oil, Mans & Benda, Home Oil, when beer trucks retrieved discarded, expended beer kegs from Art's, George's, Heinie's or Joe's places, the spent beer odor drying, caking to young nostrils not used to that tart odor. We smelled the sweat-stained, whiskey-stained pungent odor of the claypitters who seldom bathed, passing them on Upper or Lower Streets, they reeking of dried sweat, piss-stained over-alls, tobacco juice, beer, whiskey. We enjoyed the sweet fresh smell of a summer rain, the golden aroma of a fall harvest, the icy tingle of a Minnesota norther'. We enjoyed all those aromas and odors that enticed our midwestern pallet.

The village lacked awesome views of the Mississippi River as at Red Wing, Frontenac and Wacouta, the tumbling falls of Cannon Falls, the rugged bluff-laced Cannon valley of Welch, yet we relished our own views. We saw the sun set over water tank hill on clear summer nights and bitter winter evenings. We saw mist hang in low depressions on the outskirts of town when the earth's heat and air temperature collided, early fall mornings. We saw mirages beyond the white coal silo, a bluish haze hanging over the grain fields, seemingly an image of water, an illusion like the Great Salt Lake actually being a lake instead of an eons-old white salt desert. We saw striped, golden gophers skittering along dusty county roads, and blazing cerulean spring lilacs behind every house, and petunias, holly hocks, red, white and blue tulips sprouting through the crusted winter snow. We saw blazing yellow spring dandelions throughout the village, as important as later emerald-green lawns. We saw backyard vegetable gardens, side-house trellises, boulevard victory gardens, white-painted two-story frame houses, and the wobbling Dinky backing into town from Claybank over undulating rails.

Christmas and New Year's of 1960 soon passed. I found myself back in the bandroom with a renewed sense of spirit and hope that these students could become fine musicians, which they did over the next seven years. A back-to-the-basics method worked, as we built a fine program on that philosophy. As musical skills increased, understanding and love of music also increased. The more they accomplished, musically, the more they wanted to accomplish. We set "Activity March" in the archives for good to progress through finer band literature, thereby exciting the students, the super, the community, me. We even began marching and playing at the same time, so that by year two, as promised, we had participated with the now happy American Legion Corps. They dismantled their howitzer aimed at the bandroom, stopped firing broadsides at me on the street, and even made me an unofficial member of the Legion, even though I had only seen action in play wars—escape and evasion.

Throughout the sixties I continued traveling from one village to another, the two displaying little difference in basic values, philosophies and attitudes. Oh, McGregor was set in a picturesque river coulee embraced by imposing bluffs and rocky precipices skirting the vast Mississippi River, while Goodhue was set only on the high, isolated prairie. But the people were similar. I guess that's one reason those first eight years of teaching music worked so well.

Mother returned to live in the village after Bill died, preferring her adopted home to her native Red Wing home. With her settled in the antiquated Catholic parish house—Lucille up, Leone and Casey Ryan down—I again had a *real* home in the hometown instead of only a single, rented room. I returned periodically—Uncle Sam expecting my presence on the M-1 firing line for two weeks of Reserve Training every summer—plus I continued my education at the State College of Iowa. These activities left little time for returning to the village, yet Christmas, Easter and Thanksgiving remained on my visiting schedule.

These were years to reflect on the village as I moved farther into Iowa villages and music circles. What I began noticing on return visits was that the merchants, the businesses and proprietors of my youth had begun disappearing. The sixties became a decade of personal change—losing the old, accepting the new. Those changes became apparent on Lower Street, Upper Street, at the school, at church, in the neighborhoods. I was less aware that I, too, was changing. One element doesn't remain static while others change—we must have learned that in Physics class—it's only our sight, our awareness, our perception that prohibits awareness of change.

I sauntered into the village one Thanksgiving to visit with Mother working at the office of Charles Lutz Veterinary on Upper Street where she answered the phone, dispensed huge pills for cow hoof-and-mouth disease, hog cholera, liver rot, swine dysentry, and chicken distemper. She dispensed chlortetracycline and dihydrostreptomycin and oxytetracycline to eager farmers, no disease able to tolerate words like that. Lutz retired about 1966, selling out to another vet, W. P. Thompson, who dispensed even bigger horse pills and belly shots to cattle and livestock of the townships.

A couple of years earlier, Lloyd Cook printed his last issue of the *Goodhue County Tribune*, the weekly we had grown up with, the rag advertising hamburger at Heaney & Gorman for thirty-nine cents a pound, George Diercks' linen and dry goods, feed supplements at the Elevator, Ebe's haircuts, half off! The *Tribune* printed the results and scores of our GHS athletic endeavors: "Goodhue Squad wins District Tournament," (1944); "Goodhue to field new football team," (1947); "Dallas Diercks scores 144 points, Jimmy Franklin 2 in a win over Mazeppa." (1953). Years later I would become an editor of McGregor's *North Iowa Times*, est. 1856, thereby carrying on the village tradition of L. E. Cook. An honor.

One sixties' summer I returned to find Bill Huebner's Blacksmith Shop closed, a wrought iron sign hanging on a rusty nail, the smithy having decided he'd had enough anvil hammering. But the

sign saddened me, his shop a boyhood hangout where I had
gathered interesting tidbits of information around his blazing, red
hot forge and singing anvil, even hearing some words and stories
Mother didn't want me hearing.

Even the Goodhue Creamery where Dad dumped farmers'
milk cans during the forties and fifties went through several
mergers, acquisitions and churnings, eventually closing its operation by the end of the decade. Dad was long gone by the creamery's
end, but its closing seemed to be another nail in his coffin.

The Goodhue Hotel, still reeking of Pat Rowles' cigars in the
lobby, opened the Cellar Club in the early sixties offering dancing
Saturday nights till ten, plus all the gossip one could tolerate, the
club down the street from my dreaming Dreamland. The Cellar
Club offered townsfolk a place to go Saturday nights, something
to do other than watch another Lawrence Welk corny accordion
rerun on TV. Yet, it ran out of gas and money eventually, folks just
not that interested in traipsing from their cellar to another. But the
demise of the Club, the demise of the venerable Goodhue Hotel
was another loss of childhood sites. I suppose I didn't want to see
the village change. I suppose I wanted it to remain the same, to
always look the same when I returned. I suppose I wanted it
preserved as undertaker Ole Haga had preserved so many villagers. I realized that was a selfish attitude, however. New villagers,
new generations of boys, girls, folks wanted change, wanted their
own experiences, wanted their own memories. I would just have
to accept that.

By my fifth year of directing bands, Harold Lensch's Goodhue
Feed and Produce had sold out having hatched all of his eggs. I had
cleaned his chicken cages, had listened to the ruminations of
Naurice Husbyn before Lensch and Rusch bought the place, had
been chided by Naurice, endlessly, making a kid think for himself,
make judgments for himself, never knowing what prank Naurice
would pull next.

The bar scene changed, too. The old tenders who had served
my dad, uncles, cousins, kinfolk, friends and claypitters, began
tapping their last kegs. George Lucman sold his Corner Bar, Art
Haas sold his about 1962, Art, the man who *invented* happy hour.

New proprietors, new cafes, new people pushed aside *my* people. Changes.

In '62 village communications moved out of the Stone Age when the G. O. Miller Telephone provided dial service. Although more efficient I longed for the hand-crank phone and the two-party line. Some advancements don't necessarily improve a village. G. O. had been an entrepreneur in White Rock with his General Store and Telephone Company. And although long gone, V. D. Bien carried on his entrepreneurial spirit by installing the dial system. Accompanying this new-fangled contraption, the village even expanded its population in the sixties. Oh, it didn't get bigger than the 480 folks I had known; rather, its expansion was a five-digit zip code, 55027, a new address to Goodhue, Minnesota 55027. Some folks thought the number to be a secret governmental spy code branding them like Jews. At least that was the talk in the bars and cafes. But it didn't prove to be true anymore than an earlier rumor about Lutherans making a hostile attack on the Catholics. Folks soon cooled off about 55027, although a few cynics still grumbled, saying they deserved a higher number.

By far the biggest change, the most significant personal change, the one catapulting me from youth to adulthood was the sale of Swenson's Cafe. Swenson's had been our teenage hangout, our malt shop, our teen joint. Yes, we frequented Joe's place, Elsie's Cafe, Bartlett's Cafe, but always returned to Henry and Regina's. It was an indelible place of our youth, of the forties and fifties. But Heinie and Regina had had enough of fixing chocolate malts, hamburgers, fries, eggs over easy, candy by the penny, teenagers tapping the counter with nickels impatient for service, hollering, drunks and whores, although we never actually saw the whores. After one village visit with Mother, finding Swenson's closed, I returned to Iowa, older, sadder.

fter the first years I found I liked teaching music, sharing it with students. Our first band of twenty-one became sixty including oboes, bassoons, bass clarinets, baritone saxophones and french horns besides the usual army of clarinets, flutes and trumpets. We worked hard, played hard, entered solo and ensemble contests, concert band contests, marching band contests, parades and jazz ensemble festivals. Jazz education was then in its early stages, but it had been important to me a long time, since those village days listening late nights to Woody Herman, Stan Kenton, Count Basie, Lester Lanin, Benny Goodman, even Whoopee John on my bedroom radio up in the old neighborhood. I wanted my students to experience that joy, too. We began playing simple big band arrangements, not feeling the swing of Basie or Herman, but learning some jazz and swing nonetheless. Ten years later jazz education, through big bands, combos, traditional jazz groups, would sweep the nation's colleges and high schools. We were just a bit ahead of our time, thanks to dreams of dreaming the Dreamland.

I gradually focused my music education interests, eventually relinquishing the choral and general music program in favor of instrumental music, my forté. I was a faithful promoter of music education, demanding dedication and excellence from students, support from the community, firmly believing the musical experience would remain with them throughout their lives, which in retrospect, is exactly what happened.

Directing the choir, though—having sung throughout high school with Chas Wood, later with the Gregorian-chanting monks of St. John's—was a void in my profession. I recalled the operettas Wood presented at GHS, in particular singing a fearful duet with Phyllis Buchholtz. I had been in the public's eye before that tentative duet—an acolyte in front of the Holy Trinity congregation, a basketball and baseball player for village fans, a fledgling thespian in GHS class plays, an uncertain sixth grade clarinet soloist—"Believe me if all those endearing young charms," that night when I blew more gas and farts than notes. Singing in public, however, with a girl on my arms became my most difficult public performance. Oh, I sang or whistled all the time around the village while walking past Eddie's Drugstore or Huebner's Blacksmith Shop, trekking to school, on the basketball bus where everybody sang, in church singing "Holy God We Praise Thy Name," the only hymn Holy Trinity could sing . . . all the way through. Yet, soloing on stage in front of an audience was entirely different. I fretted about it for weeks, during rehearsals, nights in my room. The week of the performances finally arrived. I had no way out.

The on-stage orchestra struck up its overture to the operetta, *The Belle of Bagdad,* then segued into Act I, the chorus and actors filling lungs with song. I sang harmony with the tenors in the back row while the altos and sopranos hoarded the melody stage-front. I chorus-danced, acted in a very minor role, yet wasn't enjoying myself hidden in the back-stage chorus. That damn duet was approaching and I didn't know if I could get through it. My mouth and throat became increasingly dry as I looked across stage to duet partner Phyllis for encouragement. She was considerably more confident than me, having frequently sung stoic Luther hymns in Luther League. Also, I had to stand in front of the entire village with a girl in my arms. I was shy. Singing was bad enough, but to be seen both singing *and* with a girl would be excruciating. I was unsure of making it. Mother was unsure. Act I ended. The house lights came up. The stage curtain closed. Phyllis and I were up in Act II.

The orchestra played the prelude to Act II, my heart beating as fast and uncertain as their tempo, mouth as dry as Oscar Decker's throat after a day of digging clay. Everything shook, trembled as the love duet approached. Finally, it was time. I think I shuffled to stage-front to meet Princess Phyllistine. I reached for her hand, mine cold, clammy, hers warm and tender. She gripped my hand firmly, knowing how unstable I was. It helped some. The orchestra played the introduction. I couldn't back out now. She sang the first melody alone, like a twittering bird, as I looked into her lovely eyes like the prince I was supposed to be. I had to pee but she was singing so beautifully I couldn't abandon her by running to the toilet. She finished on a high Bb, flashed her bright eyes at me, squeezed my hand. My turn. My stomach tumbled, hands shook, both mine and hers. She steadied me as I now had only four measures before sinking . . . er, singing. I looked out into the audience, well, not *at* the audience, rather, directly into the spotlight, blinding myself so I wouldn't see them snickering, persecuting me, haranguing me, becoming the laughing stock of the village, my head to be locked in the laughing stock in front of the village jail like an ox where townsfolk and claypitters and merchants walking by would toss water in my face, spit at me, maybe even burn me at the stake like Joan of Arc. With two measures to go, I could hear women at the Ladies Aid Society, the Women's Study Club, the Civic Club, the American Legion, St. Peter's, St. Luke's, St. Columbkill's socials, Swenson's, Joe's Place, Bartlett's Cafes, Faye's Beauty Shop, the bars, all berating my voice . . .

"That kid can't sing. Maybe he can recite Latin, but he sure as hell can't carry a tune."

"I feel so sorry for his mother. Poor lady."

"He ought to stick to clarinet and leave the singing to Phyllis."

"God have mercy on his soul."

"Jesus, Mary and Joseph!" Mother intoned on her rosary.

The last introductory measure. Now sing, I thought. I opened my mouth but only a tiny voice emerged. It wasn't my voice. It wasn't the voice I was accustomed to hearing in a Swenson's booth or at Heaney's incinerator or on the basketball bus or at Holy Trinity. This was somebody else's voice. Phyllis squeezed again and held my arm whispering, "Louder, Jim. Let it come out. You can do it."

The next phrase got a little louder, the next louder yet, until by the end of my first melody, I was singing to the balcony, up to the Belle Creekers and Bellechestertonians and Belvederians and Claybankers and Featherstonians and Villagers sitting in the cheap seats, my voice not raising the roof, but sounding more like me. Phyllis smiled, nodded lightly as the orchestra played an interlude. I caught some breath. During the interlude, Wood had directed me to hug and kiss her on the cheek. I sort of did as we prepared to harmonize together. I felt more confident having Phyllis by my side as we approached the final strains of the duet. This time I sang with gusto, squeezing her hand in return, even looking directly at the audience instead of into the searing spotlight. We reached our last harmonized notes together like Enrico Caruso and Jenny Lind, held them long as the orchestra thumped its last chord with a roaring timpani roll. It was over. I had survived. Suddenly, I was surprised by clapping, applause, foot stomping, hooting. Where had that come from, I wondered, before realizing folks were applauding for Phyllis, maybe a couple for me. Phyllis bowed like a princess, I like an awkward gander before traipsing back into the shadows of the chorus, my trousers only a little damp.

The quarter notes, half notes, whole and eighth notes began falling like dominoes over the next several years. I would set them up in the guise of more challenging compositions with faster, higher, lower notes, but the students began keeping pace with me, knocking those black notes down with increasing ease. They could now rip off long streams of sixteenth notes, even thirty-second notes. They had progressed enough to impress people other than their parents and grandparents. They could now speak intelligently about the music they were playing, knowing something about Richard Wagner and his overtures to everything, including *Die Meistersingers von Nurnberg,* and *Lohengrin.* They now looked forward to playing Mozart's fine works for wind instruments, Mozart no longer a dusty old composer in a box. They anticipated new works to play by real, live composers, learning that music is a living art with newer composers building on the works of Bach and Beethoven and Brahms and Mozart.

I began looking to the future, feeling that these students had gained enough momentum to keep the ball rolling without me. This band career was great, where I wanted to be, but maybe the time had come to seek a new level. After my eighth Christmas Concert in the tiny gym, proud parents stomping and hooting just like the villagers of Goodhue County, I vacationed back in the village, deciding then to move on at the end of the school year. I would prepare for college band directing. As the Goodhue village crew pulled down the lone Christmas tree in the middle of the street by the bank, I pulled out of the village—heavy snows encasing it like an Arctic outpost—back to Iowa.

By the end of the decade the village of my youth was disappearing, and my high school teaching days were approaching their finalé. Both, however, would provide the catalyst for the next level.

Chapter 8

Loosened ties

Elsie's Cafe/Goodhue Hotel (l-r)
Lydia Moran, Lucille Franklin, Elsie, Mrs. Glen Bartlett

I HADN'T INTENDED ON ABANDONING MINNESOTA, liking it well enough for twenty-two years despite forever bitter winters, incessant humidity, voracious mosquitoes, 'you betcha' Scandinavians, and ever-lovin', everlastin' Evangelical Lutherans. Once I began teaching in Iowa, though, I became increasingly active in the farm state's extensive school band program, it following in the steps of Iowa's "Sousa," Karl King, Meredith Willson of Broadway *Music Man* fame, Bix Biederbecke of Jazz Age fame, Glenn Miller of Swing Era fame and Leo Greco, Iowa's Whoopee John. Iowa felt like home despite tolerating Iowa-Minnesota jokes for several years . . . "Why did The University of Iowa install artificial turf in their stadium? To stop the cheerleaders from grazing . . . What do you call a well-dressed Iowan? A tourist." I finally earned another degree at ISTC/SCI/UNI in Cedar Falls, that original Iowa Normal College of the forties unable to decide on a new name and stick with it. Later, I journeyed to the U of Iowa in Iowa City—not Ames, the Cow College, as Minnesotans are wont to say—to gain additional initials behind my name, sort of like an extended B. C. Majerus, MP (Master Plumber). I had accumulated, to date: Jim Franklin VAC (Village Acolyte), BA (Benedictine Acolyte), IIL (Second Louie); OCS (Officer Candidate, Supposedly), MA (Master Apprentice). I thought I may as well continue pursuing an ABD (All But Dissertation), but hopefully a Ph.D. (*Phi*nal Degree). If I were to enter the ranks of college band directors I would need another set of initials, those college academicians greatly influenced by innumerable degrees and undetermined suffix initials.

Two weeks before the University of Iowa's fall term, I found myself hot and dehydrated on the stifling Hawkeye Marching Band practice field, a graduate assistant drilling recruits in the fine art of marching while playing musical instruments. During those first weeks it seemed as if I were back at Ft. Leonard Wood drilling basic marching skills to army recruits. Some Iowa bandsmen had as much difficulty marching in step as had my army recruits. While most bandsmen were talented playing their instruments, getting them to high step in a straight line without bowing their legs—as when riding steers out on the farm—without looking as if they were stumping through the back forty after Holsteins did take some effort. My two squads were not M-1 rifle squads this time; rather, saxophone and clarinet squads. We drilled, marched and measured strides, poled intervals and executed Horns Up! Horns Down! instead of Present Arms! Right Shoulder Arms! through the sultry, corn-growing days of early September in *the* corn state. Two weeks later the 200-member band could march in block formation from one end zone to the other while simultaneously playing the *Iowa Fight Song*, they years ahead of my first high school band which could singularly execute playing and marching. The Iowa band was looking good, not so bad, as preterm practices ended, my academic classes to begin next week in pursuit of those suffixes.

The life style change returning to a full-time university campus was good. The preceding eight years teaching high school band students had thrust me into new musical challenges. I was moving forward, not because I disliked high school students; rather, because I was excited about attaining an even higher musical level just like B. C. and Cy and Dennis and George had encouraged me as a tike. I wanted to continue my profession at a small college, maybe a midsized university, maybe even a major university like the University of Iowa later in my career. Who knows. You never can tell.

I soon found that earning those new letters would be no lark, no piece of cake. St. John's Benedictine monks had been excellent educators and confessors; the State College of Iowa had proved to be more demanding than I expected. But after the first weeks at Iowa U, I knew I was in for a challenge, finding myself competing for grades, positions and recognition with talented graduate students from Mississippi, Florida, Minnesota, New York, Iowa. And the professors' expectations had also increased—readings more extensive, research papers more demanding, study load heavier, clarinet practice more frequent, marching band practice more demanding—and well, I had asked for it. It soon became apparent I would get it.

The old college spirit soon emerged, though, while interacting with new faces bent on attaining the same initials I was pursuing. They had arrived from *their* hometowns—Patrick from Dubuque, Gerry from Shell Rock, Carol from New England, Stan from Valley City, ND, or is it SD? Perry from Vicksburg, and Bill from Dallas, his great-great-grandfather, Jesse Chisholm, starting the famous Chisholm Trail running from San Antonio, Texas country to Abilene, Kansas . . .

"Yessir, Yank. I sure 'nough got me some Texas heritage," Bill said as we lounged outside the music research library on a glorious fall afternoon. He was dressed in silver-tipped, black western boots, a pearl-studded gray western shirt and a Stetson hat, this decidedly non-midwestern attire accenting a lanky, ranch-rugged frame. He had black hair, a hint of a mustache, a chiseled face, a square jaw. He could have been a Marlboro Man.

"How did you get into music, Tex?" I asked, curious how he, the great-great-grandson of Chisholm Trail fame had found his way into the world of music without the mentoring of Marldine Richter, Ben Gorman, Ole Haga or Chas Wood.

He crossed his boots at the end of long legs, the sun sparkling off his silver boot tips, "Dad played blues guitar on our Texas ranch. Mom hummed along, kind of in tune. I soon picked up the guitar and began playing blues also. Found out I was a pretty good Texas picker. Dad encouraged me, later bought me a sax, then a clarinet. Finally, I rustled myself a bassoon. Along the way I heard Bob Wills' Western Swing Band recording of 'Get With It,' you know . . .

Rhythm here, rhythm there
Rhythm floating everywhere.
Get with it, oh get with it,
Red hot rhythm now.

"Loved his western style—swing merged with good ol' Texas western. Still like Bob. One thing led to another. Here I am, podner," Bill said, "and how about you. How'd you get into music, not being from Texas nor ever hearing of Bob Wills?"

"I liked music from day one, Bill. I didn't have the exposure you had in Dallas, our village being remote and sequestered, but I might have heard Bob Wills on your Del Rio station, clear Saturday nights. I responded to music, any type of music. I'd hear it on juke boxes at Swenson's or Joe's Place or Elsie's Cafe, some western, hillbilly music spilling out the doors of the Corner Bar or Art's Bar when I walked home with a bag of groceries. And I'd pick up what big band music I could on my Crosley. I didn't think much about it other than I liked it; that is, until Chas Wood started me on sixth-grade clarinet. That was the turning point, although I was a recalcitrant musician during my grade and high school years, sports being extremely important to a fellow's stature in Goodhue."

"Sports were important to me, too. In fact, I received a semipro contract to play baseball for a Texas League team. Played a couple of years, but decided music would be a better career. Goodview? Where is that," Bill asked, picking his teeth with a long dry weed like a good Texan ranch fellow.

"Not Goodview. Goodhue! Up in Minnesota on the prairie. It's just a lonesome, dusty burg, but home," I said, trying to find a weed to join Bill.

"I grew up on a ranch outside Dallas while you began music in a lost Minnesota town. Funny isn't it where roots begin, how deep they are. I've pitched in the Texas League, wrestled long horn steers while you've gone from rustling . . . what did you wrestle, in Goodhue?"

"Hogs and steers at Heaney's Locker, Mondays, butchering day. I got some steers in my background too, Bill," I said, trying to match his Texas-sized bravura.

"Minnesota beef isn't Texas beef. Nothing like Texas long-horn steers."

"Well, Bill, you may have mighty fine steers, but we have pure black-and-white Holsteins grazing on emerald-green pastures, hefty sows, grunting, rooting hogs, pickin' chicken and dairies forever. You Texans have steers and endless, boring, dry ranches. Nothing else. We got real working family farms."

"Hell, one Texas steer is worth all your Holsteins, but we're here for music, not farming and ranching, Jim," he said, retrieving those long legs and boots. "Let's get back to the library to study Music History or we'll find ourselves back on those ranches and farms."

Saturday, week two, I rose early for pregame rehearsals outside the Iowa stadium. We were as nervous as the team, but a heck of a lot better. I had missed coach Forest Evashevski's glory days at Iowa in the fifties, but remembered the golden days of Bernie Bierman and his Minnesota Gophers. Now, the Hawkeyes had one real player in Eddie Podolak—of later Kansas City Chief's fame—and ten grazers. The band had been practicing for a month; we were confident for our first performance, but still nervous. Small town Iowa musicians accustomed to performing for 150, maybe 300 hometown folks out on the vast Iowa prairie would now march and toot before 50,000 fans. The staff didn't know if they could handle it. The bandsmen didn't know if they could handle it. Although I wasn't marching, I was nervous for my clarinets and saxophones, just like a defensive line coach. I had drilled my musical charges and was desperately hoping they would perform well during the half-time show.

The Hawkeyes were playing the Ohio State Buckeyes, Woody Hayes the perennial nemesis. The Hawks didn't stand a chance against the Buckeyes, Eddie Podolak notwithstanding, which quickly became evident. The band performed flawlessly in a short pregame, on-field show, my clarinet and saxophone squads missing nary a beat nor step.

The Hawks fumbled the opening kickoff looking much like teenage farm boys trying to grab a greased pigskin; it was down hill, down wind from then on. The Buckeyes pummeled the Hawkeyes, taunting them as if they were a junior high team—running, kicking, tackling, slamming and scoring at will. Half-time score: Buckeyes 32, Hawkeyes 0, Marching Band 0. It would be up to the band to raise the fans' spirits.

I gave a short pep talk to my charges on the sidelines as they nervously adjusted reeds, pads, slings, spats, hats. Suddenly, the drum major strutted from the end zone to midfield, back arched so low I thought he would fall onto his butt, thereby placing the band in the same league as the football team. Instead, he vaulted high into the air, stomped to a halt at the fifty yard line, tossed his 10-foot baton twirling into the air, caught it one handed while blowing a shrill, gleaming whistle and commanding the band to explode onto the field as the 50,000 crowd burst into applause. It caught me off guard. This for a band? I was to find out later that the fans came for the band in the late sixties rather than the football team. They only tolerated the team's antics until half time. What a joy, what a thrill, I thought as I nervously followed my squads' movements through the opening drill. Like a line coach, I only watched my charges instead of the entire band, anticipating their movements, fearful of a mistake—a missed assignment, a movement out of sequence, out of step. Through the first maneuver, all okay; the second, fine, followed by an intricate down field-sliding maneuver as the band blared a Mamas & Papas pop tune of the day. The next segment was a concert arrangement, no marching, just powerful brass, percussion and woodwinds screaming into the enveloping stands. It was exciting listening to them in a full stadium, fans excited, appreciative of the director's arrangements, me just a small part of it, a small kid from a small village who suddenly wondered how he got from the GHS Purple and White Band to the Iowa Black and Gold Band. I stood on the sidelines, chills running through me as the band blew scintillating full, rich chords, trumpets screeching toward the nosebleed seats, snare drums paradiddling, snapping rudimental double and triple rattamacues, tubas laying down bass lines more aggressive than the offensive line, almost a boogie beat while *my* clarinets and saxophones complemented them with biting arpeggios and floating woodwind lines. The concert arrangement ended with a thundering, rumbling cadence, the throng jumping to its feet as the band maneuvered into its last drill. The team straggled onto the sidelines fully realizing they had another half of humiliation before hitting the local bars, drinking pitchers of beer, obliterating their minds, later, screwing girlfriends, giving them what they should have given the Buckeyes, but screwing better than being humiliated by the Buckeyes.

The final half-time maneuver was the most difficult of the show. I wanted my squads to successfully complete it, to not let the band down. The band began the drill—inside, outside, concentric circles, playing, snapping, marching forward, backwards sideways, my clarinets and saxophones not missing a step . . . until a wandering clarinetist suddenly turned the wrong way, meeting an army of charging trumpets blaring down his throat. He quickly retreated like Jedidiah's great-great-grandfather Lee at Gettysburg, realizing his mistake as my throat stuck, one of my squad members missing an assignment. He recovered more quickly than me as the band reached its final position, its final show climax, the crowd again on its feet applauding for an overall thrilling performance. I was sort of happy despite one of my charges blowing an assignment. I wasn't devastated, yet disappointed. I would have to answer to the director. We'd work on that next week.

Final score: Marching Band 99, Ohio State 56, Iowa 3. I had my first Big Ten marching band performance under my belt, even though I was a lowly line sergeant, but there would be more. I was learning marching and performance and playing to fans for bigger days.

Although attending a public university I harbored that old desire for SJU's Catholic camaraderie. Four weeks into the semester I attended a campus Newman Club gathering one Friday evening after struggling through 300 pages of Renaissance Music History—Palestrina, Ockegem, Obrecht, di Lassus—not your household names; after writing boring, uninspiring eighteenth century counterpoint never to be used in a marching band arrangement; after drilling a long, cold and wet marching rehearsal. I was ready for simple monophonic Gregorian Chant, and socialization.

I joined thirty students at the Newman Campus Center to discuss being a Catholic student in a public university and what to do about it. The Center was up the hill from the stadium, a stone's throw from St. Thomas More church where sinners were no longer stoned. We sat in a huge oval doing the, "Hi, I'm John . . . Hello, I'm Jim . . . Bless you, I'm Mary Magdalene," thing until the facilitator asked us to join hands for a beginning prayer, an open-ended, creative prayer unlike the *Baltimore Catechism* prayers of my Holy Trinity youth. She spoke about the opportunities and offerings of The Center and how we could take advantage of it during our time as students. It seemed like a good idea to keep the St. John's Benedictine spirit going while continuing my pursuit of attempting to understand the Crusades, the Inquisition, papal hierarchy, sex before marriage, as well as Reformed Lutherans.

Ten minutes into the holy gathering, the holy spirit not yet appearing, a young, petite and attractive woman did appear at the door like someone seeking a room at the inn, someone seeking entrance to the inner sanctum. Because I was sitting *in* the doorway, blocking her way into the stable, like the gentleman my mother had brought me up to be, I rose, offered my chair, then scooted across the room to find another. Refocusing on her visage from across the oval gathering, I soon became interested, not listening to the director as much as pondering this blond-haired woman who accepted my chair, this woman who had come wandering in from the desert, from the dark of night. I wondered who she was, why she had come late . . . to the gathering at the inn.

It had been a long time since Becky at St. John's, Sharon in Red Wing, my energy the past years focused on teaching music and the pursuit of additional initials. I wasn't getting any younger, Mother often told me; she was getting worried, developing incessant scabs on her knees from praying countless novenas to the Blessed Virgin Mary and to St. Jude, the patron saint of lost causes, all for my salvation, and a wife. I didn't consider myself a lost cause, yet Mother fretted, as did every other village mother about *her* unmarried sons and daughters.

In our fifties' village many guys and gals married only a couple of days after high school graduation, maybe a year later. To be twenty-five and single was a mark of . . . well, townsfolk didn't say "gay" then, but they began looking at you sort of "funny." I was twenty-nine now, but Mother's novenas hadn't worked. She wasn't giving up, though. Neither had she given up spending extra money on lighting side altar votive candles on my behalf. My thirtieth was approaching. She didn't want to explain to her Bridge Club ladies that her son still wasn't married.

The facilitator stopped speaking about Newman opportunities to now encourage input from the congregation. We discussed our degree pursuits and the place of our Roman faith in that pursuit. We shared stories, experiences, desires and choices for an hour before breaking for punch and cookies. At the break I quickly approached the "chair lady" saying I was Jim, a musician-teacher, a Catholic and a Minnesotan. She said she was Terri, a teacher, a

Catholic and an Iowan. We had two out of three in common, thank God! Could've been worse. An apostolic group had surrounded the punch and cookie table, drinking and eating like it was their last supper while I chatted with Terri looking smart in a red plaid sort of two-piece pleated skirt outfit. Bill, Cynthia, Paul, plus Matthew, Mark, Luke and John surrounded the supper table, Mary Magdalene sitting forlorn in the shadows while conversations became truncated, interrupted as we bounced from one apostle to the other. But I didn't forget Sister Terri, even though Mary Magdalene poured red punch on my clean pants. ("Oh for the least of yee.") The altar bell tinkled, the incense lamp was lit as we processed back to the gathering room to generate guidelines for the fall term, forming interest groups to become involved in The Center, in ourselves.

Terri volunteered for the Liturgy Group, so I quickly joined also. I wasn't sure what a Liturgy group did, but I had had my own ideas back in the village when serving mass for Fr. Smith—ideas he nor the bishop ever incorporated. Maybe I could offer some now, ideas like limiting the priest's homily to fifteen minutes; actually *rehearsing* the congregation in the singing of hymns; requiring parishioners to move to the center of the pew instead of expecting others to step over them; permitting the congregation to drink wine in addition to partaking of the holy host (an idea way ahead of its time); reciting prayers in English instead of Latin so even I could understand them (it took Vatican II to pass that); and moving the confessional to the back of the church so the congregation wouldn't snicker as I left it. Other groups—outreach, inreach, ceremony, vestments, social, music, sex—were organized before we concluded the evening in our chosen interest group. My interest in Terri grew as we discussed what in hell or heaven we would do in the Liturgy group. Bill offered suggestions, Terri offered suggestions, and I offered my opinions of their suggestions. We agreed to meet next week, slurped watered-down punch, chomped sweetbread cookies before Mary Magdalene suggested heading to the Airliner Bar for real, unholy drink. I offered Terri a ride. She accepted. It was the beginning to the end of Mother's novenas. Mother was close to getting off her knees, close to smiling again and raising her head high at Bridge Club.

I had entered Iowa U determined to earn that "Ph.D." behind my name, not expecting an "MD" (married), too. But soon Saint Theresa began skipping onto the band practice field bringing lunch during rehearsals much to the chiding of my on-field colleagues. I set Renaissance History, Eighteenth Century Counterpoint, and the Theory of Instrumental Music Education aside periodically to attend to my non-music needs, as well as Mother's. Terri laid down her counseling books as we danced each other into a marriage, processing down the aisle of St. Thomas More to Handel's "Trumpet Voluntary," Mary Magdalene successfully pouring the wine and water, St. Luke proudly watching over the ceremony from the wings, in his wings, his success with this village fellow gaining him a higher level of heaven. Mother embraced her new daughter-in-law, then breathed a sigh of relief. She could return to the Bridge Club in the village with her head ever so high.

Nine months and a couple of weeks later, I added another initial to my growing list: FR (father), Anne Elizabeth Franklin entering the world in Iowa City on a sub zero day. The freezing, bitter February weather couldn't dampen our spirits, though, as we toted Anne home in Mother's yellow baby bunting knit back in the village especially for the occasion. I suddenly had acquired a wife, a baby daughter, a father-in-law, a mother-in-law while only coming to Iowa City for a degree. But the additions rounded out my life, made me think of something other than instrumental music, made me a father, a family . . .

"Family" had been all important in the village. Oh, it wasn't a concept we gave any particular thought to. It just was. Families were the core of the community, bachelors and spinsters, in retrospect, shunted to the side pews under dusty statues of St. Jude, to the rear pews, shunted to the hard, dusty seats in the club rooms, their names dropped to the bottom of parish rosters, sympathized with in their assumed loneliness. Being a farming village— initially existing solely for the support of farmers who shipped livestock, grains and produce from the new railroad station— township families were large with as many as eight or ten children in a household, sometimes more as in the case of Anton Rosener's twenty-six children. Catholic families were especially large, it having something to do with not understanding how to work that Rhythm Method. However, children were cheap labor on the farm, each additional child adding to the workforce. Catholics certainly didn't have a monopoly on large families, though, in the outlying townships, eastside German Lutheran "Diercks" as numerous as westside "O'Reillys." Pioneering Lutheran farmers needed that workforce as much as Catholics even if the Missouri Synod didn't expect them to implement the Rhythm Method . . .

"See the wife is carrying another load around, Harry. Guess you don't know how to turn the spicket off once you get it started."

"Know how to, don't want to," John said as they leaned on the sides of their grain trucks waiting to dump at the Elevator.

"So, how many kids you got then, anyways?" John asked, waiting his turn in the truck line behind Harry.

"Seven, number eight poppin' soon. That'll probably do it for me when this one's cooked. Got eight brothers and sisters myself, so I always figured I'd do 'bout the same. Wife's gettin' tired anyway, almost locks the door on me nights, but what the hell's a guy gonna do? Figure it'll take care of itself soon, just like my sows out on the farm. They gettin' tired, don't produce like they used to. Guess the same'll happen to the wife," John said as they jumped into their trucks to move up in the grain-dumping line.

Yes, the children kept coming over the years, filling farm-steads, filling the village, filling church pews, filling one-room school houses. They emerged from the rich, deep soil of Belle Creek, Featherstone, Belvidere, Goodhue, Hay Creek, Vasa town-ships, these the families of Allers, Banidt, Moran, Eyestone, Befort, Rowles, Campbell, Carlson, Swenson, Peterson, Thomp-son, Erickson, Olson, Swanson, Anderson, Larson, Cook, Diercks, Gorman, Ebe, Fischer, Gadient, Haga, Bien, Ingebritsen, Johnson, Haas, Nibbe, Barry, Eppen, Kehren, Deden, Kindseth, Wipper-ling, Frederickson, Bartel, Taylor, Albers, Kyllo, Huebner, Liffrig, Vieths, Ryan, Heaney, Lodermeier, Tomfohr, Buck, Lohman, Bjorngaard, McHugh, McNamara, Holm, Majerus, Goodsell, Mans, Nei, Klair, O'Reilly, O'Gorman, O'Neill, Opsahl, Parker, Swenke, Bartlett, Poncelet, Rambolt, Holst, Raasch, Mickley, Drenckhahn, Yungers, Mann, Redding, Benitt, Reese, Lensch,

Rehder, Nord, Rosener, Bremer, Rusch, Benda, Miller, Schinnert, Matthees, Jonas, Lunde, Seebach, Henning, Richter, Mehrkens, Shelstad, Buchholtz, Stemman, Husbyn, Stenlund, Dicke, Thomforde, Knutson, Manahan, Tiedemann, Schulz, Hutcheson, Vollmers, Boxrud, Voth, Warren, Zemke, Hinrichs, Zimmerman, Franklin . . . families not to be denied the wealth of the earth, not to be denied the bountiful harvest of the land, of their spirits. "Family" was close to godliness itself, its structure, its element binding people together into kith, kith and kin into a community of sharing, compromising, patience, fortitude, giving in, giving up, kinship, love developed in the close-knit family, this village, this community no different from any other, townsfolk, homefolk, villagers, farmers, ministers, toddlers, teenagers, merchants, teachers, drunks struggling to work together, to maintain a village, a community . . . then . . . now.

I was part of that village family structure, the Franklin kinfolk of the many "Davids" spreading throughout the community. Now, I was continuing that extended family, although out of Minnesota, but the tradition of family nonetheless. I cultivated those values in my new family beneath the claws of the looming Hawkeye statue. Anne Elizabeth neither knew nor cared about the difference between a Hawkeye and a Gopher in that year of 1969, but she too would graduate, a Hawkeye, twenty-two years later.

Baby Anne presented a formidable challenge to my Renaissance Music and Philosophy of Music Education studies, caring little about early composers, nor the "Study of behavioral changes in students learning to play clarinet, flute or trumpet in the public schools." She was more interested in her bottle, her crib toys, playing with blocks and balls while remaining bright-eyed into the wee hours of the morning as I attempted to gain sleep for an early class. Terri put her pending counseling degree into practice by counseling at an outlying high school. We were a small family, but family, nevertheless, on the Iowa U campus.

Year one melded into year two with innumerable classes, plus marching bands, concert bands, conducting, rehearsing, performances, tours, all dominated by that looming dissertation. You couldn't gain a doctorate without completing a dissertation. You could take all the classes, perform in bands and orchestras, but until you faced the research and dissertation monster, you would end up only an ABD, suffixes not worth a hill of beans as the village fellows used to say. The names of ABDs—students who never made the transition from reading Renaissance history, practicing clarinet and saxophone, sleeping through classes, to research and writing—litter the halls and practice rooms like inner city graffiti. I was determined to avoid that. Dodie, George and Dennis had imbued that "never-give-up" principle back at Heaney & Gorman.

By Anne's eighteenth month I was spending more time in the music library's dungeon archives searching through tomes of journal articles and countless research reports seeking an area of research interest in music education. This area would, hopefully, accompany me through a continuing career. The search wasn't easy being long, lonely deep in the aisles searching, reading, analyzing whether to pursue learning cognition, musical perception in the young child, instrumental music education in the public schools, or historical aspects of the community concert band in building community spirit, just as the Goodhue Community Concert Band had done under Marldine Richter and Chas Wood. While searching I struggled through French, German, and Statistics, all required to supposedly help my research pursuits. I enjoyed French, but detested the disarray of the German language despite Mother's Austrian-German ancestry. Mark Twain expressed my sentiments: "When the literary German dives into a sentence, that is the last you are going to see of him until he emerges on the other side of his attack with his verbs in his mouth." (*The Connecticut Yankee,* Mark Twain). Statistics slammed me to the mat, down for the count, it supposedly necessary for a pending experimental research study.

My musical genes had been well imbedded in the village, yet I pondered over the years how those mellifluous genes came about, parents appreciative but untrained. Sister Rose pounded out "Whispering," "Always," and "Nevertheless" on the parlor upright, while brother Tom mostly banged on the bass drum, off the beat, for Chas Wood's GHS band. My genes might have skipped several generations, reverting to Mother's Austrian heritage, her maternal grandmother from the Innsbruck and Imst, Tyrolian region, only a mountain valley or so from Mozart, Haydn and Beethoven's Vienna. This musing eventually led me into researching the effects of music on learning abilities, sort of behavioral research, but still fascinating. I gathered the required background research, pursed a plan of implementing an experimental research study, wrote innumerable proposals for my dissertation advisor—which he subsequently hacked to hell with his ever-sharp No. 2 yellow Ticonderoga pencil, changing my passive voice to active, clarifying my syntax and rhetoric, substituting concrete instead of inexact vocabulary—and well, I was making progress toward avoiding that ABD as I entered the final semester on the Iowa City campus; that is, until the day I received a phone call from the village.

"Jim, We've taken your mother to St. John's Hospital," Dodie Gorman yelled into the phone I picked up outside a practice room, a grocery-filtered voice I had known since childhood, immediately recognizable. "She had a spell this afternoon walking home from the grocery store. Didn't know where she was. We found her sitting on a curb outside the Methodist Church, for God's sake! Walked right past Holy Trinity. You know she must have been confused," Dodie continued, not letting me get a word in sidewise or edgewise. I had worked for Dodie, George and Dennis since eighth grade, after school, Saturdays, sweeping floors, toting garbage to the incinerator behind the Locker Plant, and sacking those innumerable potatoes for the little old ladies of the village. They had known my every move through grade school and high school, having become "adopted" parents after we buried Dad in the dry, sullen earth of St. Columbkill's Cemetery back in '51. Dodie had taken over my guidance as Mother reeled from widowhood, Lucille suddenly finding herself a forsaken widow in a village she didn't want to be a widow in. The Heaneys and Gormans were also neighbors, so Dodie had prodded me with studies, prodded me with sports, prodded me with catechism, scolded me to practice clarinet, prodded me to save *some* of my weekly pay check instead of spending it all on malts and burgers at Swenson's, this while showering every kid who worked at the store with countless Christmas clothes. I had been unfortunate losing a father at 14, but fortunate to have gained adopted parents in Dodie and George, and "Uncle" Dennis. Could've been worse.

"What happened?" I asked, finally squeezing into the conversation at the pay phone.

"We don't know, but you better come home. They're doing tests now at St. John's Hospital in Red Wing. Lucille said she was just dizzy when we found her on the curb. Said she hadn't been drinking; said she'd just been walking home saying a novena for somebody or something, maybe you. George and I drove her to the hospital. You come home right away, you hear. Bye, gotta go," and she was off the phone, gone like Dodie had lived her life in the village. She would rush into our house, then rush out just as fast, hurrying on to help somebody—brother Dennis, George, her retarded son Mike, or maybe the other nine children she brought into the village, thereby expanding its population by 20 percent.

"We're conducting tests right now, Jim, to see if we can determine what happened to your mother," the white-robed doctor said as Terri, Anne and I walked into St. John's, the same hospital I had avoided since that fateful day in '51 when the doctor met Mother, Tom and me at the door telling us that it "was all over," me for a minute thinking the apparent spell Dad just had was all over, but the doctor meaning his life was all over, Mother knowing instinctively. Now, I had returned to visit Mother, to find out why she had suddenly chosen the Methodist Church instead of the Catholic Church.

She was resting in a cranked-up hospital bed, a wet towel over her forehead as we shuffled in. "Hi, Mother. It's Jim and Terri. Anne is outside by the window," I said, approaching her at bedside, reaching for her hand.

"Hi, Jim. I've a bad headache, feel dizzy," she said, grasping my hand lightly.

"We just arrived from Iowa City. Dodie said you had joined the Methodist Church. Why would you do something like that at age seventy," I said, repositioning the towel on her forehead.

"Noooo! I was only resting by the Methodist Church. I didn't join it, Jimmy. Your joshing. I'm tired, need to sleep for awhile."

"Okay, We'll be here."

We spent the night at the Gorman's in the old neighborhood, this time with a wife and daughter instead of childhood friends. Before retiring I looked out the window, across the street to my Franklin house, it looking mostly the same, but my front-walk lamppost gone (the light post that never worked, it shorting out soon after I wired it); base paths on the side lawn near the apple tree where we had played softball and corkball through endless, drowsy, lazy afternoons, gone; the last remnants of the tree house, gone, but the scarred elm tree still standing back by Bob's sandbox, the elm surviving in spite of my abuses. Gone were most childhood remnants, but the memories remained. I fell asleep wondering about Mother and what was happening, and was her life in danger, and was my time in the village in danger.

"We're sending your mother to the Mayo Clinic, by ambulance, for more tests," the tall, white-robed doctor said to Rose, Tom, Terri and me outside her hospital room. "We're unable to determine the problem here. The Mayo Clinic will be able to determine what her problem is, but we suspect it may be neurological," he said as we stood, stunned, in the hallway. This appeared to be more than just Mother choosing to become a Methodist, more than a dizzy spell, more than being slightly tipsy after splitting several beers with the afternoon ladies in a back booth of Art's Bar. In her hospital room she was coherent, but tired, and worried, well-worn rosary beads strung through her fingers, rattling like dry corn stalks out in Belle Creek. Sister Marie Haustein had died of a brain tumor in the forties. Mother was worried about a similar fate, but we reassured her with hugs, loving touches and pats saying she would be all right and that even though I didn't favor it, she could become a Methodist if she wanted. By six o'clock Mayo Clinic doctors were examining her as Rose and I waited patiently for her test results in the immaculate waiting room.

Another white-robed doctor approached, fatigued, tired, downcast. Mother had a huge tumor growing on her brain, he said. He

needed to operate immediately, he said. Okay, we said. We waited
. . . and waited in the cold room leafing mindlessly through
*National Geographic, Field and Stream, Mechanics Illustrated,
Time* magazines. She survived the operation, but was never the
same mother again, at least for the remaining four weeks she lived
out her life back in her native Red Wing at St. John's Hospital
again. The operation had taken most of the tumor and most of her
spirit. She was no longer the mother who waited for me each day
to traipse across the back lawn through the evergreens after school
to construct a Dagwood sandwich before rushing out to play again
in the village's muddy streets. She was no longer the mother who
wet her pants during every basketball game, during every clarinet
solo, during every performance of a junior or senior class play. She
was no longer the mother who served delicious roast beef, mashed
potatoes and gravy for Sunday dinner, this after the family had
strolled to Holy Trinity. She was no longer the mother who
tolerated my childhood antics of playing basketball in the dining
room near her best china. The tumor, the operation had taken that
mother away leaving only a physical mother. Yet, she was strong,
resilient, lingering at St. John's as my "new" family returned to
Iowa City. But Dodie called again with the inevitable news.

"She didn't make it, Jim," Dodie said as I reluctantly took the
call. "Your mother died this morning. You better come home," and
Dodie was gone, again. I stood by the phone, stunned, anticipating
Mother's death, yet not prepared for it. How can one ever get ready
for a parent's death? Dad's had come too suddenly, Mother's
slower, but death, nevertheless. Endless death. I returned to the
practice room, no longer interested in practicing my scales and
études, having little energy. For the first time in my life I was
without parents. It didn't feel good. One parent had not been as
good as two, but now there were zero. I slowly picked up the
clarinet to place it into its case, but impulsively began playing
"Always," a song both Dad and Mother liked.

> *I'll be loving you, always,*
> *With a love that's true, always . . .*

I slowly placed the clarinet in its case this time, said a few Our Fathers and Hail Marys for the repose of her soul before trudging home to Anne and Terri.

Not for just an hour,
Not for just a day,
Not for just a year,
But always.

Mother's death didn't rent Holy Trinity's confessional curtain—she was saintly, not godly—and it didn't cause the earth to shake, yet the night we waked her at Lohman's Funeral Home the village witnessed one of the most catastrophic thunderstorms it had ever seen. It rained torrents for several days flooding tiny brooks and streams, rushing waters cascading over Highway 58 causing a drowning death near the Bellechester turnoff. But the folks who had known her for most of her seventy years weren't daunted by Noah's flood. They came to see her one last time, came to pay their respects just as she had done for so many during her lifetime. As at Dad's wake nineteen years earlier, they reminisced, they laughed, they cried, offering hugs and handshakes and "my sympathies" to her children, to a new daughter-in-law she hadn't had the opportunity of spending nearly enough time with. But her death's timing wasn't her choice, wasn't our choice. The Lord had said it was time to leave the village. I'm sure she said, in her last coherent moments, "Okay, Lord, you go on ahead. I'll be right there after I get my rosary and holy cards."

In her casket she *looked* like our mother, her head wrapped in a red turban like a Hindu priest, it covering that incessant tumor that had taken her life. I thought, gazing down at her on the bier, how she would have liked being here at her own wake, how she would have enjoyed her Red Wing Haustein relatives, her Belle Creek Franklin relatives, her village friends and acquaintances. She had buried two husbands, but now it was her turn. She would take the long ride to St. Columbkill's country cemetery in the morning if the ark didn't start rising.

The rains did stop but they had saturated the ground—farmers couldn't get into fields, couldn't navigate their farm yards, but they did get to the old country church. Burying Mother in the sodden ground was an uncertainty. She did well, though, as we processed her down the long aisle of St. Columbkill's for her Funeral Mass, friends and family wiping away tears, her well-worn beads strung between her fingers for eternity. Taking the front pew with sister Rose, brother Tom, Terri, I recalled standing on that altar in a white surplice fifteen years earlier, an altar boy attending her wedding to husband number two, Bill Ryan of the Ryan clan, all thirty now filling the front quarter of the church. I recalled sitting in this pew nineteen years ago when we buried Dad. I recalled lugging buckets of holy water for Fr. Smith during Holy Week. I recalled picking weeds from around headstones during summer catechism classes. I recalled standing on the front steps waiting for Mother and Dad to stop talking to parishioners so we could rush home. I recalled sleeping in these pews as a toddler during Christmas Midnight Mass. Memories of a childhood, memories of a family echoed in my ears as Father sprinkled holy water on her casket. With her mass and burial, our parents were gone, the torch, the holy water being passed to the next generation. How could it all have happened so rapidly? Where had those years gone? Why, it only seemed like yesterday, I thought, feeling like an old man, well, not an old man, but an older man as Father began a Requiem Mass for Lucille Anne Haustein Franklin Ryan. She never got that third husband, so we could bury her in one plot instead of two, next to husband number one, Dad . . .

"May her soul and the souls of the faithful departed, through the mercy of God, rest in peace. Amen."

We took the long walk down the aisle past mourning family and friends, out the creaking front doors and into a cloudy but rainless day. The procession wound across the gravel road to her cemetery plot, the same journey we had trudged too many times. Reaching the gates, I felt fourteen again, burying Dad instead of Mother. Approaching her open grave, my feet sunk into the soggy ground, water squishing into my shoes, my mind locked somewhere between 1970 and 1951. Reaching the gaping grave site—

Mother's casket placed on scaffolding—while awaiting for the priest to send her into eternity, the sight of her open grave shook me. The rains had been relentless causing the site to be more of a mud hole than a grave. But what startled me was seeing Dad's exposed vault next to Mother's grave. I couldn't believe I was viewing his vault after almost twenty years. The rains had caused the earth to collapse, exposing his vault. My mind twisted, ran amok, surged. I wiped my eyes, not accepting the sight of Mother's casket perched on the suspended vault, Dad's awaiting her arrival.

Father said his final burial prayers; we responded in kind as he circumvented the casket sprinkling it with holy water on a day we didn't need more water. Folks blessed themselves as Father intoned *Pox vobiscum* (Peace be with you), saying it was all over. Go home. But the mourners didn't want to leave Lucille. Her children didn't want to leave her. We stood in the breezy, cloudy May day trying to hold on to her and her memory, as with everyone else who had preceded her to this and other cemeteries out on the high prairies, each a life, a remnant tombstone reminding the living of the dead. And although lengthy epitaphs weren't the custom on local tombstones—as at *Spoon River*—our community recorded its own anthologies at St. Columbkill's Cemetery, Belle Creek Township . . .

William C. Ryan (1893–1957) and Julia Ryan (c. 1897–1952), Francis Ryan (1890–1958), Mary Ryan (1894–1967), Joyce Shelstad (1905–1962), J. P. Ryan (1882–1966), Dan Heaney (1895–1965), Johanna Heaney (1883–1922) and William J. Heaney (1871–1935), David Gadient (1889–1964), Tom Franklin (1894–1951) . . .

I inherited forty acres from my Father
And, by working my wife, my two sons and two daughters
From dawn to dusk, I acquired
A thousand acres. But not content.
Wishing to own two thousand acres,
I bustled through the years and with axe and plow,

Toiling, denying myself, my wife, my sons, my daughters.
Squire Higbee wrongs me to say
That I died from smoking Red Eagle cigars.
Eating hot pie and gulping coffee
During the scorching hours of harvest time
Brought me here ere I had reached my sixtieth year.
("Cooney Potter," Spoon River)

Anne McWaters (1889–1948), Jim Franklin (c. 1893–1945), Mary McHugh (1882–1966) and William McHugh (1877–1947), Ernest Gorman (1893–1967) and Mary Gorman (1890–1969), Mary Franklin (1827–1883), Tom Heaney (1868–1934), Philip Ryan (1856–1930) and Sarah Ryan (1857–1938), Patrick Rowles (1863–1958), Joseph Heaney (1859–1939), Blanche Barry (1891––1969), Lou Schinnert (1881–1947) and Anna Schinnert (1886–1967) . . .

There is something about Death
Like love itself!
If with some one with who you have known passion,
And the glow of youthful love,
You also, after years of life
Together, feel the sinking of the fire,
And thus fade away together,
Gradually, faintly, delicately,
As it were in each other's arms,
Passing from the familiar room—
That is a power of union between souls
Like love itself!
("William and Emily," Spoon River)

Patrick Kelley (1852–1900), Tom Taylor (1864–1945) and Margaret Taylor (1865–1934), Russell T. Ryan (1915–1945), Michael Kelly (1834–1913) and Catherine Kelly (1841–1906), Frank O'Gorman (1874–1957) . . .

If the excursion train to Peoria
Had just been wrecked, I might have escaped with my life—
Certainly I should have escaped this place.
But as it was burned as well, they mistook me
For John Allen who was sent to the Hebrew Cemetery
At Chicago,
And John for me, so I lie here.
It was bad enough to run a clothing store in this town,
But to be buried here—ach!
("Barney Hainsfeather," Spoon River)

Anthologies at Evergreen Cemetery, up on village hill:

Where are Elmer, Herman, Bert, Tom and Charley,
The weak of will, the strong of arm,
the clown, the boozer, the fighter?
All, all are sleeping on the hill
("The Hill," Spoon River)

Clarence Goodsell (1883–1949), Herman Diercks (1882–1955), Jesse Campbell (1885–1967), John Buck (1863–1929), John Stemman (1869–1932), Erv Stemman (1898–1944), Bill Hennings (1878–1960) and Clara Hennings (1882–1966), Fred Vieths (1890–1958), Walter Hinsch (1904–1968), Marie Bremer (1906–1965), Ole Shelstad (1836–1920) . . .

In youth my winds were strong and tireless,
But I did not know the mountains.
In age I knew the mountains
But my weary wings could not follow my vision—
Genius is wisdom and youth.
("Alexander Throckmorton," Spoon River)

Nels Skramstad (1830–1909) and Derekka Skramstad (1832–1907), Lucretia O'Gorman (1888–1958), Mary E. McHugh (1871–1934) and John McHugh (1856–1957), Fred Prahl (1875–1959), John Albers (1875–1955), Marie Albers (1881–1966), John Matthees (1888–1956), Art Holm (1894–1940), Jonathan Finney (1828–1905) and Agnes Finney (1836–1904), Glen Bartlett (1915–1965), Ray Bandit (1911–1965) . . .

The living come with grassy tread
To read the gravestones on the hill;
The graveyard draws the living still,
But never any more the dead . . .

At St. John's country cemetery, east township: Jacob Nibbe (1819–1899) and Barbara Nibbe (1844–1904), Hans Dammann (1851–1878), Catharina Matthees (1877–1879), W. M. Vomhoff (1837–1890) and Helene Vomhoff (1835–1911), Emile Matthees (1897–1965), John Luhman (1837–1903) and Metta Luhman (1849–1934), John Luhman (1877–1949) and Emma Luhman (1875–1944), Kurt Diercks (1868–1941) and Margaret Diercks (1879–1968) . . .

The verses in it say and say:
'The ones who living come today
To read the stones and go away
Tomorrow dead will come to stay . . .

John Holst (1881–1958) and Mattie Holst (1881–1958), Walter Jonas (1908–1957), Heinrich Hadler (1880–1956) and Anna Hadler (1883–1962), Peter Albers (1851–1936) and Margareta Albers (1848–1917), Detlef Scharpen (1867–1917) and Elizabeth Scharpen (1872–1969), Frau Maria Quast (1869–1903), Hein Dammann (1846–1917) and Rebecke Dammann (1842–

1917), Hinrich Bennitt (1842–1929), P. Damann (1822–1902), Deiderich Bolland (1848–1937), Maria Augustine (1800–1882), John Reese (1874–1950) . . .

So sure of death the marbles rhyme,
Yet can't help marking all the time
How no one dead will seem to come.
What is it men are shrinking from? . . .

At Grace Lutheran country cemetery, east township: Conrad Meyer (1850–1940) and Margaret Meyer (1858–1948), Margaret Daman (1840–1881), Freidrich Hinze (1828–1914), John Steffens (1879–1952) and Annie Steffens (1882–1916), Johannes Picken-pack (1871–1957), Henry Pickenpack (1874–1939), Johan Albers (1821–1893), Charles Zemke (1808–1882), Medwin Zemke (1806–1873), Anna Willers (1845–1900), Hermann Lensch (1878–1940) and Emma Lensch (1890–1958), John Buchholtz (1885–1959), George Tidemann (1887–1963).

It would be easy to be clever
And tell the stones: Men hate to die
And have stopped dying now forever.
I think they would believe the lie.
("In A Disused Graveyard," Robert Frost)

Mourners reluctantly broke away from Mother's soggy grave site. I stayed for several more moments at the final resting place of both Mother and Dad. I was only thirty-four but felt like 134.

lthough I had a wife and daughter beside me as we bounced across the uneven tracks near the village's landmark white coal silo—where in 1948 the Catholic rubber gun Crusaders had finally defeated the Evangelical Lutherans in the Showdown of the O. K. coal silo—both the irregular tracks and the moment shook me hard. I had bounced across these tracks hundreds of times when leaving the village, always to return, but this time they were rougher, more jarring as we turned south toward Zumbrota. Mother was entombed in Belle Creek's saturated earth alongside Dad. The village had been my hometown, the place I could always return to when struggling through St. John's; when escaping and evading Ft. Benning; when shooting M-1s at Ft. Leonard Wood; when beginning a music teaching career at McGregor. Mother had always been here, but no longer. Was the village my home anymore, or was this the beginning of loosened ties? Would I return, or would my new family take me to remote places, the village becoming only a memory? Passing the Bellechester turnoff I had difficulty grasping the significance of this departure. Terri wisely understood my reticence, not prodding, just holding gurgling Anne as we ventured toward Pine Island, Oronoco, Rochester, heading into Iowa.

I don't believe I spoke a word until reaching Decorah, Iowa. I was wrestling with the significance of losing a mother and driving away from the village. I felt cut loose, ties severed, the house, the hometown, gone. I hoped it wouldn't be so. I hoped I would return with that ABD . . . er, Ph.D. I didn't know where those initials would take us, maybe thousands of miles from the little whistle-stop on the high prairie. Had I been raised in Minneapolis or St. Paul or Duluth, I might not be feeling this way, those cities too big for village-like attachments. Iowa City wasn't big, but a village is a village. Cities have neighborhoods, sort of villages, but not the same.

A village is an entity, having thrust itself onto the prairies of Minnesota or Iowa or Wisconsin, communities developing out of need, supporting each other—merchants, farmers, ministers, townsfolk sharing, cooperating to make a community a community. Villages sprung up as immigrants entered this land in the 1840s and 1850s, Goodhue a bit late in starting, not incorporating until 1897, but emerging from the virgin prairie nonetheless. Vasa became an enclave for the Swedish Lutherans; Welch for itinerant Swedes and a smattering of Germans; Wanamingo and Kenyon for Norwegian Lutherans. White Willow tried to blossom; Hader tried to flower higher than its prairie wild flowers while Forest Mills struggled to hold on to its mills. Many succeeded, for a while, but most faded into history like Rice, Hader, Goodhue Centre, Ryan out by Mother's grave. Bellechester, Vasa, Zumbrota, Cannon Falls, Red Wing, Pine Island Frontenac, Sevastapol, Wacouta, sort of hung on to become villages and more.

"Village" is synonymous with the establishment of Goodhue County, with the beginning of the country. Folks of like mind, like effort, like beliefs—despite differing religious beliefs and ethnic heritage—wedded to the land to watch out for one another, to build tiny hamlets on the prairie. *Our* village was so small that when you phoned a wrong number you ended up talking for a half-hour anyway! *Our* village was so small that when a home run cleared centerfield, it cleared town! Well, small towns and "family" go way beyond blood relatives. The community *becomes* a family, caring, sharing, concerned. Mother, lying out in Belle Creek, called most ladies of the community, sisters, at least in spirit.

A village holds intangible substance. It's walking into a grocery store and having people actually interested in your answers when they ask, "How are you?" It's folks being concerned that you study, that you work hard, that you don't take drugs and engage in illicit sex, although that's open for dispute. A village is walking soft-lit Saturday nights seeing folks at home with family. It's knowing when someone is sick, in the hospital, having a baby, dying. Village connections are intangible connections, like modern-day fiber optic threads running from household to household, a community connected, monitoring every move.

A village is close, too close for some, so they move away, wanting more separation, more individuality, less homogeneity than what a village offers, demands. A village isn't perfect, all good, all a "Once Upon a Time" fairy tale. Sinclair Lewis wrote about his village's shortcomings in *Main Street* and those Sauk Centarians got mighty upset about his book. They didn't want their dirty laundry exposed. Villagers have faults, troubles, yet they seem to work them out; besides, there is usually someone to help, just as they helped me when Dad died, just as they'll help me now after Mother's death, even though I'm not a kid anymore. These thoughts raced through my head approaching Decorah as I finally remembered Terri and Anne were with me in the car. I reached over and hugged baby Anne, kissed Terri on the cheek and vowed I would return to the village, older, different, and long after circuitous journeys, but I would return.

Chapter 9

So, a long time gone, then

Ryan & Nei Implement, side street 1935

T HE LORD GIVETH AND THE LORD TAKETH AWAY.
Two weeks after we buried Mother, son Joe was born in
Iowa City. Mother lay in the saturated, bitter Belle Creek
earth having lived her entire life in Goodhue County, having
carried on the family heritage of the innumerable Red Wing

Hausteins, she forever resting out on the high, breezy prairie. She didn't get a chance to see her grandson, Joseph Daniel Franklin, and she had enjoyed only a short eighteen months with grand-daughter Anne Elizabeth. Yet, she was part of them, would be forever. Joe had been in his mother's womb when we buried his grandmother, he patiently waiting to carry on the Franklin name, the Franklin family.

Joe bounced into Iowa City and our lives on a blistering, humid, corn-growing day in June, Year of our Lord, 1970, one family member dying, another being born. The Lord taketh away and the Lord giveth . . .

Everything has a time:
There is a time for birth and a time for death,
The time for sorrow and the time for joy,
The time for mourning and the time for dancing,
The time for finding and the time for losing,
A time to laugh, a time to cry (Ecclesiastes 3:1-8)

I was experiencing mixed emotions, crying from the loss of Mother while simultaneously greeting the arrival of my second child. Love and hate, fire and ice, birth and death.

I had arrived in Iowa City alone in pursuit of that degree. Now I had a wife, a daughter and a new black haired bouncing boy who survived the sultry summer in W.W.II barracks-student housing, the heat intense, the new baby boy indifferent, but he too anticipat-ing a graduation from the university twenty years hence.

Everything was in order in our family other than having left Mother up in Belle Creek. Anne learned how to play in the sandbox, how to pour water from plastic buckets, how to swing, and how to climb the jungle gym. Joe learned how to roll over, suck on a dry bottle, suck his thumb and sleep through the night. Terri learned how to be a mother, while I learned how to become a college professor. We rolled out of Iowa City in a U-Haul toward Oklahoma Territory for our first college position, certainly not Oklahoma Sooners, more like Oklahoma Laters, but we became sort-of Okies nonetheless.

I left Iowa U an ABD but that would change. A new son and job offer enticed me from the Iowa campus after three years of pursing those initials. I hadn't finished that looming dissertation, but I *would* finish it over the next several years. The folks at Heaney & Gorman had instilled that finish-any-job-you-start quality in me. Dennis would send me to the back room of the Locker Plant to turn the sausage machine handle while Bump Schinnert filled casings for Heaney's famous sausages, Bump sliding beef or pork casings onto a hollow tube. I would get tired of turning the handle hours on end, whining for a different job. Dennis would demand I stay with the job. I would tire of wrapping beef sides and pork bellies all day, whining for a change, but Dennis would make me stick to the job. I would get cold, fingers and feet freezing when George O'Reilly, brother Tom, Frederick Rusch and I cleaned the cages deep in the catacombed locker, spending all day in the freezing dungeon sorting frozen meat packages to individual lockers. I would whine and ask for a different job, but Dennis would make me stick with the job at hand. He passed on that value he had received from his father, Will Heaney, passed it to the boys of the village who worked for him. Stick with the job. Do it right. I would stick with the dissertation, too, and do it right, in memory of Dennis Heaney.

My music career had been a long, circuitous journey since that night in '46 when Dad and Mother walked me to the old GHS gym to inspect musical instruments, Maestro Chas Wood, the veritable "music man" having recently arrived in the village to build a band program for the snotty nosed, musically illiterate children of Goodhue School. I selected the multi-piece clarinet for an un-known reason, but it had been a wise choice, nevertheless. Only later would I learn Benny Goodman had chosen the same instru-ment in his dingy, coal-sooted Chicago Southside neighborhood. Benny would become an absent mentor as well as Woody Herman and Artie Shaw, childhood musical idols of the clarinet. Chas Wood struggled teaching Bob O', Janice C, Mary B, Betty L and me, all excited about joining band and making our parents proud.

We struggled reading music, learning fingerings, adjusting reeds, playing the "Star Spangled Banner," "Activity March," and the "GHS Fight Song," *Hail, hail the purple and white.* We worked our way through *Bennett Band Book Number 1,* so that by the time we reached sixth grade we found ourselves sitting in the Concert Band next to seniors Anita and Gloria Erickson, Arlene Bremer, Regina Gadient, Velva Mae Hadler, LaDonna Opsahl and John Stueber. It wasn't a high school band; rather, an all-school band including tooters and bangers from sixth grade to senior. We honked and tooted and fingered and screeched and blared making our parents—if not Chas Wood—both exasperated and proud.

Twenty-five years later I sat at a tiny desk in my new college office preparing for the first day of classes, thinking about the long journey from the village to this new position at an Oklahoma State College. The journey had carried me through GHS, onto St. John's, then into eight years of teaching children the joy of playing musical instruments, the joy of making music. Preparing for tomorrow's first lecture in Music Theory 1, I thought about my first forays into learning Music Theory at St. John's and how difficult it had been. I thought about Marldine Richter conducting the Goodhue Town Band down by the railroad station, summer nights in the village. I thought of his John Yunger's contraption that permitted Marldine to simultaneously conduct and play the full range of the clarinet. I thought about practicing "Believe Me If All Those Endearing Young Charms," for my first sixth grade clarinet solo in front of a full, raucous auditorium, Mother wetting her pants and wondering how on earth her little boy, "the baby," could get through it, how on earth she could get through it. I made it, finally, the band and Chas Wood encouraging me, Noisy Rusch honking his tenor sax in approval, Jimmy Ryan blatting his tenor in approval, Kenny Hudson growling low on his cornet, the band stomping their feet at the conclusion, the boisterous Belle Creekers and Bellechester-tonians stomping, hollering from the cheap balcony seats. I had played the last note, looked at the audience, farted a huge Bb in relief, my face and hands drenched, Mother near collapse in the fifth row. She would go on doing that at every band concert, every operetta solo, every basketball game. But Mother was in the Belle

Creek cemetery as I prepared for my first week of college teaching. She was no longer here to worry about me, but I knew she would be with me in spirit, wringing her hands, running her rosary beads through angular fingers. I took encouragement in that as I finished my preparation before heading home to my family.

Well, it was a beginning even though I was teaching in Oklahoma, a region totally different from my beloved Midwest. I didn't realize I had crossed the Mason-Dixon line upon entering Oklahoma, but was soon made aware of it. Suddenly, I wasn't fighting the Lutherans of the Upper Midwest as I had during rubber gun wars on the village's crumbling streets and alleys. I was now battling Southern Baptists, they looking askance at a left-wing, beer-drinking, Yankee Catholic. Why, my nasal, Scandinavian-tainted voice earmarked me as soon as I opened my mouth, they wondering how this fast talking northerner had invaded their drawling Okie land.

We tolerated each other for several years as I taught Music Theory, Music History, private woodwind students, and assisted the marching band with an inept old fart who had been in the business much too long, he no longer interested or motivated in class preparation or quality, only waiting for retirement while sleeping most of the day in a cracked leather stuffed chair, the cracks on his leathered face as deep as the chair. Yet, I rescued his drowsy, prehistoric stage band from the corny, antiquated arrangements of Guy Lombardo and Lawrence Welk, turning it into a modern jazz band much to the consternation of the First Baptist Church congregation who still, in the seventies, preached jazz to be sinful. That took me back some, but I decided to fight back by evangelizing about the world of Stan Kenton, Woody Herman, Benny Goodman, Count Basie, Buddy Rich, Duke Ellington, and let the wicked notes fall where they may.

That "sinful" jazz thing did get under my skin, though, I have to admit. I was stunned that fellow music faculty members actually believed a certain arrangement of tones in a chord could produce a sinful effect. Why, if music, in and of itself, could be sinful, then back in the village I could have played certain notes or melodies on my clarinet to seduce my girlfriends, thereby using the clarinet instead of my usually ineffective words. They often liked my melodies—said I played really pretty-like—but they never began disrobing. In fact, a few put on their coats and walked out the door while I was playing. No sir, my clarinet playing wasn't sinful—bad at times, but not sinful. And Erv Richter always liked "Melancholy Baby," and "That Old Gang of Mine" when I played for him on Eddie Fischer's curb, Upper Street. Erv didn't think my melodies sinful. Father Smith never actually approached the subject of music, being focused mostly on sins of impurity, so he had offered nothing about music's lascivious influence. Some of Holy Trinity's organists and congregational singing might have approached sinfulness, but it never reached that level, at least to my acolyte knowledge. I doubt if any parishioners ever confessed to singing a major seventh chord, or singing out of tune on our meager hymns. No sir, my values didn't hold jazz to be sinful, yet three of the music faculty's six members—all members of the staid First Baptist Southern Church, I might add—thought it to be so, and they didn't like it one bit that our jazz band began playing harsh, strident, Stan Kenton-ish chords and Count Basie-ish boogie rhythms, thereby blasting the Baptists out of their staid repose. I began receiving severe glances in the hallways, at faculty meetings. I began hearing rumors about jazz and my teaching methods and my choices of musical arrangements. I began hearing the words "midwesterner," "Yankee," behind my back. I began watching my back.

Yet, just as Dennis, George and Dodie, B. C., Cy, Bill, Art and Sidney had taught me to stick to my guns as a boy, I persisted with our jazz arrangements—rehearsing, presenting concerts, touring Oklahoma Territory, even bringing mentor Woody Herman and his Thundering Herd to campus for a full day of high school clinics and concerts, much to the dismay of the First Baptist congregation. Woody played haunting blues clarinet, sang the blues, and rocked the auditorium with "Apple Honey," and "Northwest Passage," and "Early Autumn," and tooted "Woodchopper's Ball" to the musicians' delight. Our college jazz band played for Woody and his band, while visiting high school students learned about jazz from the Herman musicians. But the clinic-concert didn't earn me any points from the music faculty. They thought I was leading them down the path of evil, those jazz arrangements and thundering drums and scintillating chords and incessant Swing Era riffs leading _their_ student musicians and townsfolk into the fires of hell.

Although a state college, those Baptistery folks had considerable influence, largely ignoring the "separation of church and state" edict. They began taunting my jazz musicians and me saying I was hell and damnation itself, saying I was a bad influence on _their_ students, saying I had no place in _their_ community, saying I wasn't a good ol' boy anyway and never would be and why don't I head back across that Mason-Dixon line and never show my face in Oklahoma again. That's what they said from their holier-than-thou pedestals. They grabbed their tattered fundamentalist bibles and marched in front of my office, in front of my home frightening my children with bible stomping and marching. I got out my own bible and flung Matthew, Mark and Luke, plus a little Revelations back at them, but they were persistent and tenacious, not quite of the Ku Klux Clan ilk, but menacing in their bible thrusting nevertheless.

I fought back with brassy, discordant Stan Kenton arrangements of "Intermission Riff," and "Peanut "Vendor," and "Love For Sale" even, that arrangement really getting their dander and bibles up. I battled them with major ninth and augmented thirteenth chords, clustered notes and arrangements years beyond Guy Lombardo or Shep Fields or Lester Lanin or Lawrence Welk or the Polka Dots, Whoopee John, even. They covered their ears, fell to their knees, hoisted their bibles to the Southern Baptist heaven to deflect jazz from adulterating their ears.

Well, I won the war of the notes but eventually lost the Bible Battle in the Bible Belt. Their bible taunting got the best of me. They shoved my Chevy Nova into Lake Tishomingo—actually just a backed-up farm pond—and told me never to return to Oklahoma, to get out and take my jazz arrangements with me ... "Oh yee of your sinful jazz ways, depart from our sights, free our ears from your vile music. Let us live in peace and restful harmony. Do not taint our ears with your heathen music. Head, yee, back to your iniquitous Sodom and Gomorrah, and never, we say never, cross our doors again. In the name of our Southern God, we pray."

Their intolerance was probably a good omen anyway, as I had been too busy teaching jazz to make progress on eliminating those ABD letters from my name. I remembered Dennis' admonition about finishing jobs. We loaded that U-Haul again to head back across the Mason-Dixon line, back to the university to see what we could do about it.

A fine high school band position became available while I completed research on an experimental study in music education, so I found my myself teaching school-aged children again. The high schoolers were exuberant and played well; besides, they were Yankees who didn't think I had an accent, and they never asked if I was born again, once being enough for most midwesterners. The community appreciated our attempts at playing jazz, the "sinful" element not surfacing once. Yet, I had enjoyed the Oklahoma countryside, the Oklahoma Sooners football team, it being light years ahead of the Iowa Hawkeyes in the seventies. But it was good being back home in the Midwest. The band could play and march at the same time, something my first McGregor band couldn't do, so we participated in festivals, competitions and parades. The evening before traveling to Mason City for Iowa's biggest band festival—the home of Meredith Willson of *Music Man* fame—I sat in my study reviewing parade maneuvers, when I began reminiscing about the first festival parade I could remember in the village after W.W.II, 1947 . . .

I had only recently acquired that second digit, yet the W.W.II years are indelibly imprinted in my mind. At ten my buddies didn't possess the world perspective of parents, nor the village mayor nor the village council nor priests, ministers and rabbis, although there wasn't a rabbi within one hundred miles of the village. We also had few years under our belts with which to compare the war to other world events. Nevertheless, we *were* aware of the sacrifices, the war effort in the village. Almost everything needed to be rationed or saved or collected for the troops in Germany, France and the Pacific Operation. I wasn't around when Dad and Earl Ahern and Arnold Fredrickson and Orin Bremer of Goodhue Township fought the Kaiser in 1917–18, but I *was* in the early forties when men and women left to fight Hitler's swastika Storm Troops, Hideki Tojo's samurai troops and suicidal Mitsubishi Zeros.

Hershey chocolate bars became scarce in Swenson's candy case. Sugar was highly rationed as well as cheese, meat and chocolate chip cookies at Diercks' Grocery, Heaney & Gorman, Olson Food Market and Richter's Food Store. The village's Sunday-dressed ladies had to make do with old nylon stockings, new nylon more important for GIs parachuting behind enemy lines in France than on slender village legs and dainty ankles. Canned foods were scarce, they being more important for C Rations—cold beans on a windy hill, a lonely front line deep in the snow-laden forests at the Battle of the Bulge. Some rationing didn't bother the boys and girls, but we certainly were aware of gas rationing. Fuel was more important for tanks and jeeps. It wasn't necessary, said presidents Roosevelt and Truman, to take a Sunday afternoon drive over to Cannon Falls or Rochester or Lake Pepin or into the Welch Cannon River valley. Fuel was much too scarce to use for pleasure boating. Even the village fisherman joined forces, car pooling to hot fishing spots down on Goose Lake.

Gas rationing imprisoned villagers, sequestering us out on the high prairie. Only occasionally could we get to Red Wing for a movie to see war footage from Movietone News. We were grade school children, still able to live in a make-believe world, but parents would talk to us matter-of-factly when Private Joseph Redding, Sergeant Sidney Bodelson, Sergeant Richard Musty, Sergeant Ernest Diercks, Private Russell Ryan, Sergeant Marshall Haas, Ensign Willis Schafer or Lt. Charles O'Gorman returned to the village and township in flag-draped, pine coffins. If gas rationing didn't bring the war home to us, coffins did. We understood death. We understood it to be more than "five-minutes" dead when playing war games on the village's meandering streets and vacant, weed-infested lots.

Too many window white stars became covered with black

bunting. Goodhue County had sent hundreds of men to fight in the Civil War—Col Colvill and Minnesota's 1st Regiment engaged in the decisive Battle of Gettysburg. The county had contributed thousands of men and women to W.W.I, thousands more to W.W.II, this one county no different from others across Minnesota.

Nick Matthees contributed those seven sons to the war effort, all subsequently returning home to the high prairie, standing instead of in coffins as were the five Sullivan Brothers of Waterloo, Iowa. Others shipped out to fight the enemy so village children could live safely. Those who couldn't go worked on the home front to support the effort. Lloyd Cook supported it through *Goodhue County Tribune* service news. J. P. Ryan and tens of others planted victory gardens throughout the community. Heinie Swenson organized The Goodhue Plan, a plan acquiring volunteers to help local farmer's with farm work, manpower being short on the home front. Congress even recognized Heinie's plan. War Fund Drives and War Bond Drives were conducted to raise money for guns, bullets, ships, tanks and airplanes. The children were even asked to be on their best behavior during the village's canceled Halloween events of 1942, pranks such as tipping outhouses or soaping car windows not to be tolerated by the village fathers. Acts such as those would be considered sabotage, and the children would be shot!

For elementary students the war in Europe and the Pacific Islands continued through first, second, third and fourth grades where we battled our own wars in spelling, arithmetic, reading, geography—"Just where is France, Bob? Where is Germany, Mary? Where is Japan, Jimmy?" Teachers hung war-effort posters in the classrooms and hallways of the 1936-built, two-story Goodhue School. In third grade we heard about "D" Day, General Eisenhower, and something about an invasion across the English Channel, our teacher showing us on the tattered world map hanging from the front blackboard just underneath the green Palmer Method curlicues. She said thousands of troops and ships were massing in England to retake the European mainland from Hitler. That made Geography more interesting, more real for me. I didn't like Hitler. I didn't like Tojo. I didn't like Mussolini. I didn't like Stalin. That summer hometown GIs landed on Normandy's Omaha Beach, struggled for survival, battled to liberate France and Europe from Hitler's antics. They landed in chest-high seas, fought field-to-field for several months before reaching Berlin, before meeting the Russians approaching from the East. The Normandy invasion succeeded. Hitler was dead. The Nazi regime was finished. The village's gas rationing and sugar rationing and victory gardens and newspaper drive efforts had paid off. We had done our little part.

Yet, the world war wasn't over. Another battle still raged in the Pacific Theater. Hitler had been defeated, but General Tojo remained ensconced in the vast islands beyond Hawaii. The summer of 1945 seemed more relaxed in the village, though, as we boys felt more energy, more victorious playing "GIs," easily defeating the "Nazis" in our battles behind the Goodhue State Bank (the Reichstag), behind the Goodhue Hotel (panzer headquarters), up on water tank hill (Luftwaffe field), around Herman Diercks' Corner Store (bunkers), through the cattle pens at Heaney's Locker (prison camps), under Streater Lumber overhangs (artillery emplacements), past the Rosener Blacksmith Shop (fuel dump). We were Americans, the victors, indestructible attacking tombstones in Evergreen Cemetery (pill boxes).

Later that summer—a sultry August day—as I kicked an empty Grain Belt can along the railroad tracks near the depot, stationmaster A. B. Overby emerged shaking his legs like a beheaded chicken to ask what I was doing. I thought I was in trouble again for playing on the tracks.

"What are you doing, Jimmy? No one to play with?" he asked, adjusting his stationmaster's cap and cracking his legs, stiff from sitting long hours at the telegraph. A. B. looked old to a boy, everyone in their thirties or more looking old. He was probably only fifty, but had begun graying at the temples, crow's feet spreading from the corners of his eyes, maybe from too much squinting down the tracks waiting for the Dinky to chug into the station, something it never did, on time.

"Nothin'. Jack, Bob and Larry are all mowing lawns. I'm just knocking around," I answered, kicking that can a good ten feet across the creosoted, coal-stained ties.

He pulled a Chesterfield out of his vest pocket, lit it, retrieved a gold embossed pocket watch on a ten-foot chain, pondered it while gazing down the tracks toward Red Wing wondering if the Dinky would be on time, for once, and if it were, would there be any passengers to attend to. "Do you know much about the war effort?" he asked, his legs finally settling down.

"Some. We beat the hell out of Hitler. Workin' on Tojo now."

"Your mother wouldn't like you saying 'hell,' but . . . I just got news off the telegraph wire that last eve the U.S. dropped an atom bomb on Japan."

"An Adam and Eve bomb?" I asked, retrieving my can from the weeds.

"Not 'Adam,' Jimmy, an *atom* bomb, last evening, a nuclear device more powerful than any bomb every made," he said, drawing deeply on the Chesterfield, looking more at the endless, undulating tracks than at me. I was standing there but didn't seem to be A. B.'s main interest.

"Lots of TNT and gun powder I suppose?"

"No! Atoms being smashed together. I don't understand how it works, but my telegraph said a B-29 bomber dropped it on Hiroshima killing upwards of one hundred thousand people."

Dumbfounded, I stopped kicking the can, stood with hands in pockets and looked at A. B. who was looking at the endless tracks. I couldn't imagine it, couldn't imagine that many people killed with one bomb. Shoot! Jack and I had only "killed" a couple of the Lutheran boys with our flour bombs. An atom bomb just didn't register. "One hundred thousand? How many is that?"

A. B. meditated for a while, that number possibly being even too big for him. After a long draw and puff on the now-shortened cigarette, he answered, "That's ten, ten-thousands, 200 Goodhues," he said as we moved away from the tracks to sit on a baggage cart on the station's platform. I knew most of the villagers or a least recognized them on the street. I couldn't imagine all being dead, plus 199 other villages and towns, all of Goodhue County plus parts of Wisconsin and maybe Minneapolis. Geez!

"Washington thinks maybe it'll end the war in Japan. I sure hope so, although I'm real uncertain about using the atom bomb,"

A. B. said as he suddenly jumped from the cart and rushed into the station to receive an incoming telegraph wire, those chicken legs splaying in multiple directions. I sat on the steel-rimmed baggage wagon looking down the undulating tracks toward Claybank half expecting the Dinky to be backing into town, or maybe a coal-belching locomotive heading south toward Zumbrota. Incessant flies buzzed around my head. A hot breeze blew over the grain elevator carrying a putrid odor from a feed lot just beyond the town limits. The sun beat hard on my bare head. I was hot, yet wondered how much heat that atom bomb had generated to kill so many people. We hadn't studied anything about it in fourth grade, and I hadn't read anything about an atom bomb in Eddie Fischer's *Mechanix Illustrated* magazines. It must have been a top military secret. I sat for a long time on the baggage cart while A. B. tapped his telegraph, maybe talking to Japan for all I knew. I tired of waiting for him to return, so I began skipping up the tracks toward the lofty coal silo, kicking the beer can ahead of me. I was too young to grasp the significance of an atom bomb, yet it affected me when A. B. said it could obliterate as many as 1,000 Goodhues. That brought those deaths home. By the time I had scuffled a half mile out to the village dump, I was hoping the war would end so the men and women could return home, yet it was going to take some work to figure this atom thing out.

Several days later another B-29 dropped a second bomb on Nagasaki, A. B. said, again killing thousands of Japanese. But this one ended the war with Japan. The atom bombs did it. The men would be coming home, most marching, some riding in Jeeps holding crutches, some riding in hearses. It had been a terrible effort, a thing of terrible beauty.

I stopped daydreaming and continued reviewing parade formations in anticipation of tomorrow's Mason City parade competition. But I couldn't get the village's war effort out of my mind, including its own parade during that special village celebration, summer of 1947 . . .

" *I* s there any more business before we adjourn?" Gertrude McNamara asked at the newly formed, postwar Legion Auxiliary meeting, late October 1946.

"I have an item to introduce," Margaret Ryan declared, retrieving a loose-leaf notebook from her ever-present, overflowing purse.

"Yes, Marg, what is it?"

"I have been considering that we have recently been through a terrible four-year ordeal with the war. Would it not be nice if we organized a community celebration, a victory celebration, if you will, to recognize the servicemen and women who were on active duty, as well as those in the community who so faithfully supported the effort?" Marg asked, standing to gain the ladies' attention.

"That's a fine idea, Marg, but it sounds like considerable work to me. Just what do you have in mind?" Gertrude asked.

"I don't have the details defined yet, but a celebration that would involve the entire community: our clubs, the American Legion, school children, churches, families, the Goodhue County Artificial Breeder's Association, the Holstein Hoofer's Association, the Goodhue, Belvidere, Hay Creek and Belle Creek Township Boards, the Pure Bred Beef Association, the Girl Scouts, the Boy Scouts, the Lutherans, the Catholics, the Methodists, the Presbyterians, the Episcopalians. Everyone. No one would be left out. We could form committees during the winter months for a celebration next summer. It would be the patriotic thing to do, the least we could do," she said, taking her seat, but not releasing a firm grip on her purse, or the proceedings.

"Does anyone else support such a celebration?" Gert asked the Auxiliary members.

"I think we should discuss it with the American Legion before we go off half-baked on Marg's idea," responded Emma Kindseth, anxiously tugging on her hair net and undone coat buttons. "The Legion only organized last month. Certainly, we appreciate everyone's effort, such a great effort for so long, but do we have the manpower, I mean the womanpower, to plan and conduct such a celebration?" Emma said, fidgeting in her purse for a hanky.*

"We most certainly do," answered Marg, again standing to take command of the proceedings and ward off naysayers. "The village and neighboring townships supported the war effort through Bond Drives, rationing so many items, writing letters, and planting Victory Gardens. And we lost some of our own, one of our own even—Lucretia's son Charles," Marg said, walking over to Lucretia O'Gorman who was dabbing her eyes with a hanky, sitting alone with her private thoughts in the last row. Marg placed a hand on Lucretia's shoulder as she continued speaking to the assembled ladies. "Charles O'Gorman gave his life for us fighting in Africa three years ago. We can't bring him back for Lucretia and Frank, but we can honor his valiant effort, his supreme sacrifice. And Willis Schafer didn't come home either. Marshall Haas didn't come home. Good Lord, ladies! just for those men alone we should hold a celebration to honor them," Marg said, returning to her seat in the front row. Lucretia had been silent through this very first Auxiliary meeting, yet she forced herself to attend despite her son's death, maybe because of it. She had mixed emotions, having lost Charles in the war. Lucretia had been the village postmaster for several years, sorting letters to and from service men and women since Charles enlisted in 1941. And she had been sorting letters that terrible day the Western Union man arrived in the village to hand her a telegram. She would never forget it. She would go to her grave in

Evergreen Cemetery grieving over Charles. She cried softly in the last row as the discussion continued.

Marg had given ample thought in the privacy of her home to this celebration. She wasn't about to be deterred. "My son Philip is hoping to gain an appointment to the United States Naval Academy. It would be good for him to participate in such a celebration dressed as a navy shipman or cadet or admiral. I don't know much about the military myself, but it would be good for the entire village, help us all to recognize the effort."

"I still think it's too much work. I'm not for it," Emma said, finally finding a hanky.

"Blanche, what do you think?" Gert asked the comely Blanche Cook from the head table, her wooden gavel within easy striking distance to maintain order.

"Lloyd supported the effort editing the Goodhue County Tribune *and with paper drives. He worked hard, might be tired, but I'm mostly for the celebration if we get the American Legion to assist us, that is. The Auxiliary can't accomplish this alone."*

"How much money do we have in the treasury, Lucille?"

"We have only twenty-three dollars from our initial memberships. But we will gain more memberships soon, and maybe the city council will help," Mother said, in her new roll as treasurer.

"Let's vote on it then," Gert announced. "All in favor of a victory celebration next summer, raise your hands . . . That's seven ayes. Opposed? . . . Two nays. The ayes have it. We will be planning the Victory Celebration 1947 for next summer. Margaret, you form several committees as you see fit. I'll speak with the American Legion and we'll get this thing rolling. Now let's have some angel food cake, cookies and coffee. We've considerable work to do."

Within two days Gert had sought and gained the approval of American Legion Post 594 and its commander, the jovial, rotund J. R. Mickley. Mickley thought it a wonderful idea, an appropriate way to kick off both new service organizations. The Legion was especially complimentary of the Ladies Auxiliary for generating the idea, praise the men were not accustomed to awarding. Gert, Marg and Commander Mickley began meeting to form committees, the celebration to be held the Fourth of July. J. R. said he would get the Legion involved and seek the support of ex mayors Ed Diercks and J. P. Ryan. The steering committee developed several sub committees: parade, firing squad, float contest, band concert, hotdish bakeoff, cake bakeoff, honorary grand marshal, special float for the deceased service men, ice cream social, beer tent, games, children's carnival and activities, memorial services, flags and decorations; finally, a miscellaneous committee covering anything anyone forgot.

Marg became a whirlwind of activity throughout the glowing fall and ensuing bitter winter of 1946–47, always dressed in her finest whenever out in the village. Winter was a good time to organize and plan. She appointed chairwomen for the committees and saw to it they got to work, immediately. J. R. did the same with American Legion members, appointing chairs and following up with their work. Soon, Gert and J. R.'s enthusiasm was transferred to the Legion and Auxiliary committees as well as volunteers. Goodhue had been one of the last county towns to incorporate, this way back in 1897, but the 1946 Legion and Auxiliary were determined the village wouldn't be the most insignificant. They would show their mettle.

J. R. appointed a reluctant and restrained banker, Don Center, as parade chair. J. R. and Don chatted outside the Upper Street bank on a glorious Indian Summer day. "I'm having trouble getting the bands organized, J. R., especially encouraging bands to participate on the Fourth of July. Our Goodhue Community Band will march, maybe Zumbrota, but Red Wing is out as is Cannon Falls. I've got to have three or four bands, at least, to make a good parade," Don said as J. R. fired up a huge cigar.

"You can do it, Don," J. R. replied, tugging at a tight belt gradually losing the battle to an expanding paunch. "You're a shaker and a mover. I've confidence in you. Got to go now and see Gert about the float committee. See you soon," J. R. said, heading for his City Garage. Don had expected more empathy, but J. R. was acting just like Gen. George Patton. He didn't want excuses, only results. "Get the bands!" Don tightened a Windsor knot on his traditional blue tie and shuffled back into the bank to do just that.

"Gert? J. R. here," his greasy voice crackling over the antiquated phone lines. "How's the float committee shaping up? That's your responsibility isn't it? Don Center's organizing the bands, and the Auxiliary has the floats. Am I right 'bout that?" J. R. asked, holding the listening piece to his ear, feet and legs propped on a desk while reclining in a wooden swivel chair at his City Garage.

"Of course we're organized, J. R. I have an effective committee working on the floats, Emily Parker chairwoman. She will do an excellent job. She has already sent letters and made numerous phone calls. We are well on our way with the bakeoff contests, too. We are having a hotdish as well as cake and pie contest after the parade. What do you think of that?" Gert said through her crackling, hand-cranked telephone, a low-tech device only minimally better than Sandbox Bob's and my cup-and-string device.

"I think that's a great idea."

"Who's that on the line? Laura Mans? What are you doing? This is a private conversation."

"Oh, I just couldn't stand it. I want to be involved in the celebration. Put me on a committee. I've been listening to your phone conversation, anyway."

"Well, we can use everyone we can get," J. R. said. "Maybe we should just call all party lines for volunteers. It'd be almost better than the newspaper. Let's meet for coffee as Shelstad's Cafe in the morning, Gert, to review our plans. About quarter past eight?"

"That will be fine, J. R. Quarter past eight at Shelstad's."

When the long winter began releasing its vise grip on the village, about mid May, mountainous snow piles melted and trickled onto dirt streets, creating mud rivers and abundant potholes. Undeterred, "Victory Celebration 1947" began moving into full swing. Committees had worked faithfully during the bleak winter months, and now with improving weather, outside work could begin. Gert and J. R. were confident their committees would pull this thing off. Over the winter Don Center had received band commitments from Marldine Richter's Goodhue Community Band, Zumbrota Community Band, Zumbro Falls Village Band, Hay Creek Cowboy Band, Vasa Cornet Band, even the Welch Harmonica Band, if you could call three harmonicas and a kazoo a band. They said they would march with the famous Welch Horseshoe Team. But Don's biggest coup was the Rochester Shriner's Band and Funny Car entourage. It would be a great parade. The Auxiliary was organizing the floats. Don was also searching for a horse troop and other animals for the parade. Children loved seeing the animals.

St. Luke's, St. Peter's, Holy Trinity, Goodhue Methodist, St. Columbkill's, St. John's, and Grace Lutheran church groups began secretly planning floats for the celebration, working on distinctive floats in darkened hay barns and garages. There would be a competition for floats: first prize, ten dollars; second prize, five; third prize, a Commercial Club certificate to be redeemed Saturday nights in the village. But the prestige for a church was more important than money. The Methodists wanted to beat the Lutherans. The Lutherans hoped to beat the Presbyterians, and everyone wanted to pummel the Catholics.

"You've appointed me chair of the Miscellaneous Committee, J. R. What am I suppose to be in charge of?" the ruffled Eddie Rosener asked as he stomped into the City Garage late Friday afternoon.

J. R. dropped his feet from the desk, then swiveled to meet Eddie's eyes, head on. "Well, Eddie, just about everything that no other committees do," J. R. said, lighting up a persistent cigar.

"What's that to mean? 'Miscellaneous' don't sound like much of a committee to me," he said. "Shoot me an example, if you would, then," Eddie said, slumping into a cane-backed chair in J. R.'s dingy, oil-encrusted office across from the village elevator.

"We'll have horses in the parade, if Don can get 'em, so we'll need pooper-scoopers following the horses with shovels and buckets. That would be 'miscellaneous' " J. R. said, puffing deeply on a fresh cigar.

"I'm on the shit detail? That's all I'm good for? Damn, J. R! You kin do better than that," an exasperated Eddie resounded.

"And we'll have lots of trash after the parade. You could organize the Boy Scouts to pick it up. Everything helps," J. R. said, scratching a long wooden farmer match to relight his recalcitrant cigar. J. R. sported the looks and demeanor of Winston Churchill, portly on short legs, but a temperament unruffled in a time of turbulence, such as he was facing with Eddie.

"Hell, J. R! Why couldn't you've appointed me to do somethin' important instead of 'miscellaneous'? Don't take no brains to scoop horse shit," Eddie said, pulling out a pack of Chesterfields and lighting up two.

"Everyone has to participate, Eddie; it's the patriotic thing to do. Just be a good Legionnaire now and do your job," J. R. answered, being the diplomat as Churchill had been during the war. "I'll appreciate it and the serviceman will appreciate it and the community will appreciate. Just see to those horses and the trash."

"Ja, mein Herr, Commander!"

"I've got to see Herman Diercks about the Decoration Committee. Want to walk to Lower Street with me?"

"Sure, J. R, but why the hell couldn't you appoint me head of Decoration Committee. Sounds better than 'Miscellaneous.' "

"Come on Eddie, and quit whining. Why you whine more than the farmers out in Featherstone Township."

"B. S!"

"Hi, Herman. How's business in general in your General Store?" J. R. inquired as he and Eddie banged through Diercks' double screen door, the store teeming with dry goods, pools of thread, bolts of fabric, and assorted groceries. Herman's store, as well as Herman himself, had been a staple in the village since the thirties. He was a good community member, a supporter, a village council member. J. R. knew he could count on him.

"Pretty slow today, J. R., but Saturdays are good when folks come to town. Hi, Eddie. How are you?" the bespectacled Herman said, momentarily removing his glasses to rub tired eyes.

Eddie crunched his burnt cigarette under foot on

Herman's clean, wooden-slat floor causing Herman to wince. "Chair of the damn Miscellaneous Committee for the Victory Celebration, that's what I am. That's all J. R. thinks I'm good for. He's appointin' you Decoration chairman, ain't that right, J. R.?"

"That's right, Herman. I'd like you to be Decoration chairman for the celebration. Will you accept?" J. R. asked, approaching Herman, placing a hand on his shoulder.

"I would be honored to chair the Decoration Committee, J. R. Thank you for asking. Would you men care for a couple of sarsaparillas?"

"I certainly would," J. R. said, tugging at his ever-tightening belt.

"Got beer?" Eddie asked.

"No beer, but I've root beer, Eddie. How about that?"

"Guess it'll have to do."

The three men shuffled through narrow, overflowing aisles to the rear of Diercks' store to sit in cane-back chairs as Herman retrieved three sarsaparillas from the ancient cooler. They enjoyed cool drinks as Herman and J. R. discussed decorations: store fronts, flags in standards, flags hanging from light standards, decorations at Evergreen Cemetery. Herman Diercks was a gentleman, an easy-going, bespectacled man dressed in his ever-present double-breasted dark suit and vest with gold watch chain, certainly a sartorial man of the village. Eddie was a village smithy wearing the clothes of a blacksmith, whether tending his anvil or walking the streets. J. R. didn't dress like Herman, being a mechanic with attire attuned to changing grimy oil on Chevy trucks and greasing stubborn U-joints.

"Herman, you come up with some plans, and we'll talk more about decorating the village. It needs to be ship-shape, a real doozie. I'm sure you'll do a great job. Eddie here could help you, because he thinks he might

not have enough to do chairing the Miscellaneous Committee. Don Center's organizing the bands and animal troops for the parade, and the Auxiliary is tending to the floats and bakeoff contests. It's going to be a great celebration, two days of it, Saturday and Sunday. See you in a few days. Come on, Eddie. We've got places to go, places to be."

"Whatever."

"Regina! J. R. and I have decided that we want you from the Auxiliary and Frank Shorter from the Legion to organize the float committee. It is a big task, so you'll have to recruit helpers. You will do it, won't you?" Gert asked as the ladies sipped coffee at Swenson's Cafe.

"Float committee? That sounds like an awfully big job. Could you put me on something smaller, maybe the flower committee?" Regina asked, absentmindedly arranging her just-so permanent, momentarily surprised by the invite.

"Heavens! You're just the lady for the job, Regina. You're organized, efficient, tactful and conscientious, unlike some other ladies in the Auxiliary, and you do know who I'm talking about, don't you? Fritz Shorter at the Creamery is a good worker. The two of you will be just fine. Thanks for accepting," Gert said, patting Regina on the hand.

Regina particularly liked the comment about being conscientious. "I didn't know I had accepted, but if you really think I can do it, I'll give it a try."

"I knew I could count on you, Regina. The Victory Celebration 1947 is shaping up wonderfully. You meet with Fritz to get the ball rolling on the floats. Don's organizing the marching bands and animals, so you don't have to do that. But you and Fritz will be in charge of the entire parade. See you in a couple of days," Gert said as she skipped toward the door to meet with other committee members.

"Fritz! You're going to co-chair the float committee with Regina Swenson. I've just appointed you," J.
R. announced as he approached Fritz at the Creamery's
huge stainless steel butter churn.

"You mean I don't have any say in the matter,
Mickley?" Fritz answered, wiping his buttery hands on
a rag.

"That's right. You're just the organized and efficient fellow I need to work with Regina. You're smart,
sometimes, organized, mostly; besides, you've got handy
hands that will come in useful with the floats. You get
with Regina now to get the floats going. Got to run,
Fritz. Catch you later, if you're lucky," and J. R. was out
the back door, his portly bulk overwhelming the narrow
alley. The ignited J. R. was getting into this victory
celebration. He had already recruited numerous "volunteers" and was grabbing just about any villager he
encountered, including Art Eppen.

Art was an upright community member, a businessman owning and operating an appliance shop that
was doing especially well now, what with folks buying
new-fangled refrigerators after the war instead of
depending on old-fashioned ice boxes. Helping with
the celebration would get him out of the shop talking to
folks, something he liked doing. Art was glad to be
aboard.

J. R. waddled from the Creamery down the alley,
past the fire hall toward the Corner Bar but didn't stop
in. He had folks to see. It wasn't that long until July
Fourth. But he did stop at Eddie Fischer's Drugstore,
needing a bottle of aspirin for a growing headache.

"How's things today, Eddie?"

"Dead."

"That's nothing new, Eddie. It's always dead in the
village. Most days you could drop an atom bomb and hit
nothing, but it won't be that way for long, what with the

victory celebration we're organizing for July," J. R. said, looking over Eddie's aspirin selection which was minimal—one brand. "I'd like you to get involved in the celebration. How would you like to work with Don Center organizing horses and other animals for the parade? We'd love to have you."

The frail, wispy gray-haired Eddie pondered that for a moment before responding. "Animals? I don't know much about animals, though I did grow up on a farm in Featherstone Township. Guess I might help then, J. R. It might be good for me to get outside some," Eddie said as he wrapped a bottle of aspirin for J. R. Eddie regularly wrapped every purchase in brown wrapping paper, be it aspirin, a prescription, a girlie magazine, which I never actually had the courage to purchase, or especially feminine napkins.

"Great! You get with Don to get those animals corralled. Thanks for the aspirin."

Regina and Fritz met the next night to plan the floats. "What do you think, Fritz. How do we get started on this thing? It's overwhelming," Regina said, releasing a big sigh while fiddling with her hair in a Swenson's back booth.

"We'll be fine, Regina. You and Heinie have been in the restaurant business a long time, know lots of people. We'll contact them, inform them about the celebration, ask them to enter a float and go from there," the orderly Fritz said, laying a neat, lined yellow pad on the table. I'd say we should begin by making a list of all clubs, churches and organizations. We can type up letters, address envelopes, then follow up a couple of days later with phone calls. What do you think about that?" Fritz asked as they began planning their committee.

"You've good ideas, Fritz, but I think we should get a couple of more people to help us. Clara Hennings

is my neighbor. I'll ask her, and I'd like to get Lucretia involved, if she would. Charles' death has been so hard on her and Frank. The involvement would be good for her. I'll ask Lucretia. Who could you get?"

"I'll ask John Angus. He's got nothing better to do. Now let's start making the list. The Community Band will be in the parade, but the school should enter at least one float. Write down 'Goodhue School,' and the 'Civic Club.' The American Legion will need a big impressive float. I'll see to that."

"And the Ladies Auxiliary will have to do just as well. I'll see to that," Regina responded as she began writing names in a spiral notebook. "Let's not forget the Boy Scouts and Girl Scouts. Isn't Don Center scoutmaster? He can get them organized," Regina said as she began writing the list of float contenders.

Fritz jotted notes in his two-column yellow pad. "You know, Regina. We'll have to develop categories for float competition. And prizes will get the folks motivated to enter the parade. They like prizes and awards."

"There is the Women's Study Club, and several Bridge and Five Hundred clubs, plus the Abridged Literary Club. Do you think they'll participate, Fritz?"

"Don't know about the Bridge and Five Hundred clubs, but the Study Club should. Write them down. We need to contact every merchant in town. I'll rattle some off while you write, Regina. I'll start with the Goodhue Elevator, the Fleishmann Elevator, Creamery, Goodhue State Bank, Post Office, Chicago Great Western Railroad, the Goodhue County Tribune, *doctors Anderson and Liffrig, Heaney's Market, Diercks' General Merchandise, Richter's Foods, Herman Diercks' Corner Grocery, Marshall-Wells Hardware . . ."*

"Slow down, Fritz. I can't write that fast," Regina said, fumbling with her notebook. "I'll get some coffee while you write more merchants." Regina shuffled to

the back grill past a couple of claypitters, a transient, a stranger, a farmer or two hanging on the long bar sipping their usual 3.2 beer. She retrieved two steaming, heavy white porcelain cups of strong Hills Bros coffee, the only kind Swenson's served. Hills Bros or nothing, Heinie always said to whiners.

"I've added Buck Implement, Streater Lumber, Eppen's Electric, Majerus Gas & Appliance, and Rosener Blacksmith. Eddie Rosener's not too happy about chairing the Miscellaneous Committee, but J. R.'s going to keep him on it anyway."

"Okay, Fritz. Here's your coffee. Let's not forget Dave Franklin's City Dray Line, the Goodhue Hatchery, Swelland Produce, Mans & Benda Shell, Co-op, Home Oil, Ebe's Barber Shop, Faye's Beauty Shop, the Goodhue Hotel, Joe's Place, Al Shelstad's Cafe, Florence Taylor's Eat Shop. Goodness! We're getting quite a list here. It'll be a big parade."

"Not everyone will build a float, but at least we'll contact them and give them the Dickens if they don't. How about the Corner Bar, Art's Bar. We can't forget anyone."

"Let's see . . . Eddie's Drugstore. We wouldn't want to forget old 'step-and-a-half.' And Ole Haga, being a furniture maker, can certainly come up with something for Haga Furniture and Undertaking. Write down Tomfohr Implement, and village truckers, Erv Stemman, Bill O'Reilly, Tom Franklin, and Reinhold Schulz. They can use their trucks for floats," Fritz said, burning his tongue on the bitter coffee.

"We're on our second page, Fritz. Give me a second to organize this . . ."

"Huebner's Blacksmith Shop, John Yunger's Machine Shop, Lohman's Standard Oil, Ed Hanson's Shoe Repair, G. O. Miller Telephone, Jesse Campbell's Hardware, Fred & Frieda Vieths' General Store . . . I think I'm running out of businesses, Regina. Any more?"

"Not right now, and I'm tired. We'll think of more,
I'm sure, but this is most of them. I'll get Clara and,
hopefully, Lucretia to help me type up letters. Can you
type?"

"No, ma'am, but I can stuff and lick envelopes.
You call me when you're ready. Let's call it quits for
tonight. We're well on our way."

"Wait! We haven't included churches yet. Lordy!
We must contact St. Luke's, St. Peter's, let's see . . . St.
John's, Grace Lutheran, the Methodists . . . ,"

"Holy Trinity and St. Columbkill's out in the
country. We'll contact every church. See you later."

The village was becoming a beehive of activity—'beehive' might be stretching it some—as light, humidity-
free spring breezes arrived from White Willow or where
the ghost town had once been south of town. At least
there seemed to be more activity on the streets—folks
conversing animatedly, writing in notebooks retrieved
from tight vest pockets, merchants inspecting fifty-
year-old brick facades to decorate. Even villagers not
officially involved in the celebration were becoming
excited. It had been years since a true celebration, the
efforts of the past four years concentrated exclusively
on the war effort. Even old-timers in the saloons and
cafes were getting excited, if that were possible, sipping
boilermakers and Grain Belt beer and speculatin' that
maybe they'd get into the parade too, though they didn't
know how yet, or if they could get around to it. Several
claypitters even talked about building a float for the
parade, maybe a pile of clay on a truck bed, and they'd
ride along spading clay into buckets, throwing chunks
to the children. Everyone was happy the war had
ended. Excitement prevailed about the future of the
village. Folks began talking about the village really
exploding now that the Allies had defeated Hitler. They
thought maybe they would get some new industry in the

village, maybe start an industrial park next to Streater's Lumber or on the trash-littered vacant lots near the Goodhue Elevator. They thought maybe they'd even get a real inside movie theater instead of just free movies outside on Lower Street. Maybe a dance hall would be nice, and a fancy restaurant that served "Eye-talian" food, and maybe even oriental dishes, something other than Chung King out of the can topped with bland oriental noodles. Oh, folks liked living in the village, that was for sure, but there were things they wanted without having to drive all the way to Red Wing or Cannon Falls or the Twin Cities. Some ladies thought it would be delightful to have a millinery shop right in town, and the men thought it wouldn't be too bad if the village had an expanded hardware store. Some younger fellows wanted a hunting and fishing store, while the children dreamed about a fancy soda fountain with juke box selections you could play right from the booths, a place where they could buy heavy, thick frosty malts, maybe even a drive-in restaurant like Zumbrota's Wagon Wheel. Teenagers wanted a teen hangout where they could dance the Lindy-Hop, sip Squirt and maybe neck in the back booths, escaping the prying eyes of parents. Enthusiasm was rampant. Villagers could feel things loosening up, some of the old, stale attitudes being discarded, new freedom seeping into, especially the youngsters' minds. Folks began dreaming about what the village should have, what it could be with something to do on Sunday afternoons other than simply waiting for another dreary Monday. They were excited about the possibilities, because the war was over and gas would soon become more available and they wouldn't have to stay just in the village anymore because they could now drive to Oak Center for dances or to Lake Pepin's beaches for swimming. Mans & Benda and the Home Oil Co. and Mickley's Garage would have plentiful, cheap gas, without rationing. Folks would soon have more money in their pockets to buy things like pop-up toasters and refrigerators and electric frying pans and plastic Zenith radios with FM, and nylons and new dresses and new double-breasted suits, and maybe even a new car or one of those newfangled television sets they were reading about in the newspapers. Yes sir, things were looking good, looking up in the village, out in the townships, in James Goodhue's county. Farmers were going to be more prosperous planting more wheat and oats and barley, and dairy herds would get up to forty or fifty head and milk prices would rise, and merchants would become prosperous and Goodhue wouldn't just be Goodhue any longer. It wouldn't be just a lonely whistle-stop on the county map, a place folks bypassed on their way to somewhere else. No sir, folks would now come to the village on purpose, because there would be a reason to come. The village was going to be something and it all would start with the Victory Celebration of 1947 when thousands from throughout the county would arrive to see what a great community it was and how much they'd love it, and how often they'd come back. Victory Celebration 1947 would be a good way to face the future and head into the middle of the century, that was for sure. You could bank on it.

Edna Allers was chairing the bakeoff committee with vice-chairwoman, a reluctant Emma Kindseth. But Emma thought she'd do her job, even though she wasn't in favor of this event. She would rather work in her flower garden pruning daisies and holly hocks. Yet, Emma was a village supporter. In spite of her reluctance, she wouldn't shirk her duty.

"Emma. Let's talk about how we're going to go about this bakeoff contest. I have no experience in such a thing, have you?" Edna asked as the two women met over coffee and dainty pastries at Edna's home.

"No, I haven't, but you and I can certainly plan it. All the village women have a favorite hotdish recipe, plus a favorite cake recipe. It shouldn't be difficult," Emma said, sipping coffee from a painted cup.

"We should hold a competition for the hotdishes and a separate one for cakes and pies. We could announce it in the Tribune with the rules and procedures for entering. What do you think of that?" Edna asked, her usually beaming face more somber this day.

"Should we send out letters? That's what Regina is doing with the floats."

"Too many people for letters. I would say we just announce it through the weekly paper. Everyone subscribes to The Tribune, even though they don't read most of it," Edna said, biting into a delicate cookie. The women talked and discussed and wrote down ideas for a couple of hours at the kitchen table until they were satisfied they were well on their way. They would announce the two bakeoffs in The Tribune with rules to abide by. They would get judges for the two competitions and hold the competition immediately after the parade, maybe adjacent to the railroad station where most people would congregate. By four o'clock they had finished and, by then, even Emma was excited. It wasn't so bad, she thought. The holy hocks could wait.

J. R. and Gert met late Friday afternoon at Joe's Place to coordinate their plans. "How is the Legion progressing with its plans, J. R.?"

"I think we're well on our way, not too many problems. Could be worse. We've got the bands organized, the float committee is working hard, Herman's planning decorations, and Eddie is trying to figure out what the Miscellaneous Committee will do. How about the Auxiliary?" J. R. said, reaching for a Perfecto.

"I think we're doing fine also. I'm somewhat worried that we can get both bakeoff competitions

*organized with many ladies entering hotdishes, pies
and cakes. Keeping them fresh, out of the hot sun,
protected from flies will be a problem, but Edna and
Emma will solve it." They talked for a couple of hours,
wrote pages of notes and agreed to meet again in a
couple of days. Three weeks remained until the celebration.*

*Two weeks before "V Day" a veil of secrecy
descended over the village not unlike the buildup for
the Normandy Invasion. The village had gotten into the
celebration, everyone doing something, preparing something, building something. Church groups, 4-H clubs,
Boy Scouts, merchants were busy toiling in closed
garages, warehouses, outhouses, lean-tos, even outlying barns building floats in secrecy on every imaginable type of vehicle: hay racks and rubber wheel
wagons and honey wagons and flat-bed trucks and
pickups and tractors of every size and shape, and Red
Flyer wagons and bicycles and Mormon-sized wooden
hand carts—anything that could move became a float.
Pride was at stake for the Lutherans, the Methodists,
the Catholics, the merchants. Diercks' General Store
soon ran out of crepe paper and balloons. Woolworth's
in Red Wing was inundated with calls for rolls of crepe
paper and banners and balloons. Herman drove all the
way to St. Paul to buy flags and special decorations.
This was going to be the mother of all village celebra-
tions. You could bank on it.*

*Neither Gert nor J. R. were the type of people to get
nervous, but one week before the celebration they did
show signs of agitation. Everything had to come together; everything had to work and the responsibility
was theirs, especially Gert and Marg who had concocted this whole thing. The reputation of the village,
whatever it was, depended upon it. Could the ladies get
the hotdishes and cakes to the station for judging?
Could Don get the bands here and organized for the*

parade? Could Eddie Fischer control the goats and pigs, even Holsteins, plus a horse troop? What's more, could he contain them? There would be dogs and cats and pet rabbits and ponies in the parade. Why, so many people would participate they'd probably have to parade around the village twice just so folks could both be in the parade and watch it. Everyone had become excited about the parade, and they didn't want to be left out, free-parading Holsteins included. The Artificial Breeder's Association said it was designing a float that would surprise the audience. Eddie sort of wondered about that, and the Holstein Association said they'd be parading cows and calves, and the Belvidere Horse Troop would be riding horses in the parade and lassoing children. Eddie Fischer didn't know about that, either. Suddenly, it looked as if Eddie Rosener's Miscellaneous Committee would be more important that even he thought it would be.

The Corner Bar, Art's Bar, Swenson's Cafe, Al Shelstad's Cafe, Joe's Place and Buck's Cafe ordered extra cases of beer, extra hamburger buns, meat, soda and sarsaparilla for the coming event. It would be no time to run out. The village had gotten a head start on a war celebration, the first in the county to organize a celebration. They were proud of being first and when it was all over they wanted to be the best. They expected folks from Holden and Roscoe and Cherry Grove and Florence and Leon Townships to attend, to celebrate the victory over Germany and Japan.

Nary a garage door remained open. Nary a kitchen door was left ajar, but being closed and locked couldn't contain the aromas that began seeping throughout the village like a low-hanging mist down in the Welch valley. Ladies were testing hotdishes, endlessly, cake recipes, endlessly. Parade floats and hotdishes and cakes had to be perfect to meet the competition. Grandma's recipes were at stake. Merchants and church groups and civic organizations and, why, even faith was at stake. Secrecy was of the utmost importance as villagers toiled late into the night building, stringing banners, creating secret designs for floats, secret recipes. With only two days remaining before Saturday's opening events, tempers were becoming short in tiny, steaming kitchens, husbands' and children's stomachs bursting with hotdish and cake. There was little time left. "V" Day was almost here.

J. R. jumped . . . well, rolled out of bed Saturday at five o'clock, Gert a quarter past five. Both walked out onto their respective lawns to check on the breaking day. The sun was just edging over the eastern corn and grain fields beyond Bellechester, a low-lying mist containing more humidity than fog hovered near the ground. J. R. knew it would be a steamy day. Gert worried about the effect of humidity on the bakeoff entries, especially the cakes and pie crusts. Both, though, had anticipated this weather. July was never any different and, thank God, it wasn't raining.

Saturday's events included many for the children—a street carnival in front of the Elevator, Tilt-a-Whirl ride, a Ferris Wheel, bean bag throws, bottle throws, events children liked just as at the Goodhue County Fair. J. R. wasn't worried about the carnival. Hank Befort had volunteered to chair it. He would do a good job.

Gert needed to verify that the church booths were organized and properly set up. Each church selling faith-based ethnic foods would display dishes and various delicacies on planks and barrels on the street in front of the Goodhue Hotel, Sjoblom's Photo Studio, and Dave Franklin's Dray Line barn. Booths were to extend a full block past Sjoblom's to Eddie Rosener's Blacksmith Shop. The German Lutheran ladies would be selling lutefisk for anyone courageous enough to try it, plus lefse delicacies to eliminate the taste of the lutefisk. The Swedish Lutheran ladies would be offering their famous Swedish meatballs on hot buns. The English Lutherans would be offering goulash and Cornish pastries The Methodists would offer liver and onions, plus Kool-Aid to wash it down. Both the German Lutheran Church and St. Columbkill's Catholic would offer sauerbraten and sauerkraut with bratwurst, the local German ancestry being equally divided between Lutherans and Catholics. Holy Trinity and St. Columbkill's would be serving corned beef and cabbage plates, plus apple strudel delicacies. The competition would be intense. When Gert arrived at the hotel church ladies were already setting up their booths on the street. She needn't worry about the church ladies. They would have things well in hand. You could bank on it.

J. R. and Gert met on the crumbling hotel steps. "Well, Gertrude, this is our big day. I hope we're ready," J. R. said, sipping hot coffee.

"Me too, J. R., but just look at those ladies. Why, I probably don't need to do a thing, they're so excited and organized. They all want to put their best foot . . . er, best food forward. Reputations are at stake here," she said, checking off an item from her long notebook list. "Now, the carnival will run all day, the church booths will be offering food throughout the day, and we have children's games running all day on the school playground."

"We've a beer tent set up at the lumber yard, but it probably won't get busy until this afternoon or tonight. I've arranged for music, too. The Polka Dots will be playing at the beer garden, and the Bennett-Greten Orchestra will be playing modern-swing at the Dreamland Ballroom. Music for everyone, Gert."

"And we're offering a sewing, knitting, crocheting and quilting demonstrations in the school gymnasium,

so the ladies won't get quite so hot. It's going to be a blister today, that's for sure," Gert said as she continued checking off items.

"The Goodhue Volunteer Fireman are holding a water-barrel fighting contest this afternoon in front of the fire hall. Art Lohman and Bill Mans have organized that, Tom Franklin assisting. The firemen are setting up the wire and barrel right now. Zumbrota, Cannon Falls, Wanamingo and Hay Creek are bringing their fire departments for the competition. You can check that off your list," J. R. said, motioning toward the fire hall.

"I didn't know Hay Creek had a fire department, J. R.?"

"Well, they don't but they wanted to get in the competition anyway, so they're borrowing Frontenac's old hand pumper."

"And the bicycle decorating contest will be this afternoon for the children, although they'll ride them in the parade tomorrow," Gert said, flipping to page two. "How are the town decorations coming, J. R.?"

"Herman and his crew are starting to put them up right now. I see Bill O'Reilly and Tom Franklin down by the fire station. They're using their cattle trucks to help set the decorations. We're placing big red white and blue banners at the village's two entrances. Each light post will have a banner, and you can see merchants are beginning to hang banners and flags on their store fronts. We'll set American flag standards along the parade route. Tommy Schinnert is climbing to the top of the water tank to drape a flag; Bump Schinnert is hanging another from the coal silo. We'll be able to see them for a couple of miles. Herman's doing a great job. The town will look festive."

"All right," Gert said, checking off 'decoration.' "What about the free movies for the children tonight. Is that ready?"

"Yes, ma'am. We've Earl from Red Wing coming

out with his screen and projector. He'll set up on the side of the railroad station. Start showing a couple of movies at dusk."

"Check off 'Free movies,' " Gert responded.

"The baseball tournament? Who is chairing that?" Gert asked.

"Joyce Shelstad will be running that at the ball diamond. It'll run for two days, a double elimination tournament with teams from Welch, Belle Creek, Wabasha, Mazeppa, Goodhue and Hay Creek. They'll be busy at the diamond both days, right up to and after the parade tomorrow. Hank just needs to make sure the players don't traipse on the lawns of Janet Campbell and Blanche Barry. Blanche was bothered enough throughout the summer with baseballs bouncing into her yard, off her house from town team practices."

"Who is in charge of the Bridge and Five Hundred tournaments, Gert?" J. R. asked as they walked through the church booths, J. R. turning up his nose when he passed the lutefisk barrel.

"Mary McHugh is organizing that. The Bridge tournament will be held in the back room of the hotel, and the Five Hundred tournament at the fire hall, after they pull the trucks out for the tug of war competition. The card tournaments should be popular because folks certainly love their card games. I can check off 'Card Tournaments.' " Gert and J. R. walked along Upper Street, stopped into Joe's Place for more coffee, then continued their inspection tour along the street in front of J. P. Ryan's Hatchery, down to Herman's Corner Grocery, along Lower Street to Overby's railroad station, past Jesse's Hardware and Taylor's Eat Shop, up the side street past Heaney & Gorman and back to the hotel. By half past six the temperature had already reached the eighties, humidity the same, but folks, busy on the streets, didn't seem to mind. Soon, county folks would be buzzing into town. Everyone wanted to be

ready. J. R. and Gert knew they would be, at least they hoped to be. So far, nothing had gone wrong. They wanted things to stay that way.

By a half past nine Model A's, '39 Plymouths and '40 Chevys, most sporting two-by-four war-issue bumpers instead of chrome steel, began arriving in town. J. R. had secured several hay fields near the white coal silo as parking lots. Boy Scouts would park the cars. The fields were full of stubble, but they weren't muddy. J. R. was thankful for that. By noon cars had filled one field, another opened. County folks were shuffling through town enjoying the new look of the village, it looking sort of like a kid on the way to Sunday church, all cleaned and washed. J. R. stopped for a moment to look himself. He had been around the village a long time but had never seen the village look so good—decorations, banners, flags, balloons flying everywhere. Merchants had cleaned windows with Bon Ami *soap, swept sidewalks, and the only real dust was on the streets themselves, the village not yet being able to afford paved streets. Maybe, now that the war was over, the city council could pave and install curbs. Yet, the city maintenance workers had risen early to spray the streets from a water wagon. It would settle the dust until tramped upon.*

By early afternoon the sun was blazing, church ladies fanning themselves with dainty white handkerchiefs while visitors sought shelter wherever they could. Many men sought out the beer garden tent while ladies and children sat under sweeping elms and hard maples that had graced the village from day one. In spite of the heat, excitement prevailed. About the only "being" not affected by the excitement was Ol' Buck. He sought shade lying on his belly, panting on the side of Ebe's Barber Shop. Most events didn't excite Ol' Buck. It looked as if this celebration wasn't about to either. It was also difficult to determine whether the claypitters were excited, as they sat on high, listing stools in the saloons, early, sipping their usual beers, expressions as dour as any other day.

As Saturday afternoon wore on, the children flocked to the carnival rides, sipped pop and chomped on cotton candy. The baseball tournament had begun at the dusty diamond, Wabasha defeating Wanamingo in game one, 3–2, Goodhue leading the Belle Creek Grainers in the fifth inning of game two, 1–0. Fans lined the left field line where most of the shade was, it being too hot to sit in the right field bleachers. The Hotel Bridge tournament was in full swing, the firehouse hall Five Hundred card competition running smoothly, and the firemen's tug-of-war water fight was about to begin. Hopefully, they could contain their streams and not douse the Five Hundred players in the truck bays. J. R. was pleased with the events while on an inspection tour around town. Gert was mostly pleased, yet concerned about the bakeoff, in this heat, after tomorrow's parade.

The ladies were having a grand old time up at the school, quilting, knitting, crocheting and gossiping. Everyone was enjoying the ethnic foods at the church booths, with the exception of the lutefisk fermenting in wooden lye barrels. But the Lutheran ladies weren't worried about that. Old Norwegian stoic bachelor stalwarts would arrive soon enough to devour the lutefisk.

"J. R! We're running out of parking spaces," an excited Eddie Rosener hollered running up to J. R. at the Swedish Lutheran Church booth where J. R. was devouring a meatball sandwich."

"So, did I hear you right, then. Those two fields filled?"

"Yes, sir, J. R. Now what the hell am I gonna do? This Miscellaneous Committee thing is bigger than I thought, and the parade doesn't even begin till tomorrow," Eddie said in exasperation, placing hands on an expanding belly.

"Not to worry, Eddie. We'll figure somethin' out." J. R. opened another field, then headed back to the festivities. As he approached the hotel it seemed as if the entire county was present in this one little village, his little village. He could hardly walk, there being so many folks. And they were happy, too, excited, animated, free. He watched them drinking sodas, lemonade, beer. He was struck at how relaxed they were. Everyone had been under such intense pressure and tension the past four years that, this day, they seemed to be releasing that tension. He felt it himself, but he'd feel it more after the weekend was over. This celebration had been a good idea of Marg's, he thought. He hadn't thought of it himself, but was happy to jump on the bandwagon once she suggested it. The village had pulled together during the war. This was their reward for the hard work, for the servicemen and women who had enlisted and fought in France, Germany, North Africa, Sicily, and the Pacific Islands.

As dusk approached, children congregated near the railroad station for the free movies; the church ladies dished sauerbraten and sauerkraut, meatballs and corned beef cabbage, and yes, even the lutefisk barrel was getting lower. Men and women were becoming louder in the beer garden as the Polka Dots played polkas and mazurkas and waltzes and the "Too Fat Polka," near a pile of two-by-fours. Bennett-Greten's Orchestra swung into the "American Patrol," just like Glenn Millers' Air Force Band, the evening's events getting under way throughout the village, the day's unrelenting sun having dipped beyond the water tower and Evergreen Cemetery, the sultry air dripping with dew drops.

The evening soon took on a festive glow—both the people and village—shimmering out on the high prairie, just a little village celebrating the end of a long trauma. Some folks sat on the sidewalk sipping sodas, eating church ladies' dinners and pastries as children screamed with glee on the Tilt-a-Whirl and Ferris Wheel. Folks stood in the middle of the now dusty street, shoes, pants, dresses tainted with prairie dust, but they not minding as they talked, chatted, hugged, sang, kissed. Younger couples skipped into the shadows behind the Quast Building, behind the Goodhue Hotel, behind Eddie's Drugstore, in alleys where they hugged, kissed, explored as if it were going out of style, they experiencing new freedom, new feelings, new life in secret caresses. The beer garden tent couldn't handle the overflowing crowd, it flowing out into the street in front of Streater's, folks polkaing and schottisching to the Polka Dots on the dusty, pockmarked street while swing dancers Lindy-Hop'd to Bennett-Greten's Orchestra in the Dreamland Ballroom under a flickering, sparkling mirror. The free movies showed two features—a Tom Mix western and an Abbott and Costello comic. There was something for everyone this day, this night, and there was another entire day of joy tomorrow. You could bank on it.

"Fischer! Where do you want these Holsteins parked?" Reinhold Schulz hollered from his truck cab. He had just arrived Sunday morning with a load of fifteen braying Holsteins, compliments of the Holstein Association. Reinhold hadn't thought it a particularly good idea to parade Holsteins, but he was only the trucker, not the parade chairman. The cows would be Eddie Fischer's responsibility now.

"I've put up a snow fence corral back of the bulk oil tanks. Back 'er over there. Eddie Rosener will help unload them." Reinhold rear-gear'd toward the fence, dropped a gangplank and fifteen agitated Holsteins were corralled, braying, creating a heckuva hullabaloo, waiting to be groomed for the parade, udders and all, this the village's first udder run.

Floats of every imaginable size, shape and design were gathering on Lower Street near the Elevator, assembling along the railroad siding and stretching past the coal silo to the Home Oil Co. on Highway 58. Don Center was placing the Goodhue Band, the Cannon Falls Drum and Bugle Corps, and the Rochester Shriner's Band & Funny Cars into position, the raucous double reed Shriner oriental shawm instruments soon agitating the Holsteins accustomed to only polka-thumping accordions and tubas. Eddie Rosener helped Eddie Fischer as the Hay Creek Horse Troop, the goat group, and a varied assortment of dogs, rabbits and Shetland ponies arrived. Lower Street soon became a menagerie. Eddie Fischer soon realized he would need to call upon his youthful Featherstone farmer days for this job.

Fritz and Regina had prepared a staging plan and parade order and with the help of Clara Hennings and a reluctant Lucretia O'Gorman, were now conferring with Don Center. Regina had approached Lucretia about assisting with the floats, but Lucretia hadn't thought she had the energy to participate. She initially begged off, unable, she said, to think about anything other than son Charles' death. Her grief was unbearable. Husband Frank buried himself in attorney work, but Lucretia had been unable to accept it. The town's celebration was just another reminder of the terrible war that had robbed her of a son. She wanted to crawl into a hole, into a fox hole like her son, to escape the celebration, to escape living. She had no energy, no enthusiasm, no spirit for a celebration, but Regina had persisted, knowing it would be good for Lucretia to get out. Lucretia was on Lower Street as floats began arriving, too rapidly, the scene becoming congested. "Regina, you check the floats off as they arrive and I'll

_escort them to their staging area. That'll help," Fritz
hollered._

_Within an hour the town was overflowing with
tractors pulling hayracks, pickups pulling hayracks,
trucks of every imaginable size and condition—flat-
beds, wagons, jalopies, soup'd-up pickups, even a
couple of hosed-down honey wagons with banners
flying from their separators. Don, Regina, Clara, Lucretia, Fritz, J. R. and two Eddies scurried to get
parade floats and units in place._

_Meanwhile, the Five Hundred tournament was
progressing nicely in the firehouse; that is, until the
Welch firemen inadvertently, or later it was surmised,
sprayed the card players through the open door causing cards to scatter, shirts, dresses and permanents to
wilt and Agnes O'Reilly to lose her small slam bid of six
spades. The Welchers chortled out on the street, asking
pardon and mea culpas. But no one really believed the
incident had been inadvertent._

_Eddie Fischer was growing increasingly concerned
about his menagerie, hoping he could contain them in
the parade even though they would pull up the rear, so
to say. Church congregations had arrived with reli-
gious-based, theme floats: Christ on a cross (actually
a boy of ten in tattered shorts); Catholics offered Mary
Magdalene with a couple of Mogen David wine bottles;
Lutherans offered a replica of Martin L. nailing 95
theses to a plank (it representing the Wittenberg doors);
Methodists designed a scroll, "Words of Salvation,"
something like Burma Shave signs. The Boy Scouts
built a semaphore float with campfire, while the Girl
Scouts built a campfire, too, surrounded with girls
eating marshmallows and Girl Scout cookies. The siren
sounded "noon," but today folks didn't rush home for
dinner as they usually did. Today, it signaled the beginning of the memorial service and parade._

The committee had decided to hold a brief memo-

rial before the parade began, Legion and Auxiliary members already present. Mayor J. P. Ryan spoke with great dignity of the extraordinary sacrifices of our fallen soldiers, saying that Iwo Jima and Normandy and Omaha Beach and Guadalcanal were a long way from the village, but the sacrifices of the men would be forever remembered. Commander Mickley spoke eloquently, for him, about their fallen comrades. He honored their parents, some present today standing in the blistering sun. He said a special memorial would be engraved in the Legion Hall for all to see for all years. Gert said that women had sacrificed much, too, during the war and on the home front. They would be forever remembered. The Legion firing squad stood at somewhat attention on Swenson's corner. When Commander Mickley ordered a twenty-one gun salute, the squad fired fifteen over the elevator, drowsy pigeons suddenly startled from their high perches. They weren't American Eagles, just common barn pigeons, yet a flock flew toward the coal silo seemingly out of respect for the fallen.

The Memorial Service concluded, the American Legion Color Guard stepped off into the blistering sun, W.W.I and W.W.II helmets extra snug under double chins, shirts and khakis bursting buttons over long-earned paunches, paunches that hadn't been there a few years ago. But they were proud as they marched past Swenson's Cafe at the beginning of the parade. The Goodhue Community Band followed playing the Caisson Song *while keeping a steady, rhythmic beat for the bedecked Legion and Auxiliary. Third in line was Grand Marshall Nick Matthees, he of the seven war sons. The Victory Celebration 1947 parade had begun as the ominous Welch firemen stood at half attention adjacent to the parade route, threatening hoses in hand. Hopefully, they wouldn't use them again.*

The crowd stood two and three deep on the side-

walks waving little American flags, clapping for the American Legion, the Auxiliary, the high school band, the floats that followed in quick succession. Oh, it would be a grand parade . . . if the Welch firemen behaved, if the Holsteins could be contained, if the menagerie could be contained. The parade called for a route up town past Holy Trinity toward Heinie Swenson's house, a right flank past Tom O'Reilly's place, down past the school to Blanche Barry's street, a right flank past Blanche's, Jesse Campbell's and Bill O'Reilly's to the lumber yard, a column right past Standard Oil, down Lower Street and back to Swenson's. But neither Don, Regina nor Fritz had calculated the length of the parade units, ever measured the burgeoning floats, so that by the time the Legion Color Guard had made one pass of the circuitous route and returned to Swenson's, only a third of the units had left the staging area. The village was so small—how small was it?—that the parade encircled the village twice, because folks in the parade also wanted to see the parade. J. R. wiped his heavy brow and made a quick decision as the Color Guard bore down on him at Swenson's corner. He said, "Follow me, men," as he executed a British-style countermarch right in the middle of the street, leading the startled Color Guard and band back to the corner they had just captured. J. R. ordered a column-left and marched the Guard toward the bank. He was winging it but he needed to draw out the parade for the remaining parade units. He took charge like an infantry company commander, his troops following faithfully. But he surely better know where he was going, he thought while waving to bystanders suddenly overjoyed to see more of the parade than they had expected. J. R. and the Color Guard reached the intersection of the bank and hotel, but J. R. couldn't march right because the parade was passing through that intersection. He couldn't march left because the *parade was just starting there. He did the only thing he could; he continued uptown toward the school. But folks were loving it. They'd never seen a free-wheeling parade before. It was fun, they thought, wondering where J. R. would head next: through the City Park, through the alleys, maybe up to the German Lutheran church where he'd certainly corner himself at the dead end. The serpentine, wandering parade added a measure of unplanned excitement to the celebration.*

Naurice Husbyn's newly purchased Goodhue Hatchery had entered a highly decorated float with crepe papers and egg cartons and feed sacks and chicken photos and real, live yellow chicks in a wire cage displaying the cycles of a chicken's life from egg to roaster; the Post Office, a float with stuffed mail bags on top of a mail truck, a sign reading, "The mail will get through, mostly!" Heaney's Market presented Campbell Soup cans stacked like a pyramid, its famous Heaney's sausages hanging from a wooden rack, plus a sow being pulled behind with a sandwich board sign on its flanks stating: "I do my butchering at Heaney's." Frieda and Fred Vieths presented a float on a hayrack displaying her innumerable dry goods, and Art's Bar displayed stacked cases of Grain Belt beer, Art even handing out a few freebies as he road along the parade route. The village council presented the police car up front in the parade, so that upon finishing the route the cop could remove the village's one battery for the fire truck bringing up the rear. The Goodhue County Artificial Breeder's Association presented a life-sized stature of a cow and a calf, only implying their technical skills, they having the good sense to go no further with the float.

By now J. R. was leading the parade through the streets like the Pied Piper. He had reached the school and was about to run head long into the last third of the parade. He had to act quickly. He executed another countermarch, the Legion and band directly on his heels, and headed back toward downtown, the last third now marching up past the Methodist Church, Holy Trinity, Tom O'Reilly's, toward the old ball diamond before winding past the hotel and bank, the parade doubling back on itself like a coiled rattlesnake. The band grew tired of playing and marching, Legion paunches bounced lower as long-dormant car horns honked, folks applauded, yelled encouragement. They were having a grand time, and no one knew where or when the parade would finally end, not even J. R.

Finally, it was time for Eddie's animals to bring up the rear, to end the parade. The Hay Creek Horse Troop would lead followed by goats, rabbits, Shetlands, and finally, Holsteins at the rear.

The menagerie began beautifully—horses prancing with riders waving to the cheering crowd, even the goats cooperating with their handlers, and lastly, the Holstein Association led their gleaming, washed, scrubbed black-and-whites out of the fenced corral, each cow tether by a 4-H'r. Why, they looked good enough to enter the Goodhue County Fair. Most of the crowd had never seen Holsteins in a parade, cows normally being in stalls at the fair or just making milk out in the county's sprawling green pastures. This was unusual, they thought, but then, the war was over, a new feeling and spirit had descended upon the folks. Why not Holsteins?

The animals were behaving wonderfully, Eddie thought; that is, until the Holsteins reached City Park near the Catholic parish house. Suddenly, a huge black-and-white in the back row broke loose from its tethered escort and began running through the herd toward the horses. The goats, rabbits and horses scattered. The rampaging Holstein couldn't be caught, and in turn, excited the herd so that now they began running, first straight ahead into the rear of the parade, then *veering off through the stunned crowd onto lawns, through Victory gardens, under clothes lines. Soon, fifteen Holsteins were running, at will, throughout the village, the provoked Eddie beside himself, not knowing what to do. Even his boyhood farming days hadn't prepared him for this. Holsteins began dropping turds everywhere causing folks to slip and turn away their noses. Front lawns, even the Holy Trinity lawn, for God's sake! suddenly became pastures. They dropped loads in front of the Schriner band members who soon began slipping, sliding, falling. The only good news was that most of the parade had made its first pass and was out of the line of the rambling Holsteins. The parade was now stretched throughout the village as Holsteins suddenly appeared from behind garages, alleys, disrupting the parade at every junction, but most simply trying to break free and escape the village into the outlying fields. Children and men and even little old ladies with hickory canes began chasing Holsteins. Some skeptic later said he thought the prank- ster Eddie Rosener instigated the entire thing just so he could get a laugh, but Eddie denied it for years. Yet, the paraders were a hearty and determined group. They had just survived W.W.II. They weren't about to let a few Holsteins disrupt a long, sought-after celebration. They shooed and hollered and lassoed and shushed and shoved Holsteins away while keeping the parade go- ing, mostly, the crowd soon getting used to, even enjoying the sudden turn of events until after two hours, the last float returned to the staging area. Folks were out of breath, as well as the Holsteins. They gathered at the food booths, at the beer garden, the Holsteins having settled down under a sweeping elm on the edge of town. They just hadn't wanted to be in the parade.*

Fortunately, only one Holstein had disrupted the bakeoff entries displayed on plank tables near the depot. Edna had been guarding the entries from flies when one hell-bent-for-trouble Holstein charged her and her hotdishes, pies and cakes, but she wasn't about to let any cow disrupt her bakeoff. She waved her bonnet, hollered, shushed, and stood her ground like a matador in a bull ring. Three feet from the tables, the charging Holstein veered off toward the railroad's water tank, thereby saving both the bakeoff entries and Edna.

Folks were agog about the free-wheeling parade and Holstein debacle. They milled around downtown just as the Holsteins were now doing on the outskirts. Slowly recovering, revelers shuffled toward the reviewing wagon now parked in front of the depot. The float judges (out-of-towners Mr Sylvander, Red Wing; Mrs Gundersen, Cannon Falls; Mr Wiebusch, Lake City) had been sitting on Ole's folding chairs placed atop Uncle Dave's rubber wheeled dray wagon in front of the jail—analyzing, discussing, determining the float competition winners. It was time to divulge the results. Sylvander hollered through a borrowed GHS paper megaphone, "Ladies and gentlemen and children, I might add! The judges are happy to announce the results of the float competition. It has been extremely difficult, as all entries were exemplary, but we have . . . yes we have . . . arrived at our decisions. You will be happy to know that . . . ,"

"Get on with it judge! Save the speech. We want the winners," a beefy villager hollered, the crowd equally impatient.

"In third place, with a highly creative float, is . . . The Goodhue County Artificial Breeder's Association, their float depicting our county's lifeblood, a cow with her calf and I might add, all done in good taste," Sylvander said as he returned to his seat, Mrs Gundersen taking the megaphone. The crowd murmured, restless like the mooing Holsteins, but they didn't seem disturbed by the Breeder's third place award. Artificial

breeding was a fact of this agrarian life, and that little calf statue was kind of cute.

"I'm Mrs Gunderson from Cannon Falls and I just want to say how pleased I am to have been chosen for the high honor of judging Goodhue County's very first victory celebration in this year of 1947. My accolades to the community, to the Legion and Auxiliary, to the . . . ,"

"Get on with it, Gundersen. We know your happy, now make us happy by announcing the next winner," Beefy said, thrusting his hands into deep pockets.

"Second place float competition award goes to . . . Heaney's Market with their delightful, 'I do my butchering at Heaney's,' sandwich board and hog!" The crowd murmured lower now, all concerned about their church float entry. Certainly, the judges had seen the right and just church float, hadn't they? Certainly, our Lutherans or our Catholics or our Methodists would win first place, wouldn't they? Certainly, these out-of-town, unbiased judges would be able to see the significance of our floats, wouldn't they? The third and final judge approached the tense crowd wiping his brow with a huge red handkerchief.

"And now, ladies and gentlemen, for the moment you've all been a-waiting, the announcement of the first place winner . . . but first, let me extend my thanks and gratitude for being here, and . . . ,"

"Zip it up, judge. We want the first place winner, and it better be . . . ,"

"The first place float award goes to . . . drum roll please . . . . do we have a drummer? . . . oh well, the first place winner is none other than . . . Husbyn's Hatchery!"

Applause quickly broke out in the crowd along with low grumbling, stamping feet raising dust on Lower Street. Heavens! No church? A few cat calls emerged. All three judges stood together, linking hands, beaming at the crowd, but the crowd was obviously unsettled. "What about the church floats? We want to know which church won the competition, who's best, which faith is . . . ,"

Sylvander quickly grabbed the megaphone, "Ladies and gentlemen. The church floats were all so wonderful we have decided to award each an honorable mention."

"Well, the sonofabitches! They copped out. Everyone knew the Methodists had the best float . . . ,"

"Well, I'll be . . . I never . . . couldn't they see the Lutherans obviously had the best float."

"Damned silly, if you ask me. Catholic float was far and away the best . . . ,"

The crowd was restless, murmuring about the wimpy honorable mentions, but it soon settled down awaiting the bakeoff competition. Some realized that maybe honorable mention for all was honorable, after all.

Edna had saved her bakeoff entries from the rampaging Holstein, but she and Emma were now battling flies and bees attacking the long-planked tables of hotdish, pies and cakes. Emma was doing her best to ward of the bees, having loads of experience in her flower garden, but as the emerging crowd began walking along the display tables inspecting the entries, her task seemed hopeless. While the judges had been presenting float awards, Edna's own out-of-town judges had been inspecting, poking, looking, tasting the entries, determining the awards for the best hotdish recipe, the best cake recipe, the best pie recipe. Family heirloom recipes were at stake here, women of the village and surrounding townships mighty proud of their entries, even on this day when crusts sagged, when apple, peach and banana fillings became sodden, when frosting ran and dripped like goo.

Although Edna and Emma had organized the

bakeoff extremely well, it now seemed like chaos as the invading crowd began poking, tasting, destroying all evidence. Revelers simply couldn't keep their hands off hotdish, any kind of hotdish, protruding fingers, notwithstanding. Fortunately, the judges had finished their deliberations, now comparing notes and sticky fingers, nearing the time of announcement.

Family recipes were next to godliness, to some folks, even surpassing it. Their religious convictions were undaunted. Their family recipes handed down through generations were almost undaunted. Family pride, family honor was at stake with mothers', grandmothers', great-grandmothers' hotdish, cake and pie recipes being tested. For generations these recipes had been ruthlessly scrutinized at family reunions, wakes, funerals, weddings. They had withstood church suppers and baby showers, threshing bees and neighbors' carping. Families guarded their secrets in dark closets, none more valuable than recipes. Oh, when the ladies congregated at church they shared "some" of their recipe, but not all of it. To share all was to divulge grandmother's secret, who had in turn gotten it from her Scandinavian mother, her German mother, her Irish, maybe even her Bohemian mother. Each lady held something back when writing a recipe for her neighbor. She held back a secret ingredient, something that set her recipe apart from the others. That's the way it was. Share and share a- . . . well . . not alike.

The assembling crowd soon devoured the evidence: tater-tot hotdish, round steak hotdish, oriental noodle hotdish, hamburger hotdish; pound, iced, baked, chocolate and angel food cakes; banana, lemon creme, minced meat, cherry and apple pie. Edna and Emma weaved through the crowd to Uncle Dave's wagon. Before the crowd had anticipated the announcement, Edna dived right in, no preliminaries, no long-winded speeches like the float judges. She was all business. By the time she and her committee had made the an-nouncements, the hotdish first place had been awarded to Mrs Hepplemann of Bellechester, second place to a Mrs Chandler of Belle Creek and third place to Florence Taylor of the village, this after the usual grumbling about the unfairness of the judges.

Mary McHugh of the village took first place in the cake bakeoff; second place went to the Vasa Swedish Lutheran Church Monday Night Bible-Study Women, of all things, and third place to a third-generation Featherstone of Featherstone Township.

Finally, pie awards had been presented to Mrs Majerus of Bellechester, Estelle Shelstad of the village (Joe's Place), and Mrs Holst from Claybank. Many in the crowd beamed with happiness and pride as they accepted blue, red and white ribbons from Emma, while others appeared crestfallen by their displacement. Oh, no one came right out and said a recipe was bad, bitter or tasteless. It was just that some hadn't won. But hope was eternal and grandmother's recipe had survived generations. It would surely survive more.

Evening, Tommy and Bump Schinnert climbed to the top of the white coal silo to fire army-procured fireworks as folks milled around looking up in amazement and awe at the exploding show, these fires of joy instead of destruction. The ten-minute show concluded the celebration. Clara Hennings and Lucretia stood with Gert, tears in Lucretia's eyes as the fireworks burst over the coal silo, Lucretia's emotions running as rampant as the afternoon's Holsteins. How could she ever find joy again? This celebration had brought joy to most villagers, yet she couldn't feel it. It would be irreverent to feel joy when Charles was in a grave, she thought. It would be sacrilegious to find peace in celebrating a war that had caused his death, she thought. Giving a son to the country brought her no comfort, she thought. She tried not to be bitter, to blame others, but she didn't know how to continue living without Charles. Regina moved closer to Lucretia, laid an arm around her shoulders and just held her as the final blazing red, bursting white and blue streamers spiraled into the black sky.

During the final bursts over the silo, Eddie Fischer shuffled up to J. R. standing with the ladies viewing the fireworks. "Sorry about the Holsteins, J. R. and Gert. I was worried something might happen, and surely it did. My apologies," Eddie said, head downcast.

"Don't you worry one bit about it," J. R. said, placing a hand on Eddie's scrawny shoulder.

"That's right, Eddie. It wasn't your fault; besides, it added a measure of excitement to the parade and did no real harm. Folks will be talking about the Holstein parade for years to come. They rambled around town at will, that's for sure, but maybe, Eddie, in a few years the village might even sponsor a real Udder Run ... and it all began here in 1947."

I had been doodling marching band formations for so long while daydreaming about the 1947 celebration that Anne and Joe had gone to bed, and Terri was watching the Johnny Carson Show. I closed my notebook hoping tomorrow's Mason City Parade wouldn't be quite as eventful as the village's Celebration of 1947.

Chapter 10

Tar'd & defeather'd

Whistling Down County Rd. No. 9

E SCAPING THE FUNDAMENTALISTS OF OKLAHOMA
proved beneficial, in retrospect, because once back "up
north" I replaced those "ABD" suffixes with "Ph.D." This
final academic requirement catapulted me into a higher, higher
education faculty appointment in the Motor City just down the

street from General Motors' world headquarters and Barry Gordy's Motown Studios. We were keeping U-Haul in business, but Michigan seemed like a good state, not Upper Midwest, but at least Upper Near Midwest.

As Anne and Joe entered grade school in Motown's suburbs, I found myself again sweating on a marching band field performing Saturday afternoons in a blighted inner city Detroit stadium for bored fans and proud parents. Even our uplifting marching efforts couldn't help the Wayne State U team, their efforts so boring, they so inept that only parents and grandparents could enjoy them. Thankfully, we escaped that stadium once a year to perform for the Detroit Lions NFL team on Thanksgiving Day in the barn-sized Silverdome (one hundred Cueball Holst barns), its air-inflated ceiling rising 400 feet higher than Cueball's out on County Rd. No. 9. Annually, the band hoped for national TV exposure, but was always superseded by Miller Beer half-time commercials, plus Chevrolet, Ford and Cadillac ads. This was Motor City, baby, and don't you forget it.

My new appointment included more than directing the marching band, though. I was soon ensconced in teaching prospective band directors about the vagaries of public school teaching, debating philosophies of music education, directing field-based instrumental music classes deep in the bowels of Detroit City—Hamtramck, a Polish enclave I loved with a name I couldn't pronounce—thereby continuing a long tradition begun with Chas Wood's GHS school band.

Detroit was as far from the village as Mars from Earth. Terri wondered why on earth I accepted an appointment in this blighted, inner city university, my roots so rural, so provincial, so uncitified, so backwoods—she didn't actually say "backwoods." I told her it would be a good position, one enhancing my record; besides, maybe we could show those Detroiters a thing or two as we settled into a cozy suburban neighborhood twenty-five miles from the sprawling university, twenty-five miles from the withering inner city.

Although a country bumpkin from the high prairie, I was fascinated by Detroit's condition, frequently escaping my ivory tower to supervise student teachers in decaying inner city schools. On visitations I would drive through the *real* Detroit, well off the beaten paths, well off the main thoroughfares. I saw the gritty Detroit, not the gleaming Renaissance Center on the sludge-filled Detroit River, not the towering GM headquarters, not Henry Ford's headquarters, not the bilious Silverdome nor the entrancing, touristy Greek Town. I saw earthy Detroit, Rosa Parks' Detroit—endless miles of blighted houses, burned out shells where families once struggled to live, some surviving, many not. I saw decaying, fire-encrusted buildings collapsing like ancient barns out on County Roads 4 and 7, scarred remnants of Detroit's earlier, glory days when Henry Ford offered men five dollars a day to make Model T's. Some of those "T's" were now decaying in the shadow of General Motors offering a contrast so starling I couldn't grasp it. I saw burned out V-8 engines manufactured in the Motor City, auto skeletons stripped of all meaning—fenders, tires, hoods ripped off to be bolted to a different vehicle, thereby creating grass roots hybrid cars. I drove past fire-bombed cars abandoned to decay on the street for years, never towed, forsaken to blight eyes, hearts, spirits. I visited student teachers in depressing, gray high schools protected by gun-toting policeman trying to protect students brave enough to attend school, yet those inner city students often more polite and well behaved than the pretentious progeny of Grosse Pointe, neighbors of the Fords, the Buicks, the Dodges, the Studebakers, the Chryslers.

Driving the neighborhoods, I speculated on how I might have turned out had I been raised here instead of in the vast Minnesota hinterland. Would I have had the good sense to behave properly? Would I have had the good sense to be a Boy Scout—honest, truthful, trustworthy? Would I have had mentoring and tutoring from folks like Dennis, George, Dodie, Frank O', B. C, Cy, Bill, Luverne, Heinie, Joyce, Lucille and Tom, plus a horde of Belle Creek Franklins and Red Wing Haulsteins. I wondered how important that was, something I had taken for granted during those years in the village.

On Woodward Avenue I viewed row upon row of garages, houses and outhouses collapsing, desecrating, untouched, unmaintained for decades, depressed mothers, crying children sitting on stoops trying to survive. I snaked through endless neighborhood battlefields, through Rosa Parks' post Montgomery, Alabama, neighborhood, Rosa standing up in the bus and saying, "Dammit, I'm not going to take it anymore," or something like that. She was a gallant woman trying to right a terrible wrong. I wondered if I could have done the same. Would I have been courageous enough to withstand withering discrimination? Oh, the Lutheran taunting we Catholic children received would sometimes sting, get under our Roman Catholic collars, but it was nothing compared to what Rosa Parks withstood. Where had she received her values? Were they from parents, the products of transplanted southerners. Was her courage innate or did it come from her environment? Certainly, no one would ever utter "Goodhue, Minnesota" and "Detroit, Michigan" in the same sentence. Yet, was there a connection, a comparison? I wondered, driving Gratiot Street past former speakeasies, brothels, adult bookstores, past the Graystone Ballroom where Jean Goldkette and his Band of Renown catapulted the nation into the Jazz Era even before my beloved Benny Goodman kicked of "Let's Dance," this Detroit City then more than a motor city. I drove crumbling streets littered with broken wine bottles, broken lives.

I pondered the impact of environment on a person. Would I have been different, would I hold different values had I not worked at Heaney & Gorman sacking potatoes (separating the good from the bad, the wheat from the chaff), sweeping floors of sawdust, burning garbage in the alley incinerator, stomping wool into fifteen-foot sacks, chasing wild hogs along Upper Street and through dusty alleys, those hogs determined not to become chops or bacon or pork bellies. What if I had not turned sausage handles for Bump Schinnert, stacked grocery shelves with Sally Schinnert, chomped watermelon during lunch under the sweeping elm with Donnie Luhman, George O'Reilly, Fred Rusch and brother Tom? What if I hadn't had that structure, that tutoring, that mentoring, even that chiding. Men and women of the village watched over me after Dad died, they automatically taking on a surrogate parent role trying to keep me on the straight and narrow path in spite of my efforts to get off. Fr. Smith exorcised his best priestly efforts with my sins of impurity, disobeying mother, cussing, particularly a propensity to utter the "F" word out behind the old diamond's right field deep into the fifth row of burgeoning corn. Dodie had done her best encouraging me to save *some* of my Heaney & Gorman weekly check instead of spending it all at Swenson's on malts and burgers. Dennis did his best by chiding me when I arrived five minutes late, gently letting me know it wouldn't be tolerated and that on-timeness would benefit me if I ever left the village. George did his best fathering me when I sliced a beef roast against the grain instead of with it, when I was less than polite waiting on Agnes O'Reilly or Edna Allers or even Oscar Decker, when I sloughed off instead of staying on the task at hand. Those admonitions were more than admonitions. They were values being instilled by folks who cared, because Dad wasn't around anymore to do it. And Uncle Dave always had advice, too, helping me find jobs around the village, assisting him whether scaling and painting the Standard Oil bulk tanks, scraping and painting Streater's Lumber Yard, digging graves at St. Columbkill's Cemetery, or working together at Bookie's pea viners. B. C. advised me. Cy advised me. Casey Ryan advised me. Leone Ryan advised me. Emma Kindseth advised me. Clara Hennings advised me. Bill Mans advised me. Julius Ebe chided me. And way back in grade school, Sidney Berg patiently listened to my stories with a sympathetic ear while he sewed new soul into my childhood soles.

What would I be today, I thought, if I hadn't been exposed to those people, if instead, I had been born into the teeming, high-rise, broken streets of Detroit City. Would I have "turned out all right?" Approaching the Diana Ross Grade School for a student teacher visit, I doubted I would have, but then, I didn't really know. Was I a product of the village or myself? Was *myself* because of the village or in spite of it? Walking into Diana's school in Rosa Park's neighborhood, I wondered if I had Rosa's courage? I'd find out a few short years down the road.

The WSU Marching Band improved. Neither the WSU football team nor the Detroit Lions did. Year one lead to year two, three to four, four to five, most events at the university and at home appearing to be heading in the right direction, although I had noticed Terri shying away from my home-coming hug more often. I pondered that coolness some, but dismissed it to midwestern, stoic displacement. The children soon acquired friends, neighborhood children flooding our home for weekends and stayovers. Terri worked in the community as I entered year six at the university, a year to approach the daunting task of applying for tenure, a process whereby the powers-that-be make a decision on whether they want you around any longer. They might not like your dress, your speech, even your religion—like those Okie Fundamentalists. The music faculty, the Liberal Arts College faculty, and assorted ivory soap deans would put heads together to make a determination about that Franklin fellow, to consider granting or withholding a teaching license at WSU. Officially, I had to submit reams of paper about supposed accomplishments in the classroom, out of the classroom, bettering the university and myself by studying, writing, researching, and most importantly, publishing in dusty academic journals later to be stashed in the basement archives of every university library across the country, the tomes never again seeing the light of day. If the truth be told, the real decision would be made while tenured professors looking like Mark Twain and Theodore Roosevelt sipped Jack Daniels whiskey and puffed on foot-long Cuban cigars in a secret smoke-filled room off the Dean's office. The question entering year six was, would I perish or publish, or vice versa?

I dedicated considerable time to preparing a portfolio, requesting letters of endorsement and support, and writing a rationale why they should keep me and not send me back to the pea viners. After months of preparation I finally toted my box of materials to the music faculty dean. He signed for it while looking askance over the top of his glasses, I wondering what that look meant. He said he would forward it to the music tenure committee, then, if I were lucky, on to the Liberal Arts College tenure committee, the dean, and if I were further lucky, to the provost, the president of the university, the speaker of the U.S. House, the Senate, the vice-president, the president of the. U.S., and finally to God himself. They'd let me know in a couple of months if God responded.

I was pleased with my tenure effort, pleased to have it submitted so I could again concentrate on classroom teaching and music making. Over the following weeks and months, I gave the application little thought until summoned late one Friday after-noon to the music dean's office.

"Sit down, Jim. Cup of coffee?" Dean said, again peering over those horn-rimmed glasses.

"Thanks. Always have enjoyed a cup of coffee, ever since drinking my first cup at Swenson's Cafe," I said, settling into a stuffed chair in Dean's office.

"Swenson's? Where is that?" he asked, offering a steaming cup.

"Back in my Minnesota village. Swenson's was my child-hood and teenage hangout. The only place in town really. Had my first cup of coffee there," I said, wondering what he wanted to see me about. Certainly, it wasn't to question me about Swenson's— Hills Bros or nothing—coffee.

"I received a determination today on your tenure application, Jim. I'm sorry to inform you it didn't fly at the Liberal Arts College level. The music faculty supported your work, but your application failed with the Liberal Arts committee. It's not good news for you or the music department, but . . . well . . . ," Dean murmured while sipping on his coffee, mine suddenly turned bitter.

I was stunned. I hadn't expected this. Things had been going well in the music department; besides, I knew no one in the Liberal Arts hierarchy, the university being so large I seldom escaped the music department. Suddenly, Dean's coffee turned sour, worse even than Swenson's on a bad day, this pill bitter to swallow. Since sixth grade and my first clarinet lesson, my music career had been going upward and outward. Abruptly, a lynching group was blocking my progress just as 'the boys" had done to Chas Wood.

Dean fiddled with desk pencils, fiddled while Rome burned, said nothing. I looked out his window, cigarette wrappers blowing down the desolate street stacking up against the door of the adult bookstore. When I regained my composure I asked, "What next, Dean? You say the music faculty supported my application but the Liberal Arts committee didn't? Run that by me again."

"Affirmative. They indicated they needed to see more research, more publications in national journals instead of only Michigan journals. They appreciate your efforts with school band directors, and your work in computer-assisted music instruction . . . you get a second chance next year. Let's see if we can strengthen your portfolio by then. See me this summer. We will begin working on your second application."

Dazed, I wobbled out of the dean's office, the music department suddenly looking different. It didn't look as bright as I struggled up three flights of stairs to my office, sitting for a couple of hours trying to absorb this news.

I hadn't had any bad news for a long time, not since Dodie called me that day at Iowa University about Mother being confused, sitting on the Methodist Church stoop instead of Holy Trinity's. I had gotten accustomed to, maybe even complacent about receiving good news: better teaching positions, marriage, a daughter, a son, a Ph.D. I had cried profusely at Dad's death and burial, and Mother's cancerous tumor and death. For a moment, I felt like crying, but repressed it, crying not appropriate I thought, but uncertain what in hell that was all about. A couple of salty tears did escape as I looked toward the abandoned marching field and vacant stadium, pondering this unexpected turn of events. Folks I had never laid eyes on had now said they didn't like me, said they didn't want me around, said I wasn't good enough for them. No one had said that since my first dating attempts back in the village when I'd ask girls for a date and they simply turned away snarling, "Get lost, little boy!" That would hurt for a couple of minutes, but I'd try again, often getting the same response from a cute sophomore or junior in Assembly Hall . . . "Get lost, Franklin." . . . "Are you kidding, Jim? I wouldn't date you if you were the last boy in Goodhue, and there are only three boys in town!" I'd slink off to the locker room, lace my Converse Chuck Taylor All Stars and soon forget dating, a basketball more comfortable, feeling better than a dumb old girl any old time.

But this sudden repulsion was sticking in my throat as I finally abandoned the darkened office to drive home to my family, a long, lonely, twenty-five miles down the littered freeway. At least I had my family, I thought, pulling into the driveway. I reached for Terri as I entered the kitchen, she again pulling away, not encouraging an embrace.

"How was your day?" she asked, quickly retrieving the cheese and crackers, snapping open a can of Stroh's for me.

"Not so good. Dean called to inform me that my tenure application didn't pass. It got shot down at the Liberal Arts level. He said I had one more year to apply again," I said, taking my first gulp of beer, it cold, soothing, momentarily pacifying me. For the next two hours we discussed the events of tenure as the children did whatever it is that children do when parents retire to the secrecy of a closed room, they with ears glued to the door knowing something important is being discussed. I had been a child in 1949 when I was shunted to a leeward porch, aunts and uncles speaking in hushed voices about Uncle Don Haustein being diagnosed with tuberculosis and needing to enter the Cannon Falls Sanitarium for a couple of years, and how was Hazel and the family going to survive and could we help. I had been on the other side of that door. We finished our discussion. I reached out for a warm hand, finding instead a welcoming ear, but cold hand. I wondered about that.

I regrouped over the next several days as the end of spring term approached, sort of like regrouping after being rejected for a high school date. I didn't have a basketball for comfort now, that team sport replaced by my singular running, my family, my music. Maybe I could *run* this thing off, gain a better perspective after ten miles . . . *forget my troubles and just be happy* . . . these troubles that had suddenly crept into my life not unlike the village's troubles when struggling to rise from the virgin Minnesota prairie. It wasn't all that easy becoming a village, as I heard so often sitting around the potbellied stove, Saturday nights, at Heaney & Gorman . . .

F rank O'Gorman, his well-worn rumpled suit and face both full of wrinkles, puffed on long, dark cigars as he slumped in a cane-bottom chair around the potbellied stove, Saturday nights during the forties. Frank—his full, bushy mustache stained yellow on the edges from years of smoking cigars, his longer-than-acceptable village hair, his craggy, warm face lined with wisdom and knowledge—was one of the old-timers in town, one of the learned, a local philosopher who earned a law degree, then returned to the village to hang out a wooden shingle, second floor, Quast Building, Upper Street. That shingle appeared about 1907, only a few years after the village had incorporated in 1897.

"Yes, sir, fellows. It warn't easy getting the village up and going in those years. (Frank, the learned attorney knew that "warn't" warn't proper English, but outside his office, when telling stories or chatting to townsfolk, he acted like a country-bumpkin lawyer. No airs. No pretentiousness. But put Frank behind a law desk, get him in court against you, and you would surely find yourself up against a shrewd man, one who then used the King's English.)

"Not sure myself why I came back to the burg to begin practicin' law. Guess 'cause it was home. Might have gone to Red Wing or Lake City, even to St. Paul, make more money, but hell, I returned to do what I could for the locals about gettin' the village up and going." Frank twisted his shaggy mustache, drew long and hard on his cigar, taking time with the story, choosing his words carefully.

"But it warn't easy a'tall, to paraphrase Mark Twain, gentlemen. No sir, warn't easy," Frank said, drawing in a deep breath, brushing his heavy Mark Twain-ish silver hair, dispensing several white smoke rings toward the already crowded ceiling. Uncle Dave, Dennis, Tommy O'Rourke, Pat Rowles, Dad and me were listening to Frank expound. I'd only been around for eight or nine years by then, but I'd join Mother and Dad on their weekly downtown Saturday night saunter to buy groceries, to talk with townsfolk and farmers about the price of wheat, the price of milk, the per pound price of steers up at the South St. Paul Stockyards. While Mother shopped for groceries, meats and dry goods, Dad and I sauntered toward the stove to sit a spell. Frank fascinated me, he being probably the smartest person I'd run into, so far. I didn't know what God looked like, but I thought it wouldn't be all bad if he looked like Frank O'Gorman. "Fellers, Goodhue was known around the county as a lawless burg back 'round the turn of the century and before. Some folks wanted the township to be dry. Others wanted it wet, so sometimes the village sported several saloons, other times none. That's when the blind pigs showed up," Frank said, adjusting his rumpled suit coat, one that fit him to a *T*, shaped to every bulge and contour of his ancient body. I wasn't expected to talk in such prestigious company, but that blind pig thing got my attention. I suddenly spoke up, "What's a blind pig doing in the village, Frank?" I asked as Dad looked askance at me in the circle, slightly raising his arm toward my head before Frank began answering me.

"Do know what a blind pig is, Jimmy?"

"Sure, Mr O'Gorman. It's a pig that can't see. I know that."

"Not quite, Jimmy. It's a pig that's wearin' cataracts, can't see worth a damn," Uncle Dave offered, guffawing and slapping his knee and smiling at the circle of men, some smoking cigarettes, some cigars. "Dogs sometimes can't see either, Jimmy. What do you call a seeing-eye dog with cataracts?"

Shoot! I didn't know a cataract from a catapult, but I followed Dave's lead, "What?"

"A sore for sight-eyes! Get it, Jimmy, a sore for sight-eyes! Ha! Ain't that a good one, Jimmy?"

I understood some of the joke, but missed most, yet persisted with the blind pig story. "Mr O'Gorman, I'd like to know about blind pigs," I said, scooting over to a chair next to him.

"'Blind pig' is a misnomer, Jimmy. You know what a misnomer is?"

"No, sir."

"A misnomer is a word that isn't what you think it is. A misnomer is a euphemism for something else, in this case an illegal liquor store," Frank said, turning to look directly into my eyes.

"A you . . . fizz . . . him? What's that?"

"Euphemism, Jimmy. Means an easier, softer way of saying something unpleasant. For example: Many folk in these here parts like to say 'passed away' when someone dies. They don't like to say 'died' or 'dead 'cause it sounds too everlasting."

"Well, dying is dead, isn't it, Mr O'Gorman?"

"That it is, Jimmy, that it is, but lots o' folks don't want to actually say the word. A euphemism is a way of avoiding an unpleasantry. You remember that now, because you got yourself an inquisitive mind. Have you ever heard a lady say, 'In a family way?'"

"Sure. Mom and my aunts are always saying that. We got lots of family ways."

"Do you know what it means, 'In a family way?'"

"Means having family fun, I guess." Dad looked at Frank and Dave and Dennis and Pat in the circle. They all had smiles on their faces, all suppressing chuckles.

"'In a family way' means . . . well . . . the ladies say 'pg,' but that in itself is a euphemism for 'pregnant.' Do you know what 'pregnant' means, Jimmy?"

"Yup. The O'Neill boys out in Belle Creek say it sometimes when talking about their heifers and mares and sows. I guess it means that a heifer is going to have a calf, or a sow's gonna have piglets. The O'Neill boys usually say 'knocked up,' though. I think it means about the same, don't it Dennis?" I asked as I thought this whole conversation about blind pigs confusing.

"It means about the same, Jimmy, but Frank, finish your story about the blind pigs," Dennis said.

"Back in 1897 or '98, village had a reputation as a rowdy town, a place where township fellows and stragglers came to buy liquor, drink, brawl in the saloons, on the streets, fighting, cussing. The law would get mad and shut the saloons down, bring the sheriff in from Red Wing, but that didn't stop the saloon keepers from selling hootch. They concocted a plan whereby they'd sell liquor through a wooden window. Folks'd shuffle up to the back of a building in a dark alley, knock three times on the window, lay some money down on the counter, wait a few minutes before the window'd open. They'd get a bottle of booze without ever seein' who or where it came from. Blind pigs were an early version of the twenties' speakeasies, Jimmy, long before you were hatched. What year were you born?"

"Nineteen thirty-six, Mr O'Gorman. Just made it though, by a couple of days. I'm eight."

"Well, Jimmy, you just do what your dad says, and Uncle Dave, too. We need nice boys like you in the village. Didn't always have them, though. Area newspaper editors liked to chide the village about its lawlessness. They liked taking the village to task for its blind pigs and pigs running wild and pig pens in back lots, smelled pretty darn putrid. Tarnation! I set up my law office on the second floor of the Quast Building. Tried to help folks and merchants with their legal doings. I played some saxophone with Lucretia, dances in the Dreamland Ballroom, Monday nights, mostly. Even visited a few blind pigs myself," Frank said, settling back into his chair as Mother approached the men's circle.

"Are you ready to go home, Jimmy? I've finished my grocery shopping."

"Oh, Mom, Mr O'Gorman is telling some good stories about blind pigs. Can't I stay for awhile," I pleaded.

"What do you think, Tom? Is he being a good boy?"

"Sure, Lucille. You've more shopping to do on Upper Street don't you? Go on up to Diercks' General and the Drugstore. Jimmy and I'll be along shortly."

Frank drew a second breath before launching into a related story. "The saloons 'n' rowdy behavior of their patrons, particularly bums and itinerants who hopped off the freights, was an exasperatin' circumstance for our new village. Tramps camped by the station 'longside the tracks after buying booze at saloons on Lower Street, 'Broadway' to uppity folk. They also got it at the blind pigs when the saloons were locked up and shut down. Town Marshall didn't like it; townsfolk didn't like it. Even the *Goodhue Enterprise* took the village to task, but it warn't easy getting rid of blind pigs. Cannon Falls, Red Wing, even Zumbrota had incorporated years ahead of Goodhue, so they had the law in better shape by the time Goodhue incorporated. Well now, listen to me, Jimmy, the troubles for darn sure exploded one night back in 1905 when Henry Prolow bounded into town, a Wisconsin tippler who'd way to much to drink at Zemke's Saloon on Lower Street. Zemke finally told Prolow he'd had enough whiskey and Zemke wasn't going to sell one more shot o' liquor. Prolow got damn mad about that, Jimmy. Stormed out of the bar mad as a wet hen, cackling, cussing, calling Zemke a sonofabitch and other words too tart for your young ears. But that warn't the end of it, Jimmy. No siree. Prolow returned later with a gun. Walked up to Zemke at the bar, learned over it and shot him four times, blank range. Killed Zemke over booze. Killed him in his own saloon. Town Marshal apprehended the culprit and they slammed Prolow into prison for life. Zemke was dead, long time dead at age 31. Left a wife, a family, a village. The town was in an uproar over the commotion. Pierce, editor of *The Enterprise*, ranted and raved in his editorials about lawlessness and rowdiness and the troubles booze caused this town. Now look what's happened, Pierce wrote, a death right here in the village! Only one ever happened, far as I know," Frank said as Dennis left the circle to retrieve frozen meat from the Locker.

"Killed him?" I asked. "In Goodhue?" I asked

"That's fer sure, Jimmy. Fact is, Prolow later tried to hire me as his attorney, get him off the hook, but I deferred, sending him to a Red Wing attorney instead. The incident was too close to home for me. So watch the booze, Jimmy. It can get you in trouble, too much, fer sure, it can."

My summer recess was a good respite—a time to momentarily forget tenure troubles, a time to mow the lawn, remodel the house, play golf, play with Anne and Joe, and spend some quality time with Terri, although she seemed that summer to prefer the company of her flower garden to me. I pondered that some, but as long as she was happy planting and pruning I figured it was good for both of us. We worked together, separately, around the house, on the lawn, in the garden, and after a few weeks I regained the energy and motivation to tackle my portfolio. The immediate pain of rejection had dissipated, and I was again acquiring the energy to

face my troubles head on, just as I had been taught by folks in the
village, Mr Frank O'Gorman among others. Yet, there were storm
warnings on the horizon, although nothing like the troubles a
township undertaker had in the thirties. Frank O'Gorman told the
story one night around Heaney & Gorman's potbellied store. I was
there . . .

"You see, Seamus O'Kelly croaked one day while threshing
wheat out on his farm. Terrible hot day it was, late August or
September I reckon, don't rightly recall, but the threshing team
was there that day, struggling in the heat. Men were cutting hay,
gathering the sheaves into shocks, pitching bundles onto horse-
drawn hay racks, pitching it onto long conveyors before stacking
the straw. Well now, the temperature must have been in the 90s,
humidity 'bout the same. Now, you know Seamus was a big man,
liked his meat and potatoes 'n' beer, too. He must of run 'bout 250
pounds, maybe more. But the men had been threshing for each
other for years, O'Kelly too. This year warn't any different until
about three o'clock in the afternoon, that is, when Seamus suddenly dropped his pitch fork, grabbed his chest, let out a huge cry
before collapsing onto the revolving conveyor, his hatless head
heading toward the grinders. The fellow engineering the steam
tractor saw it happen, quickly shut down the steam machine, but
Seamus was dead even before he reached the grinders. He was hot,
dry, threshing dead. And he was so heavy the men could hardly get
him down. Terrible tragedy. Left a wife and eight kids plus a
mortgage on the homeplace. You talk about trouble, Jimmy? That
family was beset with troubles. If you ever have troubles of your
own later in life, you just remember this story. Well, Seamus' dyin'
wasn't the end of it all at all, even though it were the end of him.
The men took him to the undertaker shop, threw a hell of a wake
for him, stayin' up all night with the corpse chatting, devouring
roast beef and cake and drinking beer. Next day they gathered to
bury him. The Mrs was beside herself, bawling, hollering, carrying
on something terrible, the children in tears hanging onto the Mrs'
dress as the undertaker and pallbearers hoisted the wooden casket
down from the hearse. They was a-shuffling slowly toward the
church, mourners lining both sides, three deep, Seamus being a

popular and well-known farmer. Folks was there to pay their last respects, all dressed in black—black hats, black suits, black shoes, black dresses even on a hot, sultry day. The Mrs and children followed the casket and pallbearers toward the church steps, but as the pallbearers reached the third of about eight steep steps, that casket—now at a 45 degree angle—suddenly began creaking, a nauseating sound filling the church yard, and dammit, Jimmy, I'm here to tell you, Seamus fell right out of the bottom of that casket, his body tumbling down the steps toward the Mrs and children. She shrieked and fell to the ground, right on top of Seamus. The children shrieked, mourners gasped, ten ladies in black, covered veils fell like dominoes. Poor Seamus had been too heavy for that casket. He came right out the bottom. You think you might have troubles some day, Jimmy, you just remember this. Well, the priest thought fast, removed his surplice and covered poor Seamus laying on the step, not hurt cause he was already dead, you see. The Mrs and children were quickly shunted off to the vestibule while the mourners turned away in horror. The undertaker was taken aback, or taken under. They asked everyone to depart momentarily as they recovered Seamus, tipping the casket over and replacing him upside down on the cover. They carted him back to the hearse, announcing that the burial would be momentarily delayed. That's trouble, Jimmy, real trouble. That undertaker never conducted another burial service in the township again. He dug his own grave that day, that's fer sure."

The summer ended much too quickly, it being a better summer for Terri's flowers than for me as they received more attention, more tender loving care. I headed back to the marching band field and music education classes, but saved enough personal time to prepare another tenure application. I honed and edited and deleted and added and wrote an improved rationale for keeping me at WSU instead of sending me back to the village on a Cub Farmal tractor. By November I had officially reapplied, then waited four months while the powers-that-be in their ivory tower of the Liberal Arts College deliberated my future.

I wanted to take my application to them directly, to confront them, to throw it in their faces, to let off steam, but I reconsidered. There would be time enough if they denied me again. I recalled the old biblical philosopher, Ecclesiastes, writing: "There is a time for everything." Difficult as it was, I refocused my energies on teaching, my academic career in limbo. Anyway, I had much practice in being patient.

I had learned patience over the years, it being a natural, inherent value in the village where nothing happened fast, everything moving at a snail's pace. A village that had begun in the horse and buggy days hadn't been in a hurry to enter the twentieth century, to embrace the horseless carriage. It hadn't been in a hurry to incorporate, this occurring some twenty years after the site graduated from "Goodhue Center" on the breezy prairie to the actual village of "Goodhue" in 1897. Certainly, patience was a virtue of village settlers. They needed patience waiting for almost everything. Telephone service was long in arriving. When it finally did there was only one line in and out of town, folks lining up in the rear of the bank building to talk on it, voices speeding all the way to Red Wing or Rochester. White Rock's G. O. Miller strung a few more lines in 1907; a competitor strung even more through the townships, but even then folks had to settle for party lines, three and four families trying to talk on the same wire at the same time. Patience.

Villagers waited years before getting paved streets, before escaping the mud area, their streets dotted with mud holes, potholes, horse, cow and pig turds. Oh, they were a patient lot.

Moving pictures had been shown briefly in Anderson's Hall during the early twenties, but that didn't last long. For several later decades villagers saw free movies on a tattered movie screen blowing in the high prairie wind. Even today some townsfolk wait patiently for a real movie house, but most have given up.

We patiently awaited school buses to bus the country bumpkins to town, this in the late forties long after neighboring school districts had buses. But we were mighty proud when they did arrive, two buses for the Goodhue District, "Goodhue School" emblazoned on each side.

We patiently waited for our first football team in 1947 when Butch Jonas, Hilbert Reese, Arnie Jonas, Clarence Lunde, Jr., Sigvard Stenlund, Harold Lensch, Terri Shelstad, Harold Ramboldt, John Yungers, Duane Hinsch and Harlin Reese finally rambled onto the gridiron, this long after the Golden Gophers had pounded Big Ten foes Michigan and Illinois and Wisconsin for years. We learned patience.

I practiced patience waiting for Dad to finish talking with farmers on his milk route out in Belvidere, Belle Creek and Goodhue Townships, early dew-laden mornings. I liked riding in his blazing red International truck, but I was wasn't expected to join in conversations as he talked with farmers alongside their milk houses. I was to wait, be patient before getting on the road again.

We would occasionally ask our parents to drive to Red Wing's Colvill Park swimming pool, but it took patience waiting for Mother and Dad to make up their minds. I'd saunter toward water tank hill kicking stones, meandering past Supt. Eyestone's hill house, Naurice Husbyn's house, through Evergreen Cemetery reading headstones of villagers I'd never known—Nels Skramstad, Jonathan Finney, Ole Shelstad—folks who had arrived in the township in the 1850s and 1860s, dying long before I arrived. I'd mosey down County Rd. No 9 toward Finney's Woods, then just another dusty, bumpy gravel road, kicking stones, bees and flies buzzing my ears, butterflies floating lazily in the breeze through the pines of Evergreen. I was practicing patience.

I practiced enjoyable patience, though, fishing with Dad and brother Tom at the Welch Dam, the Cannon River's blue water gently flowing in easy cascades over the dam while we waited for a sunfish, a perch, a crappie to drag our bobbers into the swirling stream. Fishing teaches patience. Impatient men raced stock cars and shot guns. Impatient men don't fish.

I practiced patience when trying to get a date with the high school girls. Sometimes I'd ask a cute blonde for a date outside the Assembly Hall. She would take forever to answer . . . minutes passing as she gazed about, pondered, chewed her pencil, twisted her hair . . . excruciating . . . "What is she thinking," I wondered. "Why is she taking so long to answer," I thought. I'm standing right here in front of her. Is she weighing her options waiting for Bob or Larry or Jack or Tom or Fred or George or Dallas or Hutch to come up and displace me? I'd lean on one leg, then another before she would see a girlfriend, run off without ever answering me. Patience.

I practiced patience waiting for Heinie Swenson to wait on me, my nickels and dimes burning my hands, they needing to be released for a chocolate bar, an ice cream cone.

I practiced patience waiting for Emma Kindseth or Mrs Goodsell or Mary McHugh to leave Eddie's Drugstore so I could continue sneaking a glance at the girlie magazines. That took considerable patience, because Emma would look at everything in the store before buying something. I had interminable patience as Eddie slowly wrapped her package in brown paper before tying it with long string. Patience.

I practiced patience as Miss Cree conjugated verbs and talked endlessly about phrases and sentences and the subjunctive and adjectives and verbs and prepositions and dangling participles and grammar things I didn't care about. I was impatient, wanting to get out to the ball diamond, to the gym to bounce or hit a ball. Patience.

I learned patience in the confessional, waiting forever it seemed, after reciting my litany of sins, for Father to dispense my penance so I could scoot out of Holy Trinity into fresh, secular air and freedom. The time dragged interminably, me wondering what was so bad about a few sins of impurity, what was taking him so long to devise a penance. Was he conferring with the bishop in St. Paul, the pope in Rome? I learned patience. Maybe that was my penance.

During the early seventies, while encamped in Okie Muscogee land with the Bible Belt Baptistery Brethren, Terri and I were enthralled with "All In The Family," and Archie Bunker's bigoted opinions. A particular episode that sticks in my mind was an inane episode whereby Archie ostracizes son-in-law Meathead for putting on and removing his shoes and socks wrong, according to Archie. Archie advocated putting on both socks before shoes, but Meathead didn't understand that approach. He favored a sock and a shoe, a sock and a shoe. Archie also advocated removing both shoes instead of dropping a shoe and a sock, thereby leaving the other foot with a shoe and sock. That episode came back to haunt me two weeks before the end of the school year, year seven, when the first shoe fell . . .

> I REGRET TO INFORM YOU THAT I, THE PROVOST OF WAYNE STATE UNIVERSITY, HAVE DETERMINED THAT YOU, JAMES L. FRANKLIN, HAVE NOT MET THE REQUIREMENTS FOR TENURE AT OUR ESTEEMED UNIVERSITY. WE APPRECIATE YOUR EFFORTS DURING YOUR BRIEF STAY HERE AND WISH YOU SUCCESS IN YOUR CONTINUING ACADEMIC CAREER.
>
> SINCERELY,
> PROVOST OF THE UNIVERSITY

Translation:
We're goddamn happy to tell you to get your ass out of our university. Don't ever dirty our classrooms, our lily-white academic institution, our ivory tower with your absurd, provincial midwestern countenance again. You're nothing but a piece of shit, not worthy of teaching our students, not worthy of even talking with our fucking esteemed faculty. Get your ass out of the university, out of Detroit as soon as your last class is completed. And I hope to hell you burn in hell.

Get lost you sonofabitch!
Esteemed provost

Meathead was right. That shoe fell hard, loud, banging through my ears, my head, my mind. Suddenly, I was left unbalanced with only one shoe and sock, uneven, wavering as I trudged up three flights of stairs that suddenly felt like thirty, and this wearing only one shoe! I collapsed in a chair, stunned as I had never been before.

Being rejected for high school dates, losing a close basketball game to Janesville by one point in the final second of the 1953 sub district tournament had stunned my cager friends, losses in retrospect, nothing like this. This felt more like the day Supt. Hubert came down to the boy's locker room to get me as I dressed for phys-ed class, he on the stairs saying my dad wasn't doing so well at St. John's Hospital and that I should go with brother Tom and Mother with George Gorman to Red Wing where, when walking in, the doctor was waiting and saying it was all over and I was glad because Dad was now feeling better because his spell was over but Mother bursting into hysterical tears, she realizing "all over" meant all over. Then, crying in the ante room of St. John's because my dad had just died.

In my office I felt my heart racing, my face flush, sweating, hands trembling. I couldn't believe this was happening. I couldn't believe it had happened—a shoe dropping, my academic career crashing. I wanted a beer, maybe even a shot of Jack Daniels, but I had only water and it was much too weak for my present condition. What had gone wrong, I wondered. I thought my second application greatly improved, yet it didn't fly. Oh, an addendum at the end of the fucking provost letter said that this application had passed through the Liberal Arts Tenure Committee, but the L. A. Dean hadn't supported it. But the rules of academia said it must be forwarded to the provost in his gleaming tower, who then in his almighty realm, supported the fucking Dean. That was obvious. That was like Catholics supporting Catholics, Lutherans supporting Lutherans, Democrats supporting Democrats. What was so fucking unique about a provost supporting another administrative dean? Where was John L. Lewis when I needed him? Where was Jimmy Hoffa when I needed him? Somewhere on the bottom of the Detroit River entombed in five tons of cement, that's where. Hoffa had stood up for the working man, the working class, a guy like me, not management, not the administration, not a fucking dean. Come back, Shane!

Stunned, angry, depressed sitting in a chair gazing out at the deserted football stadium I'd not march on again, GM headquarters casting its dark shadow across the university campus, I knew

I had to get a grip on myself, keep that other shoe on. I didn't want to return home to tell Terri I had failed, that I no longer had a job. I had dragged her to Michigan, the children to new schools. Now, I had let them down, hadn't shown the way, hadn't shown the light. Husbands and dads are supposed to show the way. I trudged through the disturbingly silent hallway for a drink of water, shuffling, pacing back and forth as dusk invaded the campus. I couldn't make sense out of it. I might have anticipated it, but as anticipating death, nothing compares. Dead is dead. Non tenured is non tenured. I still had my life but what was I going to do with it? I now had a scarlet mark on my face for all to see, my family, the rest of academia. Would I ever get another teaching position? Over and over these thoughts bombarded me, not letting me alone, attacking, biting like the worst mosquito infestation in Minnesota. Thoughts buzzed at me from every direction, snarling, biting, injecting poison into my system. I couldn't escape the stinging thoughts racing through my mind. I finally rushed out of my office to escape, slammed the door shut, hurtled down the steps two at a time past a startled colleague, out to my car and began racing down the freeway, the wrong way—Wrong way Corrigan—three miles before reversing my direction.

Terri met me at the back door with a can of cold Stroh's, just another day of the wage earner arriving home, but again she stepped backward instead of toward me—Why does she do that? "How was your day, Jim? Classes go all right today?" she asked, retrieving the cheddar cheese, crackers, other hors d'oeuvres. I hardly saw her as I stumbled toward a chair wearing only one sock, one shoe. She hadn't noticed my lost shoe and sock.

"Are you all right, Jim. You're gray, not good coloring in your face. Have a beer and maybe you'll feel better," she said, placing cheese and crackers on the table. I hadn't even reached for my beer yet, highly unusual for me, when she came over slowly and placed her hand on my shoulder, something she hadn't done for a very long time. I noticed. "Did you hear from the tenure committee today?" she asked softly while rubbing my neck. I was tongue-tied, just like Archie Bunker when he had been locked in the basement alone, realizing there that Jefferson's God was, indeed, African-

American. I couldn't speak for a minute, but Terri was patient, as usual, waiting . . .

"I . . . ah . . . got . . . well . . . I received a letter . . . from the p . . . provost today. I . . . I'm out of a job. No tenure," I blurted, finally reaching for a long gulp of Stroh's. There, it was out, someone knew besides that sonofabitching provost and me. Terri rubbed my shoulder for a long time, even came close to giving me a hug, but detoured at the last second to only a pat on my back. I told her about the contents of the letter as we retired to the study for an hour or so, mostly gazing, little talking. What could we say? The children played outside, again locked outside the door, outside their parents' lives.

I don't believe I slept that night nor the next, but I did struggle to the university to finish teaching my classes with integrity. I was bruised but my integrity intact. After the shock wore off I would need to get a hold of myself, to readjust, to find a direction again. I just hoped I could keep that other shoe on. Hard times . . .

My mother told me,
'Fore she passed away,
Said, son, when I'm gone,
Don't forget to pray.

'Cause there'll be hard times,
Lord, those hard times,
Who knows better than I?

B. C. Majerus drove a pickup with things forever falling off— galvanized pipe, copper tubing, propane gas tanks, a bumper, a wayward fender, a rear view mirror, a hubcap. You could locate him by simply following his trail. As Terri worked feverishly on her flower garden that summer, I thought of B. C. and his truck. I felt like that now. Something had fallen off and I pondered how I could get it back on. Like Terri, I too sought therapy working on the house, the lawn, the deck, the two of us working together, separately, toward an undetermined future.

For some unknown and odd reason I thought often about

dancing at the Skyline Ballroom, Friday or Saturday nights after a
GHS basketball game. I'd get in a couple of hours of swing
dancing, fox trots, a couple of polkas, even some cheek-to-cheek
slow waltzing with a sweet-smelling, full-breasted sophomore, if
I were lucky. I suppose I found comfort, relief in recalling high
school days. That way I didn't have to face my uncertain future. It
seemed easier thinking of slow waltzing at the Skyline or at the old
GHS gym than searching for the shoe that had fallen off. Terri, by
now, noticed my unstableness as I stumped around the lawn and
house with only one shoe and sock.

A week later, while repairing the roof so rains wouldn't seep
into the living room, Terri called me down for lemonade and a
sandwich on the rear deck. I was ready for a break, the June heat
already building along the Great Lakes. We sat on the deck sipping
cool lemonade, the children off to swimming lessons or tennis
lessons or somewhere lessons. It was nice, just the two of us. That
didn't happen often. I wouldn't call Terri reticent, but I thought she
more quiet than usual as we sipped and admired her beautiful
gladiolus, impatiens, daises. She didn't seem to be enjoying the
respite as much as me, but maybe she hadn't worked hard enough
yet today.

"I don't want to live with you anymore. I want a separation!"

B O O O O M! A bomb exploded, as powerful as Harry
Truman's atom bomb over Hiroshima. It swept over me, the blast
burning my face, searing my eyes, piecing my heart. It continued
in waves, knocking me to the deck. I couldn't breathe. I couldn't
see. I had been radiated, it attacking, blistering, destroying. The
other shoe had fallen.

T wo weeks later I was sleeping in my beat-up, hard riding,
rusted, cramped 1980 Chevette somewhere in Michigan—
Terri gone, the children gone, the house gone, the neighborhood gone, my job gone. I felt like B. C.'s truck. I felt like Erv
Richter on one of his worst nights in the village. I sat on the fender
of the Chevette looking at the moon, wondering how all this had
happened so suddenly. Which way would I turn now? How was I

going to keep from going crazy, a state I was rapidly approaching. I had purchased the Chevette a couple of years ago after being rear-ended by a drunken lady on a Detroit freeway, this after she had spent an afternoon sloshing wine and whiskey at Leo's Bar & Grill on South Gratiot. She had demolished my beloved Beetle, forcing me into a working man's car, the worst car General Motors ever made, discounting the "unsafe at any speed Corvair," of course. Tonight, peering at the sliding blue moon, I hoped, desperately, the Chevette would hold together better than B. C.'s truck. I was hoping the wheels wouldn't come off the Chevette as they had in my life.

For the next several weeks I pounded the road to nowhere, driving, wandering like one of Moses' horde, drinking bitter coffee at truck stops, chomping on greasy hamburgers and smelling the sour farts of 18-wheel truckers at roadside diners. I was down, moving in a trance, pissing with the big boys at every truck stop and dive somewhere in the Great Lakes or Midwest. Who cared? I was on a road to nowhere. Where the fuck was Jack Kerouac when I needed him? I didn't shave. I didn't change clothes. I didn't brush my teeth. I only emptied my bladder whenever or wherever convenient, usually pissing on the Chevette's wheels to wash them of the grime I was accumulating on the endless road. If I'd had a longer dong I'd have turned it on myself, washed the grime off myself, piss on myself. Why not, everyone else was? Who the hell cared anymore. The fucking provost didn't care. Terri didn't care. Everything I had worked for, everything I had loved was now gone. Just me and this fucking Chevette. I felt and smelled like hobos that frequented the tracks by the village station in the first decades of the century. They camped along the tracks, sometimes in tents, sometimes in box cars, sometimes on front lawns, exasperating the townsfolk as they too pissed in the weeds behind the T. B. Sheldon Grain Elevator, tossing trash anywhere. Why not, I thought. What the hell difference did living make—being neat, being clean. I'd been there, done that. Maybe a hobo's life would be the next thing in my life. Maybe I could head back to the village, visit the Dreamland Ballroom. Maybe, tonight, I'd begin . . . slow waltzing back to Goodhue.

I had no plan. I drove through the night, oncoming lights appearing like locomotives ready to devour me, to end my life. I was hoping they would. I could see, but I couldn't think. I had lost my ability to think, to reason. I tried a few Hail Marys and Our Fathers, but even they seemed shallow. I tried thinking of Job and his troubles, but I couldn't concentrate on Job. At least Job had friends to talk to, I thought. Yet, I could feel, feel hurt deep in my gut which was rolling and reeling with every bounce of the Chevette. I devoured packages of Rolaids every day, my bitter stomach attacking my tender throat, my dry tongue. I didn't even listen to music, only stared endlessly down the long road, humped over the wheel like Jesse Campbell driving home after a day at Campbell's Hardware. I had no map, no itinerary. I turned when I felt like it. Didn't turn when I felt like it. I had cried the first few days, but now was dried up. I think I drove around Chicago, but wasn't sure. I think I entered northern Illinois, but wasn't sure. I slept in roadside parks, humped over in a hard-ass Chevette. I slept in truck stops and outside diners and cafes. I didn't care. I didn't read the newspaper. I didn't listen to the radio. The world was incidental. I was on the road to somewhere, but the road to nowhere. Hard times . . .

Well, I soon found out,
Just what she meant,
When I had to pawn my clothes,
Just to pay the rent.

Talkin' 'bout hard times,
Lord, those hard times,
Who knows better than I?

"You's is lookin' pretty bedraggled, hon," the blond-tussled waitress said while pouring me a cup of steaming coffee without asking at Somewhere, Somewhere, U.S.A. "Lookin' like you's could use a good cleanin' up. You might'n not look so bad underneath if you'd get some o' that grime off'n you's, maybe some clean clothes too or somethin'. Got a shower out a-back there with them truckers. Don't cost none but fifty cents. Make you feel better, hon. I'll be back to take yer order when you's had a chance to look the menu over," and she was gone, sidling down the plywood-topped, ancient counter pouring steaming coffee to paunchy truckers, seed-cap farmers, greasy plumbers, two-by-four carpenters, itinerant carpetbaggers, and wandering hobos like me. I sipped the coffee slowly, stared straight ahead, not picking up the newspaper—Who the hell cares what happens in Iran, in India in South America? I looked at Nesbitt Orange signs and Beech Nut chewing tobacco signs and Wrigley's gum signs, and . . . well . . . I wasn't right with the world. I wasn't right with myself and I knew it.

"Whatchagonna have then, hon? Make up you's mind yet?"

"What mind?" I said cynically. I was surly but had the good sense not to take it out on Miss Congeniality. "Sorry, Miss, I wasn't thinking so good. Didn't mean to be impolite. I haven't looked at the menu yet. Give me another five," I said, reaching for the catsup-stained menu.

"Think some 'bout that shower, hon. Do you good," she said, bounding down the counter—full-sized hips bouncing off the counter—pouring coffee to snarly truckers staring down that long, lonely road just like me. At least they had something to live for, a purpose, even if it was only driving an 18 wheeler to nowhere. Their direction was better than mine. And why did Miss Congeniality care whether I took a shower or not? Why she or anyone else would care was beyond me at that moment. I didn't care. Why should they?

"What'll it be then, hon?" she asked, returning more quickly than I anticipated, but I had no sense of time. She twisted a long pencil in her bun hair, chewed Wrigley's gum faster than I'd ever seen a lady chew, even back at Joe's Place or Bartlett's.

"Two eggs up, sunny side, fried potatoes like they make at Swenson's, and more coffee . . . please," I said, sliding the menu down the worn linoleum-topped counter to the next trucker who obviously already had it memorized from his frequent stops here.

"Swenson's? Where's that, hon?" she said, bending over

toward me, chewing furiously, revealing a small amount of cleavage over her apron.

"Minnesota, out in the village."

"Village in Minnesota? Then what you doin' in Ioway?" she asked, straightening up and taking her cleavage with her. At least I noticed that. I must still be alive.

"Iowa? Didn't I know I was in Iowa. Just been driving all night, every night, days, nights. Going nowhere fast," I said. "Take some more coffee here, Miss? . . . ,"

"Name's Burnadette, Mr?"

"Jim here. Just Jim from nowhere, going nowhere," I mumbled, slumping on the stool.

"Well, Mr Jim from nowhere. You eat your eggs then. I'm gonna knock fifty cents off and push you to the shower after you's et. Make you feel a whole lot better," she said, heading for the hot grill. I didn't want a shower. I didn't want to comb my hair. I wanted my wife and family back. I wanted my job back. Who the fuck cared about a shower?

"Well now, ain't you sumpthin'," Miss Congeniality said as I emerged from the shower, grimy clothes intact, but a clean body and hair. I didn't want to admit it, but I did feel a little better.

"Thanks, Burnadette. Thanks for your persistence. You're just like my mother," I said, patting her on the shoulder.

"Where's this village you keep talkin' about, Mr Jim."

"Up in Minnesota, southern Minnesota. Can't be too far from here. Where am I, anyway?"

"You's in Dorchester, Ioway, 'bout 15 miles from the Minnesota border. But you could hang around here fer awhile, if'ns you wanted to. How about it?"

"Got to hit the road, Burnadette. Don't know why, don't know where, but I'm on the road again," I said, dropping two quarters into her apron, briefly feeling the warmth of her hip on my hand. For a moment I wondered if I should hang around.

"Well, hon, you stop back again when you's in the territory. Take care of yourself, Mr Jim. You's don't look so bad, cleaned up," she said as I shuffled through the creaking door to my ever-patient, waiting Chevette hunkered in the parking lot like a horse tied to a hitching post in the village, a lot of years ago.

I was emotionally numb but the shower had felt good, and Burnadette was nice to me . . . for some unknown reason. Why would she be nice to me? For a brief moment—sitting in the Chevette alongside an 18 wheeler loaded with stinking hogs headed for the Sioux City Stockyards, dust blowing through the dirt lot into my window—for just a moment I felt hope in the guise of a yellow-winged butterfly fluttering through my open window. I reached for it, but it fluttered out as quickly as it had come in. I grasped for it again, but couldn't hold it in my hands. I ground the gears into first and second, then headed onto the road to Nowhere, Nowhere, U.S.A.

I meandered along the back roads of Iowa and Minnesota, driving about the speed of a farmer and his pickup through Houston and Fillmore Counties, turning on a whim, turning or not turning as I chose. Continuous driving was an attempt to clear my mind, a mind that had only gained a degree or two in the past several weeks. I didn't even know how many weeks had passed since the second shoe fell. I had lost track of everything, including time. Gradually, though, I learned not to think about the future. I trained myself to concentrate only on the next hour. That was easier. An entire day was too much to consider, certainly a week or the future. I began marking the hours. Slowly, my body began healing, it long before my mind. I didn't know if my mind would ever heal. I had a cancer of the heart, of the soul. I had to find a reason to live again, yet I doubted if I would. I began driving longer hours, deep into the night, the dark evening hours mesmerizing space and time, offering some comfort, as if in a time warp, a tunnel to outer space. During sunlight hours everything was too bright, too stark, too real. But at night I could escape the real world of people working, families sitting down to eat dinner. At night, now driving through western Minnesota, I was able to escape and I certainly wanted to escape.

Weeks passed, I guess, the Chevette chugging along, retaining most items other than a couple of hubcaps that had escaped into cornfields down in Iowa. I gradually began taking better care of myself, at least washing my hands and face more, brushing my teeth daily, combing my hair, although my clothes were grimy. I stopped at laundromats to wash my clothes, waiting patiently in the bathroom, in my shorts, while they tumbled dry. Something was pulling me back to reality. I slowly began caring about how I looked, how I smelled, even if no one else did.

I began wondering about my survival skills and where they had come from, if in fact, I had any. Was the will to live innate or had I inherited it from Lucille and Tom, the Franklin and Haustein hordes and all the folks in the village and townships. What had they contributed to my survival skills? What values of living had they offered? Was it simply because I had seen them praying at church, dragging recalcitrant children like me along because it was good for us, like eating spinach and peas. What *was* good for me? Was it because I saw folks tending to daily work, working a good day for a good day's pay? Weren't those things everyone, everywhere did? Were those values any different in the village? Why did I do the things I did? How much influence had the village had on me, on my friends, on others? What was detrimental about the village? How had it stunted my growth? My college friends from the Twin Cites had had many advantages when I met them at St. John's. Were their values the same? Were they different? Why was I Catholic and not English Lutheran? Why Roman Catholic and not German Lutheran? Was I Catholic only because my parents were? Had I ever really worked out that theology, that philosophical belief by myself? Why was I a Democrat and not a Republican? Had I thought that out by myself? Why did I feel compelled to give a good day's work for a good day's pay, as at Bookie's pea viners? Was it because of Bookie, Dennis Heaney, the Gormans, because of Luverne Haas and Art Lohman and Art Eppen and Harold Wipperling, and . . . well, everybody else I saw working hard, so I might as well too? What made me believe in things the way I did? Why was I feeling terrible now about losing a job? Hell! Lots of guys never wanted to work in the first place. The village had had its share of tramps, bums, hobos during the Great Depression. Was it because of Dad's values, his beliefs? He had only attended grade school in a one-room school out in Goodhue Township. Hell! I had a Ph.D. but was worse off than him with his eighth grade education. What sense did that make? What would Dad tell me now if he were here? What would Mother tell me if she were alive? Maybe I should drive out to St. Columbkill's Cemetery to ask them what to do. They'd know.

How much had I changed since living in the village? Certainly, the village wouldn't be the same if I waltzed back there now. It had been many years, twenty-five or more since I had been around, another generation or two having replaced me. Would village values be the same? Would they still be concerned about their children—if they wore clean underwear, if they cleaned under their finger nails, if they said their prayers, if they were nice to their teachers, their ministers, their dogs, their pet Holsteins, their ministers, their priests, their church. What were values about? What were my values about living? I'd surely need to find out if I were going to get both shoes on again, if I were going to keep the wheels on this old Chevy.

I continued meandering, that butterfly of hope flitting in and out the window, staying momentarily, then floating off, but gradually appearing more often. Somewhere around Northfield it appeared again, the landscape now becoming more familiar as I headed into the eastern sunrise. For the first time since leaving Michigan I flipped on the radio pulling in Faribault's KDHL. I didn't want old-time music, not after having earned a degree in *real* music. I didn't want to hear corny schottisches and polkas, but then a nice waltz squeaked through my tinny speakers, a pleasant old bittersweet waltz I'd danced to at Oak Center, at high school proms, at the Skyline Ballroom. The lyrics were poignant. For the first time since that second shoe fell, I thought of Terri without anger in my heart. I began humming along, softly at first, this the first time I'd sung, hummed or whistled since both shoes had fallen. It felt good to be . . . whistling down County Road No. 9.

I'll . . . see . . . you again,
Whenever spring . . . breaks . . . through again,
Time may lie heavy between,
But what has been,
Is past forgetting . . .

I had reached Highway 52, the last perimeter between Goodhue County Lutheranism and Catholicism. Apparently, I was heading for the village without having realized it, without having made a decision to do so. I'd not made *any* decisions since my shoe strings had come untied. I crossed Highway 52 onto No. 9 and into Belle Creek Township. As I passed the turnoff to St. Columbkill's country church and cemetery, that yellow-winged butterfly of hope flew in the window and landed on my shoulder . . .

> *This . . . sweet . . . memory,*
> *Across the years . . . will . . . come to me,*
> *Tho my world may go awry,*
> *In my heart will ever lie,*
> *Just the echo of a sigh . . .*

> *Good-bye.*

Photo Credits

Credits

Popcorn Press
Forthcoming *Books*
by Jim Franklin

Folk Dancing out on the High Prairie
Upper Midwest Settlement
HISTORICAL FICTION
PUBLICATION 2006

A Real Slow Drag in Upper Mulberry
A Midwestern Small Town Novel
PUBLICATION 2008

Wheeling & Whistling on the Open Road
Living by 12-Volt
PUBLICATION 2010

Dancing Along the Upper Mississippi
HISTORICAL NOVELLAS
CATALOG 1997

About Popcorn Press

Our publishing plans and the answer
to the question . . . Why did you call your
book publishing company Popcorn Press?

Slow Waltzing Back To Goodhue is the third book published by
Popcorn Press: Books of the Upper Midwest, an independent,
small press publisher based in McGregor, Iowa. We published
Last Waltz In Goodhue, and *Dancing Along The Upper Mississippi* in 1997. We will continue with these trade size, creative
nonfiction and fiction books, plus adding *Popcorn Press' Popular History Series of the Upper Mississippi Valley,* historically
accurate books with abundant photographs. Each year should
see at least one new publication; thereby, establishing a catalog
of books about Upper Midwest life.

 Slow Waltzing Back To Goodhue is part II of T H E
G O O D H U E T R I L O G Y, highlighting Jim's years after high
school. The thread of the book follows his college and later
years, but it is really a book about the village, everyone's
village.

 Last Waltz In Goodhue was the first published book in
T H E G O O D H U E T R I L O G Y, its publication coinciding
with the Goodhue Centennial celebration, summer 1997. We
patiently waited for that centennial to arrive, but folks thought it
was about time the book was published. They didn't want to
wait another one hundred years.

 Whistling Down County Road No. 9, part III of T H E
G O O D H U E T R I L O G Y was originally part II, but . . . well,
things change, it now being rewritten for its rightful order, No.
3 in the trilogy. Publication is 2004.

 Folk Dancing out on the High Prairie will be a historical
fiction book about pioneer settlement in the Upper Midwest,
more specifically some of the townships of Goodhue County,

Minnesota. It will tell the story of several ethnically-diverse families settling in the 1840s and 1850s.

A Real Slow Drag in Upper Mulberry will be a small town novel depicting life found in any small Upper Midwest town whether Minnesota, Wisconsin, Iowa or the Dakotas. We would like to say it will be another *Winesburg, Ohio*, or *Main Street*, or maybe *Lake Wobegon,* but time moves pretty darn slow in Upper Mulberry. It'll just have to settle for being itself.

Wheeling & Whistling on the Open Road: Living by 12-Volt is a departure from the above books, more in the vein of Steinbeck's *Travels With Charley*, Bill Bryson's travel series and Moon's *Blue Highways*. Some folks think we're biased about life in the Upper Midwest. This book will be for those naysayers.

The Popcorn Press Popular History Series of the Upper Mississippi Valley is a series of five books covering the river and its communities from Dubuque, Iowa to St. Paul, Minnesota. The books will be historically accurate, full of photographs, and written in an accessible, travelogue style.

As a boy in Minnesota, my older brother, Tom, and I operated a popcorn wagon in the village. We parked it next to Jesse's Hardware on Saturday nights to serve popcorn, soda and candy bars to the folks watching the free movies projected onto the side of the railroad station. Then on Sunday afternoons we pulled it to the dusty old ball diamond to serve the local clientele as they lounged under the spreading elm out in left field, watching their heroes play ball. And we would pull it out County Road No. 9 to serve popcorn and pop to folks attending a farm auction at Walt's or Carl's place. Popcorn Press. It fits.

Go ahead and fill out the form on the last page to order current books and to place your name on the mailing list for our catalog and direct mail notices of forthcoming books.

A guy could do a lot worse.

Colophon

Typeface: Times Roman
Paper: 60# Booktext Natural, Acid Free
Cover: 10pt. C1S, Film Lamination-Matte
Design: Popcorn Press & Chris L. Shelton
Printer: Sheridan Books, Ann Arbor, MI
Composed in Pagemaker on a Macintosh Computer

Order Form

Please send the books I have checked below.
Telephone orders:(563) 516-1135
Mail orders: Popcorn Press, Main Street
               P.O. Box 237, McGregor, Iowa 52157

[ ] *Slow Waltzing Back To Goodhue: Once Upon a
Time in a Village* by Jim Franklin. Part II of
THE GOODHUE TRILOGY. Creative autobiography.
448 pp.
          (No.)_____ copies at $22.95: $_____

[ ] *Last Waltz In Goodhue: Adventures of a Village
Boy* by Jim Franklin. Part I of THE GOODHUE
TRILOGY. Creative autobiography. 328 pp.
          (No.)_____ copies at $20.95: $_____

[ ] *Pioneering Goodhue County* by Jim Franklin.
No. I of The Popcorn Press Historical Series.
Popular history. 275 pp, photos.
          (No.)_____ copies at $23.95: $_____

          Subtotal books: $_____
          Sales Tax: 6%, IA residents only $_____
          Shipping: $2.00 first book.
          $ .50 each additional book. $_____
          TOTAL to Popcorn Press $_____

Name:_____
Address:_____
City:_____State:_____Zip:_____

[ ] Please place my name on the mailing list for notice
of forthcoming books from Popcorn Press.

Popcorn Press
Main Street
P.O. Box 237
McGregor, Iowa 52157
Phone & Voice Mail orders (563) 516-1135

Forthcoming Books
Popcorn Press
by Jim Franklin

Folk Dancing out on the High Prairie
Upper Midwest Settlement
HISTORICAL FICTION
PUBLICATION 2006

A Real Slow Drag in Upper Mulberry
A Midwestern Small Town Novel
PUBLICATION 2008

Wheeling & Whistling on the Open Road
Living by 12-Volt
PUBLICATION 2010

Dancing Along the Upper Mississippi
HISTORICAL NOVELLAS
CATALOG 1997

433

POPCORN PRESS' POPULAR HISTORY
SERIES OF THE UPPER MISSISSIPPI VALLEY
by Jim Franklin

A multi-volume series telling the story, through historical accounts and photos, of the hearty, courageous people and benchmark events in the Upper Mississippi River Valley.

No. 1___
Pioneering Goodhue County
The villages, burgs, hamlets, whistle-stops, ghost towns, townships and good folks of Goodhue County, Minnesota
Publication 2002

No. 2___
Settling Lake Pepin's Shores
The majestic lake, steamboats, rafting, anchoring towns
Publication 2003

No. 3___
Pike's Peak and the Five Rivers' Valley
The Mississippi, Wisconsin, Kickapoo,
Turkey and Yellow Rivers

Publication 2003

No. 4___
Grand Excursion 2004
Paddlewheelers, sidewheelers, captains, pilots, roust-abouts, scoundrels again ply the Upper Mississippi River
Publication 2004

Popcorn Press

presents

THE GOODHUE TRILOGY

by Jim Franklin

One boy finds meaning growing up, later moving beyond a tiny, dusty village out on the rolling prairie. His adventures and escapades are those of universal youth. Relive your own in this heartwarming, whimsical trilogy. Come along.

Part I
Last Waltz in Goodhue
Adventures of a Village Boy
Publication 1997

Part II
Slow Waltzing Back to Goodhue
Once Upon a Time in a Village
Publication 2002

Part III
Whistling Down County Road No. 9
Remembering a Village
Publication 2004

435